WRITER
PAUL JENKINS

"EMBEDDED"

PENCILER
RAMON BACHS

INKER
JOHN LUCAS

COLORIST
LAURA MARTIN

"SLEEPER CELL"

PENCILER
LEE WEEKS

INKERS
ROB CAMPANELLA, SANDU
FLOREA, LEE WEEKS &
NELSON

COLORIST
SOTOCOLOR'S J. BROWN

COLLECTION EDITOR
JENNIFER GRÜNWALD

ASSISTANT EDITORS
MICHAEL SHORT &
CORY LEVINE

ASSOCIATE EDITOR
MARK D. BEAZLEY

"THE ACCUSED"

ARTIST
STEVE LIEBER

COLORIST
JUNE CHUNG

"WAR
CORRESPONDENCE"

ARTISTS
KEI KOBAYASHI, KANO,
DAVID AJA, SEAN CHEN &
RICK MAGYAR, ROY ALLEN
MARTINEZ & JORGE LUCAS

COLOR ART
CHRISTINA STRAIN,
DEAN WHITE
JOSE VILLARRUBIA &
SOTOCOLOR'S A. CROSSLEY

SENIOR EDITOR,
SPECIAL PROJECTS
JEFF YOUNGQUIST

SENIOR VICE PRESIDENT
OF SALES
DAVID GABRIEL

PRODUCTION
JERRY KALINOWSKI

"THE PROGRAM"

ARTIST
LEANDRO FERNANDEZ

COLORIST
DAN BROWN

LETTERER
VC'S RANDY GENTILE
WITH CORY PETIT

COVER ART
JOHN WATSON

ASSISTANT EDITORS
MOLLY LAZER &
AUBREY SITTERSON

EDITORS
TOM BREVOORT &
CORY SEDLMEIER

BOOK DESIGNER
DAYLE CHESLER

VICE PRESIDENT OF CREATIVE
TOM MARVELLI

EDITOR IN CHIEF
JOE QUESADA

PUBLISHER
DAN BUCKLEY

WAR
FRONT LINE

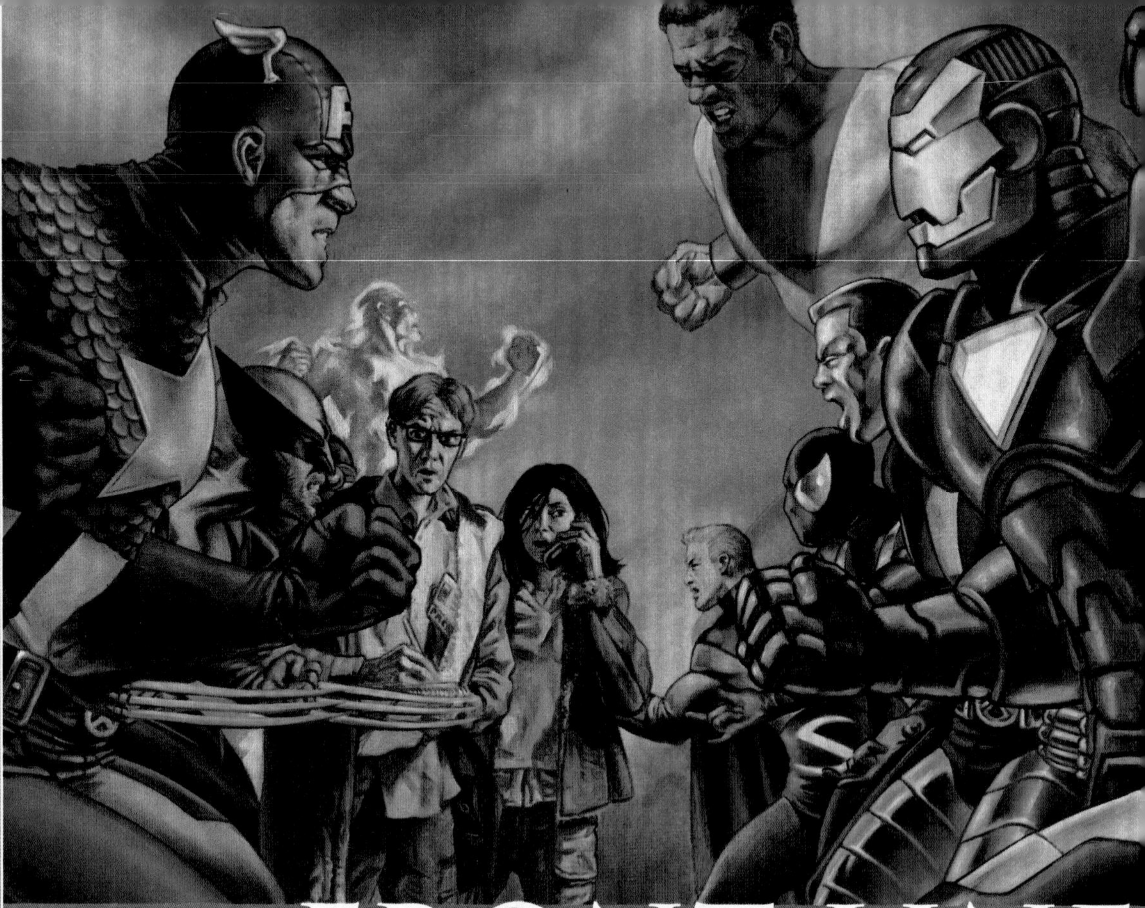

FRONT LINE

A MARVEL COMICS EVENT

CIVIL WAR

CIVIL WAR: FRONT LINE #1

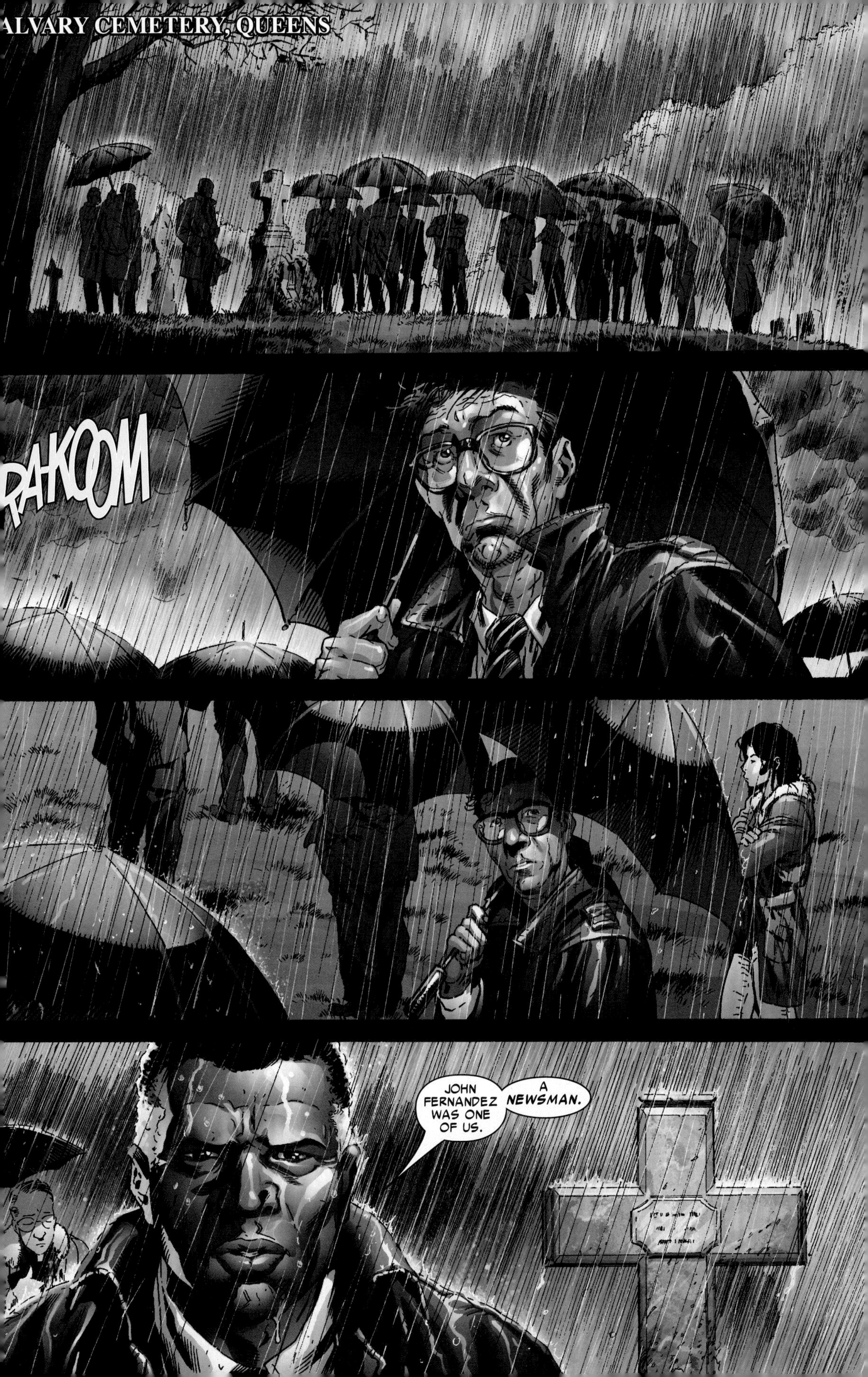
ALVARY CEMETERY, QUEENS
RAKOOM
JOHN FERNANDEZ WAS ONE OF US.
A NEWSMAN.

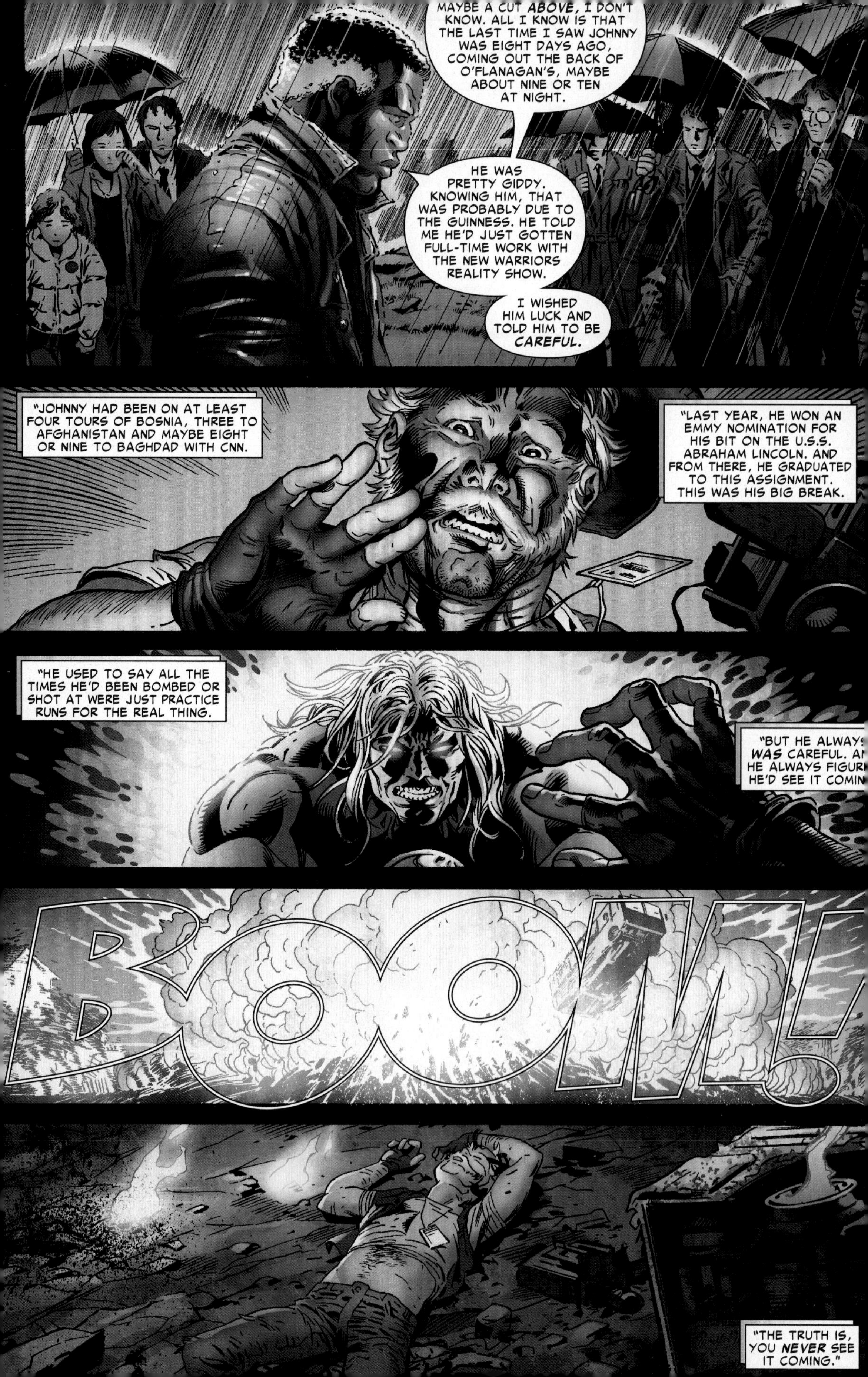

MAYBE A CUT ABOVE, I DON'T KNOW. ALL I KNOW IS THAT THE LAST TIME I SAW JOHNNY WAS EIGHT DAYS AGO, COMING OUT THE BACK OF O'FLANAGAN'S, MAYBE ABOUT NINE OR TEN AT NIGHT.
HE WAS PRETTY GIDDY. KNOWING HIM, THAT WAS PROBABLY DUE TO THE GUINNESS. HE TOLD ME HE'D JUST GOTTEN FULL-TIME WORK WITH THE NEW WARRIORS REALITY SHOW.
I WISHED HIM LUCK AND TOLD HIM TO BE CAREFUL.
"JOHNNY HAD BEEN ON AT LEAST FOUR TOURS OF BOSNIA, THREE TO AFGHANISTAN AND MAYBE EIGHT OR NINE TO BAGHDAD WITH CNN.
"LAST YEAR, HE WON AN EMMY NOMINATION FOR HIS BIT ON THE U.S.S. ABRAHAM LINCOLN. AND FROM THERE, HE GRADUATED TO THIS ASSIGNMENT. THIS WAS HIS BIG BREAK.
"HE USED TO SAY ALL THE TIMES HE'D BEEN BOMBED OR SHOT AT WERE JUST PRACTICE RUNS FOR THE REAL THING.
BOOM!
"THE TRUTH IS, YOU NEVER SEE IT COMING."

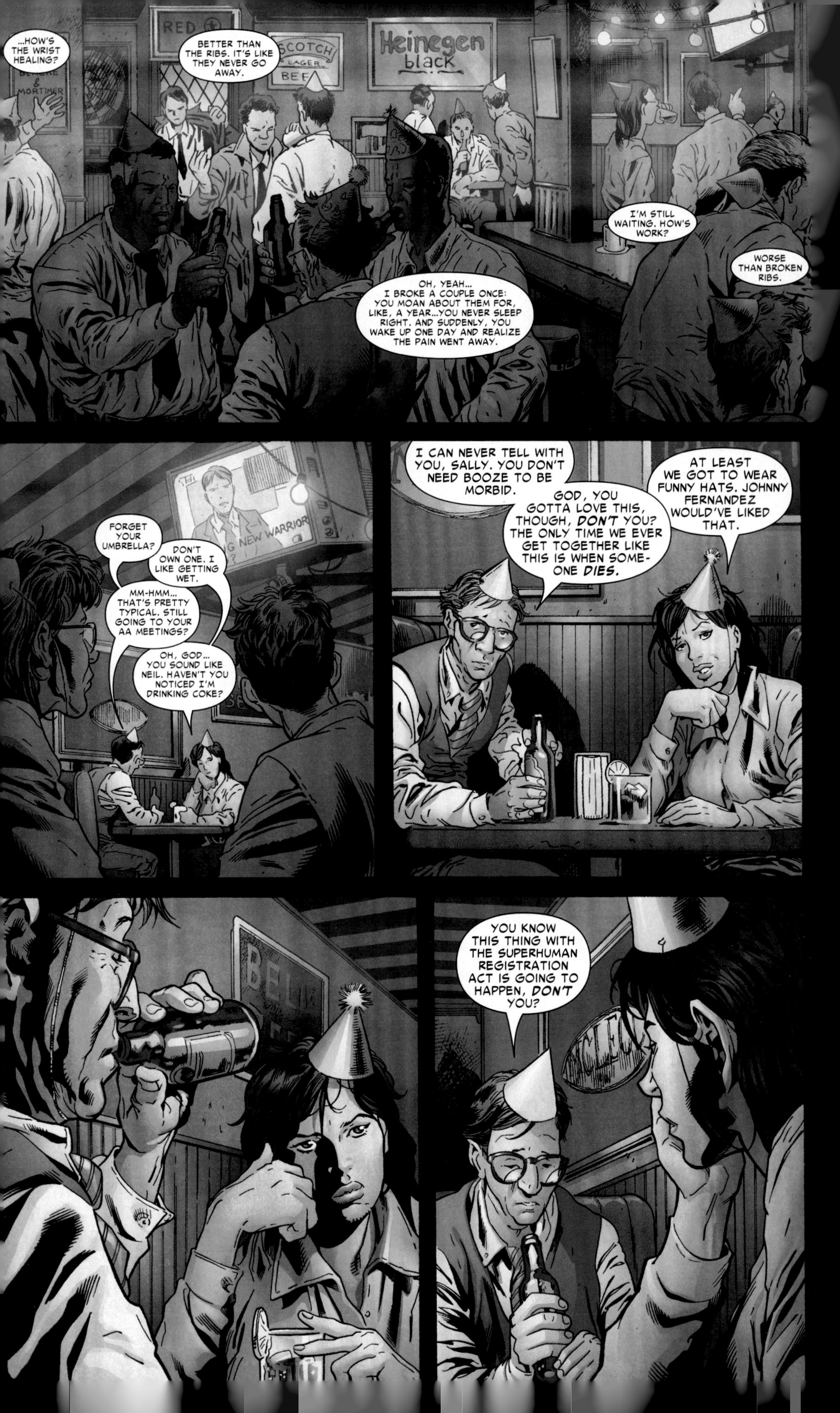

...HOW'S THE WRIST HEALING?
BETTER THAN THE RIBS. IT'S LIKE THEY NEVER GO AWAY.
OH, YEAH... I BROKE A COUPLE ONCE: YOU MOAN ABOUT THEM FOR, LIKE, A YEAR...YOU NEVER SLEEP RIGHT. AND SUDDENLY, YOU WAKE UP ONE DAY AND REALIZE THE PAIN WENT AWAY.
I'M STILL WAITING. HOW'S WORK?
WORSE THAN BROKEN RIBS.
FORGET YOUR UMBRELLA?
DON'T OWN ONE. I LIKE GETTING WET.
MM-HMM... THAT'S PRETTY TYPICAL. STILL GOING TO YOUR AA MEETINGS?
OH, GOD... YOU SOUND LIKE NEIL. HAVEN'T YOU NOTICED I'M DRINKING COKE?
I CAN NEVER TELL WITH YOU, SALLY. YOU DON'T NEED BOOZE TO BE MORBID.
GOD, YOU GOTTA LOVE THIS, THOUGH, *DON'T* YOU? THE ONLY TIME WE EVER GET TOGETHER LIKE THIS IS WHEN SOME-ONE *DIES*.
AT LEAST WE GOT TO WEAR FUNNY HATS. JOHNNY FERNANDEZ WOULD'VE LIKED THAT.
YOU KNOW THIS THING WITH THE SUPERHUMAN REGISTRATION ACT IS GOING TO HAPPEN, *DON'T* YOU?

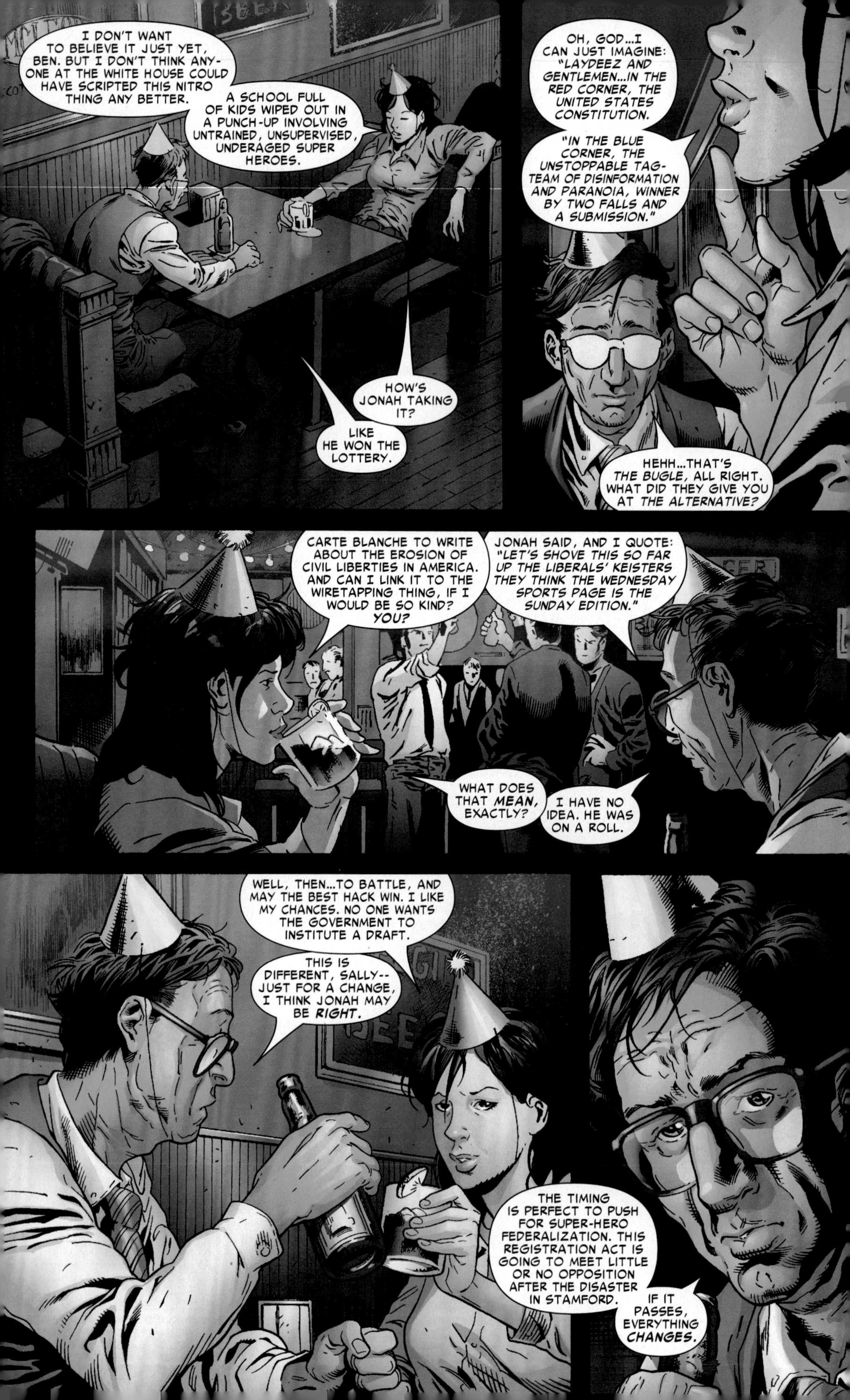
I DON'T WANT TO BELIEVE IT JUST YET, BEN. BUT I DON'T THINK ANY-ONE AT THE WHITE HOUSE COULD HAVE SCRIPTED THIS NITRO THING ANY BETTER.
A SCHOOL FULL OF KIDS WIPED OUT IN A PUNCH-UP INVOLVING UNTRAINED, UNSUPERVISED, UNDERAGED SUPER HEROES.
HOW'S JONAH TAKING IT?
LIKE HE WON THE LOTTERY.
OH, GOD...I CAN JUST IMAGINE: "LAYDEEZ AND GENTLEMEN...IN THE RED CORNER, THE UNITED STATES CONSTITUTION.
"IN THE BLUE CORNER, THE UNSTOPPABLE TAG-TEAM OF DISINFORMATION AND PARANOIA, WINNER BY TWO FALLS AND A SUBMISSION."
HEHH...THAT'S *THE BUGLE*, ALL RIGHT. WHAT DID THEY GIVE YOU AT *THE ALTERNATIVE?*
CARTE BLANCHE TO WRITE ABOUT THE EROSION OF CIVIL LIBERTIES IN AMERICA. AND CAN I LINK IT TO THE WIRETAPPING THING, IF I WOULD BE SO KIND? ***YOU?***
JONAH SAID, AND I QUOTE: *"LET'S SHOVE THIS SO FAR UP THE LIBERALS' KEISTERS THEY THINK THE WEDNESDAY SPORTS PAGE IS THE SUNDAY EDITION."*
WHAT DOES THAT *MEAN*, EXACTLY?
I HAVE NO IDEA. HE WAS ON A ROLL.
WELL, THEN...TO BATTLE, AND MAY THE BEST HACK WIN. I LIKE MY CHANCES. NO ONE WANTS THE GOVERNMENT TO INSTITUTE A DRAFT.
THIS IS DIFFERENT, SALLY-- JUST FOR A CHANGE, I THINK JONAH MAY BE ***RIGHT***.
THE TIMING IS PERFECT TO PUSH FOR SUPER-HERO FEDERALIZATION. THIS REGISTRATION ACT IS GOING TO MEET LITTLE OR NO OPPOSITION AFTER THE DISASTER IN STAMFORD.
IF IT PASSES, EVERYTHING ***CHANGES***.

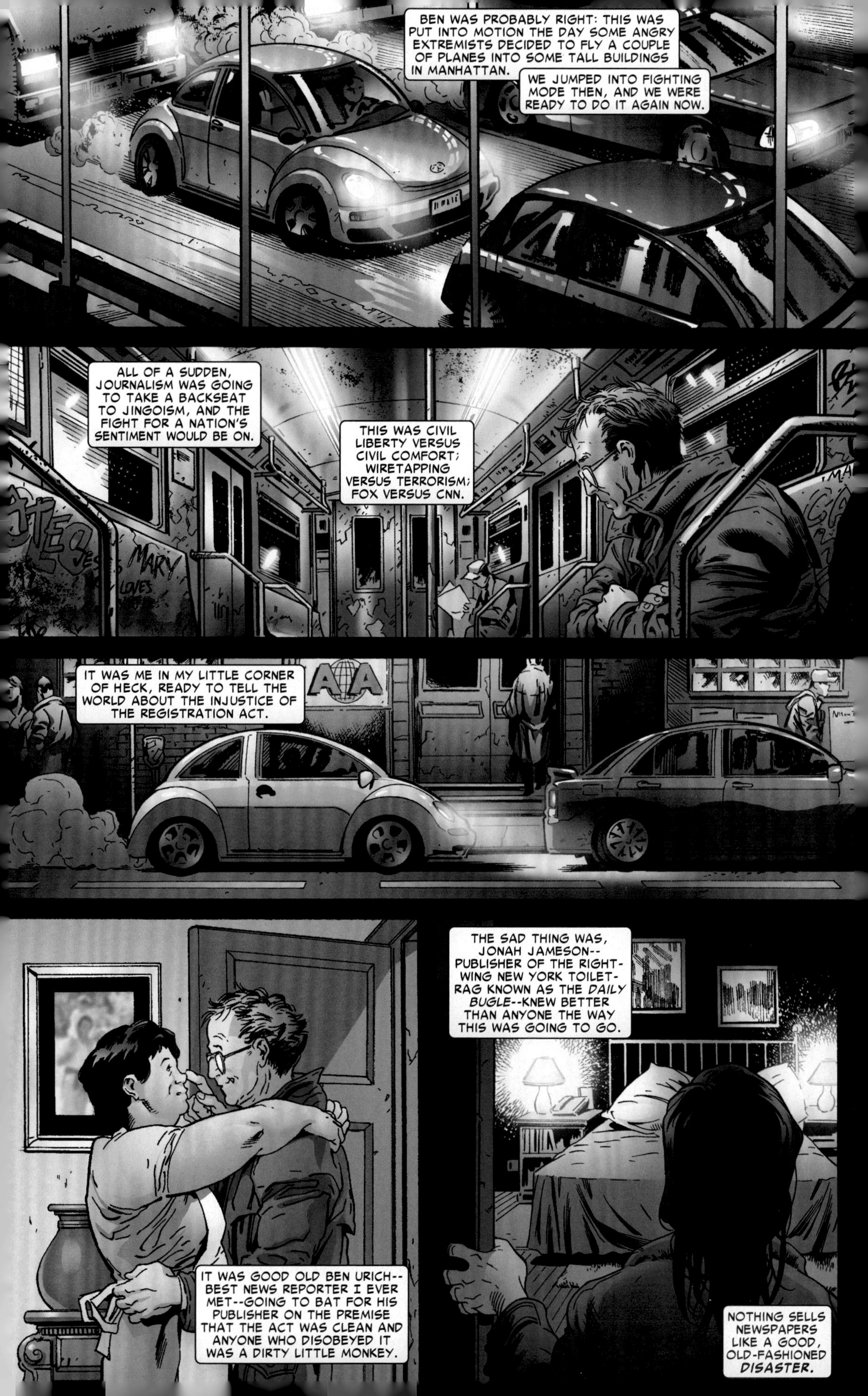
BEN WAS PROBABLY RIGHT: THIS WAS PUT INTO MOTION THE DAY SOME ANGRY EXTREMISTS DECIDED TO FLY A COUPLE OF PLANES INTO SOME TALL BUILDINGS IN MANHATTAN.
WE JUMPED INTO FIGHTING MODE THEN, AND WE WERE READY TO DO IT AGAIN NOW.
ALL OF A SUDDEN, JOURNALISM WAS GOING TO TAKE A BACKSEAT TO JINGOISM, AND THE FIGHT FOR A NATION'S SENTIMENT WOULD BE ON.
THIS WAS CIVIL LIBERTY VERSUS CIVIL COMFORT; WIRETAPPING VERSUS TERRORISM; FOX VERSUS CNN.
IT WAS ME IN MY LITTLE CORNER OF HECK, READY TO TELL THE WORLD ABOUT THE INJUSTICE OF THE REGISTRATION ACT.
IT WAS GOOD OLD BEN URICH--BEST NEWS REPORTER I EVER MET--GOING TO BAT FOR HIS PUBLISHER ON THE PREMISE THAT THE ACT WAS CLEAN AND ANYONE WHO DISOBEYED IT WAS A DIRTY LITTLE MONKEY.
THE SAD THING WAS, JONAH JAMESON--PUBLISHER OF THE RIGHT-WING NEW YORK TOILET-RAG KNOWN AS THE *DAILY BUGLE*--KNEW BETTER THAN ANYONE THE WAY THIS WAS GOING TO GO.
NOTHING SELLS NEWSPAPERS LIKE A GOOD, OLD-FASHIONED *DISASTER.*

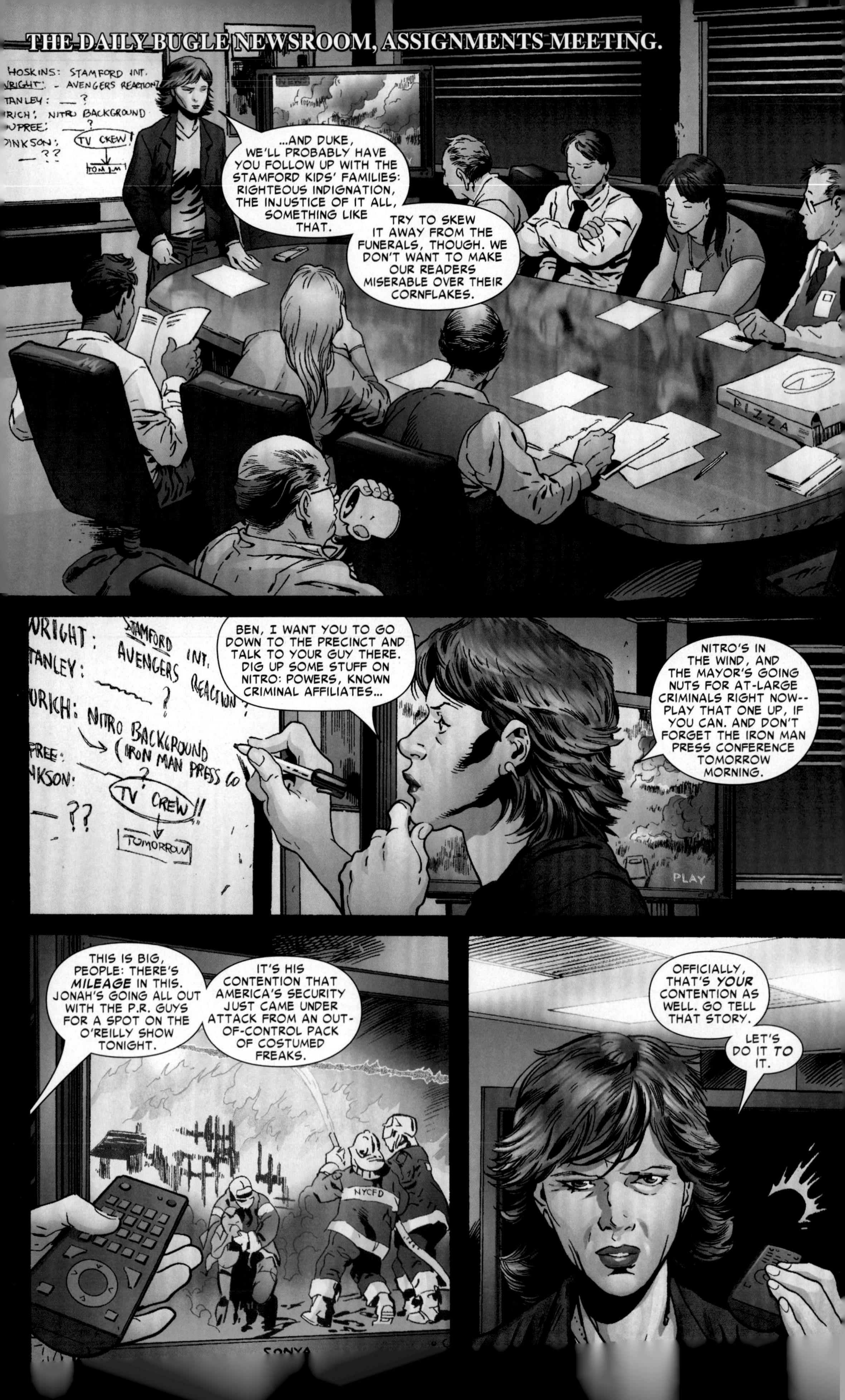
THE DAILY BUGLE NEWSROOM, ASSIGNMENTS MEETING.
...AND DUKE, WE'LL PROBABLY HAVE YOU FOLLOW UP WITH THE STAMFORD KIDS' FAMILIES: RIGHTEOUS INDIGNATION, THE INJUSTICE OF IT ALL, SOMETHING LIKE THAT.
TRY TO SKEW IT AWAY FROM THE FUNERALS, THOUGH. WE DON'T WANT TO MAKE OUR READERS MISERABLE OVER THEIR CORNFLAKES.
PIZZA
BEN, I WANT YOU TO GO DOWN TO THE PRECINCT AND TALK TO YOUR GUY THERE. DIG UP SOME STUFF ON NITRO: POWERS, KNOWN CRIMINAL AFFILIATES...
NITRO'S IN THE WIND, AND THE MAYOR'S GOING NUTS FOR AT-LARGE CRIMINALS RIGHT NOW-- PLAY THAT ONE UP, IF YOU CAN. AND DON'T FORGET THE IRON MAN PRESS CONFERENCE TOMORROW MORNING.
PLAY
THIS IS BIG, PEOPLE: THERE'S *MILEAGE* IN THIS. JONAH'S GOING ALL OUT WITH THE P.R. GUYS FOR A SPOT ON THE O'REILLY SHOW TONIGHT.
IT'S HIS CONTENTION THAT AMERICA'S SECURITY JUST CAME UNDER ATTACK FROM AN OUT-OF-CONTROL PACK OF COSTUMED FREAKS.
NYCFD
OFFICIALLY, THAT'S *YOUR* CONTENTION AS WELL. GO TELL THAT STORY.
LET'S DO IT *TO* IT.

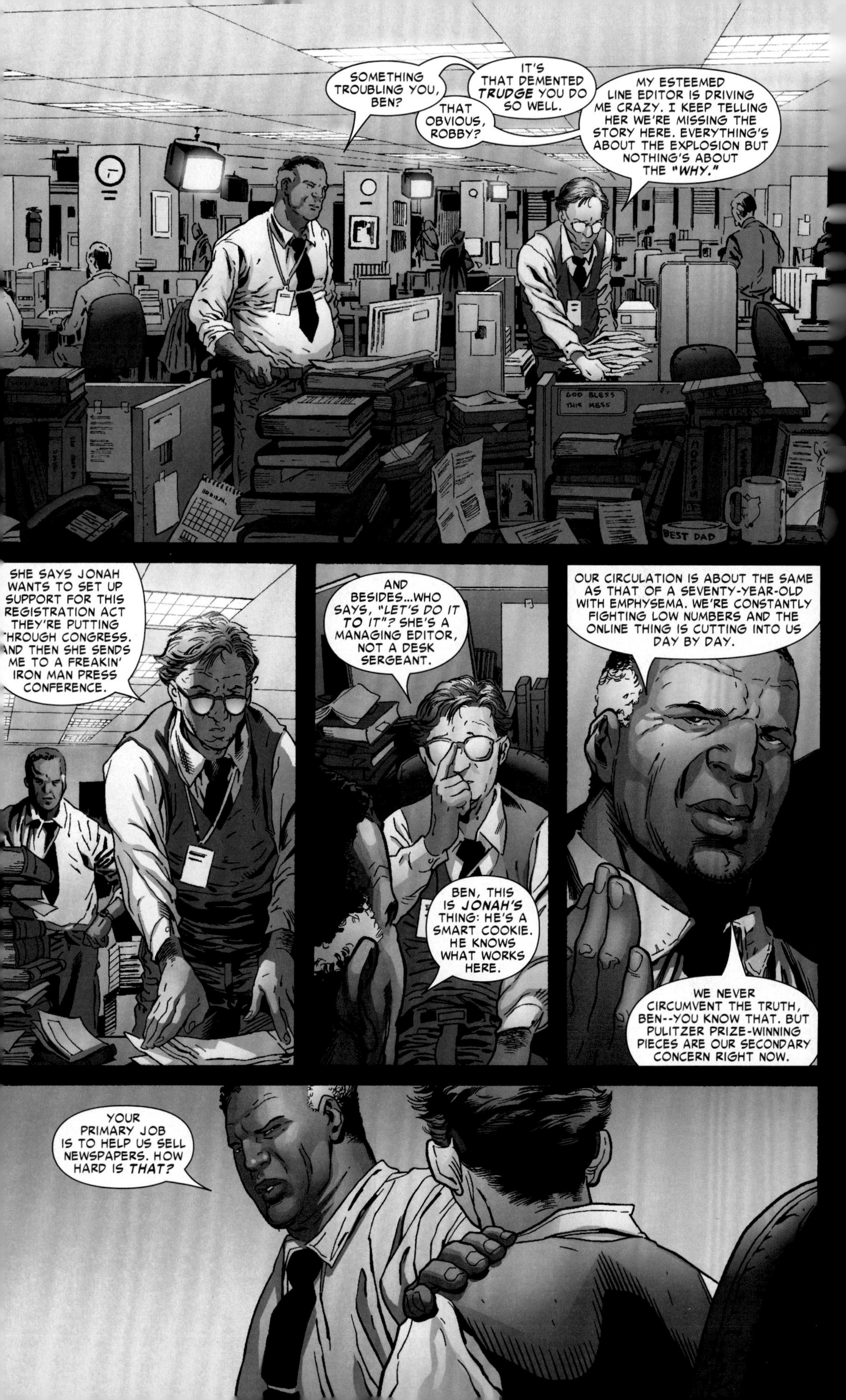
SOMETHING TROUBLING YOU, BEN?
THAT OBVIOUS, ROBBY?
IT'S THAT DEMENTED TRUDGE YOU DO SO WELL.
MY ESTEEMED LINE EDITOR IS DRIVING ME CRAZY. I KEEP TELLING HER WE'RE MISSING THE STORY HERE. EVERYTHING'S ABOUT THE EXPLOSION BUT NOTHING'S ABOUT THE "WHY."
GOD BLESS THIS MESS
BEST DAD
SHE SAYS JONAH WANTS TO SET UP SUPPORT FOR THIS REGISTRATION ACT THEY'RE PUTTING THROUGH CONGRESS. AND THEN SHE SENDS ME TO A FREAKIN' IRON MAN PRESS CONFERENCE.
AND BESIDES...WHO SAYS, "LET'S DO IT TO IT"? SHE'S A MANAGING EDITOR, NOT A DESK SERGEANT.
BEN, THIS IS JONAH'S THING: HE'S A SMART COOKIE. HE KNOWS WHAT WORKS HERE.
OUR CIRCULATION IS ABOUT THE SAME AS THAT OF A SEVENTY-YEAR-OLD WITH EMPHYSEMA. WE'RE CONSTANTLY FIGHTING LOW NUMBERS AND THE ONLINE THING IS CUTTING INTO US DAY BY DAY.
WE NEVER CIRCUMVENT THE TRUTH, BEN--YOU KNOW THAT. BUT PULITZER PRIZE-WINNING PIECES ARE OUR SECONDARY CONCERN RIGHT NOW.
YOUR PRIMARY JOB IS TO HELP US SELL NEWSPAPERS. HOW HARD IS THAT?

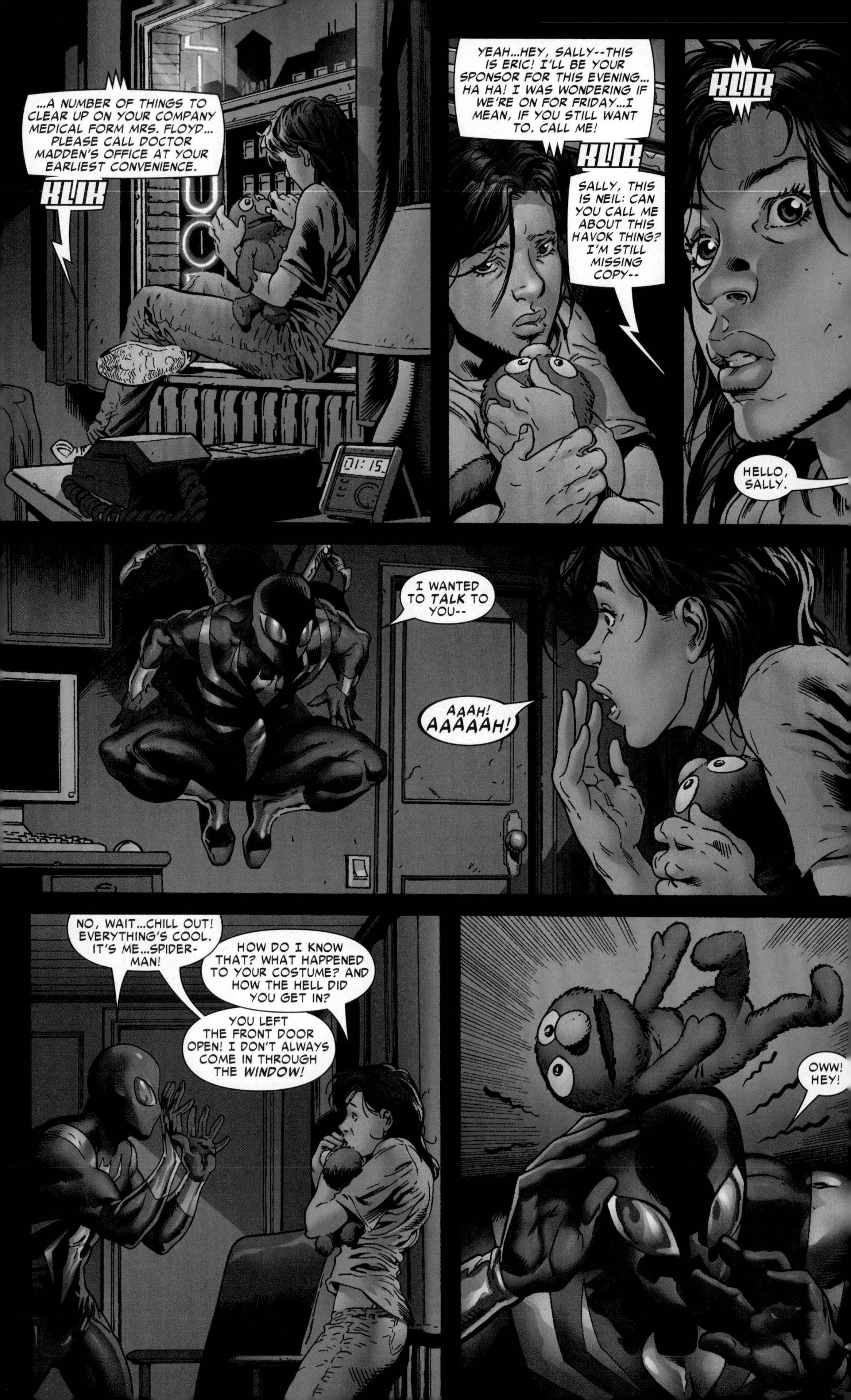
...A NUMBER OF THINGS TO CLEAR UP ON YOUR COMPANY MEDICAL FORM MRS. FLOYD... PLEASE CALL DOCTOR MADDEN'S OFFICE AT YOUR EARLIEST CONVENIENCE.
KLIK
YEAH...HEY, SALLY--THIS IS ERIC! I'LL BE YOUR SPONSOR FOR THIS EVENING... HA HA! I WAS WONDERING IF WE'RE ON FOR FRIDAY...I MEAN, IF YOU STILL WANT TO. CALL ME!
KLIK
SALLY, THIS IS NEIL: CAN YOU CALL ME ABOUT THIS HAVOK THING? I'M STILL MISSING COPY--
KLIK
HELLO, SALLY.
I WANTED TO TALK TO YOU--
AAAH! AAAAAH!
NO, WAIT...CHILL OUT! EVERYTHING'S COOL. IT'S ME...SPIDER-MAN!
HOW DO I KNOW THAT? WHAT HAPPENED TO YOUR COSTUME? AND HOW THE HELL DID YOU GET IN?
YOU LEFT THE FRONT DOOR OPEN! I DON'T ALWAYS COME IN THROUGH THE WINDOW!
OWW! HEY!

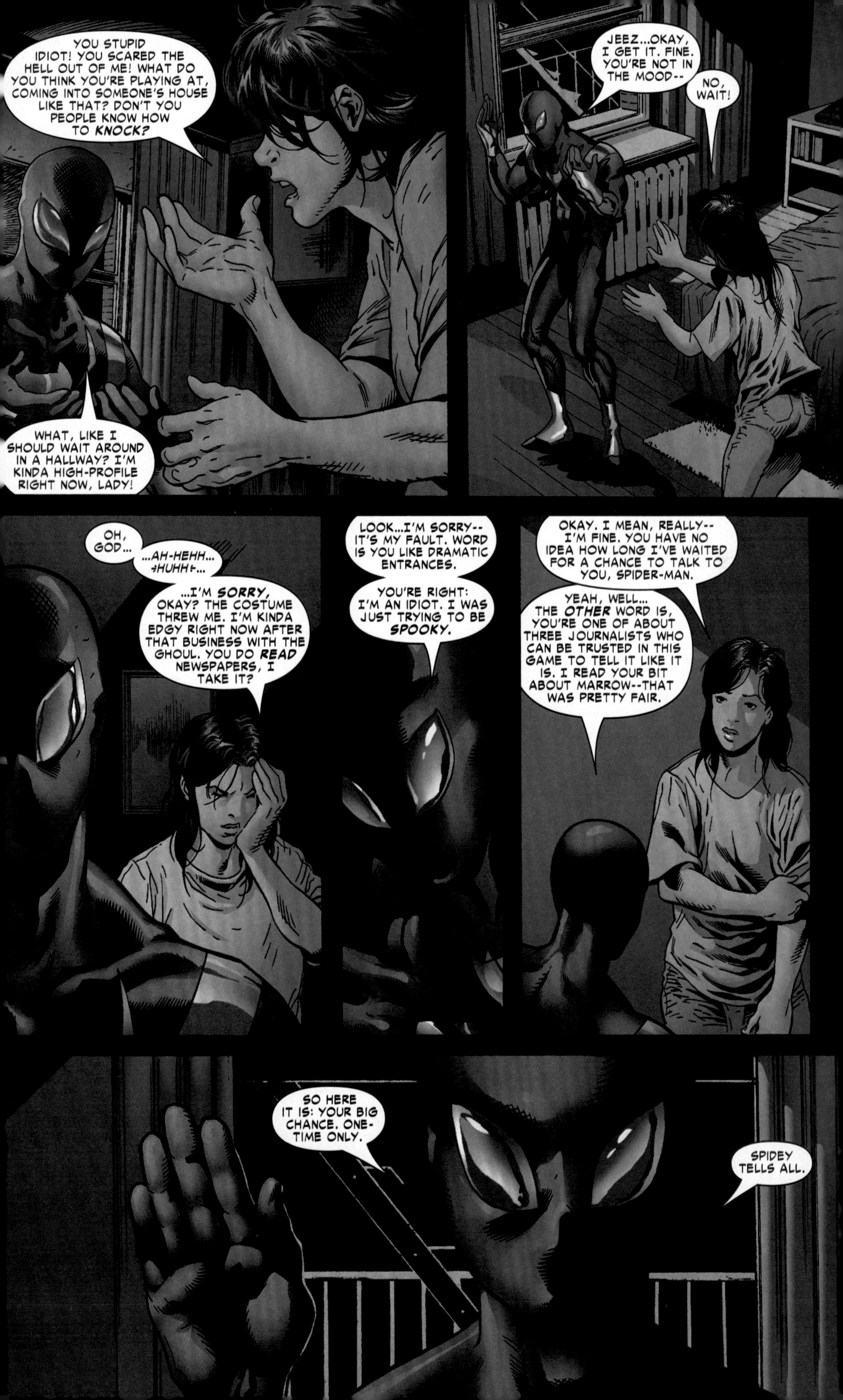

YOU STUPID IDIOT! YOU SCARED THE HELL OUT OF ME! WHAT DO YOU THINK YOU'RE PLAYING AT, COMING INTO SOMEONE'S HOUSE LIKE THAT? DON'T YOU PEOPLE KNOW HOW TO KNOCK?
WHAT, LIKE I SHOULD WAIT AROUND IN A HALLWAY? I'M KINDA HIGH-PROFILE RIGHT NOW, LADY!
JEEZ...OKAY, I GET IT. FINE. YOU'RE NOT IN THE MOOD--
NO, WAIT!
OH, GOD...
...AH-HEHH... HUHH...
...I'M SORRY, OKAY? THE COSTUME THREW ME. I'M KINDA EDGY RIGHT NOW AFTER THAT BUSINESS WITH THE GHOUL. YOU DO READ NEWSPAPERS, I TAKE IT?
LOOK...I'M SORRY-- IT'S MY FAULT. WORD IS YOU LIKE DRAMATIC ENTRANCES.
YOU'RE RIGHT: I'M AN IDIOT. I WAS JUST TRYING TO BE SPOOKY.
OKAY. I MEAN, REALLY-- I'M FINE. YOU HAVE NO IDEA HOW LONG I'VE WAITED FOR A CHANCE TO TALK TO YOU, SPIDER-MAN.
YEAH, WELL... THE OTHER WORD IS, YOU'RE ONE OF ABOUT THREE JOURNALISTS WHO CAN BE TRUSTED IN THIS GAME TO TELL IT LIKE IT IS. I READ YOUR BIT ABOUT MARROW--THAT WAS PRETTY FAIR.
SO HERE IT IS: YOUR BIG CHANCE. ONE-TIME ONLY.
SPIDEY TELLS ALL.

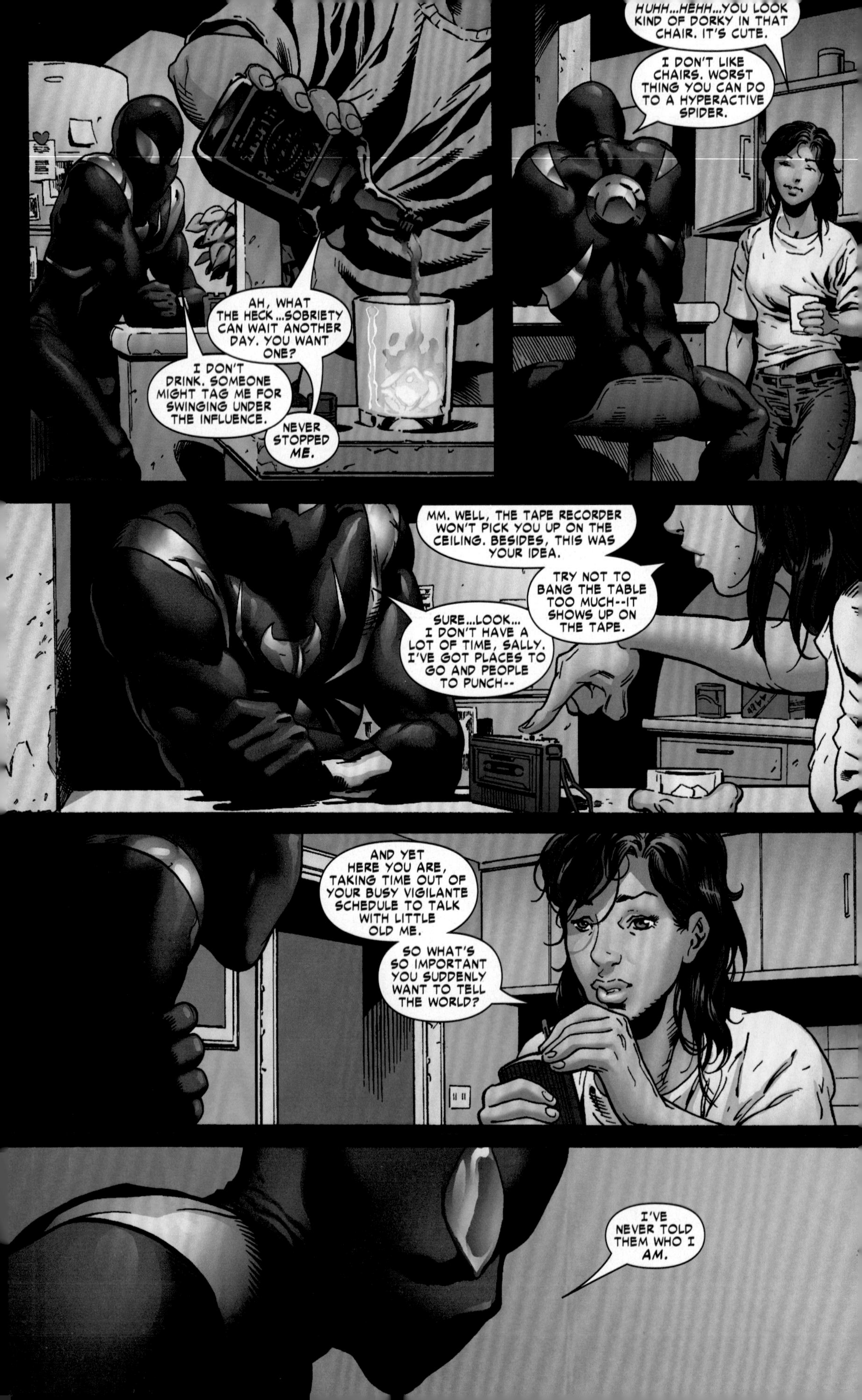
AH, WHAT THE HECK...SOBRIETY CAN WAIT ANOTHER DAY. YOU WANT ONE?
I DON'T DRINK. SOMEONE MIGHT TAG ME FOR SWINGING UNDER THE INFLUENCE.
NEVER STOPPED ME.
HUHH...HEHH...YOU LOOK KIND OF DORKY IN THAT CHAIR. IT'S CUTE.
I DON'T LIKE CHAIRS. WORST THING YOU CAN DO TO A HYPERACTIVE SPIDER.
MM. WELL, THE TAPE RECORDER WON'T PICK YOU UP ON THE CEILING. BESIDES, THIS WAS YOUR IDEA.
TRY NOT TO BANG THE TABLE TOO MUCH--IT SHOWS UP ON THE TAPE.
SURE...LOOK... I DON'T HAVE A LOT OF TIME, SALLY. I'VE GOT PLACES TO GO AND PEOPLE TO PUNCH--
AND YET HERE YOU ARE, TAKING TIME OUT OF YOUR BUSY VIGILANTE SCHEDULE TO TALK WITH LITTLE OLD ME.
SO WHAT'S SO IMPORTANT YOU SUDDENLY WANT TO TELL THE WORLD?
I'VE NEVER TOLD THEM WHO I AM.

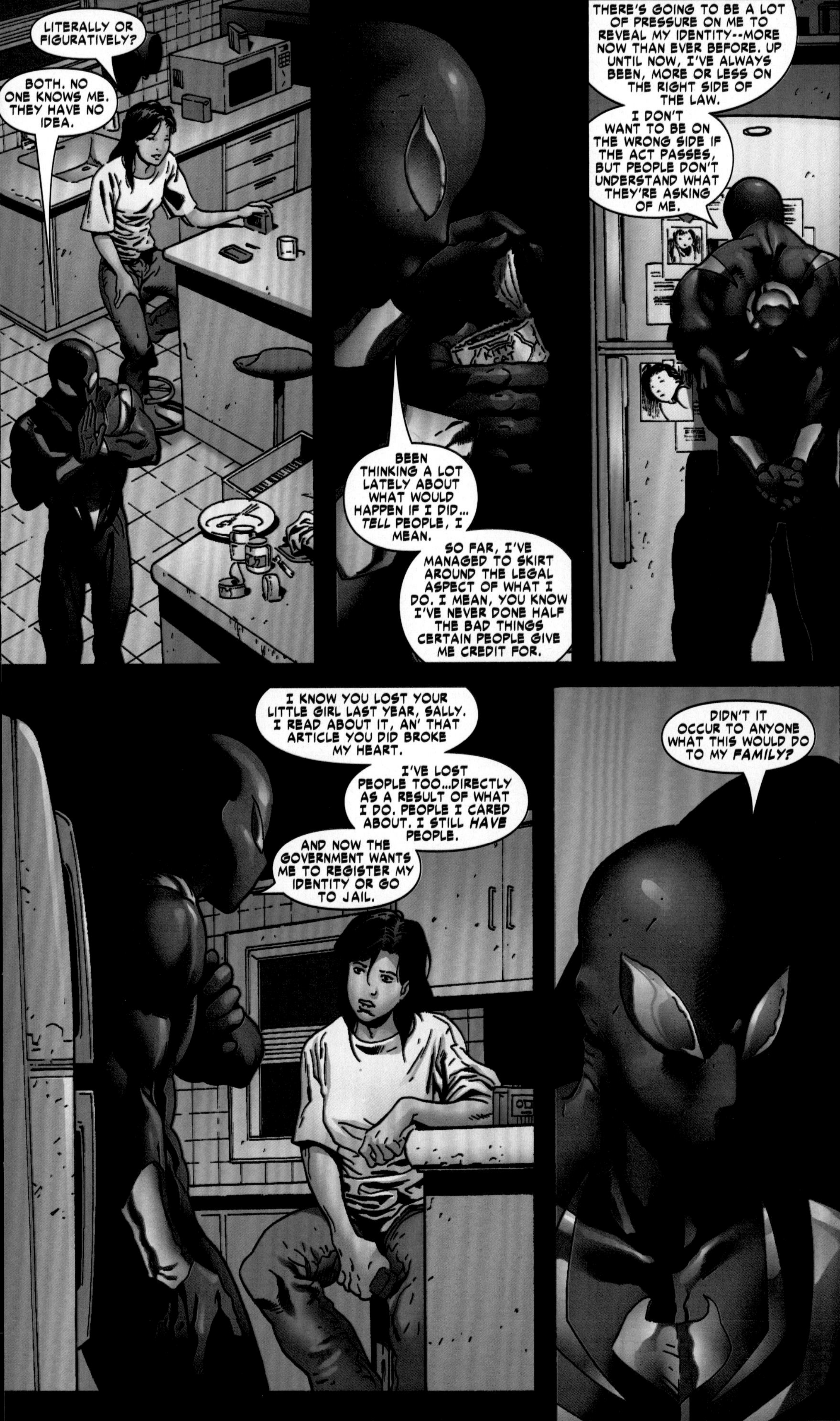
LITERALLY OR FIGURATIVELY?
BOTH. NO ONE KNOWS ME. THEY HAVE NO IDEA.
BEEN THINKING A LOT LATELY ABOUT WHAT WOULD HAPPEN IF I DID... *TELL* PEOPLE, I MEAN.
SO FAR, I'VE MANAGED TO SKIRT AROUND THE LEGAL ASPECT OF WHAT I DO. I MEAN, YOU KNOW I'VE NEVER DONE HALF THE BAD THINGS CERTAIN PEOPLE GIVE ME CREDIT FOR.
THERE'S GOING TO BE A LOT OF PRESSURE ON ME TO REVEAL MY IDENTITY--MORE NOW THAN EVER BEFORE. UP UNTIL NOW, I'VE ALWAYS BEEN, MORE OR LESS ON THE RIGHT SIDE OF THE LAW.
I DON'T WANT TO BE ON THE WRONG SIDE IF THE ACT PASSES, BUT PEOPLE DON'T UNDERSTAND WHAT THEY'RE ASKING OF ME.
I KNOW YOU LOST YOUR LITTLE GIRL LAST YEAR, SALLY. I READ ABOUT IT, AN' THAT ARTICLE YOU DID BROKE MY HEART.
I'VE LOST PEOPLE TOO...DIRECTLY AS A RESULT OF WHAT I DO. PEOPLE I CARED ABOUT. I STILL *HAVE* PEOPLE.
AND NOW THE GOVERNMENT WANTS ME TO REGISTER MY IDENTITY OR GO TO JAIL.
DIDN'T IT OCCUR TO ANYONE WHAT THIS WOULD DO TO MY *FAMILY?*

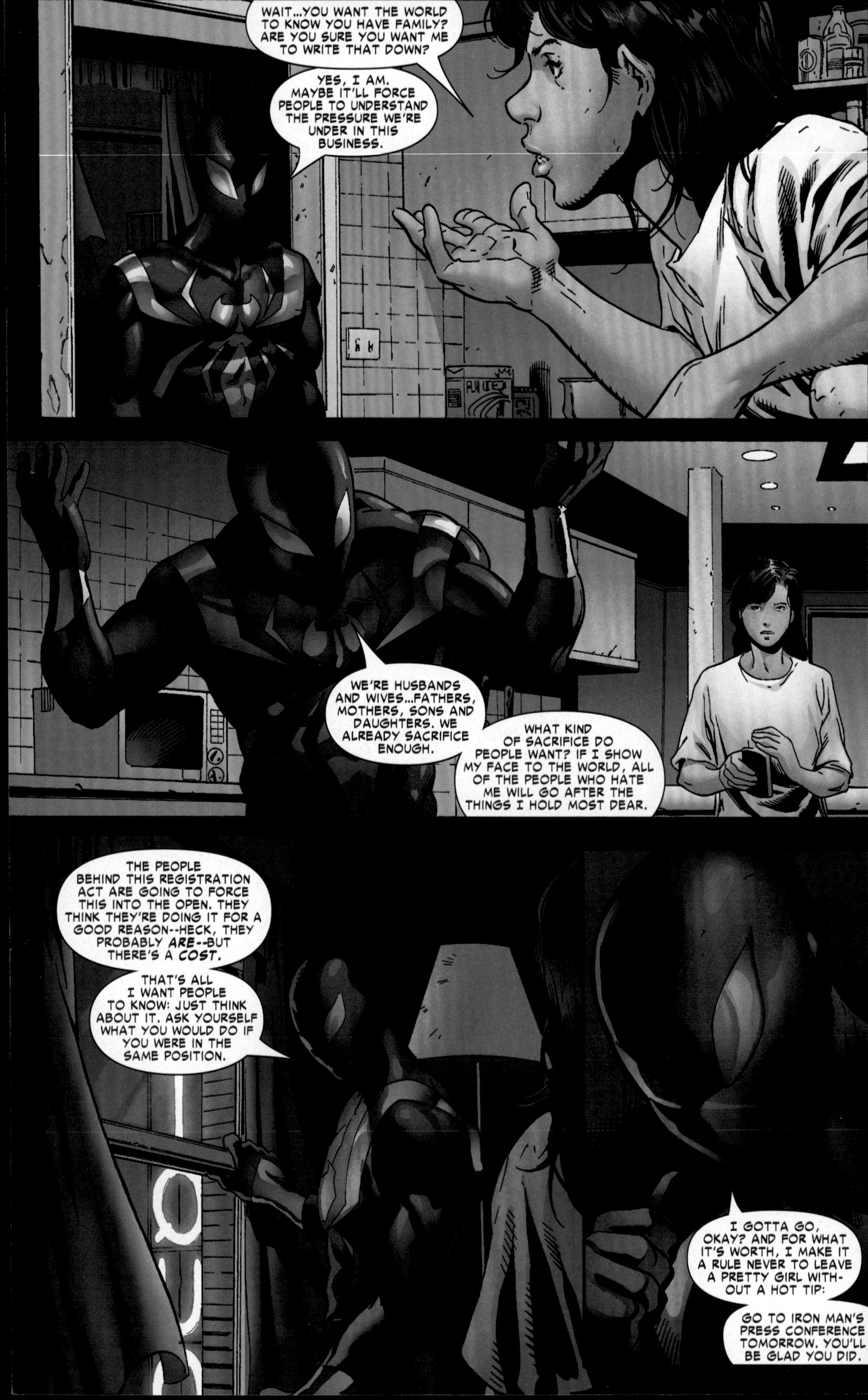
WAIT...YOU WANT THE WORLD TO KNOW YOU HAVE FAMILY? ARE YOU SURE YOU WANT ME TO WRITE THAT DOWN?
YES, I AM. MAYBE IT'LL FORCE PEOPLE TO UNDERSTAND THE PRESSURE WE'RE UNDER IN THIS BUSINESS.
WE'RE HUSBANDS AND WIVES...FATHERS, MOTHERS, SONS AND DAUGHTERS. WE ALREADY SACRIFICE ENOUGH.
WHAT KIND OF SACRIFICE DO PEOPLE WANT? IF I SHOW MY FACE TO THE WORLD, ALL OF THE PEOPLE WHO HATE ME WILL GO AFTER THE THINGS I HOLD MOST DEAR.
THE PEOPLE BEHIND THIS REGISTRATION ACT ARE GOING TO FORCE THIS INTO THE OPEN. THEY THINK THEY'RE DOING IT FOR A GOOD REASON--HECK, THEY PROBABLY *ARE*--BUT THERE'S A *COST*.
THAT'S ALL I WANT PEOPLE TO KNOW: JUST THINK ABOUT IT. ASK YOURSELF WHAT YOU WOULD DO IF YOU WERE IN THE SAME POSITION.
I GOTTA GO, OKAY? AND FOR WHAT IT'S WORTH, I MAKE IT A RULE NEVER TO LEAVE A PRETTY GIRL WITH-OUT A HOT TIP:
GO TO IRON MAN'S PRESS CONFERENCE TOMORROW. YOU'LL BE GLAD YOU DID.

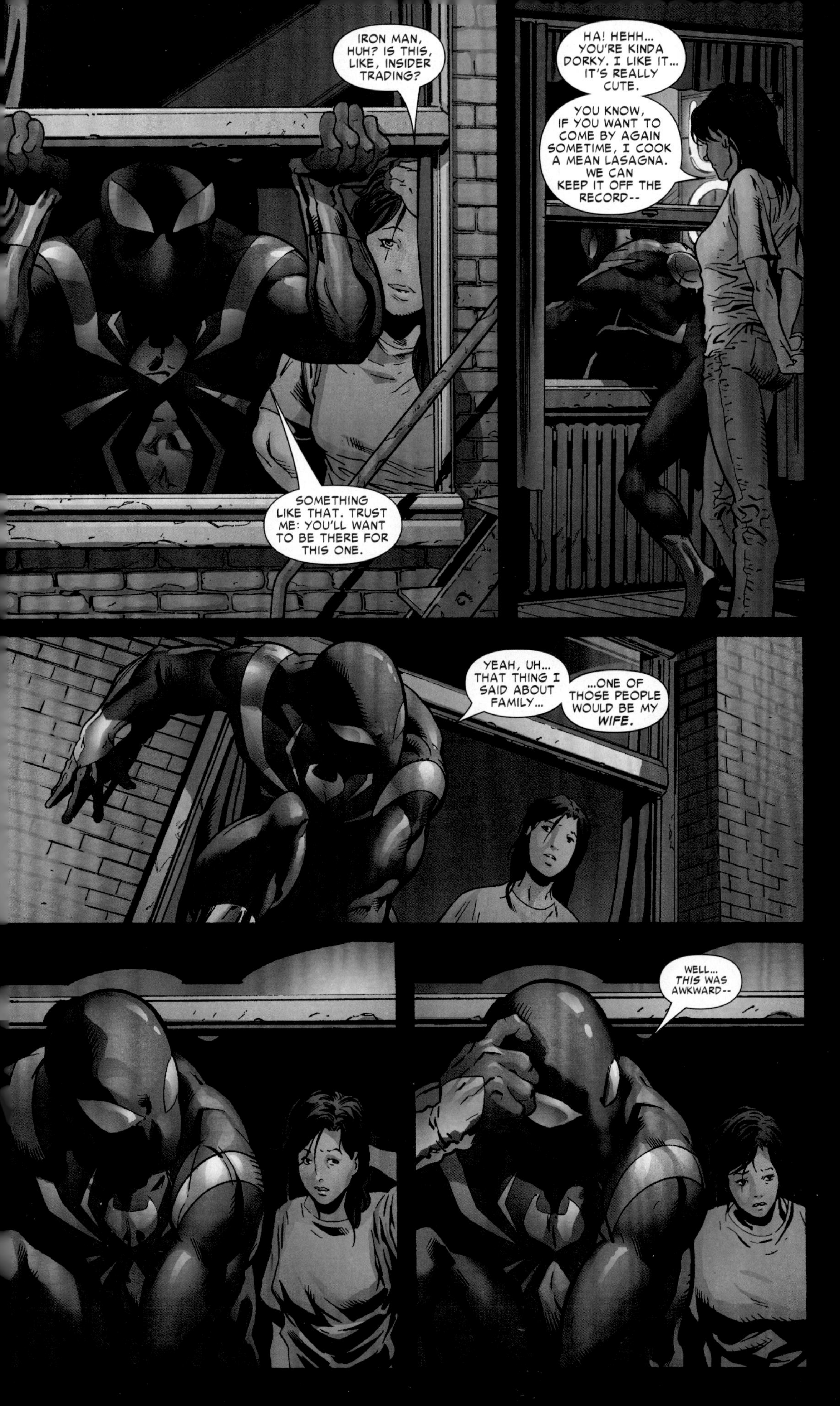
IRON MAN, HUH? IS THIS, LIKE, INSIDER TRADING?
SOMETHING LIKE THAT. TRUST ME: YOU'LL WANT TO BE THERE FOR THIS ONE.
HA! HEHH... YOU'RE KINDA DORKY. I LIKE IT... IT'S REALLY CUTE.
YOU KNOW, IF YOU WANT TO COME BY AGAIN SOMETIME, I COOK A MEAN LASAGNA. WE CAN KEEP IT OFF THE RECORD--
YEAH, UH... THAT THING I SAID ABOUT FAMILY...
...ONE OF THOSE PEOPLE WOULD BE MY *WIFE.*
WELL... *THIS* WAS AWKWARD--

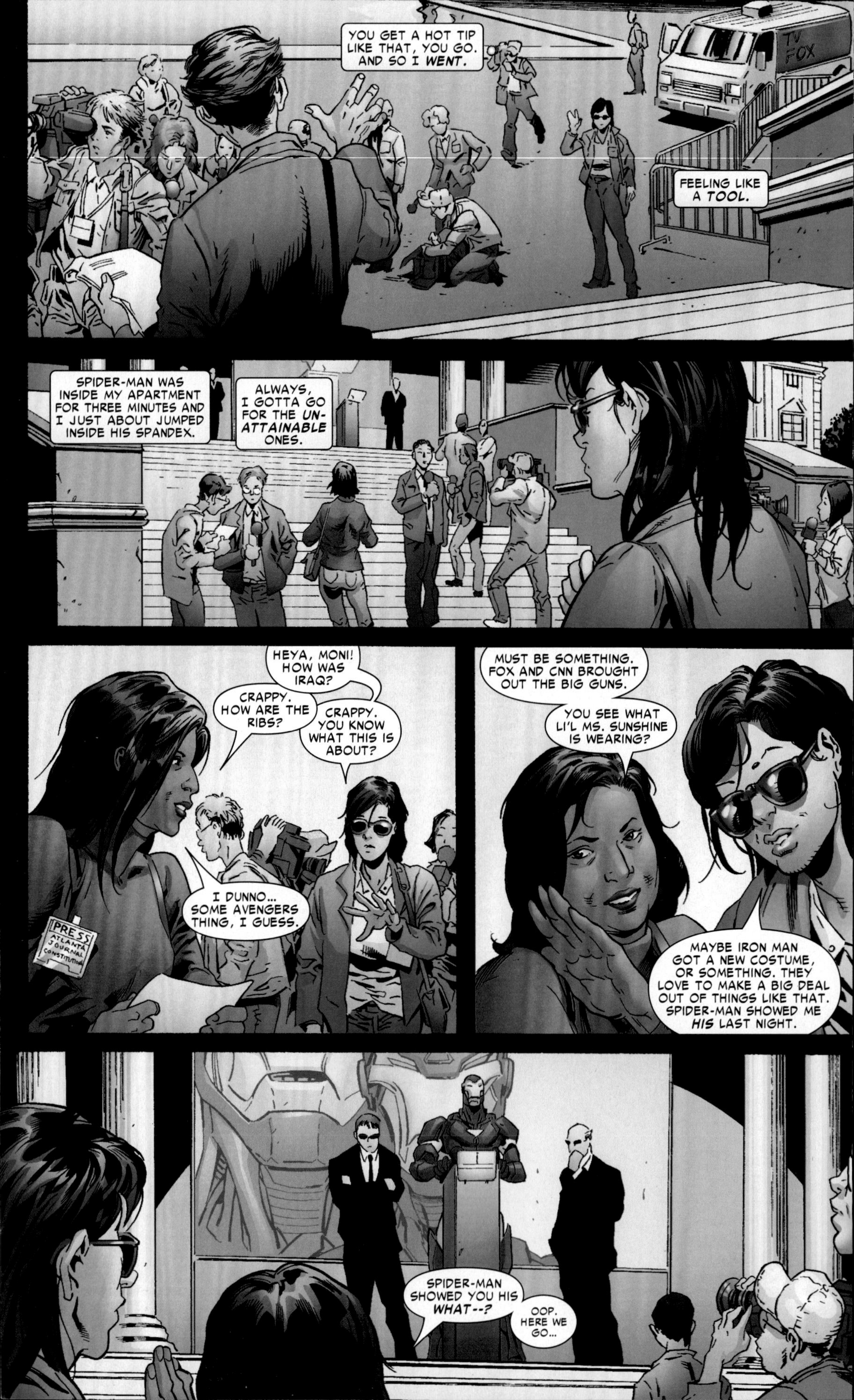
YOU GET A HOT TIP LIKE THAT, YOU GO. AND SO I WENT.
FEELING LIKE A TOOL.
TV FOX
SPIDER-MAN WAS INSIDE MY APARTMENT FOR THREE MINUTES AND I JUST ABOUT JUMPED INSIDE HIS SPANDEX.
ALWAYS, I GOTTA GO FOR THE UN-ATTAINABLE ONES.
HEYA, MONI! HOW WAS IRAQ?
CRAPPY. HOW ARE THE RIBS?
CRAPPY. YOU KNOW WHAT THIS IS ABOUT?
I DUNNO... SOME AVENGERS THING, I GUESS.
PRESS ATLANTA JOURNAL CONSTITUTION
MUST BE SOMETHING. FOX AND CNN BROUGHT OUT THE BIG GUNS.
YOU SEE WHAT LI'L MS. SUNSHINE IS WEARING?
MAYBE IRON MAN GOT A NEW COSTUME, OR SOMETHING. THEY LOVE TO MAKE A BIG DEAL OUT OF THINGS LIKE THAT. SPIDER-MAN SHOWED ME HIS LAST NIGHT.
SPIDER-MAN SHOWED YOU HIS WHAT--?
OOP. HERE WE GO...

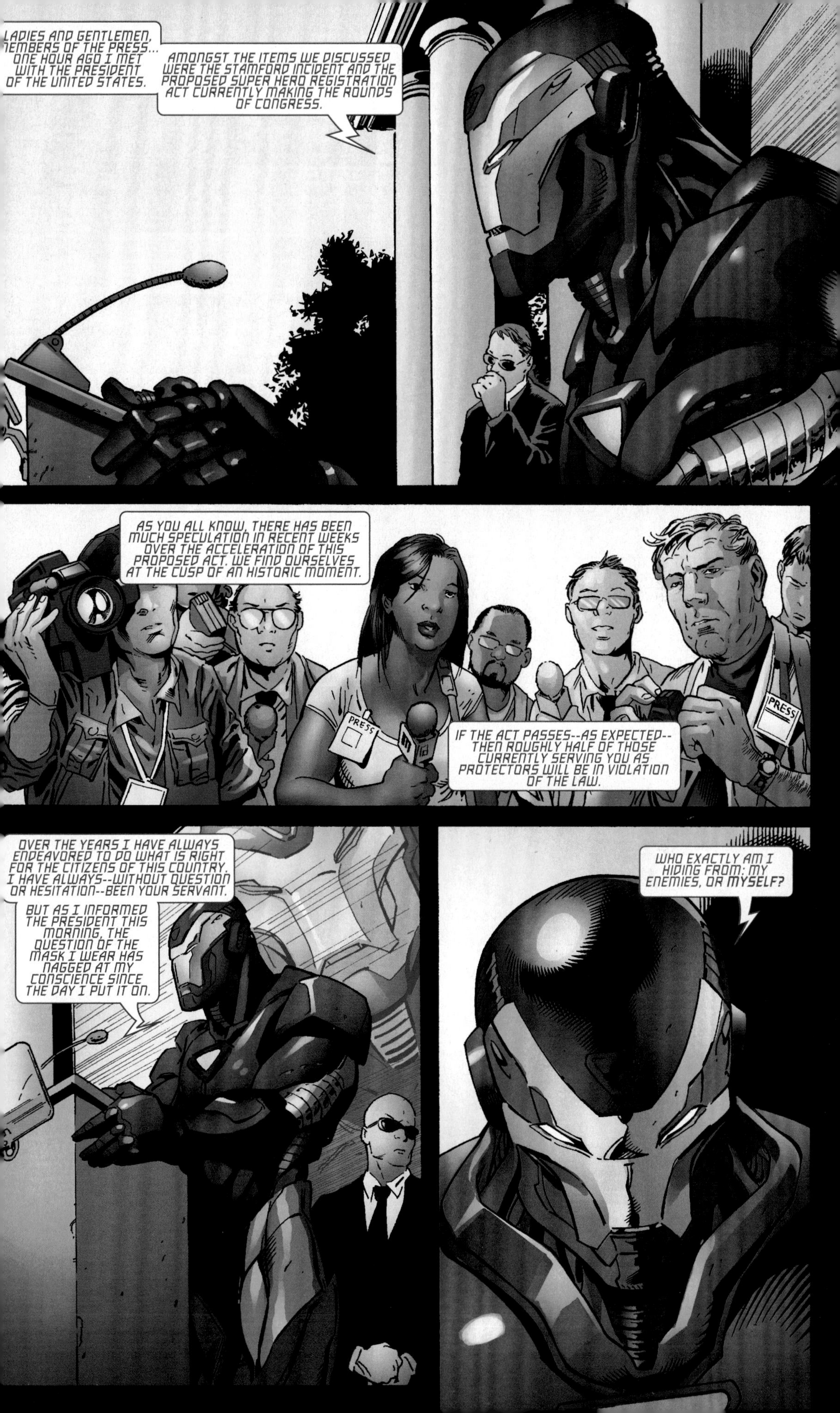
LADIES AND GENTLEMEN, MEMBERS OF THE PRESS... ONE HOUR AGO I MET WITH THE PRESIDENT OF THE UNITED STATES.
AMONGST THE ITEMS WE DISCUSSED WERE THE STAMFORD INCIDENT AND THE PROPOSED SUPER HERO REGISTRATION ACT CURRENTLY MAKING THE ROUNDS OF CONGRESS.
AS YOU ALL KNOW, THERE HAS BEEN MUCH SPECULATION IN RECENT WEEKS OVER THE ACCELERATION OF THIS PROPOSED ACT. WE FIND OURSELVES AT THE CUSP OF AN HISTORIC MOMENT.
IF THE ACT PASSES--AS EXPECTED--THEN ROUGHLY HALF OF THOSE CURRENTLY SERVING YOU AS PROTECTORS WILL BE IN VIOLATION OF THE LAW.
OVER THE YEARS I HAVE ALWAYS ENDEAVORED TO DO WHAT IS RIGHT FOR THE CITIZENS OF THIS COUNTRY. I HAVE ALWAYS--WITHOUT QUESTION OR HESITATION--BEEN YOUR SERVANT.
BUT AS I INFORMED THE PRESIDENT THIS MORNING, THE QUESTION OF THE MASK I WEAR HAS NAGGED AT MY CONSCIENCE SINCE THE DAY I PUT IT ON.
WHO EXACTLY AM I HIDING FROM: MY ENEMIES, OR MYSELF?

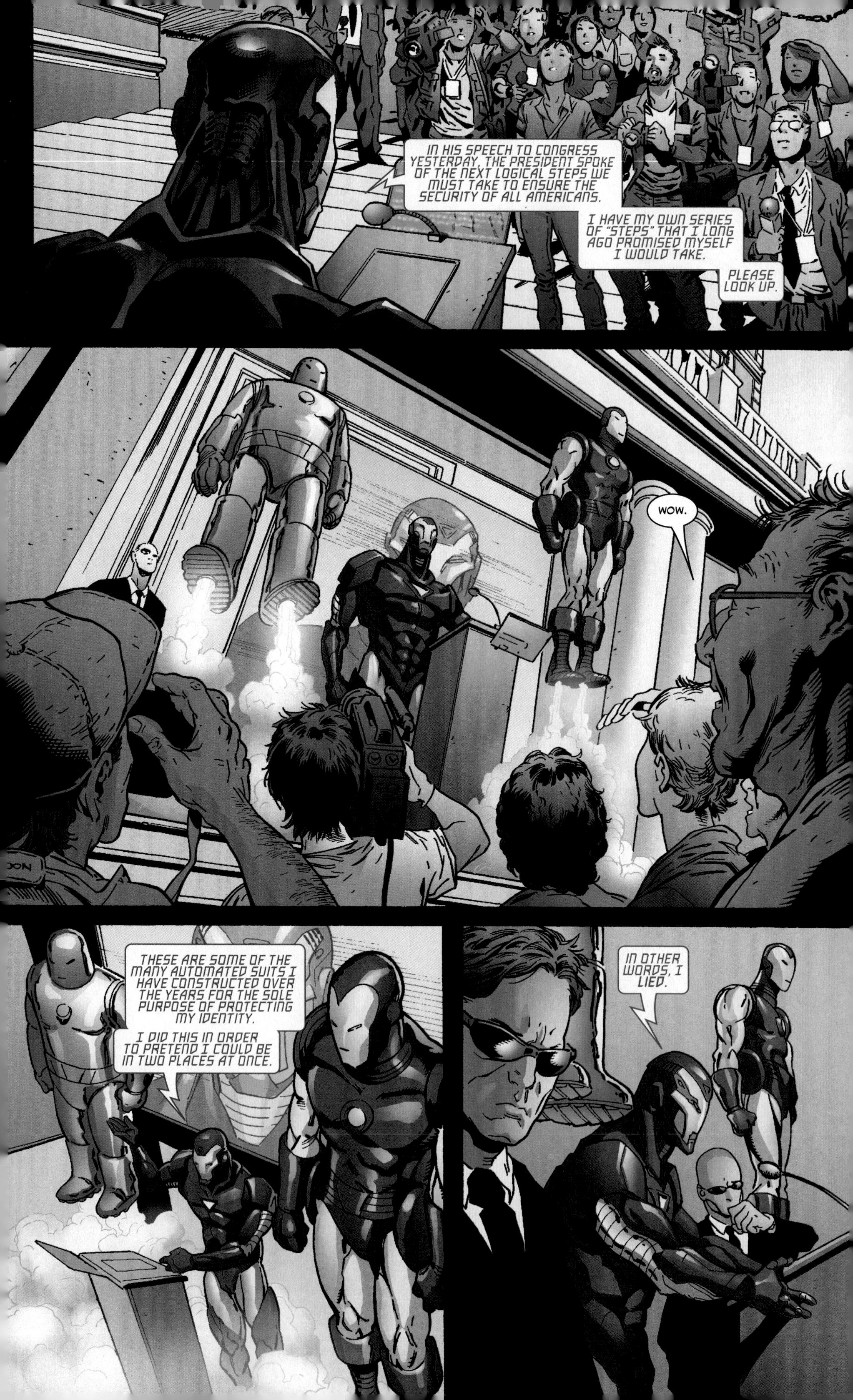
IN HIS SPEECH TO CONGRESS YESTERDAY, THE PRESIDENT SPOKE OF THE NEXT LOGICAL STEPS WE MUST TAKE TO ENSURE THE SECURITY OF ALL AMERICANS.
I HAVE MY OWN SERIES OF "STEPS" THAT I LONG AGO PROMISED MYSELF I WOULD TAKE.
PLEASE LOOK UP.
WOW.
THESE ARE SOME OF THE MANY AUTOMATED SUITS I HAVE CONSTRUCTED OVER THE YEARS FOR THE SOLE PURPOSE OF PROTECTING MY IDENTITY.
I DID THIS IN ORDER TO PRETEND I COULD BE IN TWO PLACES AT ONCE.
IN OTHER WORDS, I LIED.

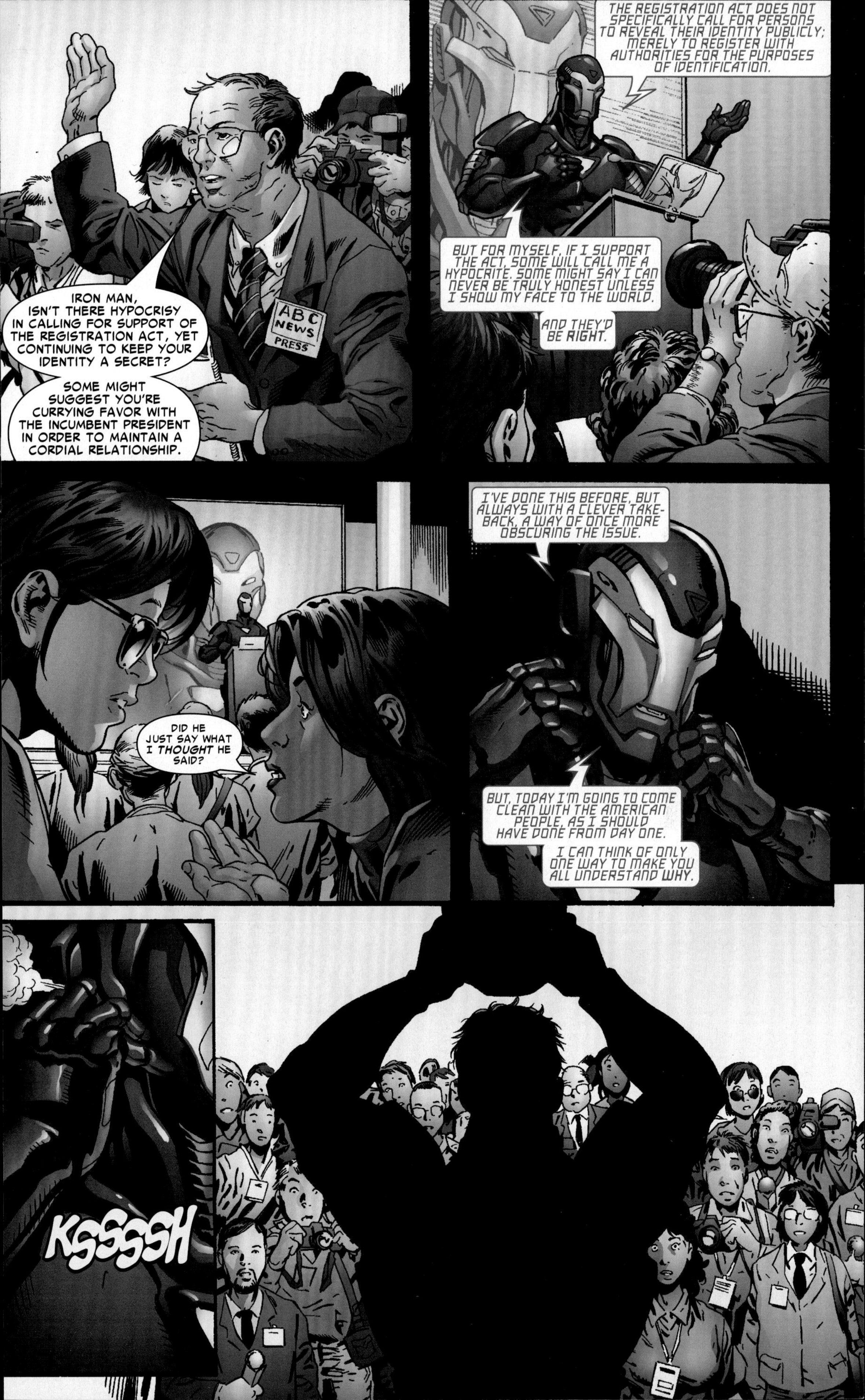

IRON MAN, ISN'T THERE HYPOCRISY IN CALLING FOR SUPPORT OF THE REGISTRATION ACT, YET CONTINUING TO KEEP YOUR IDENTITY A SECRET?
SOME MIGHT SUGGEST YOU'RE CURRYING FAVOR WITH THE INCUMBENT PRESIDENT IN ORDER TO MAINTAIN A CORDIAL RELATIONSHIP.
ABC NEWS PRESS
THE REGISTRATION ACT DOES NOT SPECIFICALLY CALL FOR PERSONS TO REVEAL THEIR IDENTITY PUBLICLY; MERELY TO REGISTER WITH AUTHORITIES FOR THE PURPOSES OF IDENTIFICATION.
BUT FOR MYSELF, IF I SUPPORT THE ACT, SOME WILL CALL ME A HYPOCRITE. SOME MIGHT SAY I CAN NEVER BE TRULY HONEST UNLESS I SHOW MY FACE TO THE WORLD.
AND THEY'D BE RIGHT.
DID HE JUST SAY WHAT I THOUGHT HE SAID?
I'VE DONE THIS BEFORE, BUT ALWAYS WITH A CLEVER TAKE-BACK, A WAY OF ONCE MORE OBSCURING THE ISSUE.
BUT, TODAY I'M GOING TO COME CLEAN WITH THE AMERICAN PEOPLE, AS I SHOULD HAVE DONE FROM DAY ONE.
I CAN THINK OF ONLY ONE WAY TO MAKE YOU ALL UNDERSTAND WHY.
KSSSSH

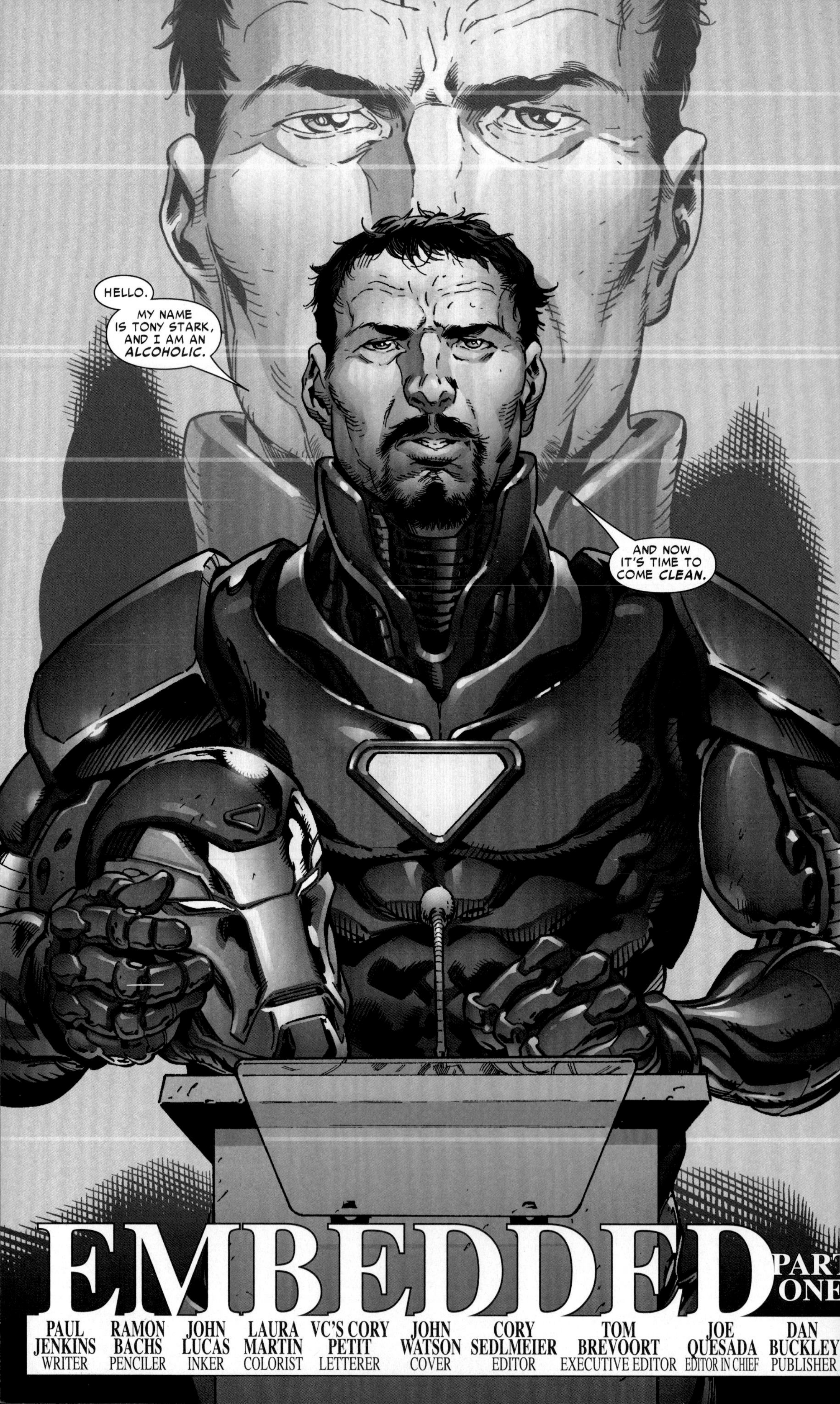
HELLO.
MY NAME IS TONY STARK, AND I AM AN *ALCOHOLIC.*
AND NOW IT'S TIME TO COME *CLEAN.*
EMBEDDED PART ONE
PAUL JENKINS WRITER
RAMON BACHS PENCILER
JOHN LUCAS INKER
LAURA MARTIN COLORIST
VC'S CORY PETIT LETTERER
JOHN WATSON COVER
CORY SEDLMEIER EDITOR
TOM BREVOORT EXECUTIVE EDITOR
JOE QUESADA EDITOR IN CHIEF
DAN BUCKLEY PUBLISHER

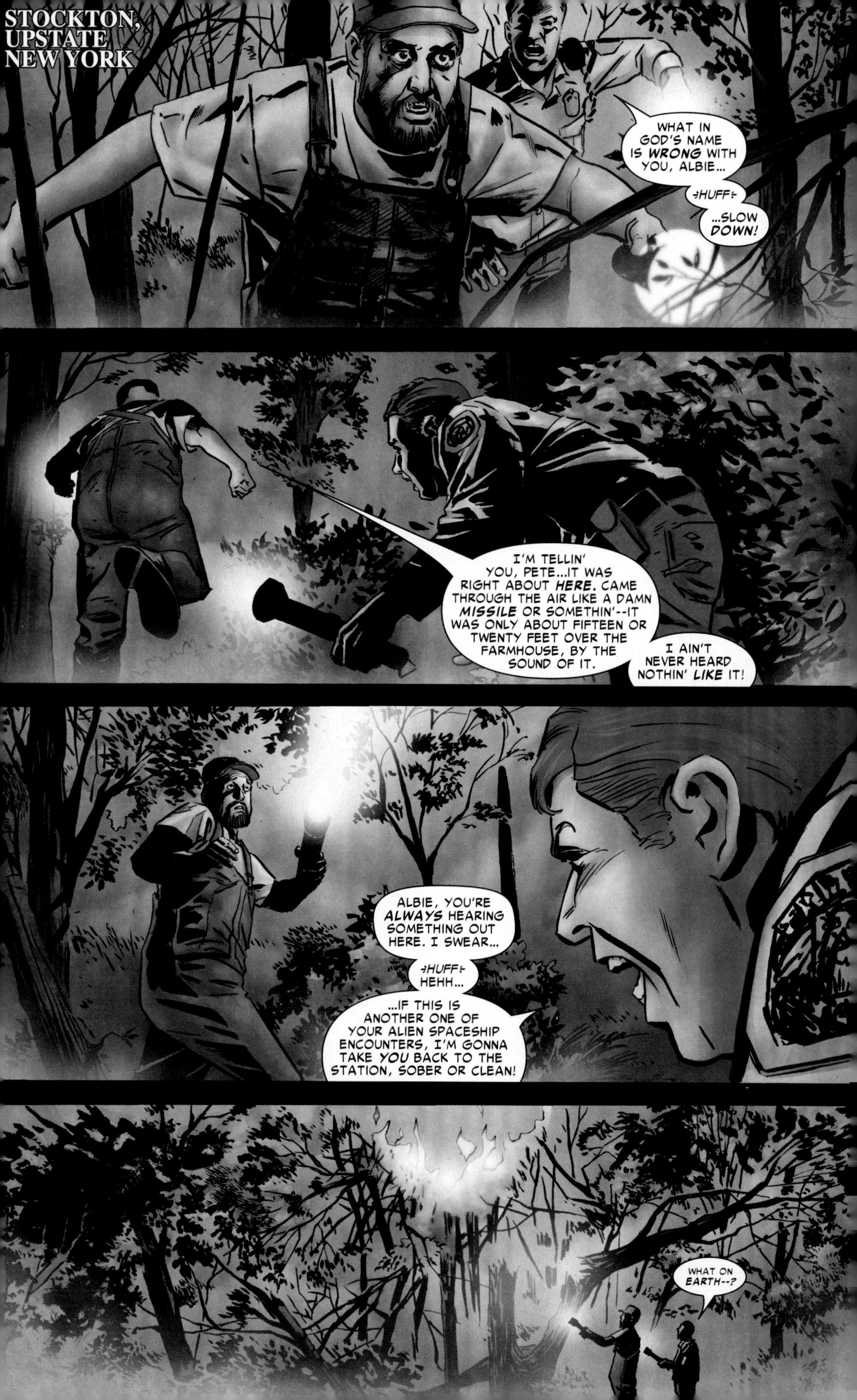
STOCKTON, UPSTATE NEW YORK
WHAT IN GOD'S NAME IS WRONG WITH YOU, ALBIE...
HUFF
...SLOW DOWN!
I'M TELLIN' YOU, PETE...IT WAS RIGHT ABOUT HERE. CAME THROUGH THE AIR LIKE A DAMN MISSILE OR SOMETHIN'--IT WAS ONLY ABOUT FIFTEEN OR TWENTY FEET OVER THE FARMHOUSE, BY THE SOUND OF IT.
I AIN'T NEVER HEARD NOTHIN' LIKE IT!
ALBIE, YOU'RE ALWAYS HEARING SOMETHING OUT HERE. I SWEAR...
HUFF HEHH...
...IF THIS IS ANOTHER ONE OF YOUR ALIEN SPACESHIP ENCOUNTERS, I'M GONNA TAKE YOU BACK TO THE STATION, SOBER OR CLEAN!
WHAT ON EARTH--?

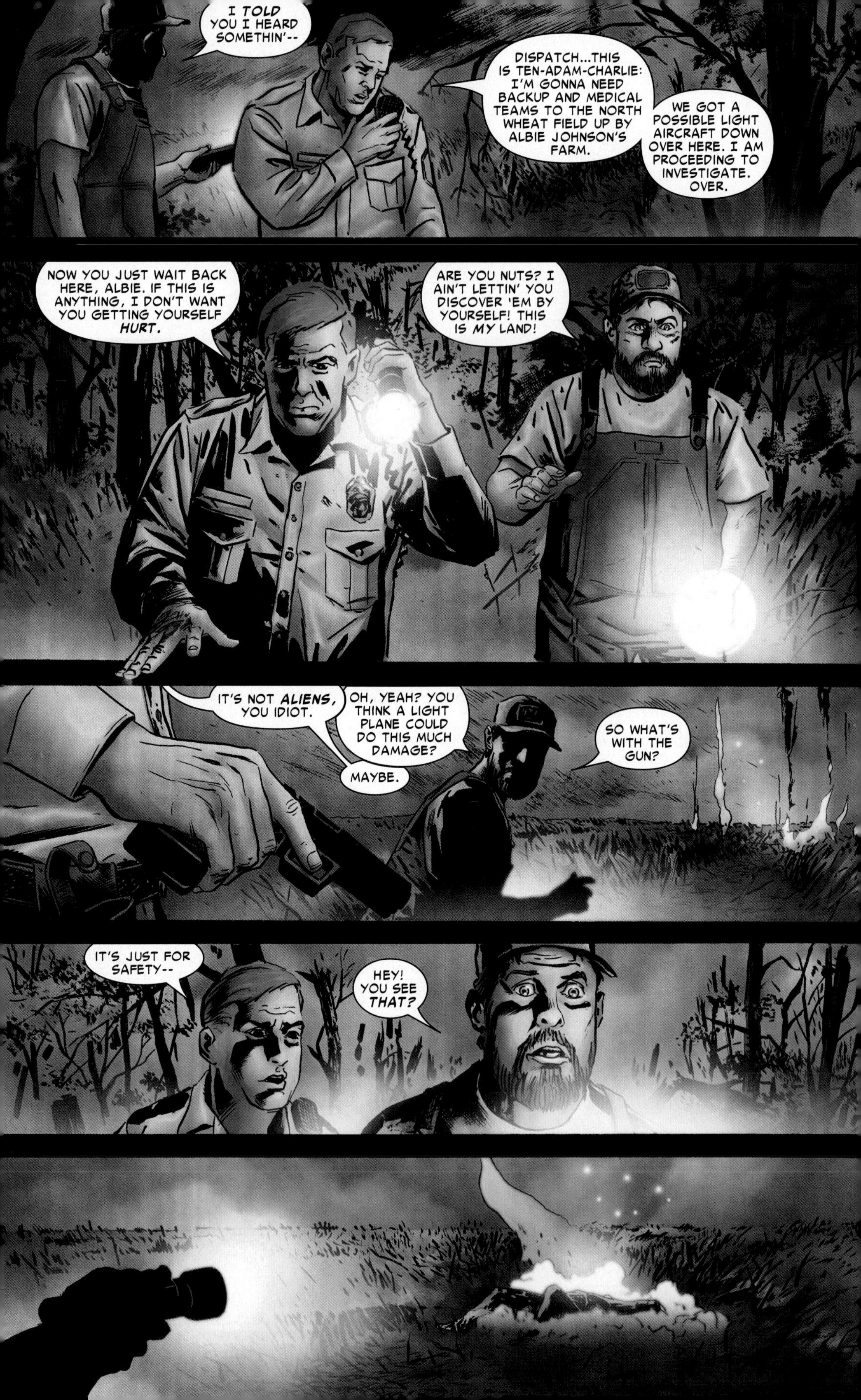
I TOLD YOU I HEARD SOMETHIN'--
DISPATCH...THIS IS TEN-ADAM-CHARLIE: I'M GONNA NEED BACKUP AND MEDICAL TEAMS TO THE NORTH WHEAT FIELD UP BY ALBIE JOHNSON'S FARM.
WE GOT A POSSIBLE LIGHT AIRCRAFT DOWN OVER HERE. I AM PROCEEDING TO INVESTIGATE. OVER.
NOW YOU JUST WAIT BACK HERE, ALBIE. IF THIS IS ANYTHING, I DON'T WANT YOU GETTING YOURSELF HURT.
ARE YOU NUTS? I AIN'T LETTIN' YOU DISCOVER 'EM BY YOURSELF! THIS IS MY LAND!
IT'S NOT ALIENS, YOU IDIOT.
OH, YEAH? YOU THINK A LIGHT PLANE COULD DO THIS MUCH DAMAGE?
MAYBE.
SO WHAT'S WITH THE GUN?
IT'S JUST FOR SAFETY--
HEY! YOU SEE THAT?

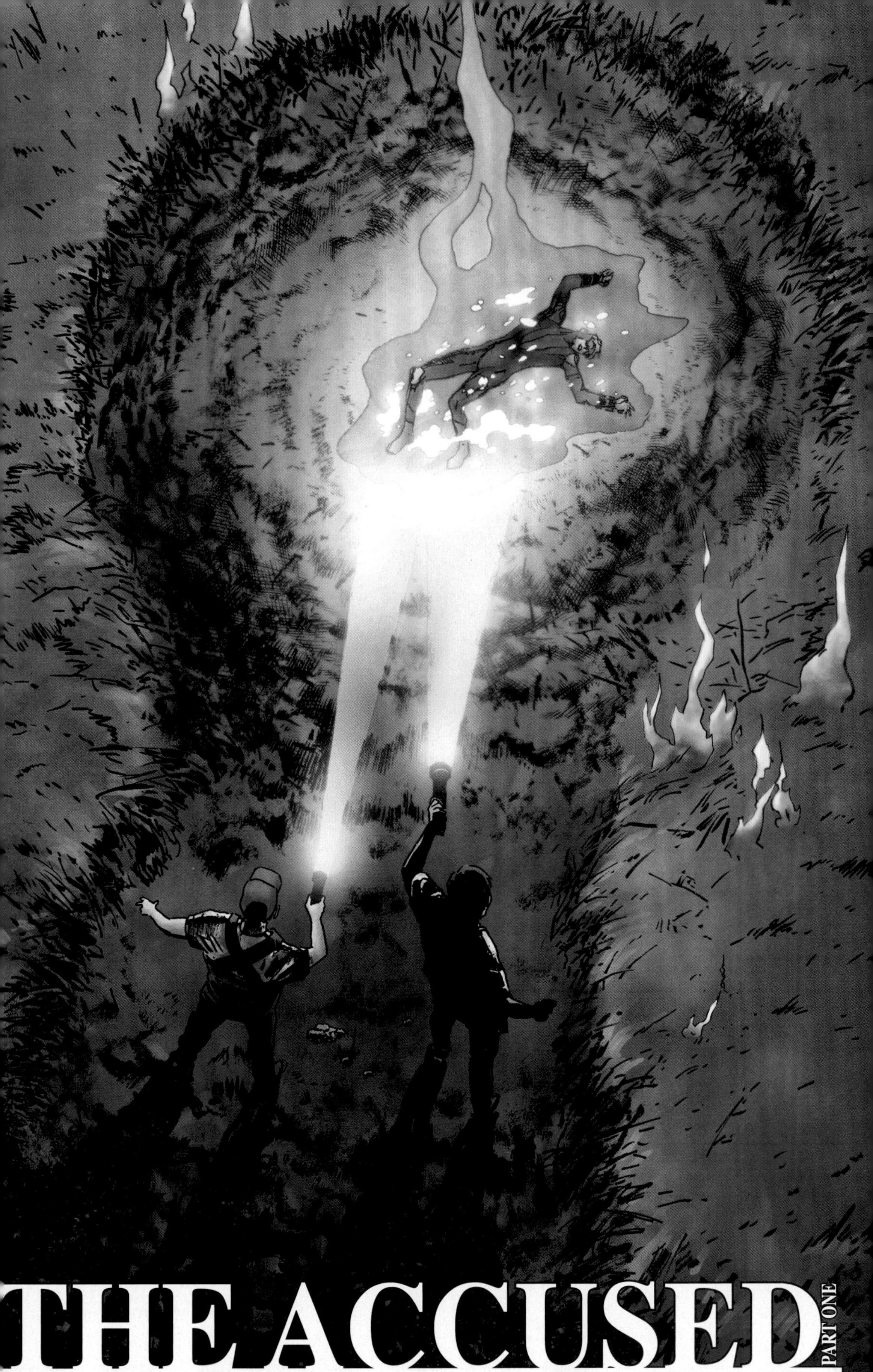

THE ACCUSED PART ONE

PAUL JENKINS WRITER
STEVE LIEBER ARTIST
JUNE CHUNG COLORIST
VC'S RANDY GENTILE LETTERER
CORY SEDLMEIER EDITOR
TOM BREVOORT EXECUTIVE EDITOR
JOE QUESADA EDITOR IN CHIEF
DAN BUCKLEY PUBLISHER

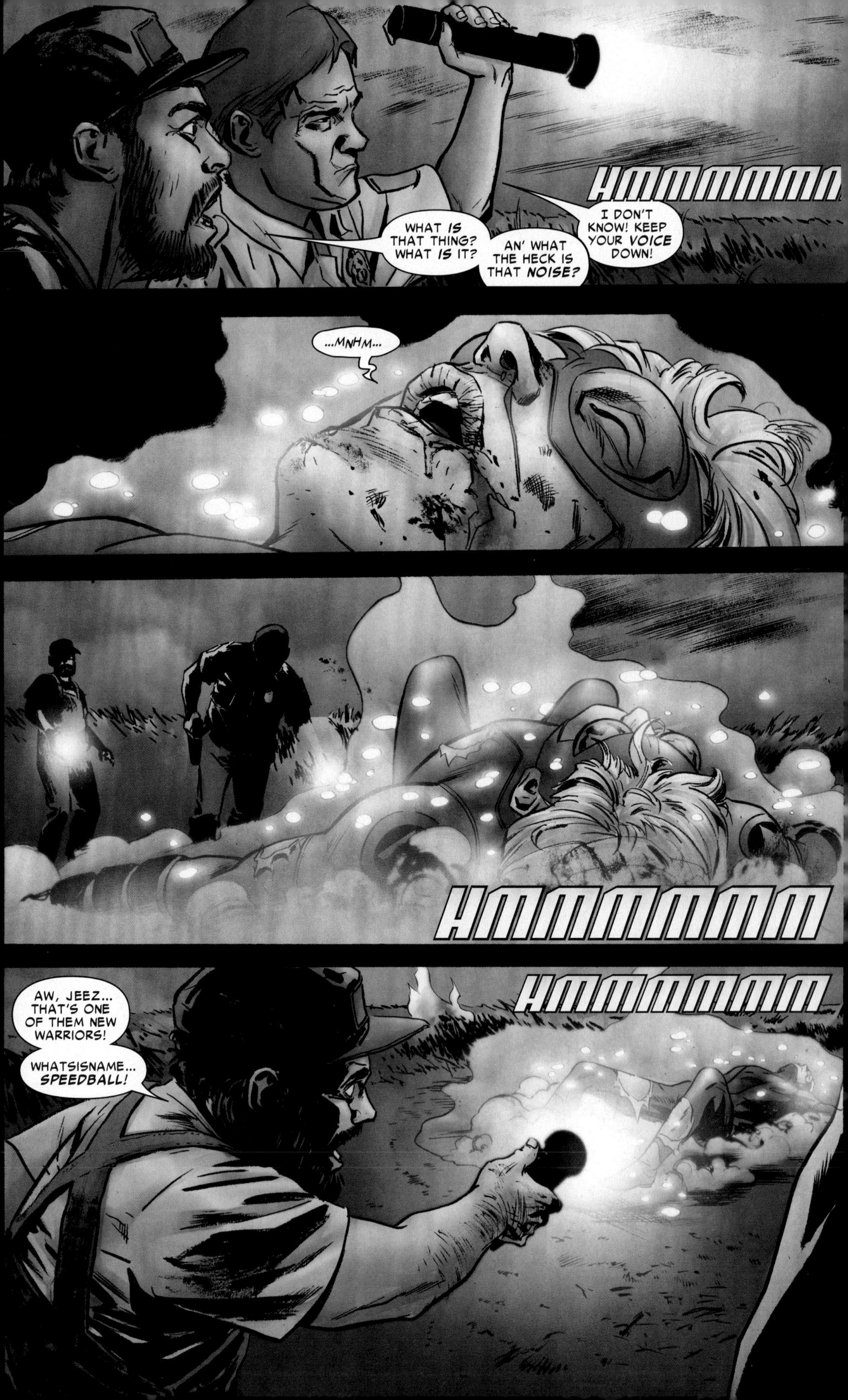
HMMMMMMM
WHAT IS THAT THING? WHAT IS IT?
AN' WHAT THE HECK IS THAT NOISE?
I DON'T KNOW! KEEP YOUR VOICE DOWN!
...MNHM...
HMMMMMMM
HMMMMMMM
AW, JEEZ... THAT'S ONE OF THEM NEW WARRIORS!
WHATSISNAME... SPEEDBALL!

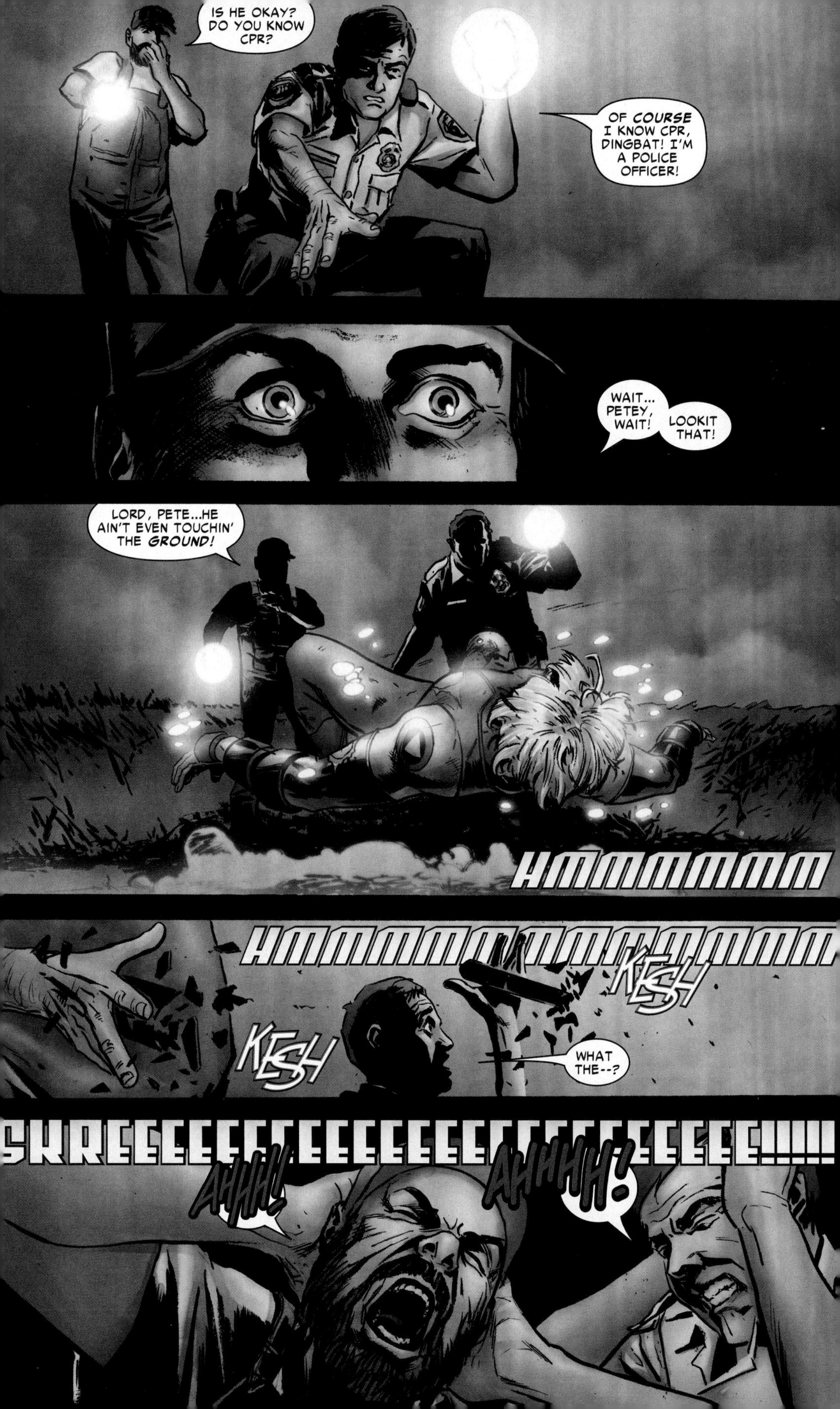
IS HE OKAY? DO YOU KNOW CPR?
OF COURSE I KNOW CPR, DINGBAT! I'M A POLICE OFFICER!
WAIT... PETEY, WAIT!
LOOKIT THAT!
LORD, PETE...HE AIN'T EVEN TOUCHIN' THE GROUND!
HMMMMMMM
HMMMMMMMMMMMMMM
KESH
KESH
WHAT THE--?
SKREEEEEEEEEEEEEEEEEEEEEEEEEEE!!!!!
AHHH!
AHHHH!

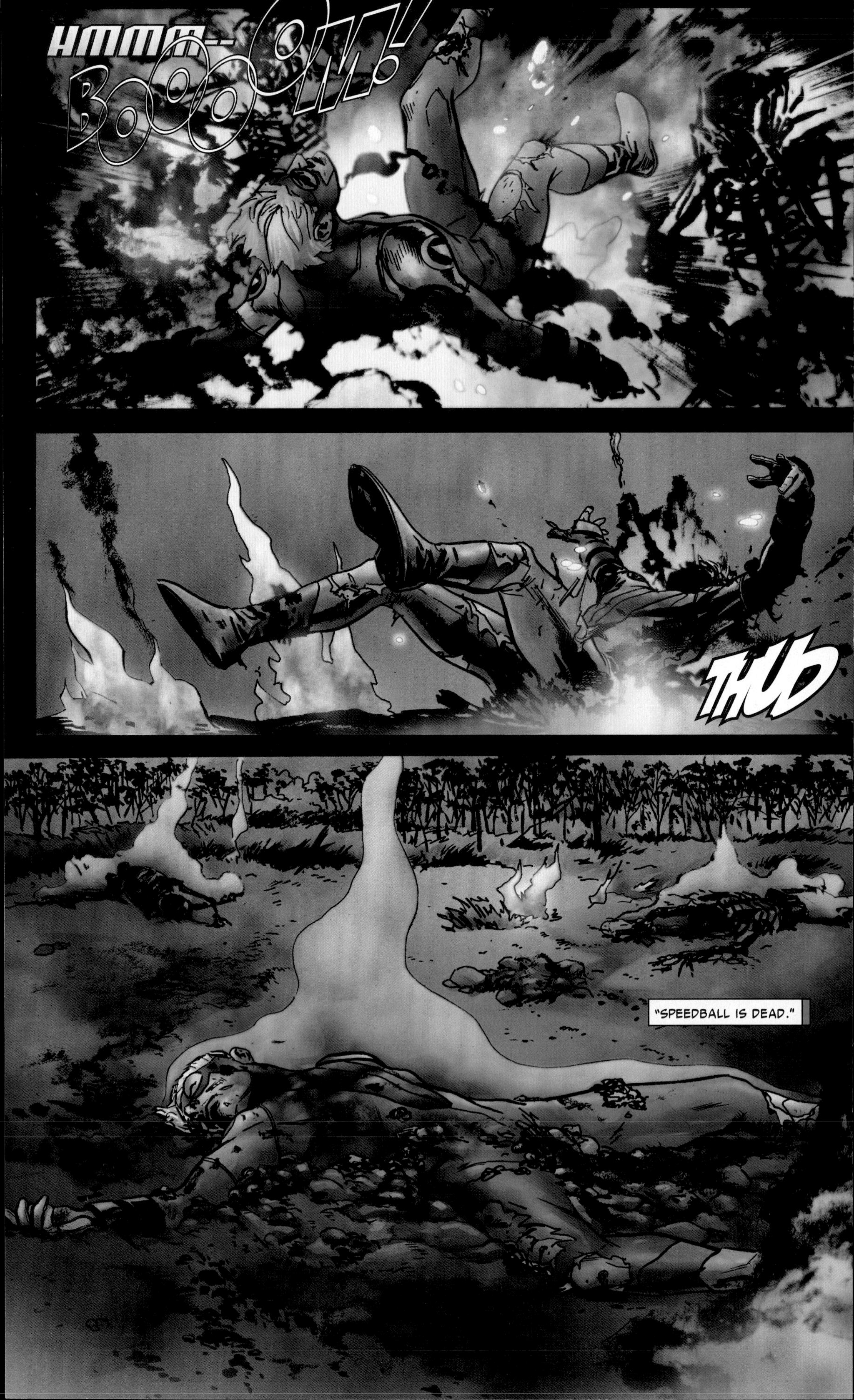
HMMM--
BOOOOOOM!
THUD
"SPEEDBALL IS DEAD."

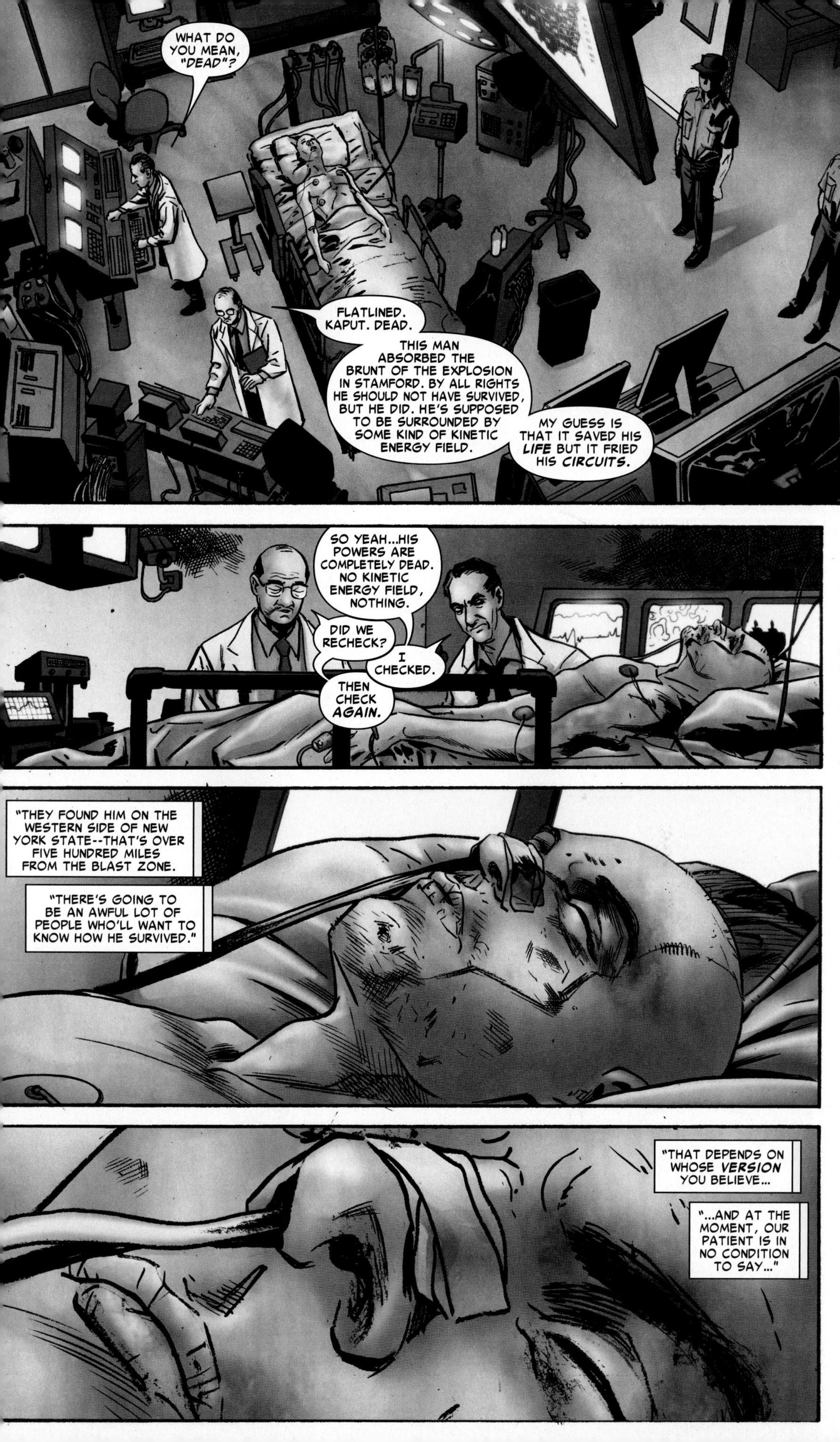
WHAT DO YOU MEAN, "DEAD"?
FLATLINED. KAPUT. DEAD.
THIS MAN ABSORBED THE BRUNT OF THE EXPLOSION IN STAMFORD. BY ALL RIGHTS HE SHOULD NOT HAVE SURVIVED, BUT HE DID. HE'S SUPPOSED TO BE SURROUNDED BY SOME KIND OF KINETIC ENERGY FIELD.
MY GUESS IS THAT IT SAVED HIS *LIFE* BUT IT FRIED HIS *CIRCUITS*.
SO YEAH...HIS POWERS ARE COMPLETELY DEAD. NO KINETIC ENERGY FIELD, NOTHING.
DID WE RECHECK?
I CHECKED.
THEN CHECK *AGAIN.*
"THEY FOUND HIM ON THE WESTERN SIDE OF NEW YORK STATE--THAT'S OVER FIVE HUNDRED MILES FROM THE BLAST ZONE.
"THERE'S GOING TO BE AN AWFUL LOT OF PEOPLE WHO'LL WANT TO KNOW HOW HE SURVIVED."
"THAT DEPENDS ON WHOSE *VERSION* YOU BELIEVE...
"...AND AT THE MOMENT, OUR PATIENT IS IN NO CONDITION TO SAY..."

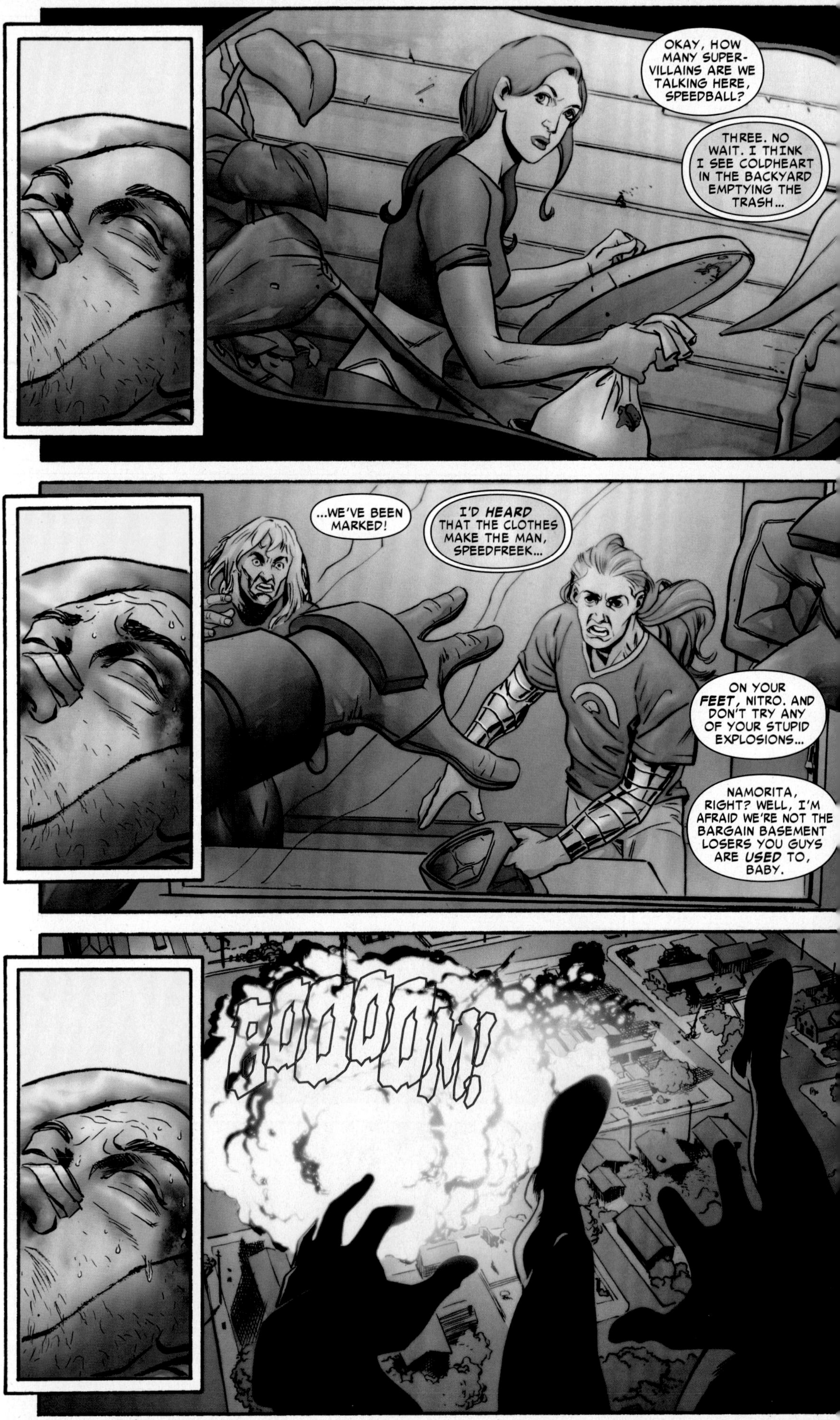
OKAY, HOW MANY SUPER-VILLAINS ARE WE TALKING HERE, SPEEDBALL?
THREE. NO WAIT. I THINK I SEE COLDHEART IN THE BACKYARD EMPTYING THE TRASH...
...WE'VE BEEN MARKED!
I'D *HEARD* THAT THE CLOTHES MAKE THE MAN, SPEEDFREEK...
ON YOUR *FEET*, NITRO. AND DON'T TRY ANY OF YOUR STUPID EXPLOSIONS...
NAMORITA, RIGHT? WELL, I'M AFRAID WE'RE NOT THE BARGAIN BASEMENT LOSERS YOU GUYS ARE *USED* TO, BABY.
BOOOOM!

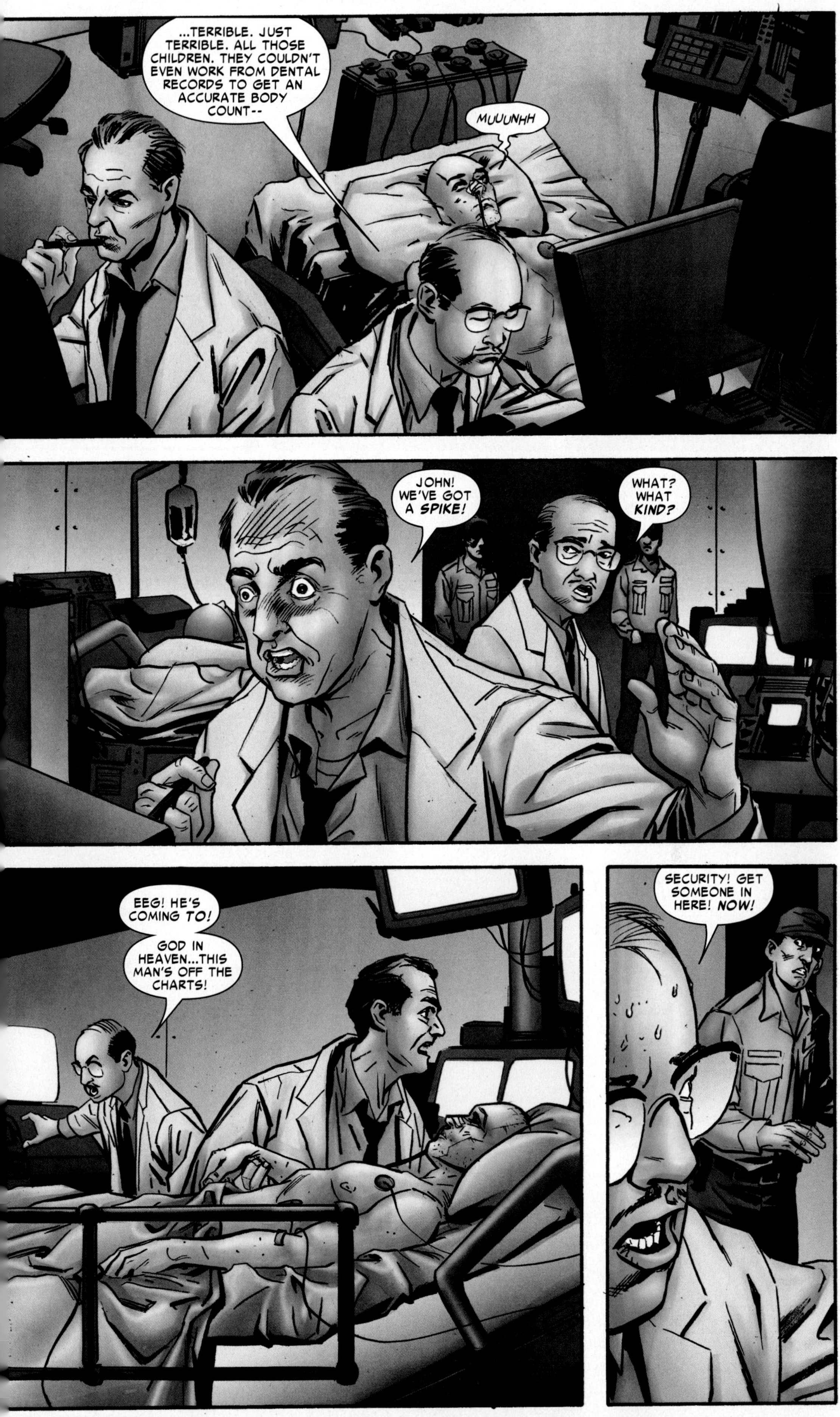
...TERRIBLE. JUST TERRIBLE. ALL THOSE CHILDREN. THEY COULDN'T EVEN WORK FROM DENTAL RECORDS TO GET AN ACCURATE BODY COUNT--
MUUUNHH
JOHN! WE'VE GOT A SPIKE!
WHAT? WHAT KIND?
EEG! HE'S COMING TO!
GOD IN HEAVEN...THIS MAN'S OFF THE CHARTS!
SECURITY! GET SOMEONE IN HERE! NOW!

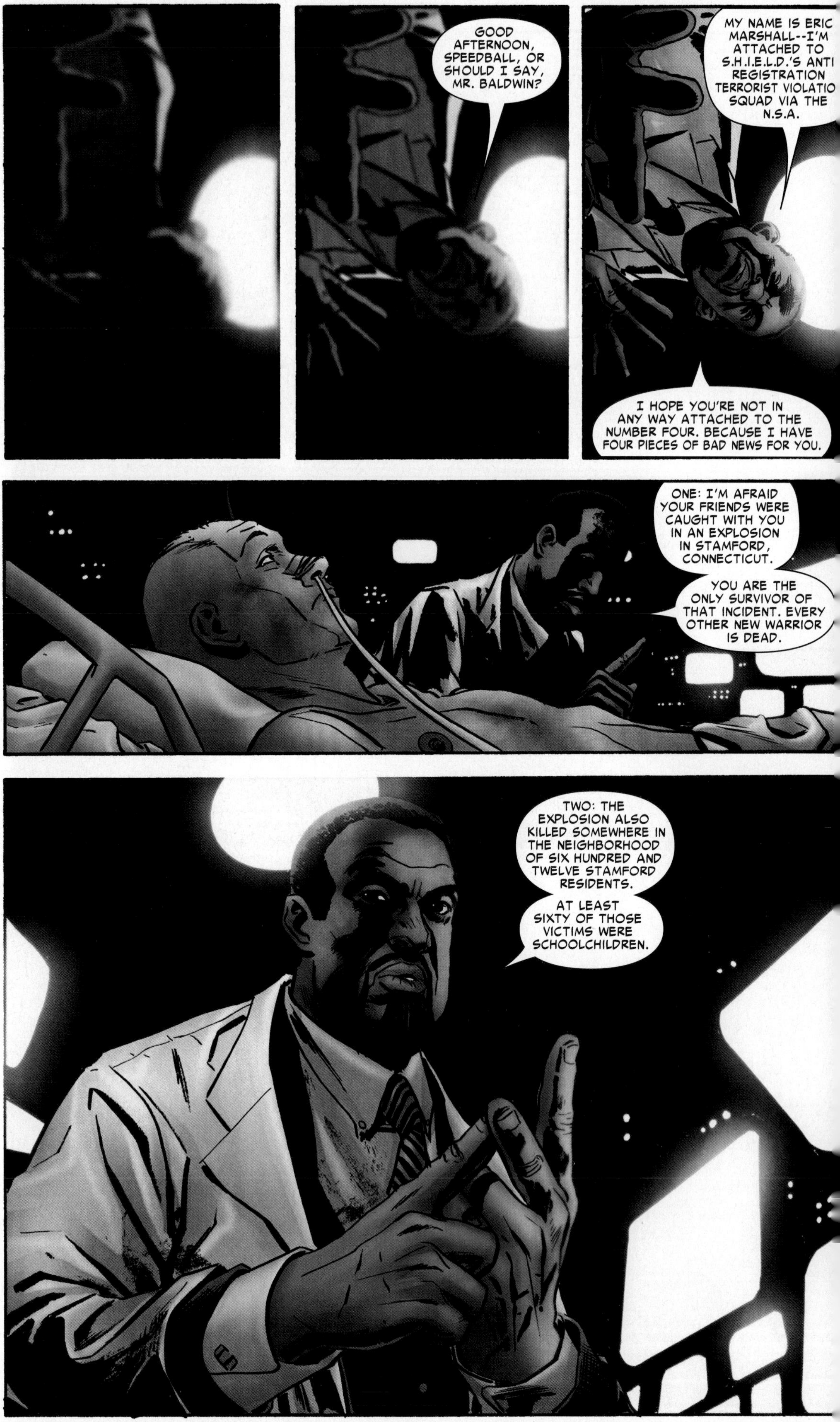
GOOD AFTERNOON, SPEEDBALL, OR SHOULD I SAY, MR. BALDWIN?
MY NAME IS ERIC MARSHALL--I'M ATTACHED TO S.H.I.E.L.D.'S ANTI REGISTRATION TERRORIST VIOLATIO SQUAD VIA THE N.S.A.
I HOPE YOU'RE NOT IN ANY WAY ATTACHED TO THE NUMBER FOUR. BECAUSE I HAVE FOUR PIECES OF BAD NEWS FOR YOU.
ONE: I'M AFRAID YOUR FRIENDS WERE CAUGHT WITH YOU IN AN EXPLOSION IN STAMFORD, CONNECTICUT.
YOU ARE THE ONLY SURVIVOR OF THAT INCIDENT. EVERY OTHER NEW WARRIOR IS DEAD.
TWO: THE EXPLOSION ALSO KILLED SOMEWHERE IN THE NEIGHBORHOOD OF SIX HUNDRED AND TWELVE STAMFORD RESIDENTS.
AT LEAST SIXTY OF THOSE VICTIMS WERE SCHOOLCHILDREN.

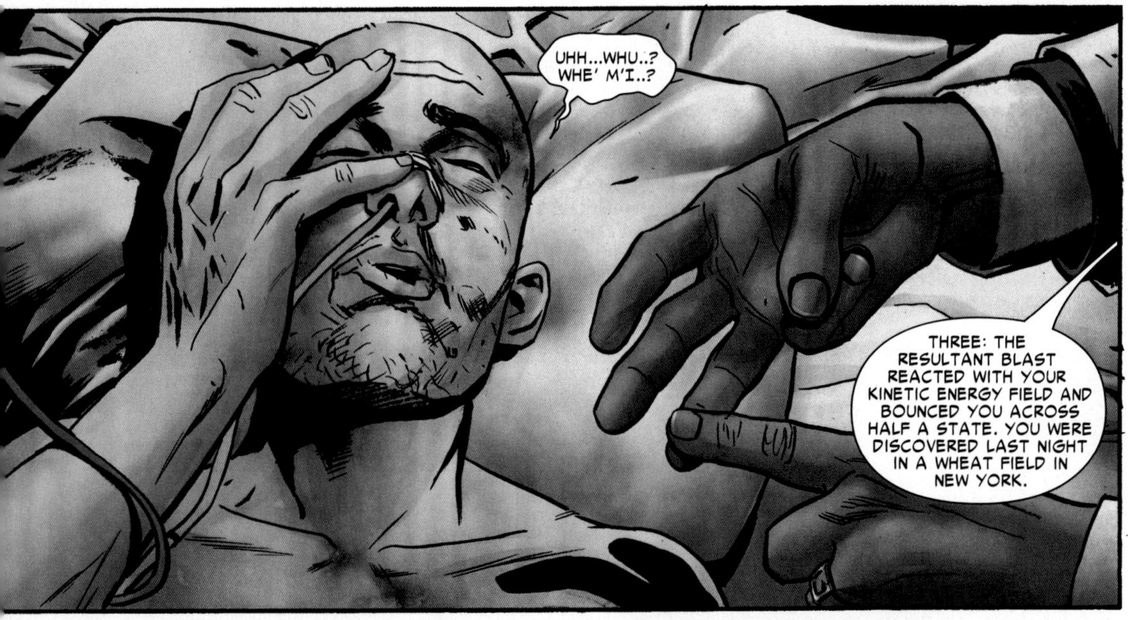
UHH...WHU..? WHE' M'I..?
THREE: THE RESULTANT BLAST REACTED WITH YOUR KINETIC ENERGY FIELD AND BOUNCED YOU ACROSS HALF A STATE. YOU WERE DISCOVERED LAST NIGHT IN A WHEAT FIELD IN NEW YORK.

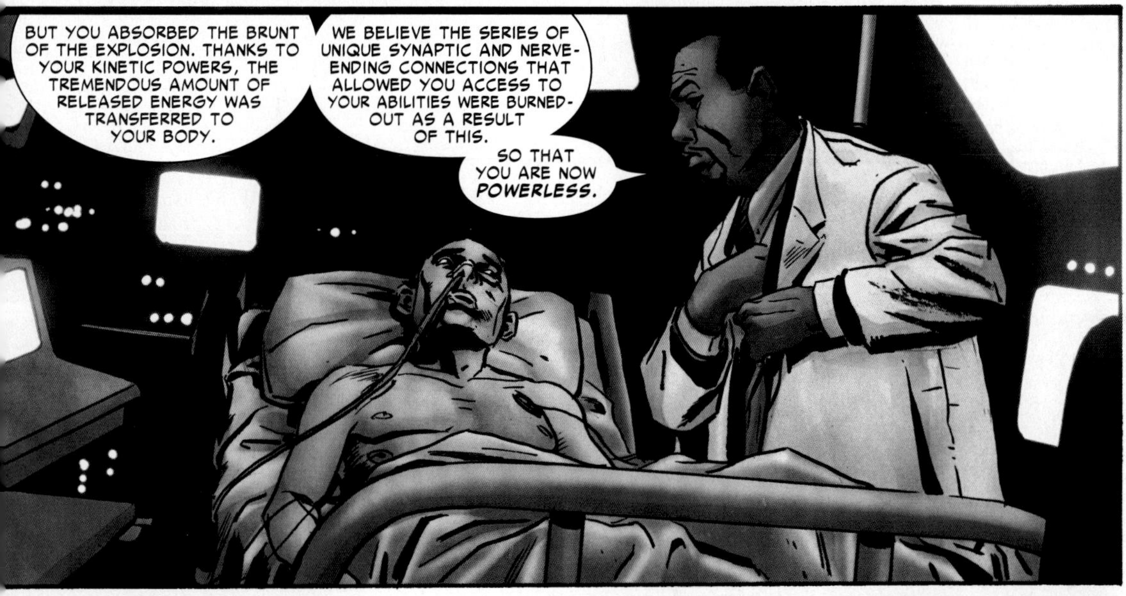
BUT YOU ABSORBED THE BRUNT OF THE EXPLOSION. THANKS TO YOUR KINETIC POWERS, THE TREMENDOUS AMOUNT OF RELEASED ENERGY WAS TRANSFERRED TO YOUR BODY.
WE BELIEVE THE SERIES OF UNIQUE SYNAPTIC AND NERVE-ENDING CONNECTIONS THAT ALLOWED YOU ACCESS TO YOUR ABILITIES WERE BURNED-OUT AS A RESULT OF THIS.
SO THAT YOU ARE NOW POWERLESS.

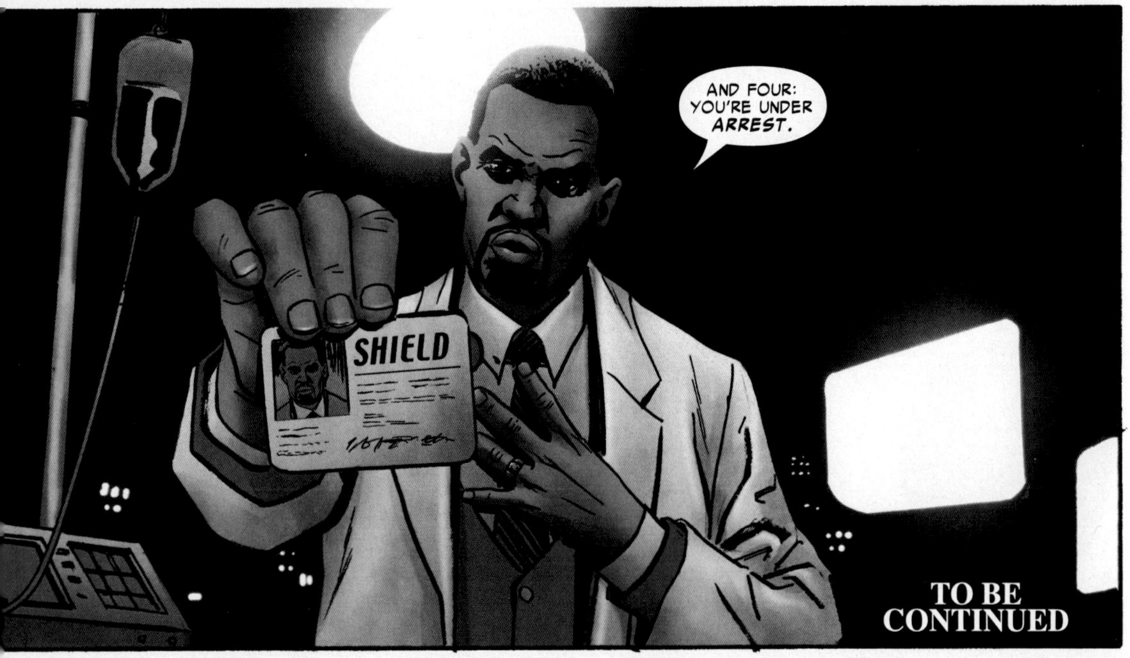
AND FOUR: YOU'RE UNDER ARREST.
SHIELD
TO BE CONTINUED

In 1942, concerned by a possible invasion of the West Coast, the President of the United States signed Executive Order 9066, precipitating one of the largest controlled migrations in history. Over 110,000 people of Japanese descent were moved from their homes near the Pacific Coast into 10 wartime communities under the jurisdiction of the Wartime Relocation Authority.

Most of these people were American Citizens of Japanese ancestry with little or no allegiance to the Japanese Emperor. Over half were children. They were forced to leave behind ove two hundred million dollars' worth of real estate and possessions, though a later law permitted some of these people to renounce their citizenship and return to their former homes.

In the interests of fairness, it can be noted that while they provided very sparse accommodation, these relocation centers had the highest live-birth rate and the lowest death rate in wartime United States. The Japanese in the centers received free food, lodging, medical and dental care, clothing allowance, education, hospital care, and all basic necessities. The government even pai travel expenses and assisted in cases of emergency relief.

The following poem--written anonymously--was circulated at Poston War Relocation Camp during the summer of 1943.

PAUL JENKINS WRITER | KEI KOBAYASHI ARTIST | CHRISTINA STRAIN COLORIST | VC'S RANDY GENTILE LETTERER | CORY SEDLMEIER EDITOR | TOM BREVOORT EXECUTIVE EDITOR | JOE QUESADA EDITOR IN CHIEF | DAN BUCKLE PUBLISHE

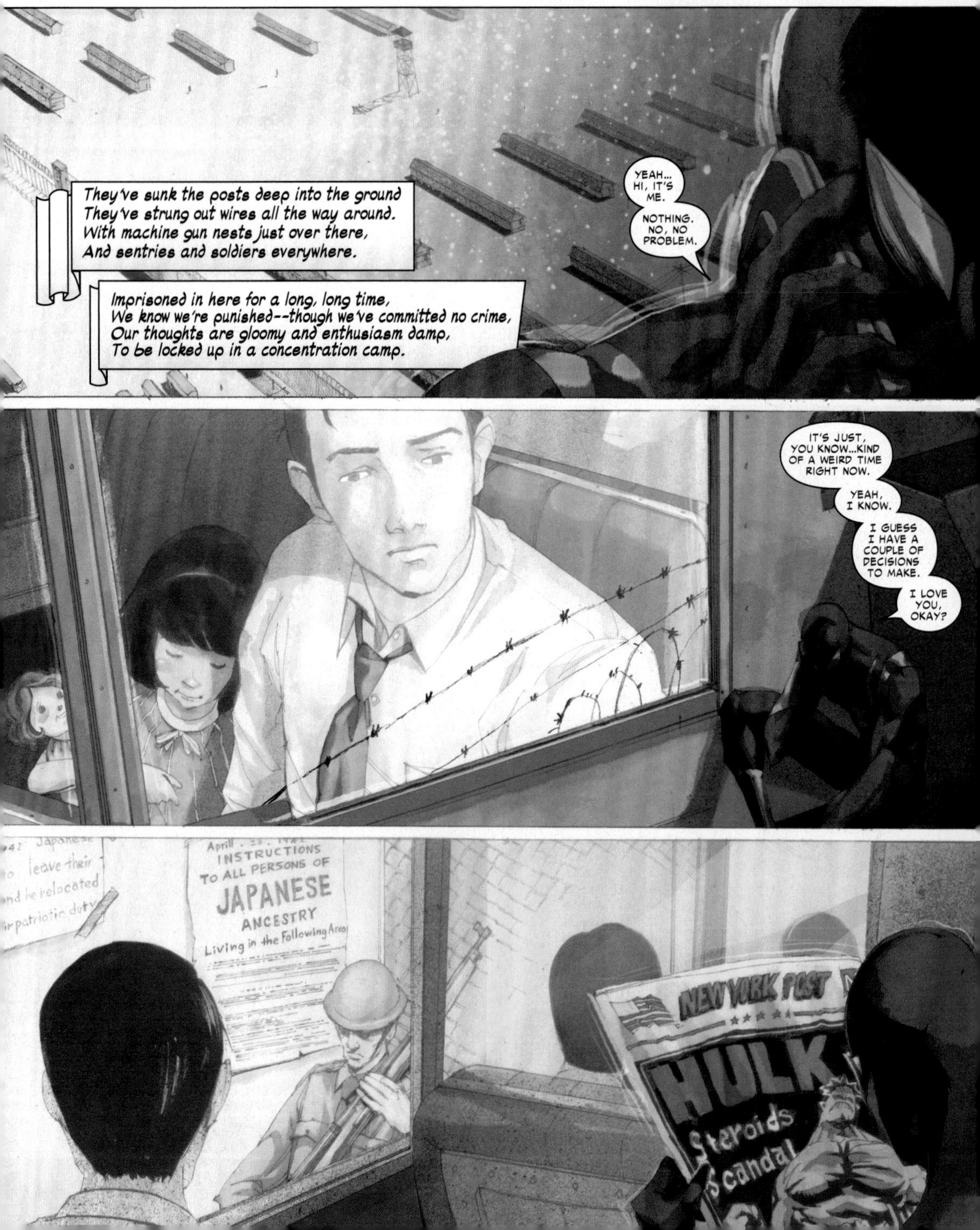
They've sunk the posts deep into the ground
They've strung out wires all the way around.
With machine gun nests just over there,
And sentries and soldiers everywhere.
YEAH... HI, IT'S ME.
NOTHING. NO, NO PROBLEM.
Imprisoned in here for a long, long time,
We know we're punished--though we've committed no crime,
Our thoughts are gloomy and enthusiasm damp,
To be locked up in a concentration camp.
IT'S JUST, YOU KNOW...KIND OF A WEIRD TIME RIGHT NOW.
YEAH, I KNOW.
I GUESS I HAVE A COUPLE OF DECISIONS TO MAKE.
I LOVE YOU, OKAY?
INSTRUCTIONS TO ALL PERSONS OF JAPANESE ANCESTRY Living in the Following Area
NEW YORK POST
HULK
Steroids Scandal

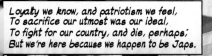

Loyalty we know, and patriotism we feel,
To sacrifice our utmost was our ideal,
To fight for our country, and die, perhaps;
But we're here because we happen to be Japs.

DADDY... WHEN CAN WE GO HOME?

THIS IS OUR HOME, KIMIKO.

I DON'T LIKE IT HERE.

HUSH NOW, DARLING. YOU'LL FRIGHTEN MOMMY.

We all love life, and our country best,
Our misfortune to be here in the West,
To keep us penned behind that damned fence,
is someone's notion of national defense.

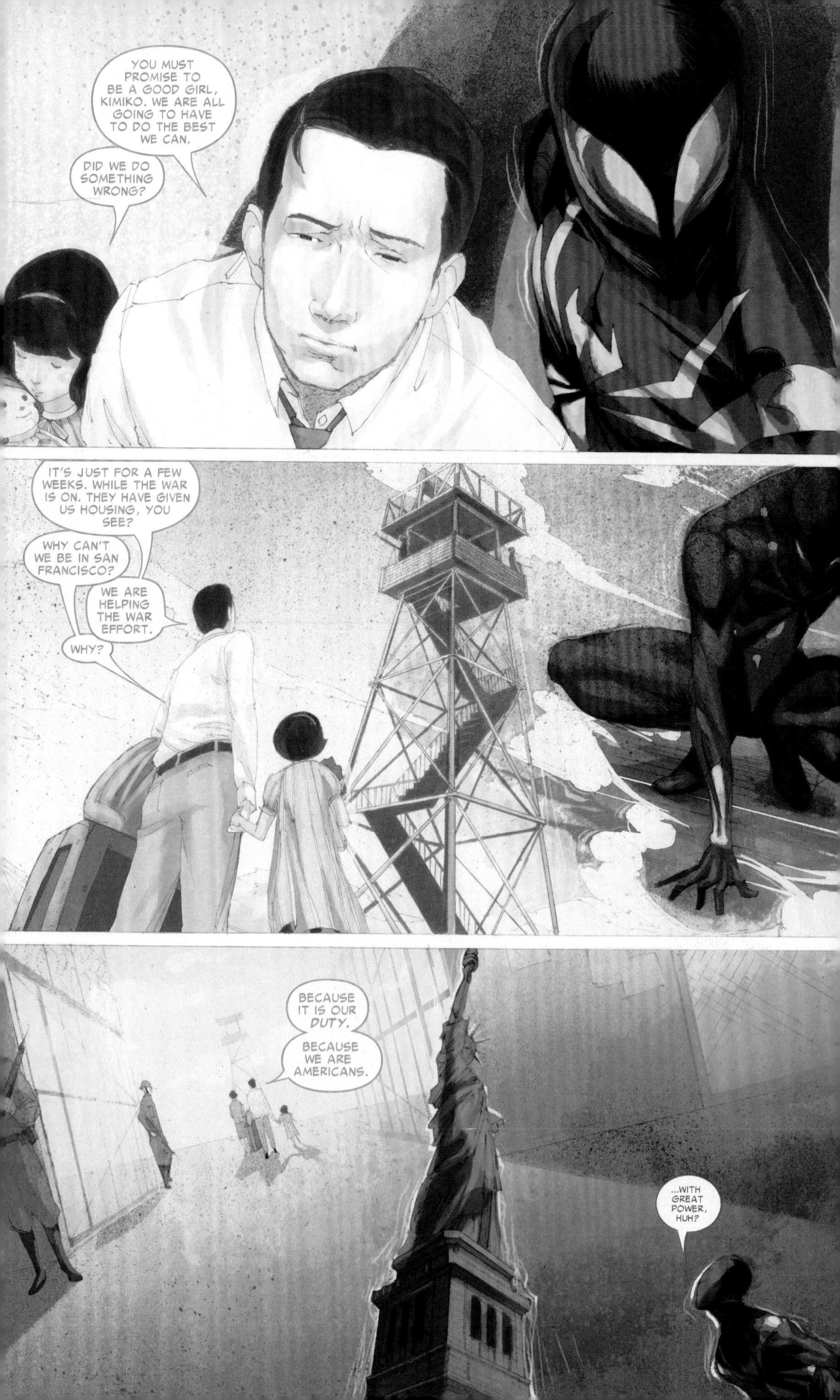

YOU MUST PROMISE TO BE A GOOD GIRL, KIMIKO. WE ARE ALL GOING TO HAVE TO DO THE BEST WE CAN.
DID WE DO SOMETHING WRONG?
IT'S JUST FOR A FEW WEEKS. WHILE THE WAR IS ON. THEY HAVE GIVEN US HOUSING, YOU SEE?
WHY CAN'T WE BE IN SAN FRANCISCO?
WE ARE HELPING THE WAR EFFORT.
WHY?
BECAUSE IT IS OUR DUTY.
BECAUSE WE ARE AMERICANS.
...WITH GREAT POWER, HUH?

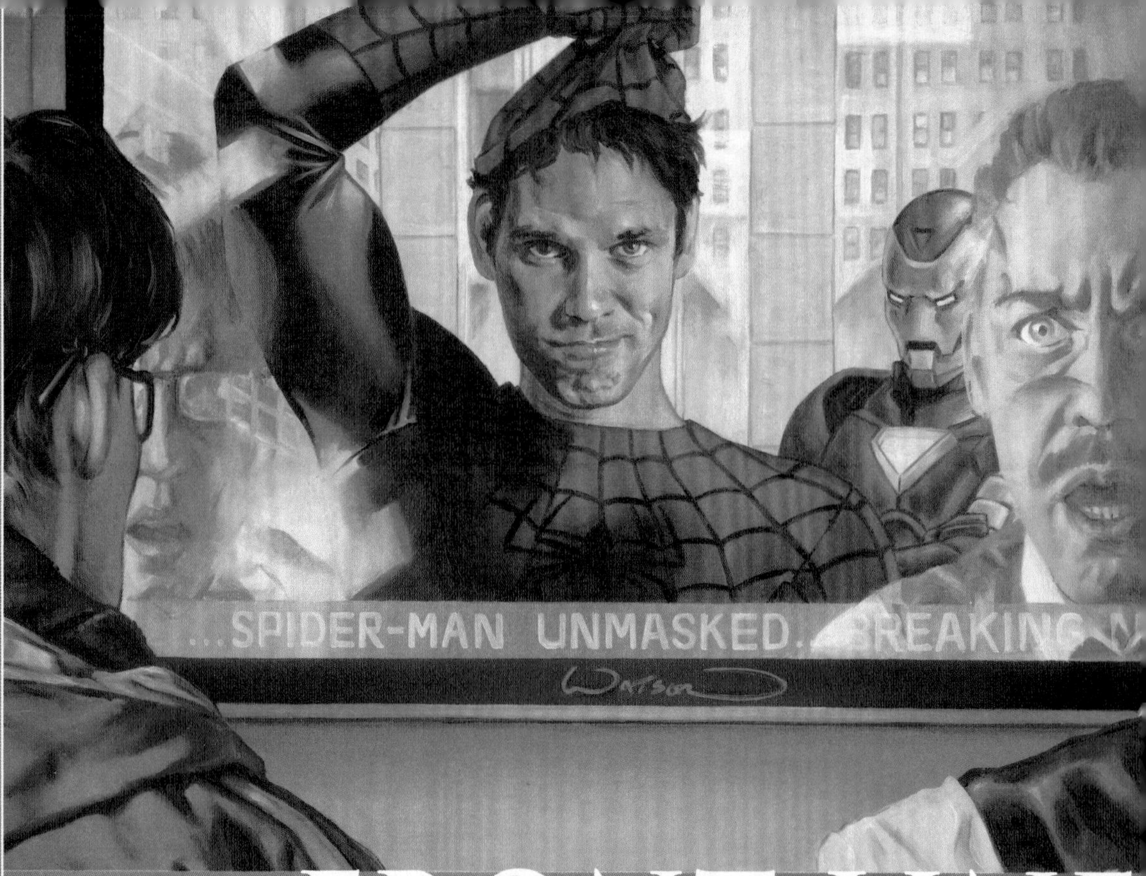
...SPIDER-MAN UNMASKED... BREAKING N
WATSON

FRONT LINE

A MARVEL COMICS EVENT

CIVIL WAR

CIVIL WAR: FRONT LINE #2

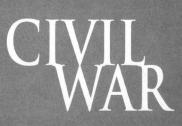

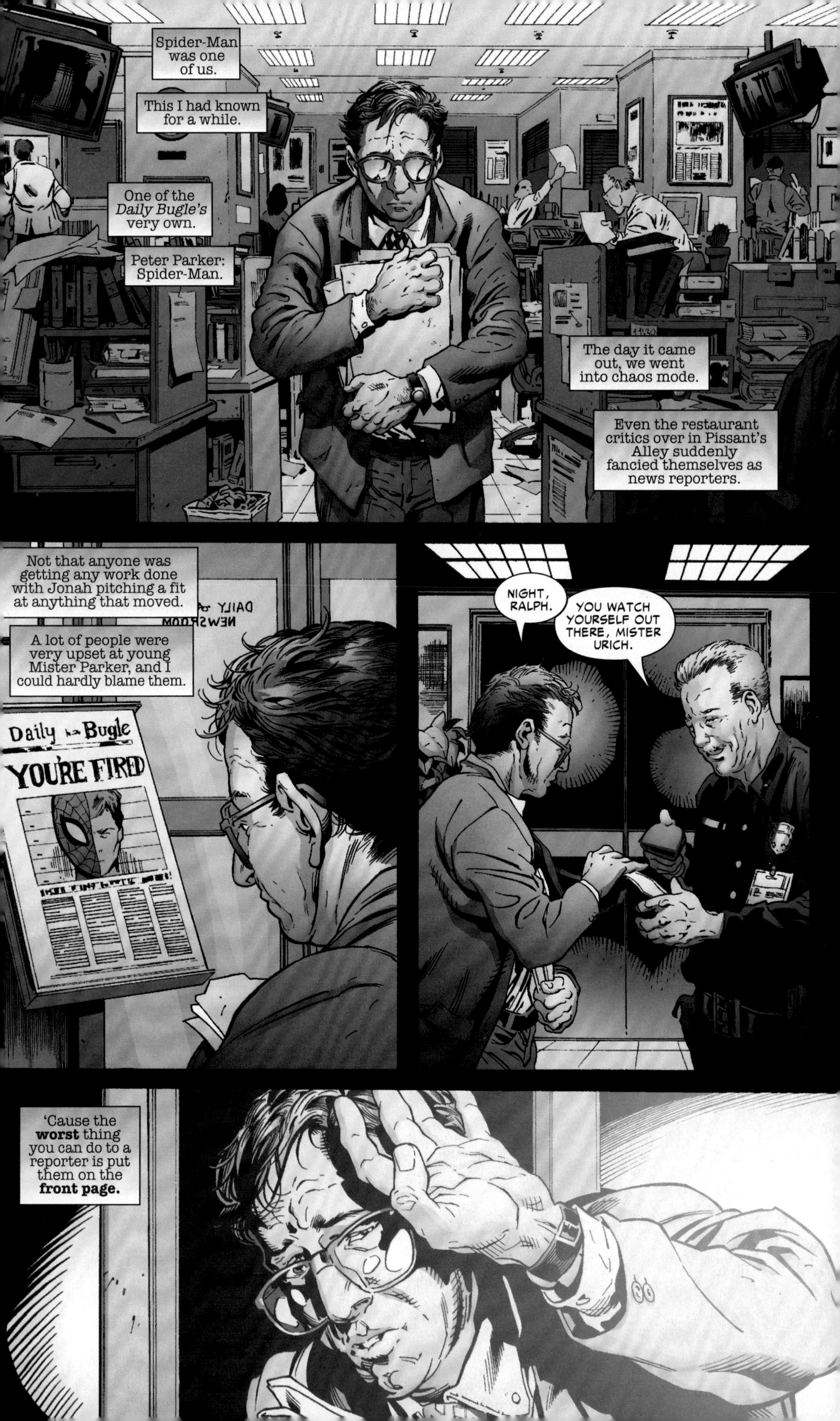

Spider-Man was one of us.
This I had known for a while.
One of the *Daily Bugle's* very own.
Peter Parker: Spider-Man.
The day it came out, we went into chaos mode.
Even the restaurant critics over in Pissant's Alley suddenly fancied themselves as news reporters.
Not that anyone was getting any work done with Jonah pitching a fit at anything that moved.
A lot of people were very upset at young Mister Parker, and I could hardly blame them.
Daily Bugle
YOU'RE FIRED
NIGHT, RALPH.
YOU WATCH YOURSELF OUT THERE, MISTER URICH.
'Cause the **worst** thing you can do to a reporter is put them on the **front page.**

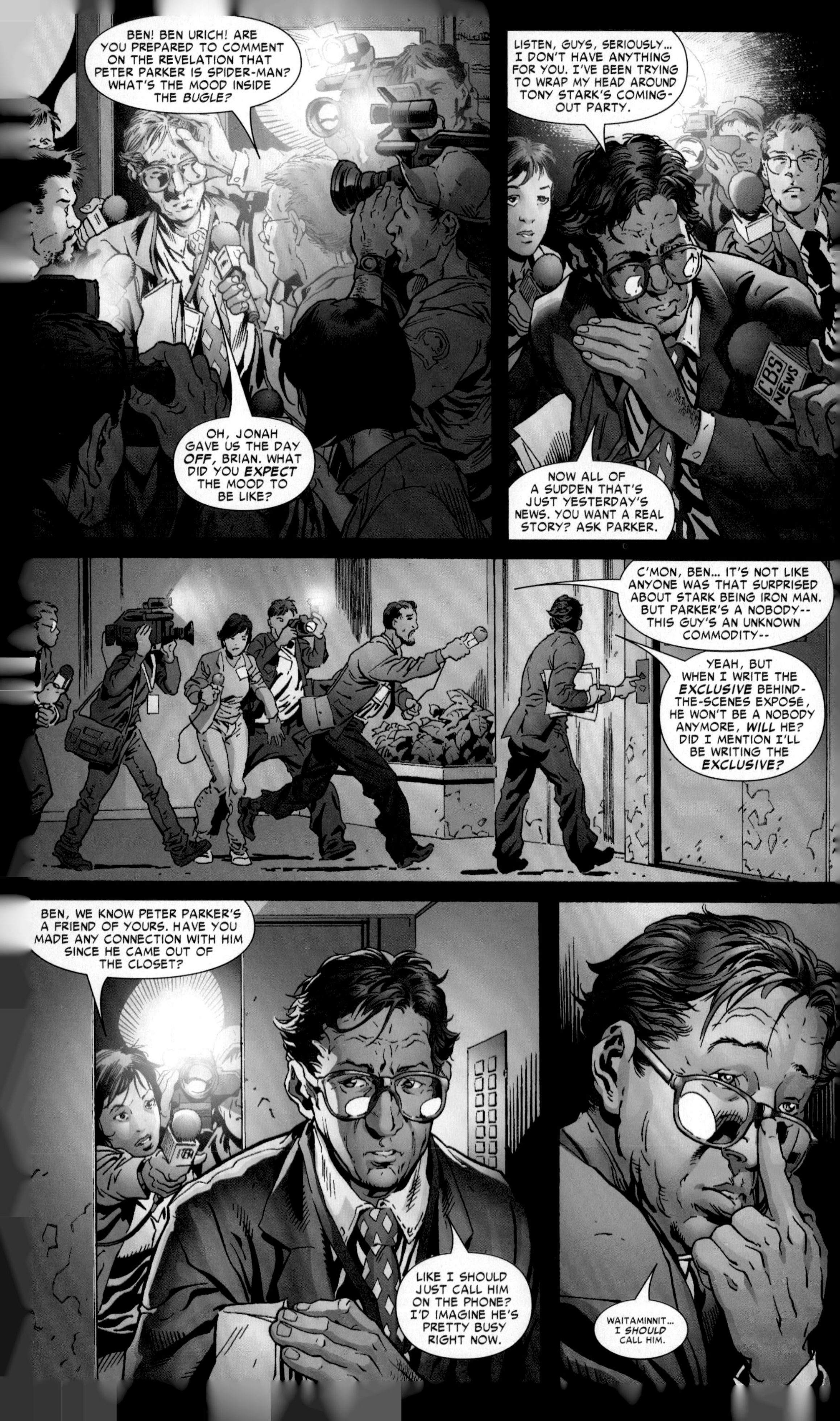

BEN! BEN URICH! ARE YOU PREPARED TO COMMENT ON THE REVELATION THAT PETER PARKER IS SPIDER-MAN? WHAT'S THE MOOD INSIDE THE *BUGLE?*
OH, JONAH GAVE US THE DAY *OFF,* BRIAN. WHAT DID YOU *EXPECT* THE MOOD TO BE LIKE?
LISTEN, GUYS, SERIOUSLY... I DON'T HAVE ANYTHING FOR YOU. I'VE BEEN TRYING TO WRAP MY HEAD AROUND TONY STARK'S COMING-OUT PARTY.
CBS NEWS
NOW ALL OF A SUDDEN THAT'S JUST YESTERDAY'S NEWS. YOU WANT A REAL STORY? ASK PARKER.
C'MON, BEN... IT'S NOT LIKE ANYONE WAS THAT SURPRISED ABOUT STARK BEING IRON MAN. BUT PARKER'S A NOBODY-- THIS GUY'S AN UNKNOWN COMMODITY--
YEAH, BUT WHEN I WRITE THE ***EXCLUSIVE*** BEHIND-THE-SCENES EXPOSÉ, HE WON'T BE A NOBODY ANYMORE, ***WILL*** HE? DID I MENTION I'LL BE WRITING THE ***EXCLUSIVE?***
BEN, WE KNOW PETER PARKER'S A FRIEND OF YOURS. HAVE YOU MADE ANY CONNECTION WITH HIM SINCE HE CAME OUT OF THE CLOSET?
LIKE I SHOULD JUST CALL HIM ON THE PHONE? I'D IMAGINE HE'S PRETTY BUSY RIGHT NOW.
WAITAMINNIT... I *SHOULD* CALL HIM.

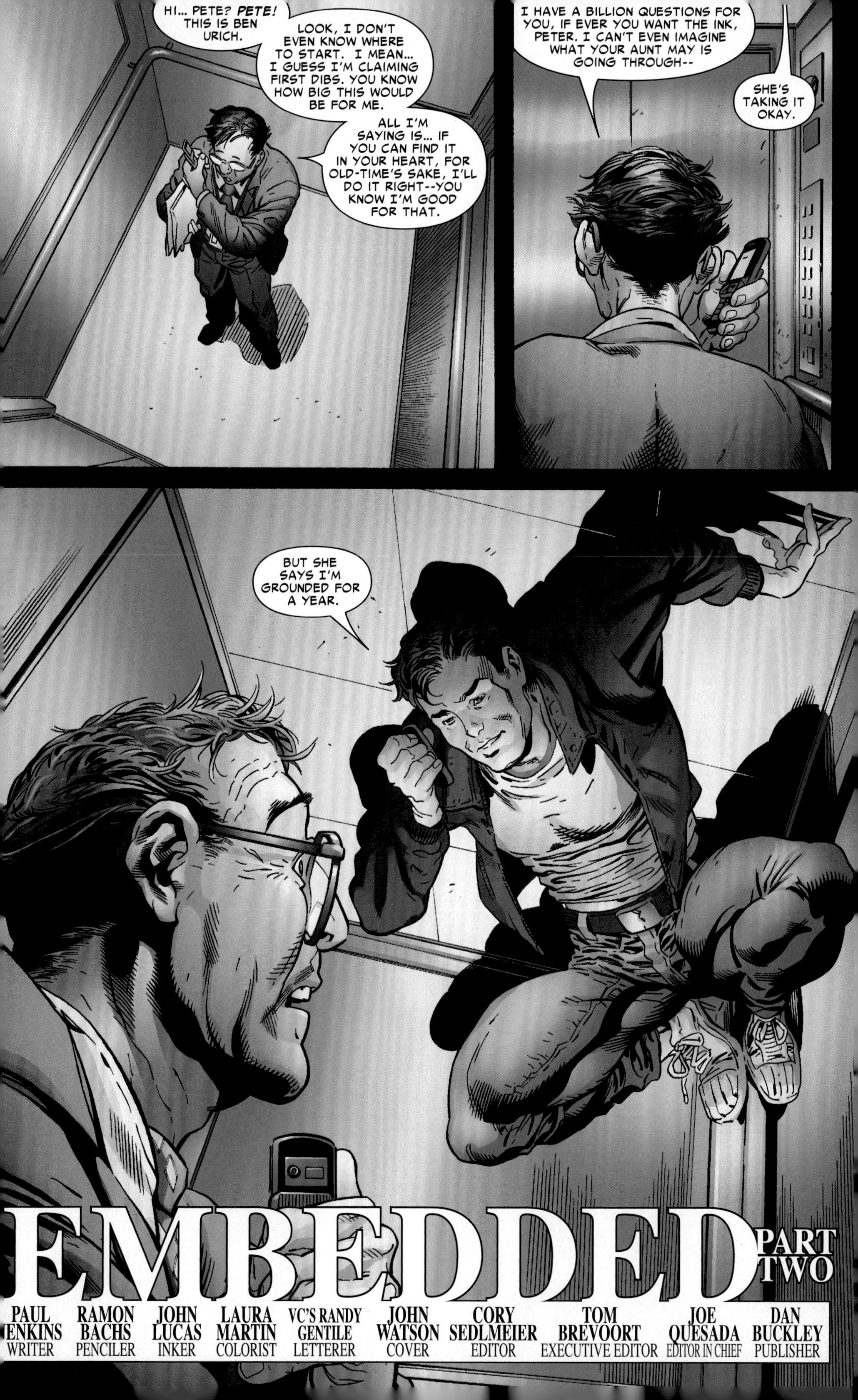

HI... PETE? *PETE!* THIS IS BEN URICH.
LOOK, I DON'T EVEN KNOW WHERE TO START. I MEAN... I GUESS I'M CLAIMING FIRST DIBS. YOU KNOW HOW BIG THIS WOULD BE FOR ME.
ALL I'M SAYING IS... IF YOU CAN FIND IT IN YOUR HEART, FOR OLD-TIME'S SAKE, I'LL DO IT RIGHT--YOU KNOW I'M GOOD FOR THAT.
I HAVE A BILLION QUESTIONS FOR YOU, IF EVER YOU WANT THE INK, PETER. I CAN'T EVEN IMAGINE WHAT YOUR AUNT MAY IS GOING THROUGH--
SHE'S TAKING IT OKAY.
BUT SHE SAYS I'M GROUNDED FOR A YEAR.
EMBEDDED PART TWO
PAUL JENKINS WRITER
RAMON BACHS PENCILER
JOHN LUCAS INKER
LAURA MARTIN COLORIST
VC'S RANDY GENTILE LETTERER
JOHN WATSON COVER
CORY SEDLMEIER EDITOR
TOM BREVOORT EXECUTIVE EDITOR
JOE QUESADA EDITOR IN CHIEF
DAN BUCKLEY PUBLISHER

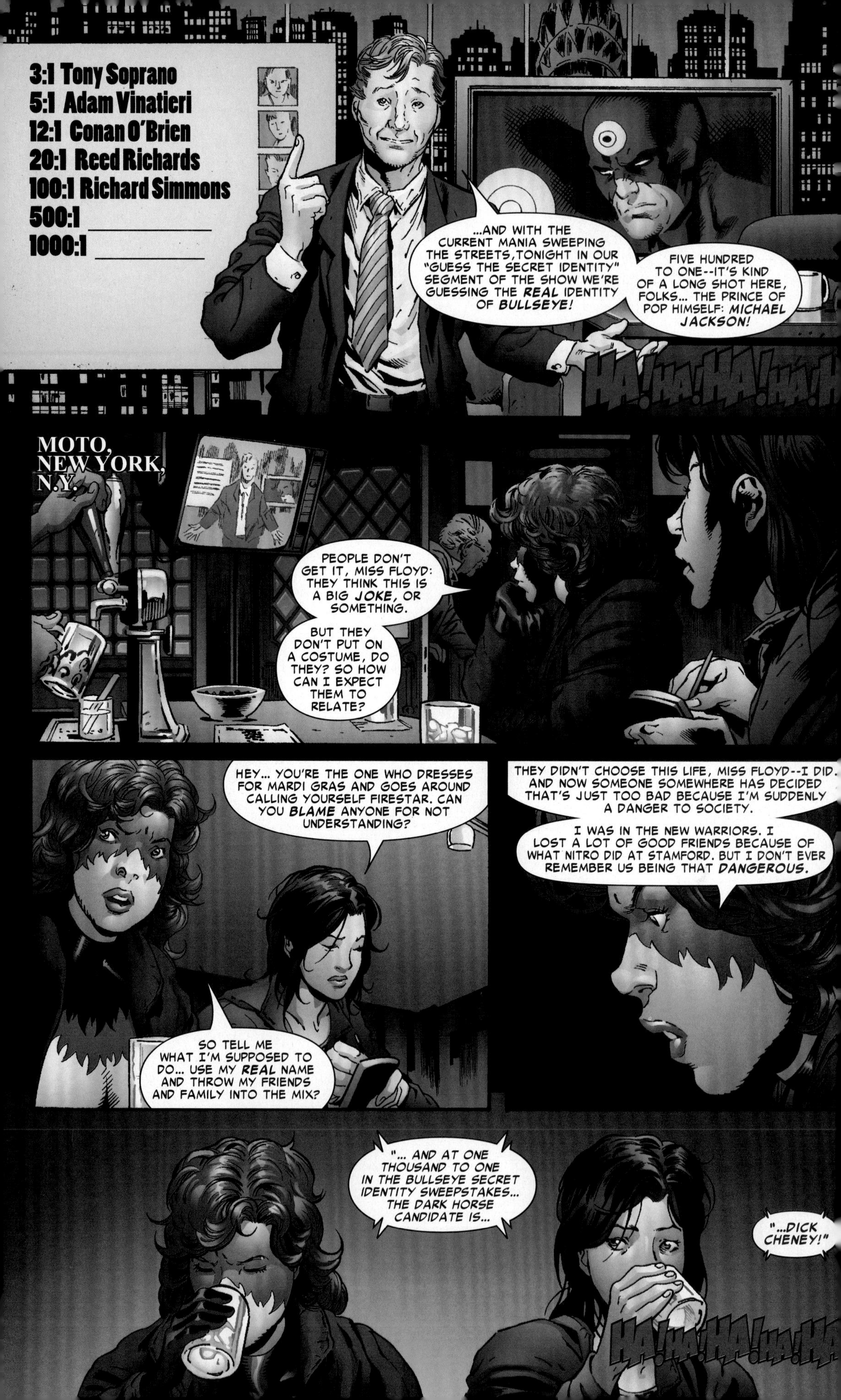

3:1 Tony Soprano
5:1 Adam Vinatieri
12:1 Conan O'Brien
20:1 Reed Richards
100:1 Richard Simmons
500:1
1000:1
...AND WITH THE CURRENT MANIA SWEEPING THE STREETS, TONIGHT IN OUR "GUESS THE SECRET IDENTITY" SEGMENT OF THE SHOW WE'RE GUESSING THE REAL IDENTITY OF BULLSEYE!
FIVE HUNDRED TO ONE--IT'S KIND OF A LONG SHOT HERE, FOLKS... THE PRINCE OF POP HIMSELF: MICHAEL JACKSON!
HA! HA! HA! HA! H
MOTO, NEW YORK, N.Y.
PEOPLE DON'T GET IT, MISS FLOYD: THEY THINK THIS IS A BIG JOKE, OR SOMETHING.
BUT THEY DON'T PUT ON A COSTUME, DO THEY? SO HOW CAN I EXPECT THEM TO RELATE?
HEY... YOU'RE THE ONE WHO DRESSES FOR MARDI GRAS AND GOES AROUND CALLING YOURSELF FIRESTAR. CAN YOU BLAME ANYONE FOR NOT UNDERSTANDING?
SO TELL ME WHAT I'M SUPPOSED TO DO... USE MY REAL NAME AND THROW MY FRIENDS AND FAMILY INTO THE MIX?
THEY DIDN'T CHOOSE THIS LIFE, MISS FLOYD--I DID. AND NOW SOMEONE SOMEWHERE HAS DECIDED THAT'S JUST TOO BAD BECAUSE I'M SUDDENLY A DANGER TO SOCIETY.
I WAS IN THE NEW WARRIORS. I LOST A LOT OF GOOD FRIENDS BECAUSE OF WHAT NITRO DID AT STAMFORD. BUT I DON'T EVER REMEMBER US BEING THAT DANGEROUS.
"... AND AT ONE THOUSAND TO ONE IN THE BULLSEYE SECRET IDENTITY SWEEPSTAKES... THE DARK HORSE CANDIDATE IS...
"...DICK CHENEY!"
HA! HA! HA! HA! HA

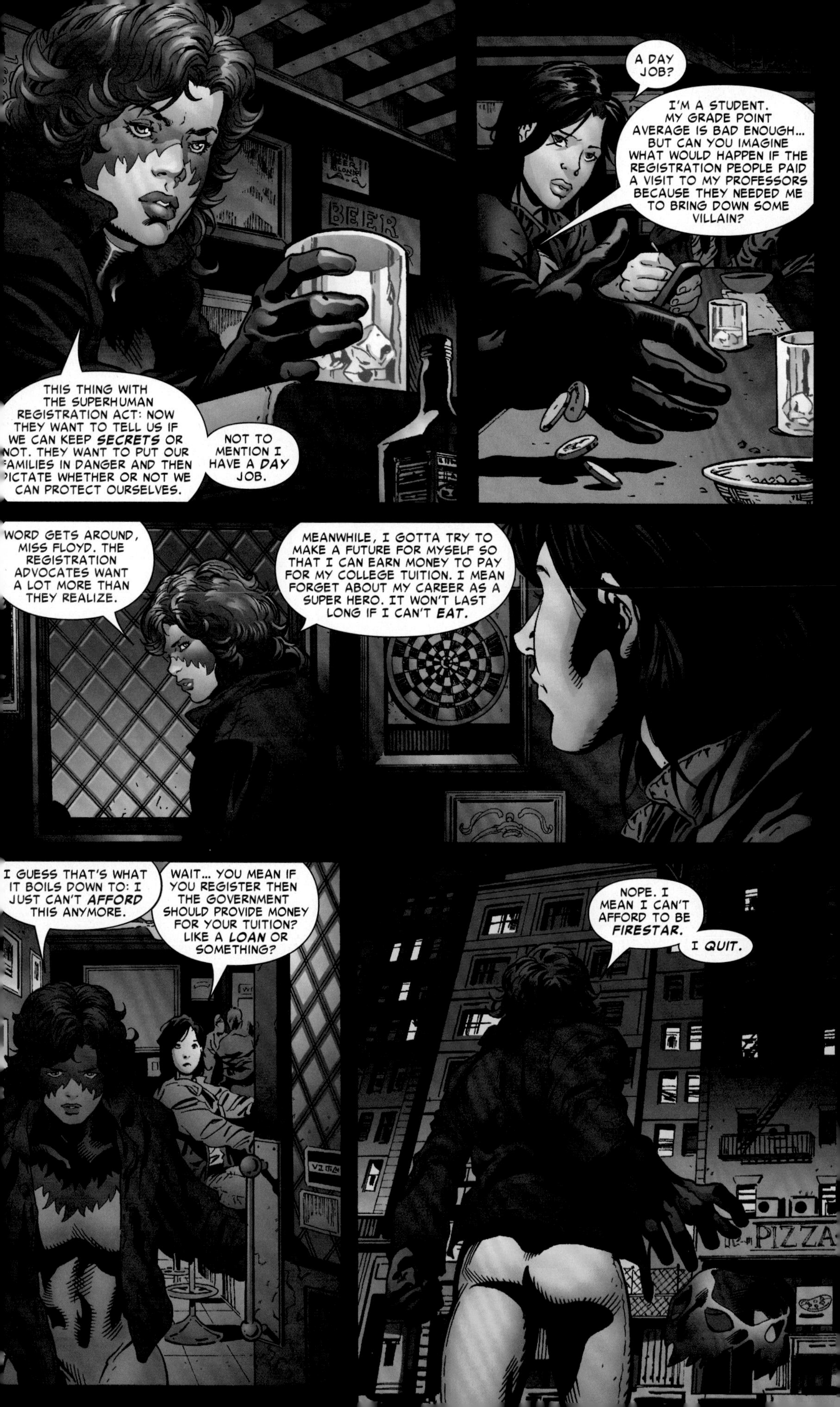
THIS THING WITH THE SUPERHUMAN REGISTRATION ACT: NOW THEY WANT TO TELL US IF WE CAN KEEP SECRETS OR NOT. THEY WANT TO PUT OUR FAMILIES IN DANGER AND THEN DICTATE WHETHER OR NOT WE CAN PROTECT OURSELVES.
NOT TO MENTION I HAVE A DAY JOB.
A DAY JOB?
I'M A STUDENT. MY GRADE POINT AVERAGE IS BAD ENOUGH... BUT CAN YOU IMAGINE WHAT WOULD HAPPEN IF THE REGISTRATION PEOPLE PAID A VISIT TO MY PROFESSORS BECAUSE THEY NEEDED ME TO BRING DOWN SOME VILLAIN?
BEER
WORD GETS AROUND, MISS FLOYD. THE REGISTRATION ADVOCATES WANT A LOT MORE THAN THEY REALIZE.
MEANWHILE, I GOTTA TRY TO MAKE A FUTURE FOR MYSELF SO THAT I CAN EARN MONEY TO PAY FOR MY COLLEGE TUITION. I MEAN FORGET ABOUT MY CAREER AS A SUPER HERO. IT WON'T LAST LONG IF I CAN'T EAT.
I GUESS THAT'S WHAT IT BOILS DOWN TO: I JUST CAN'T AFFORD THIS ANYMORE.
WAIT... YOU MEAN IF YOU REGISTER THEN THE GOVERNMENT SHOULD PROVIDE MONEY FOR YOUR TUITION? LIKE A LOAN OR SOMETHING?
NOPE. I MEAN I CAN'T AFFORD TO BE FIRESTAR.
I QUIT.
PIZZA

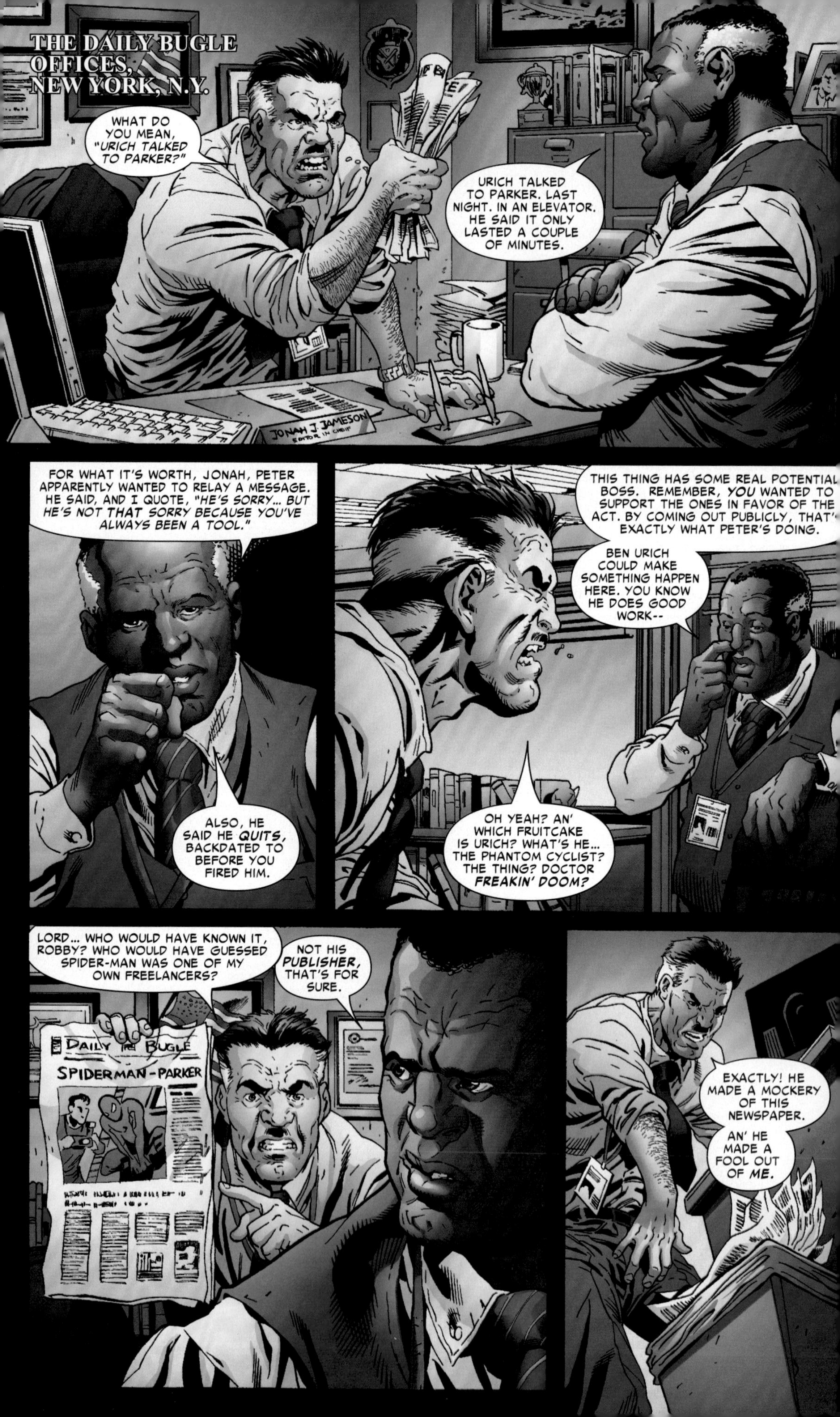

THE DAILY BUGLE OFFICES, NEW YORK, N.Y.
WHAT DO YOU MEAN, "URICH TALKED TO PARKER?"
URICH TALKED TO PARKER. LAST NIGHT. IN AN ELEVATOR. HE SAID IT ONLY LASTED A COUPLE OF MINUTES.
JONAH J. JAMESON EDITOR IN CHIEF
FOR WHAT IT'S WORTH, JONAH, PETER APPARENTLY WANTED TO RELAY A MESSAGE. HE SAID, AND I QUOTE, "HE'S SORRY... BUT HE'S NOT THAT SORRY BECAUSE YOU'VE ALWAYS BEEN A TOOL."
ALSO, HE SAID HE QUITS, BACKDATED TO BEFORE YOU FIRED HIM.
THIS THING HAS SOME REAL POTENTIAL BOSS. REMEMBER, YOU WANTED TO SUPPORT THE ONES IN FAVOR OF THE ACT. BY COMING OUT PUBLICLY, THAT' EXACTLY WHAT PETER'S DOING.
BEN URICH COULD MAKE SOMETHING HAPPEN HERE. YOU KNOW HE DOES GOOD WORK--
OH YEAH? AN' WHICH FRUITCAKE IS URICH? WHAT'S HE... THE PHANTOM CYCLIST? THE THING? DOCTOR FREAKIN' DOOM?
LORD... WHO WOULD HAVE KNOWN IT, ROBBY? WHO WOULD HAVE GUESSED SPIDER-MAN WAS ONE OF MY OWN FREELANCERS?
NOT HIS PUBLISHER, THAT'S FOR SURE.
DAILY BUGLE
SPIDERMAN-PARKER
EXACTLY! HE MADE A MOCKERY OF THIS NEWSPAPER.
AN' HE MADE A FOOL OUT OF ME.

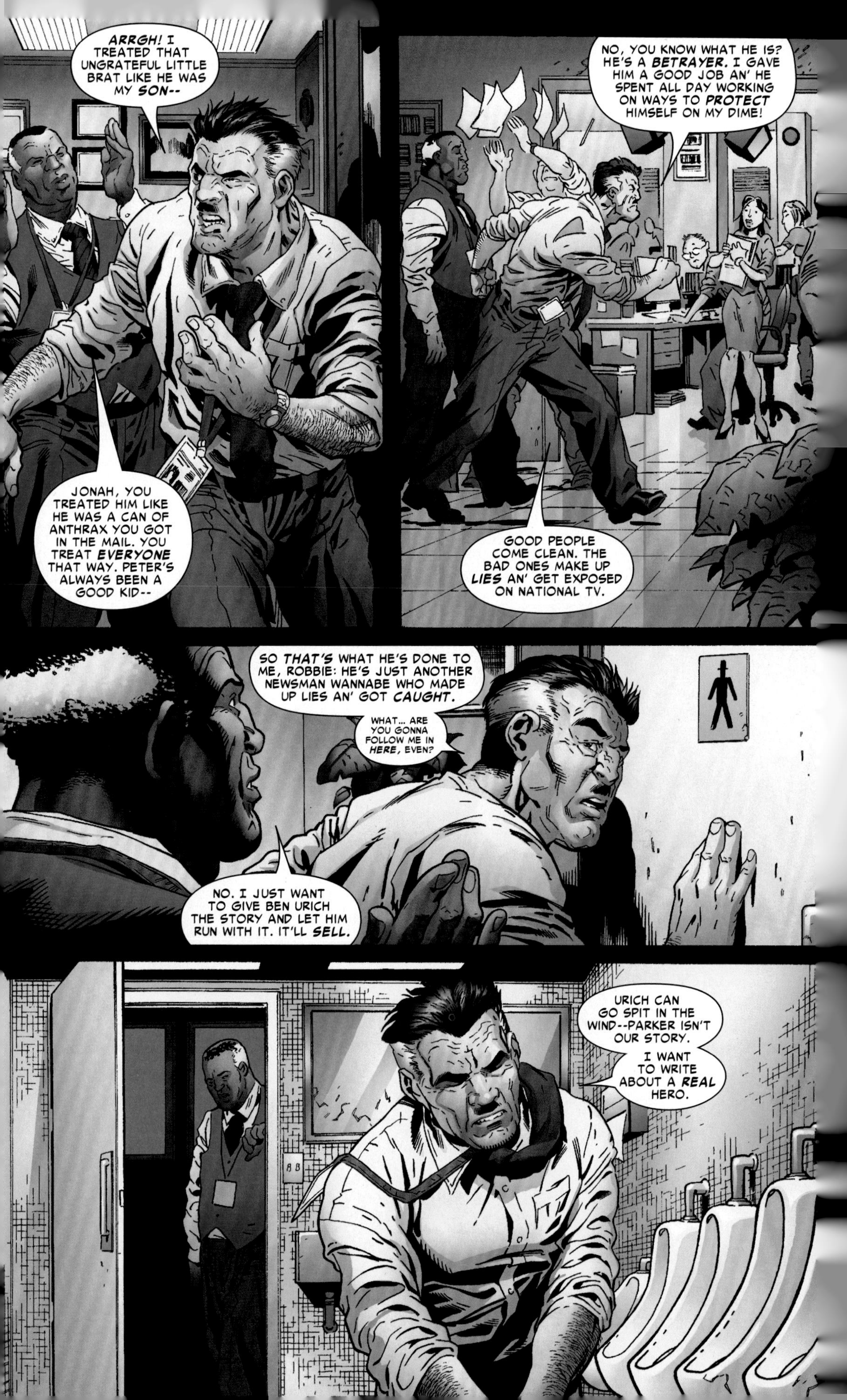
ARRGH! I TREATED THAT UNGRATEFUL LITTLE BRAT LIKE HE WAS MY SON--
JONAH, YOU TREATED HIM LIKE HE WAS A CAN OF ANTHRAX YOU GOT IN THE MAIL. YOU TREAT EVERYONE THAT WAY. PETER'S ALWAYS BEEN A GOOD KID--
NO, YOU KNOW WHAT HE IS? HE'S A BETRAYER. I GAVE HIM A GOOD JOB AN' HE SPENT ALL DAY WORKING ON WAYS TO PROTECT HIMSELF ON MY DIME!
GOOD PEOPLE COME CLEAN. THE BAD ONES MAKE UP LIES AN' GET EXPOSED ON NATIONAL TV.
SO THAT'S WHAT HE'S DONE TO ME, ROBBIE: HE'S JUST ANOTHER NEWSMAN WANNABE WHO MADE UP LIES AN' GOT CAUGHT.
WHAT... ARE YOU GONNA FOLLOW ME IN HERE, EVEN?
NO. I JUST WANT TO GIVE BEN URICH THE STORY AND LET HIM RUN WITH IT. IT'LL SELL.
URICH CAN GO SPIT IN THE WIND--PARKER ISN'T OUR STORY.
I WANT TO WRITE ABOUT A REAL HERO.

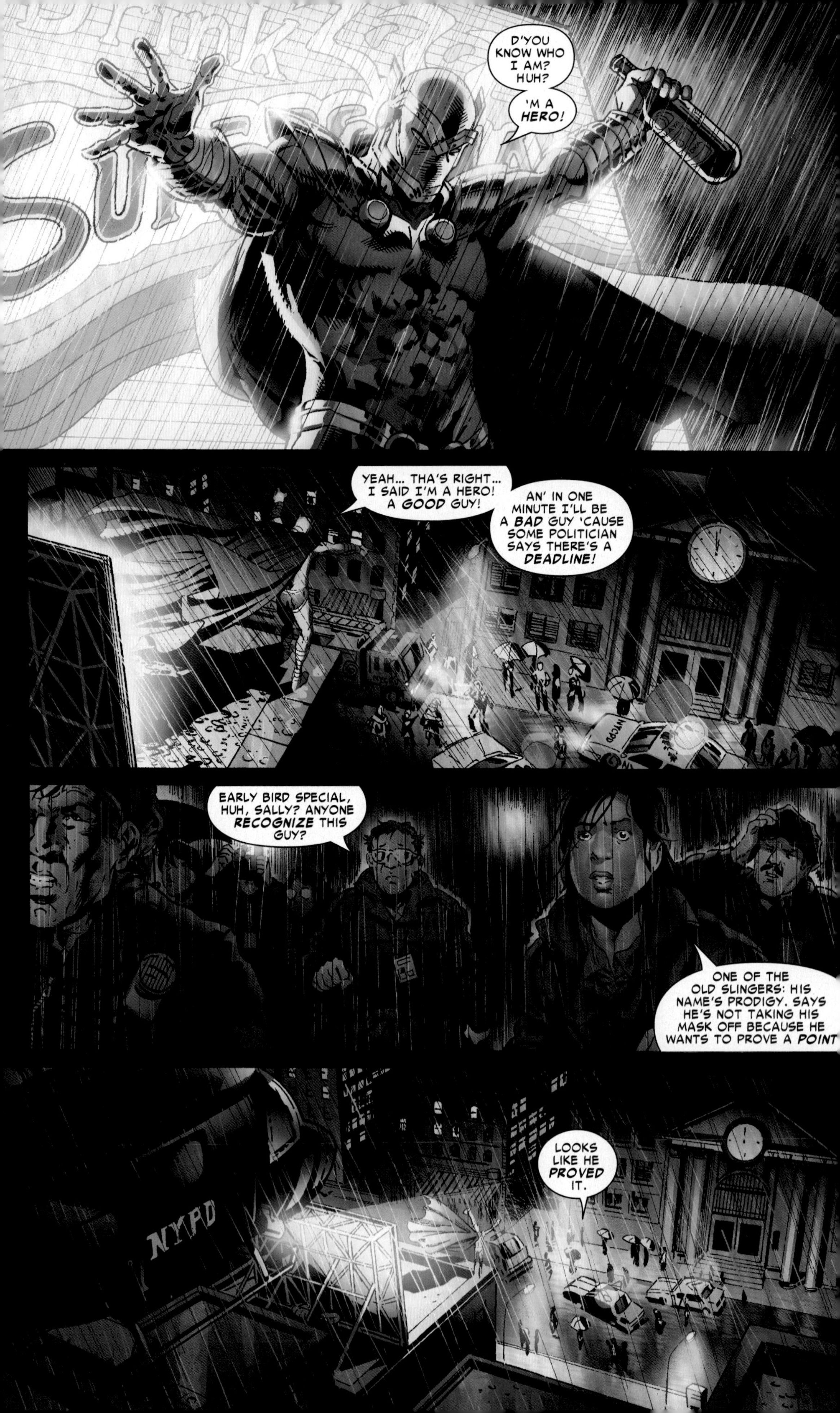
D'YOU KNOW WHO I AM? HUH?
'M A *HERO!*
YEAH... THA'S RIGHT... I SAID I'M A HERO! A *GOOD* GUY!
AN' IN ONE MINUTE I'LL BE A *BAD* GUY 'CAUSE SOME POLITICIAN SAYS THERE'S A *DEADLINE!*
NYCPD
EARLY BIRD SPECIAL, HUH, SALLY? ANYONE *RECOGNIZE* THIS GUY?
ONE OF THE OLD SLINGERS: HIS NAME'S PRODIGY. SAYS HE'S NOT TAKING HIS MASK OFF BECAUSE HE WANTS TO PROVE A *POINT*
LOOKS LIKE HE *PROVED* IT.
NYPD

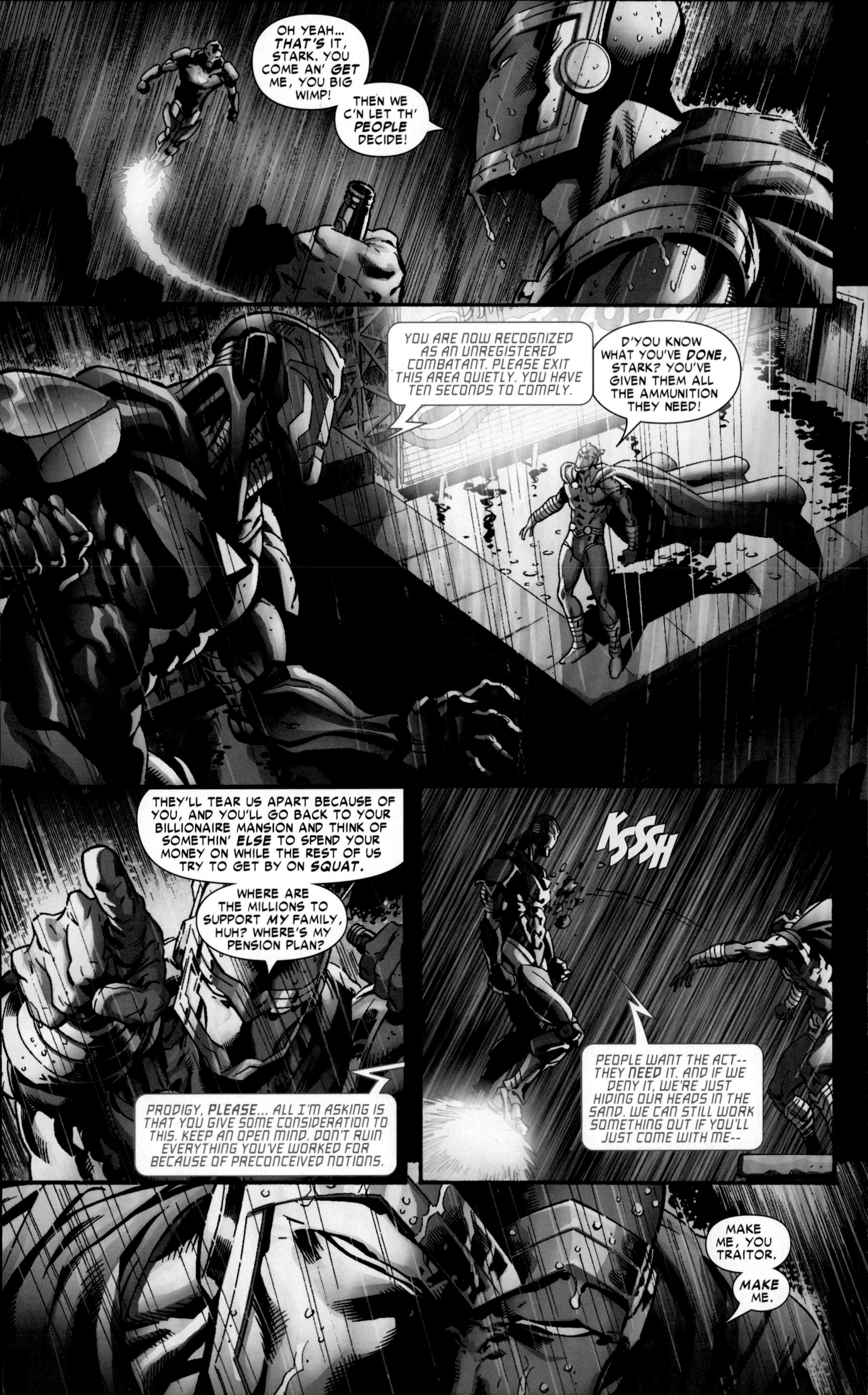
OH YEAH... THAT'S IT, STARK. YOU COME AN' GET ME, YOU BIG WIMP!
THEN WE C'N LET TH' PEOPLE DECIDE!
YOU ARE NOW RECOGNIZED AS AN UNREGISTERED COMBATANT. PLEASE EXIT THIS AREA QUIETLY. YOU HAVE TEN SECONDS TO COMPLY.
D'YOU KNOW WHAT YOU'VE DONE, STARK? YOU'VE GIVEN THEM ALL THE AMMUNITION THEY NEED!
THEY'LL TEAR US APART BECAUSE OF YOU, AND YOU'LL GO BACK TO YOUR BILLIONAIRE MANSION AND THINK OF SOMETHIN' ELSE TO SPEND YOUR MONEY ON WHILE THE REST OF US TRY TO GET BY ON SQUAT.
WHERE ARE THE MILLIONS TO SUPPORT MY FAMILY, HUH? WHERE'S MY PENSION PLAN?
PRODIGY, PLEASE... ALL I'M ASKING IS THAT YOU GIVE SOME CONSIDERATION TO THIS. KEEP AN OPEN MIND. DON'T RUIN EVERYTHING YOU'VE WORKED FOR BECAUSE OF PRECONCEIVED NOTIONS.
KSSSH
PEOPLE WANT THE ACT-- THEY NEED IT. AND IF WE DENY IT, WE'RE JUST HIDING OUR HEADS IN THE SAND. WE CAN STILL WORK SOMETHING OUT IF YOU'LL JUST COME WITH ME--
MAKE ME, YOU TRAITOR.
MAKE ME.

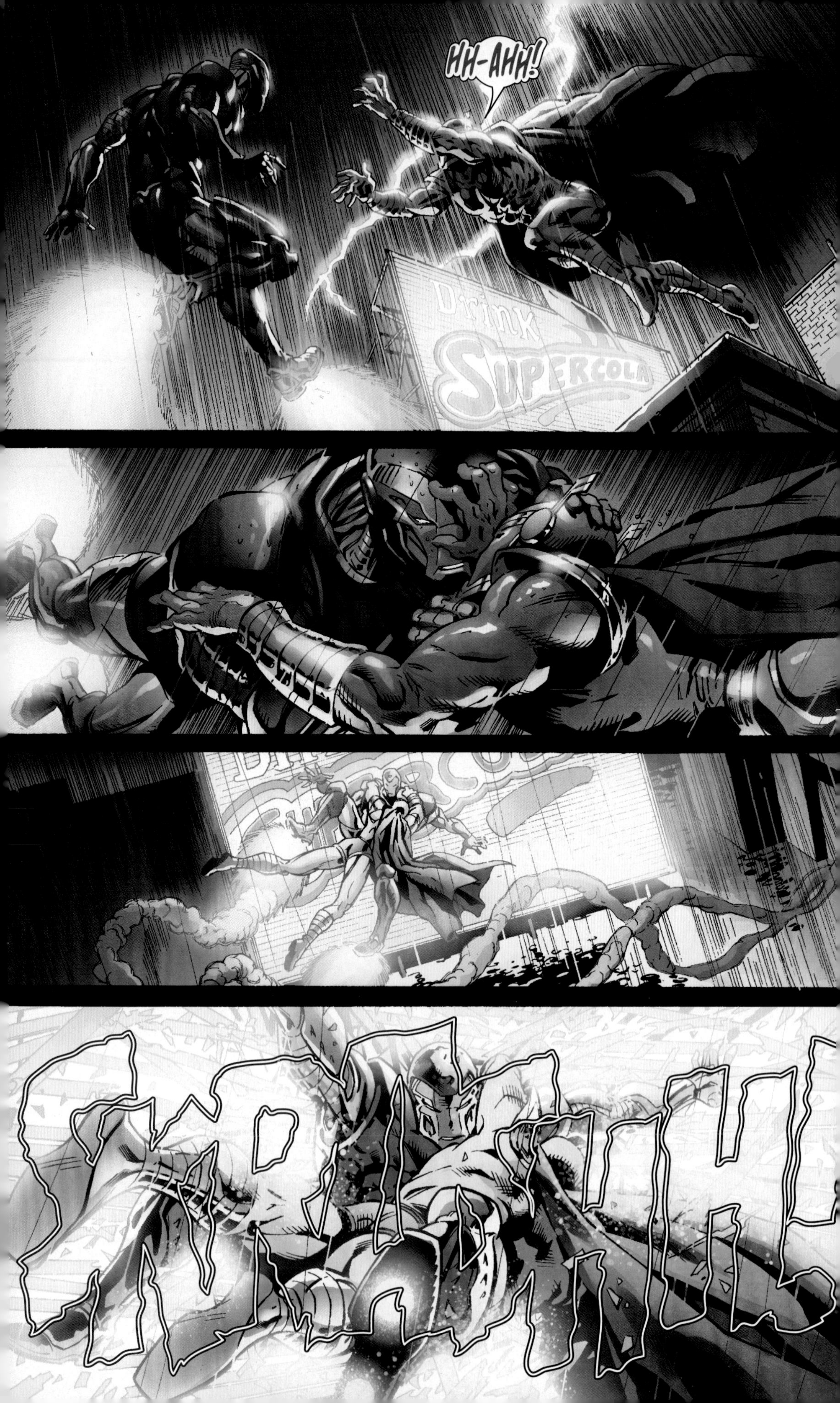
HH-AHH!
Drink
SUPERCOLA

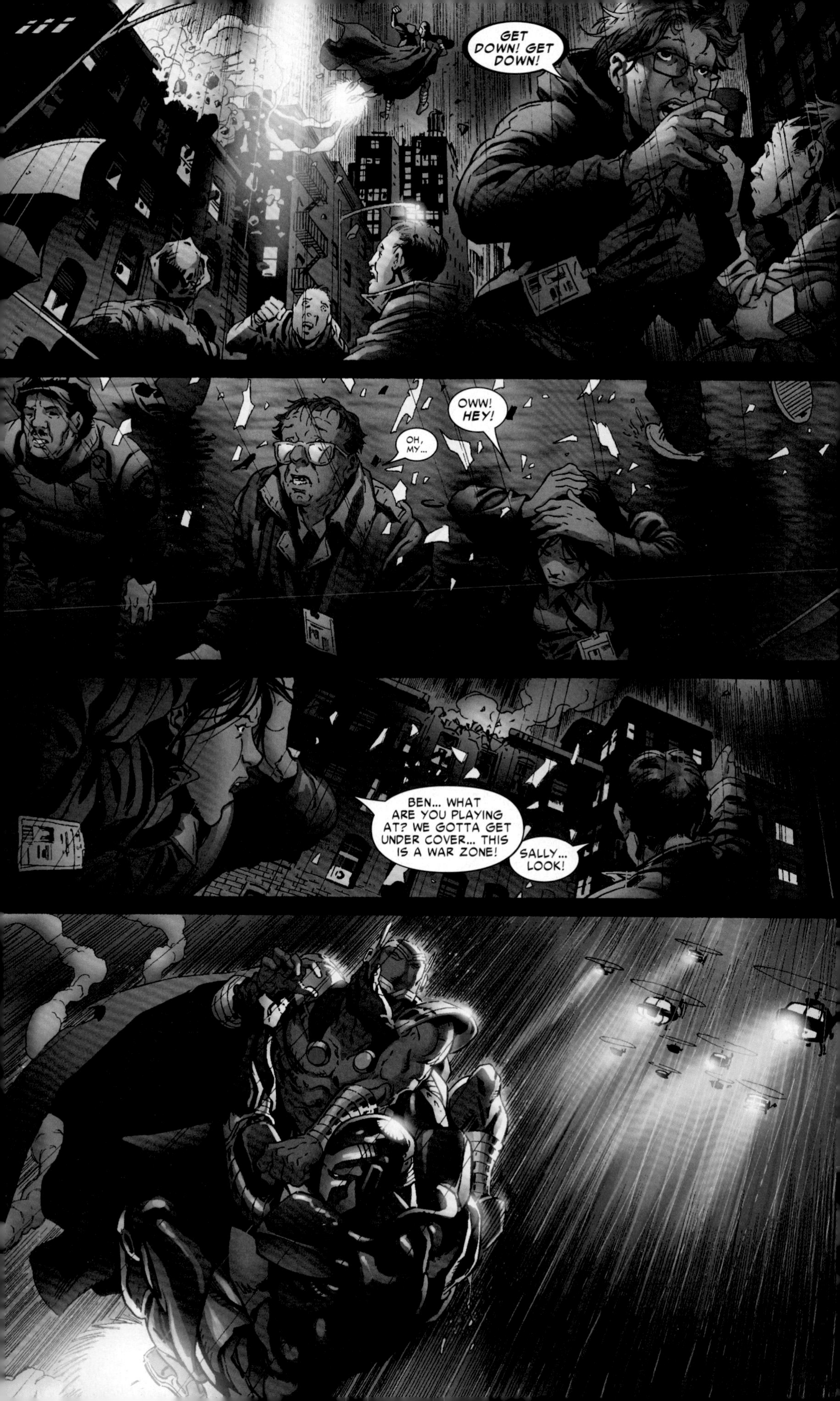
GET DOWN! GET DOWN!
OWW! HEY!
OH, MY...
BEN... WHAT ARE YOU PLAYING AT? WE GOTTA GET UNDER COVER... THIS IS A WAR ZONE!
SALLY... LOOK!

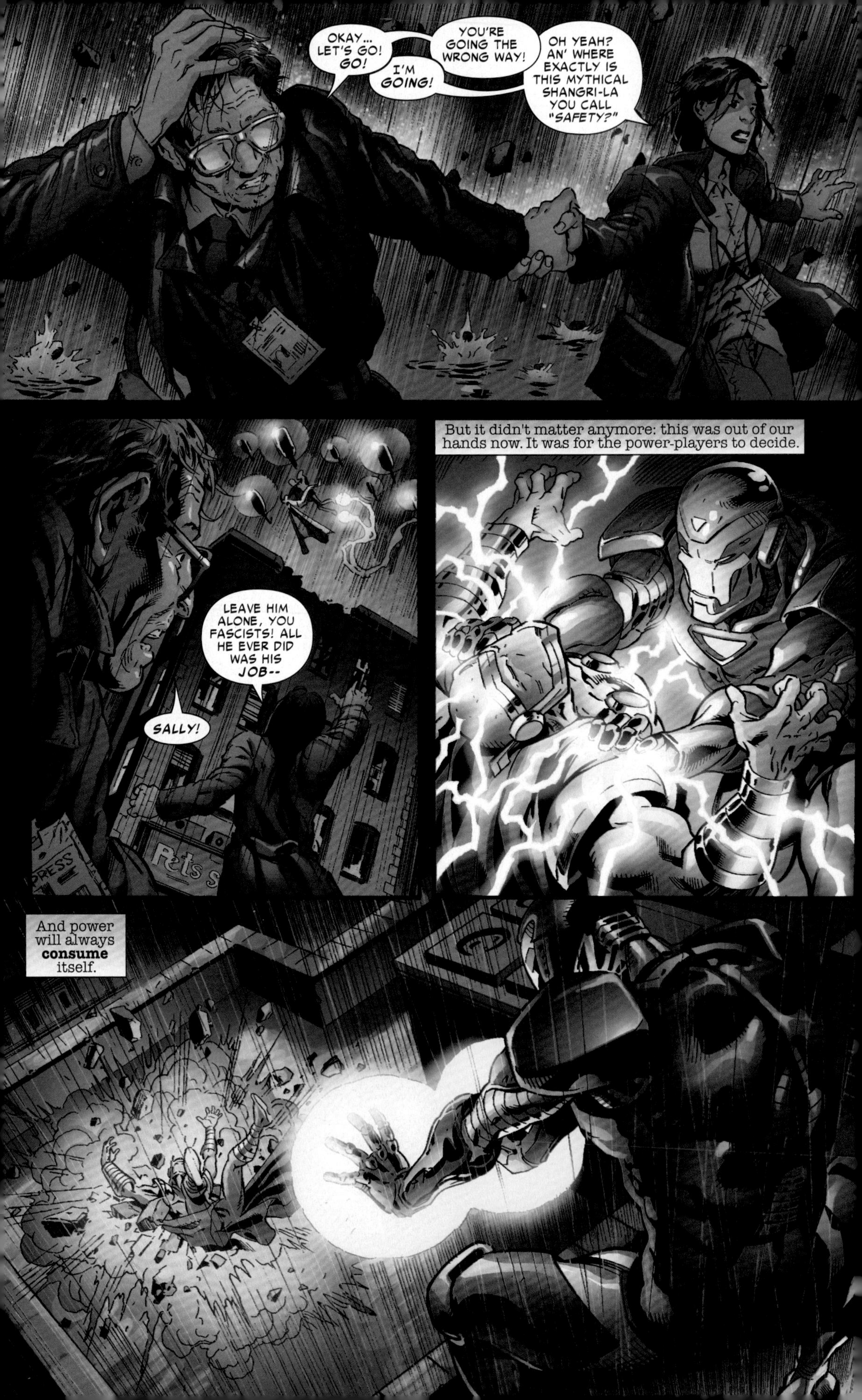
OKAY... LET'S GO! GO!
YOU'RE GOING THE WRONG WAY!
I'M GOING!
OH YEAH? AN' WHERE EXACTLY IS THIS MYTHICAL SHANGRI-LA YOU CALL "SAFETY?"
LEAVE HIM ALONE, YOU FASCISTS! ALL HE EVER DID WAS HIS JOB--
SALLY!
But it didn't matter anymore: this was out of our hands now. It was for the power-players to decide.
And power will always consume itself.

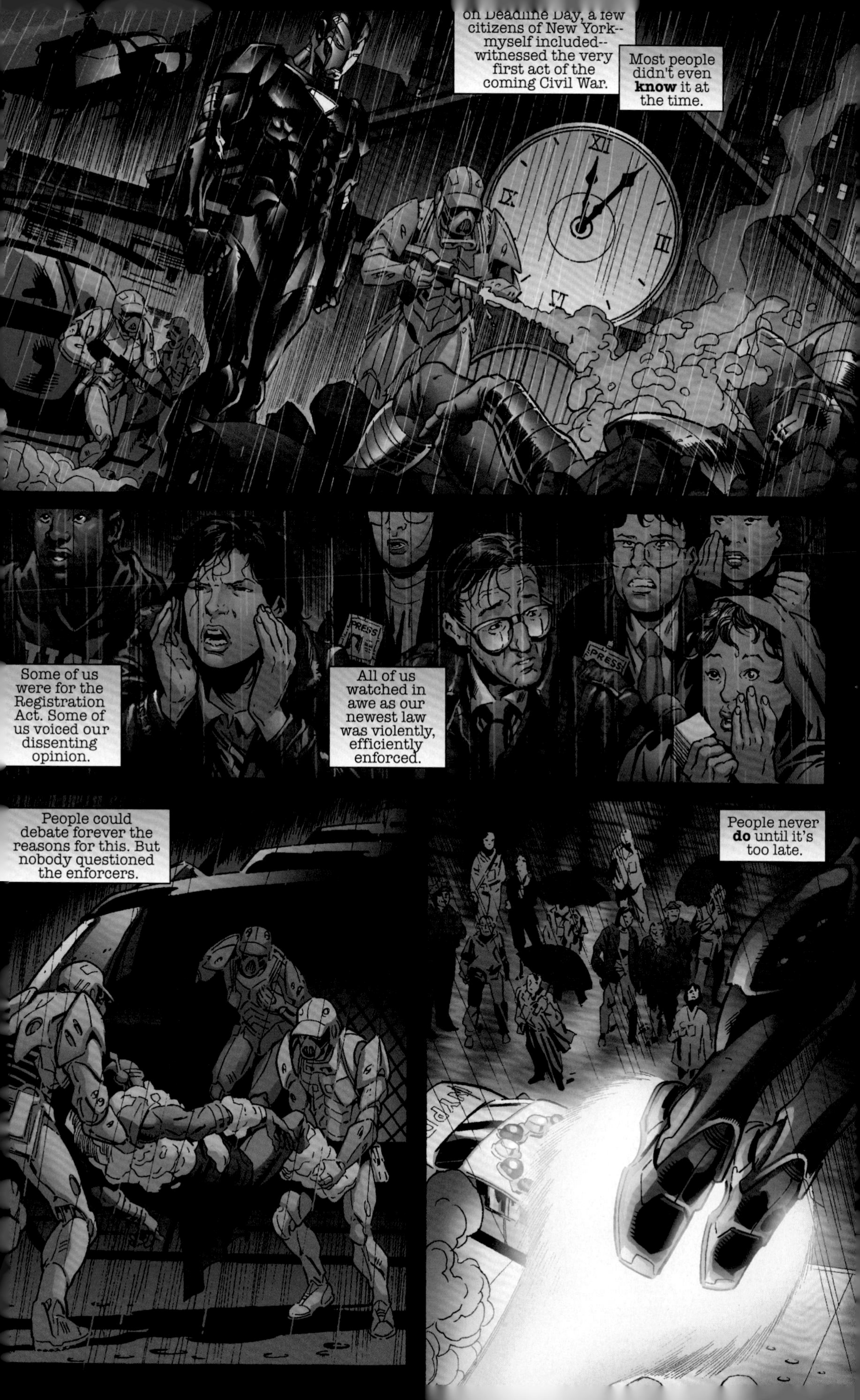
On Deadline Day, a few citizens of New York--myself included--witnessed the very first act of the coming Civil War.
Most people didn't even **know** it at the time.
PRESS
PRESS
Some of us were for the Registration Act. Some of us voiced our dissenting opinion.
All of us watched in awe as our newest law was violently, efficiently enforced.
People could debate forever the reasons for this. But nobody questioned the enforcers.
People never **do** until it's too late.

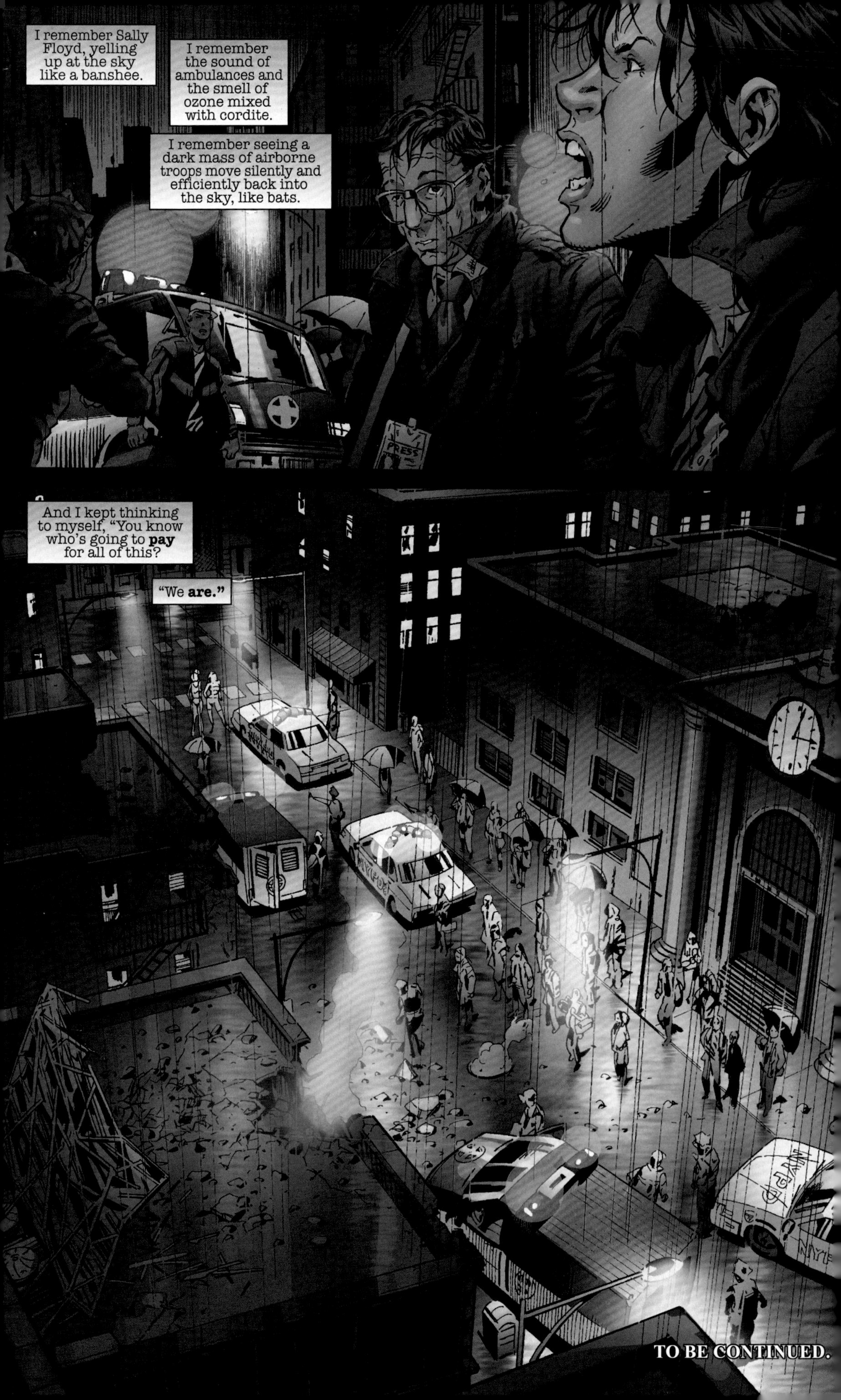
I remember Sally Floyd, yelling up at the sky like a banshee.
I remember the sound of ambulances and the smell of ozone mixed with cordite.
I remember seeing a dark mass of airborne troops move silently and efficiently back into the sky, like bats.
PRESS
And I kept thinking to myself, "You know who's going to **pay** for all of this?
"We **are.**"
TO BE CONTINUED.

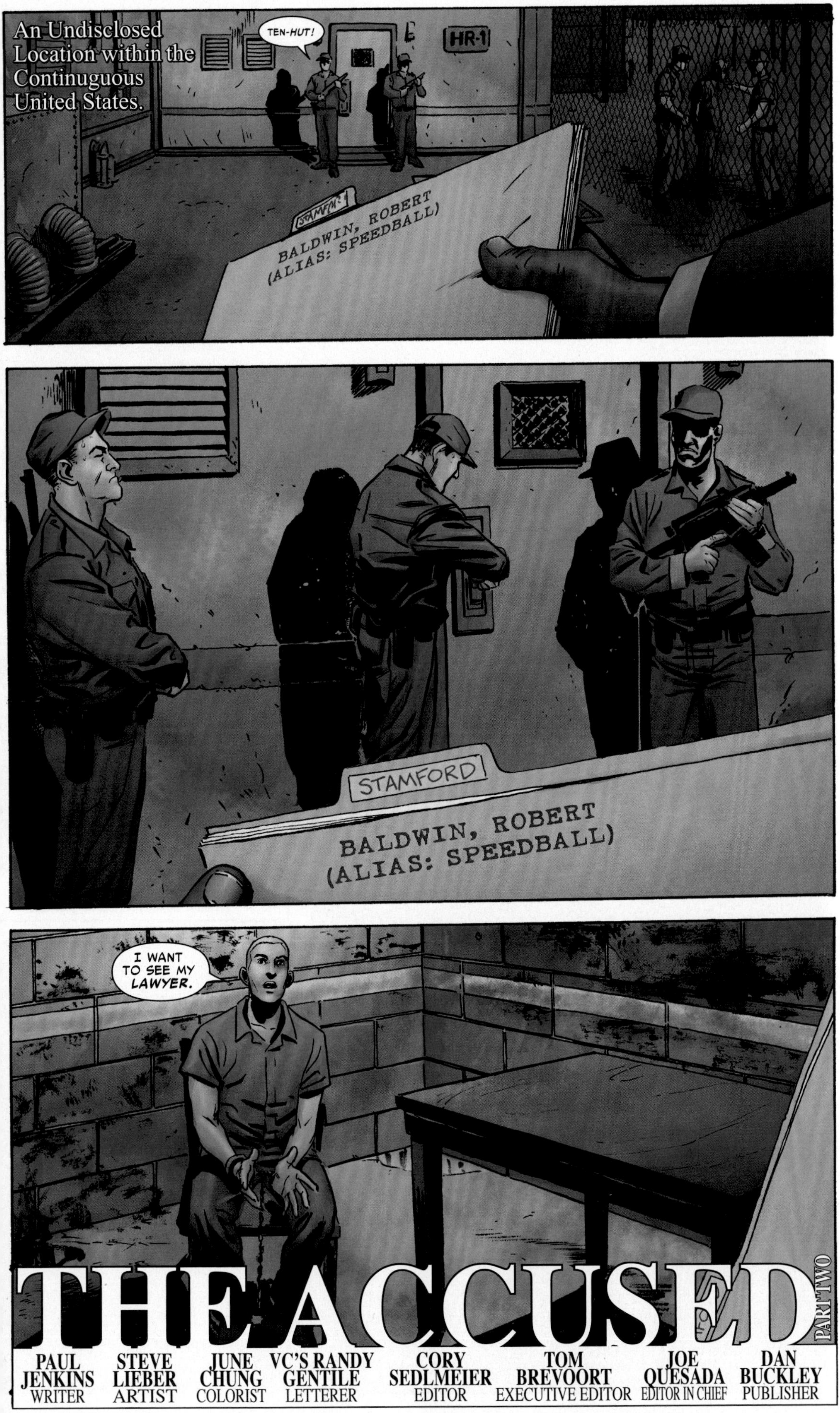

An Undisclosed Location within the Continuguous United States.
TEN-HUT!
HR-1
BALDWIN, ROBERT (ALIAS: SPEEDBALL)
STAMFORD
BALDWIN, ROBERT (ALIAS: SPEEDBALL)
I WANT TO SEE MY LAWYER.
THE ACCUSED
PART TWO
PAUL JENKINS WRITER
STEVE LIEBER ARTIST
JUNE CHUNG COLORIST
VC'S RANDY GENTILE LETTERER
CORY SEDLMEIER EDITOR
TOM BREVOORT EXECUTIVE EDITOR
JOE QUESADA EDITOR IN CHIEF
DAN BUCKLEY PUBLISHER

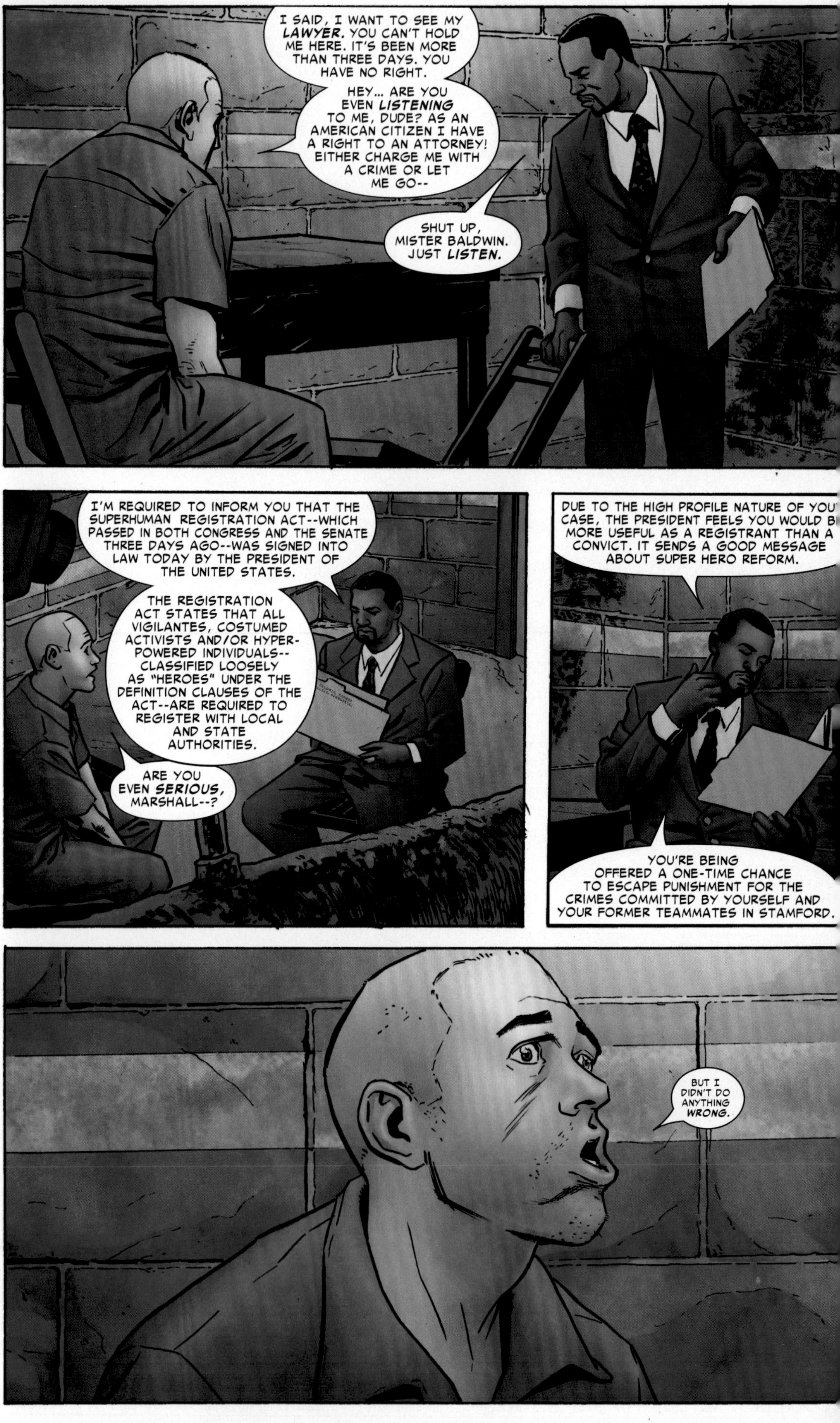
I SAID, I WANT TO SEE MY LAWYER. YOU CAN'T HOLD ME HERE. IT'S BEEN MORE THAN THREE DAYS. YOU HAVE NO RIGHT.
HEY... ARE YOU EVEN LISTENING TO ME, DUDE? AS AN AMERICAN CITIZEN I HAVE A RIGHT TO AN ATTORNEY! EITHER CHARGE ME WITH A CRIME OR LET ME GO--
SHUT UP, MISTER BALDWIN. JUST LISTEN.
I'M REQUIRED TO INFORM YOU THAT THE SUPERHUMAN REGISTRATION ACT--WHICH PASSED IN BOTH CONGRESS AND THE SENATE THREE DAYS AGO--WAS SIGNED INTO LAW TODAY BY THE PRESIDENT OF THE UNITED STATES.
THE REGISTRATION ACT STATES THAT ALL VIGILANTES, COSTUMED ACTIVISTS AND/OR HYPER-POWERED INDIVIDUALS--CLASSIFIED LOOSELY AS "HEROES" UNDER THE DEFINITION CLAUSES OF THE ACT--ARE REQUIRED TO REGISTER WITH LOCAL AND STATE AUTHORITIES.
ARE YOU EVEN SERIOUS, MARSHALL--?
DUE TO THE HIGH PROFILE NATURE OF YOU CASE, THE PRESIDENT FEELS YOU WOULD B MORE USEFUL AS A REGISTRANT THAN A CONVICT. IT SENDS A GOOD MESSAGE ABOUT SUPER HERO REFORM.
YOU'RE BEING OFFERED A ONE-TIME CHANCE TO ESCAPE PUNISHMENT FOR THE CRIMES COMMITTED BY YOURSELF AND YOUR FORMER TEAMMATES IN STAMFORD.
BUT I DIDN'T DO ANYTHING WRONG.

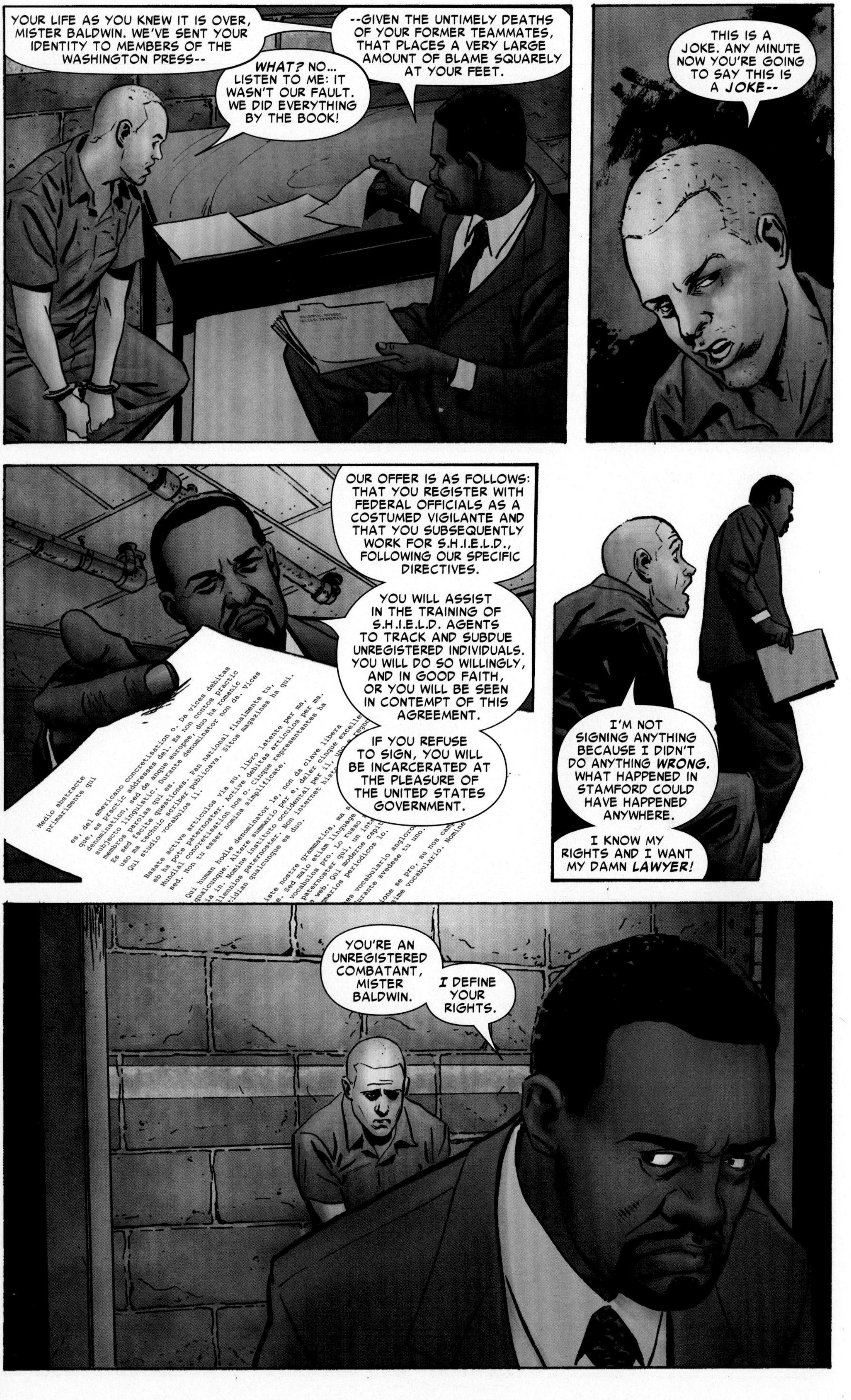
YOUR LIFE AS YOU KNEW IT IS OVER, MISTER BALDWIN. WE'VE SENT YOUR IDENTITY TO MEMBERS OF THE WASHINGTON PRESS--
--GIVEN THE UNTIMELY DEATHS OF YOUR FORMER TEAMMATES, THAT PLACES A VERY LARGE AMOUNT OF BLAME SQUARELY AT YOUR FEET.
WHAT? NO... LISTEN TO ME: IT WASN'T OUR FAULT. WE DID EVERYTHING BY THE BOOK!
THIS IS A JOKE. ANY MINUTE NOW YOU'RE GOING TO SAY THIS IS A JOKE--
OUR OFFER IS AS FOLLOWS: THAT YOU REGISTER WITH FEDERAL OFFICIALS AS A COSTUMED VIGILANTE AND THAT YOU SUBSEQUENTLY WORK FOR S.H.I.E.L.D., FOLLOWING OUR SPECIFIC DIRECTIVES.
YOU WILL ASSIST IN THE TRAINING OF S.H.I.E.L.D. AGENTS TO TRACK AND SUBDUE UNREGISTERED INDIVIDUALS. YOU WILL DO SO WILLINGLY, AND IN GOOD FAITH, OR YOU WILL BE SEEN IN CONTEMPT OF THIS AGREEMENT.
IF YOU REFUSE TO SIGN, YOU WILL BE INCARCERATED AT THE PLEASURE OF THE UNITED STATES GOVERNMENT.
I'M NOT SIGNING ANYTHING BECAUSE I DIDN'T DO ANYTHING WRONG. WHAT HAPPENED IN STAMFORD COULD HAVE HAPPENED ANYWHERE.
I KNOW MY RIGHTS AND I WANT MY DAMN LAWYER!
YOU'RE AN UNREGISTERED COMBATANT, MISTER BALDWIN.
I DEFINE YOUR RIGHTS.

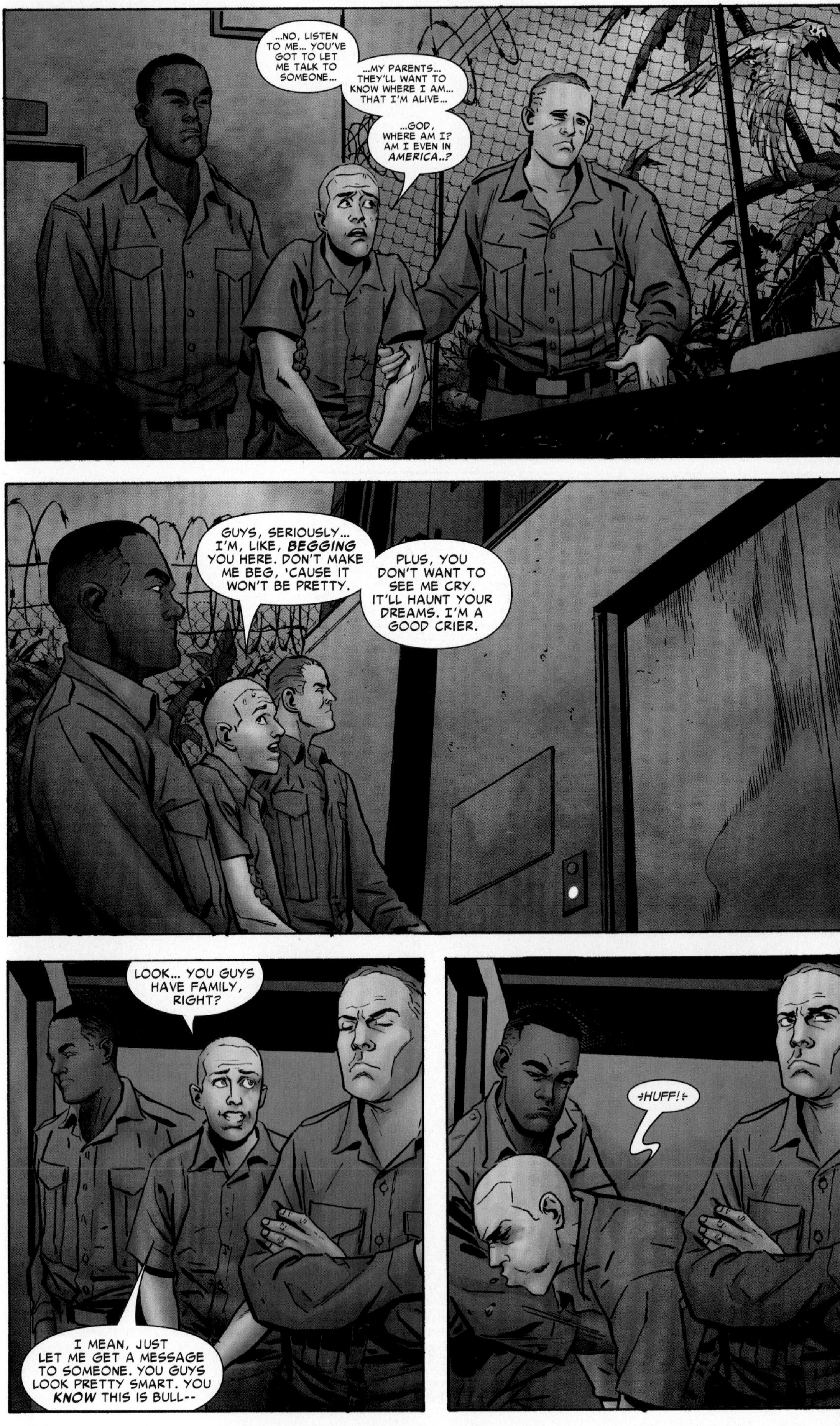
...NO, LISTEN TO ME... YOU'VE GOT TO LET ME TALK TO SOMEONE...
...MY PARENTS... THEY'LL WANT TO KNOW WHERE I AM... THAT I'M ALIVE...
...GOD, WHERE AM I? AM I EVEN IN AMERICA..?
GUYS, SERIOUSLY... I'M, LIKE, BEGGING YOU HERE. DON'T MAKE ME BEG, 'CAUSE IT WON'T BE PRETTY.
PLUS, YOU DON'T WANT TO SEE ME CRY. IT'LL HAUNT YOUR DREAMS. I'M A GOOD CRIER.
LOOK... YOU GUYS HAVE FAMILY, RIGHT?
I MEAN, JUST LET ME GET A MESSAGE TO SOMEONE. YOU GUYS LOOK PRETTY SMART. YOU KNOW THIS IS BULL--
HUFF!

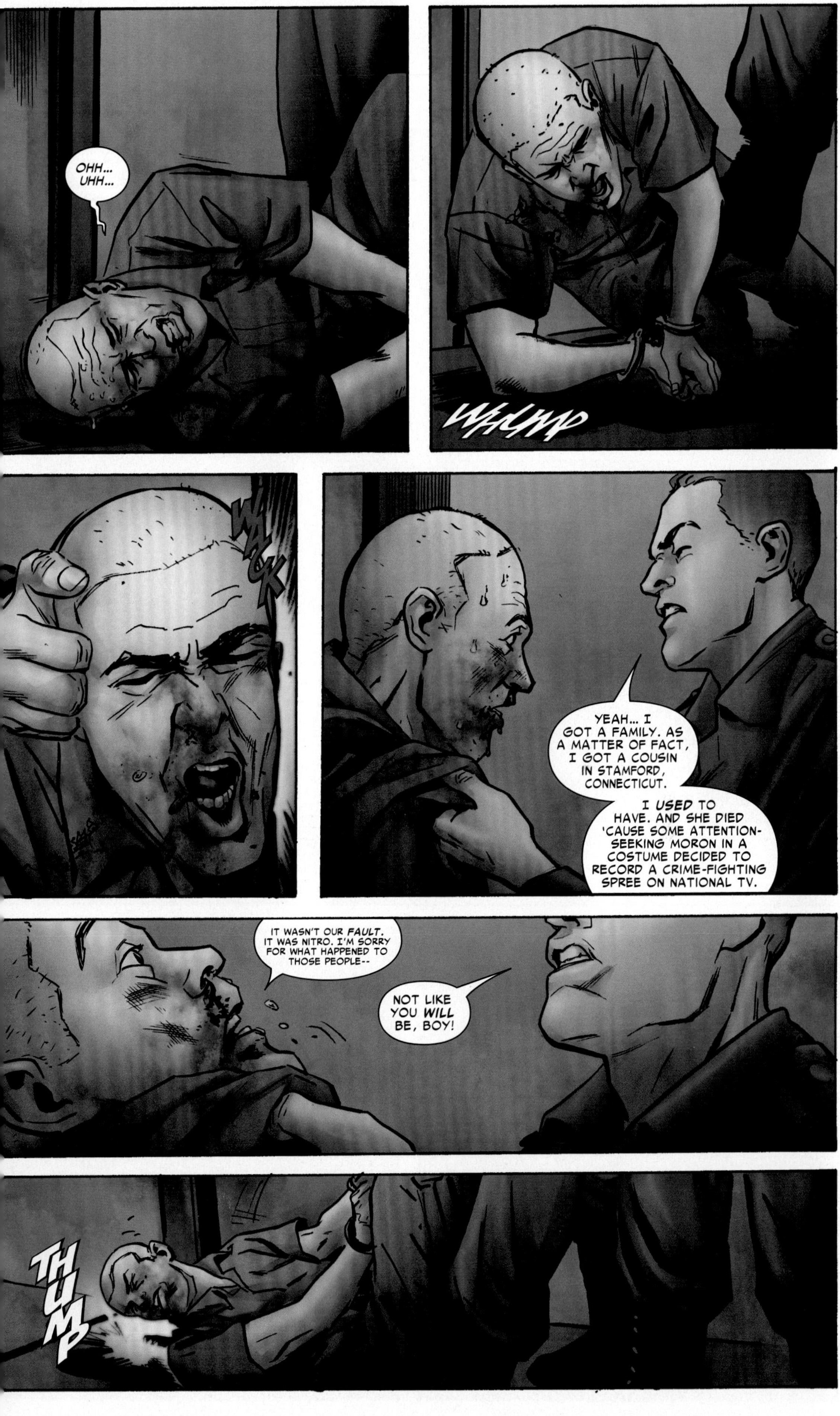
OHH... UHH...
WHUMP
WACK
YEAH... I GOT A FAMILY. AS A MATTER OF FACT, I GOT A COUSIN IN STAMFORD, CONNECTICUT.
I USED TO HAVE. AND SHE DIED 'CAUSE SOME ATTENTION-SEEKING MORON IN A COSTUME DECIDED TO RECORD A CRIME-FIGHTING SPREE ON NATIONAL TV.
IT WASN'T OUR FAULT. IT WAS NITRO. I'M SORRY FOR WHAT HAPPENED TO THOSE PEOPLE--
NOT LIKE YOU WILL BE, BOY!
THUMP

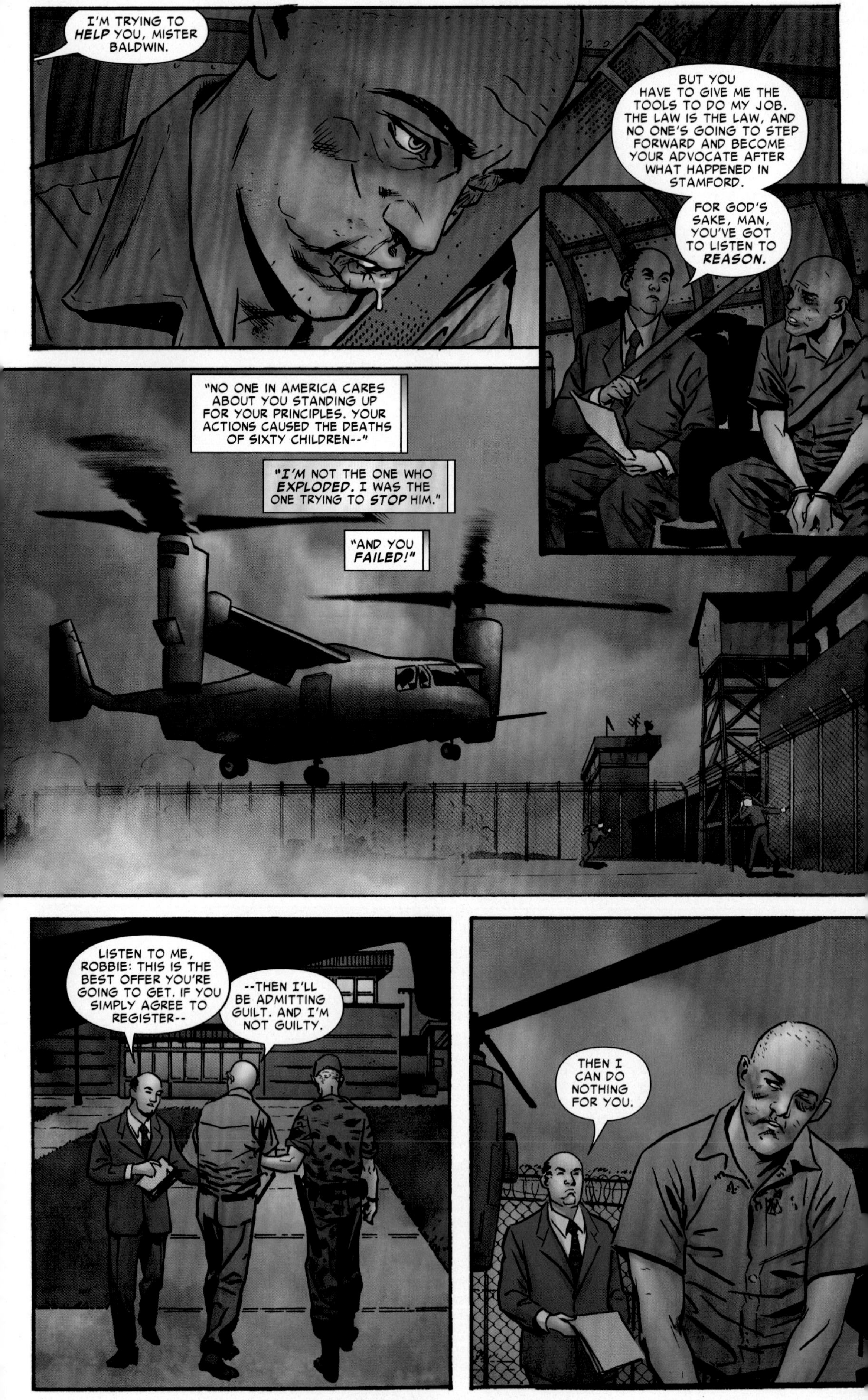

I'M TRYING TO HELP YOU, MISTER BALDWIN.
BUT YOU HAVE TO GIVE ME THE TOOLS TO DO MY JOB. THE LAW IS THE LAW, AND NO ONE'S GOING TO STEP FORWARD AND BECOME YOUR ADVOCATE AFTER WHAT HAPPENED IN STAMFORD.
FOR GOD'S SAKE, MAN, YOU'VE GOT TO LISTEN TO REASON.
"NO ONE IN AMERICA CARES ABOUT YOU STANDING UP FOR YOUR PRINCIPLES. YOUR ACTIONS CAUSED THE DEATHS OF SIXTY CHILDREN--"
"I'M NOT THE ONE WHO EXPLODED. I WAS THE ONE TRYING TO STOP HIM."
"AND YOU FAILED!"
LISTEN TO ME, ROBBIE: THIS IS THE BEST OFFER YOU'RE GOING TO GET. IF YOU SIMPLY AGREE TO REGISTER--
--THEN I'LL BE ADMITTING GUILT. AND I'M NOT GUILTY.
THEN I CAN DO NOTHING FOR YOU.

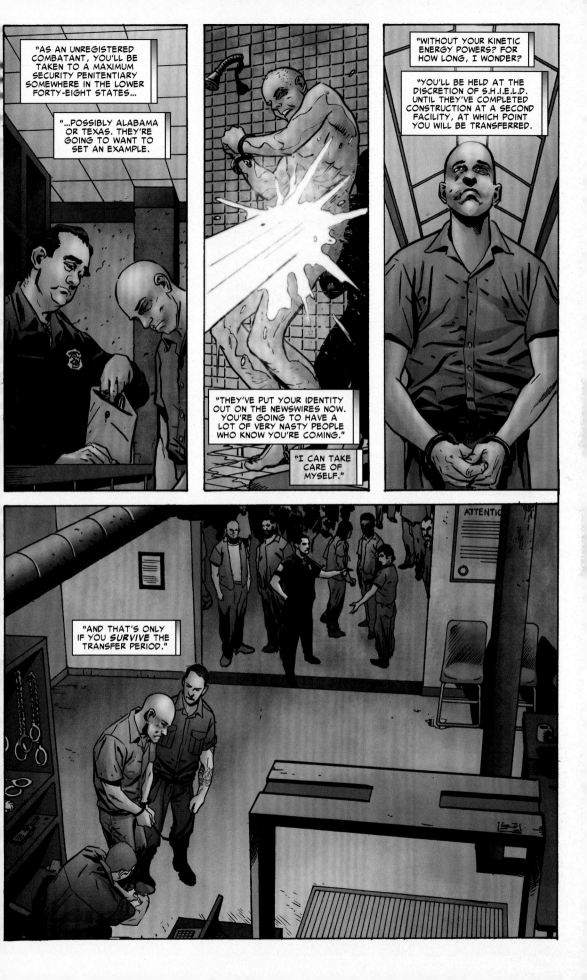

"AS AN UNREGISTERED COMBATANT, YOU'LL BE TAKEN TO A MAXIMUM SECURITY PENITENTIARY SOMEWHERE IN THE LOWER FORTY-EIGHT STATES...

"...POSSIBLY ALABAMA OR TEXAS. THEY'RE GOING TO WANT TO SET AN EXAMPLE.

"THEY'VE PUT YOUR IDENTITY OUT ON THE NEWSWIRES NOW. YOU'RE GOING TO HAVE A LOT OF VERY NASTY PEOPLE WHO KNOW YOU'RE COMING."

"I CAN TAKE CARE OF MYSELF."

"WITHOUT YOUR KINETIC ENERGY POWERS? FOR HOW LONG, I WONDER?

"YOU'LL BE HELD AT THE DISCRETION OF S.H.I.E.L.D. UNTIL THEY'VE COMPLETED CONSTRUCTION AT A SECOND FACILITY, AT WHICH POINT YOU WILL BE TRANSFERRED.

"AND THAT'S ONLY IF YOU *SURVIVE* THE TRANSFER PERIOD."

ATTENTIO

PRISONER INCOMING! CLEAR THE DOORS!

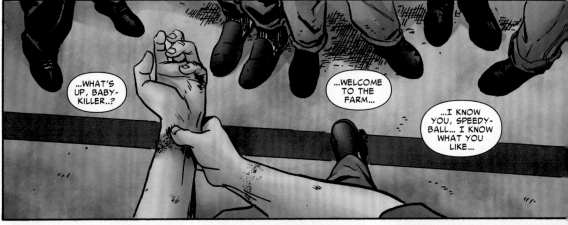

...WHAT'S UP, BABY-KILLER..?

...WELCOME TO THE FARM...

...I KNOW YOU, SPEEDY-BALL... I KNOW WHAT YOU LIKE...

...GONNA SHOW YOU AROUND, BOY...

...SHOW YOU A GOOD TIME...

...LIKE YOU SHOWED THEM KIDS...

TIK

HH-UHH!

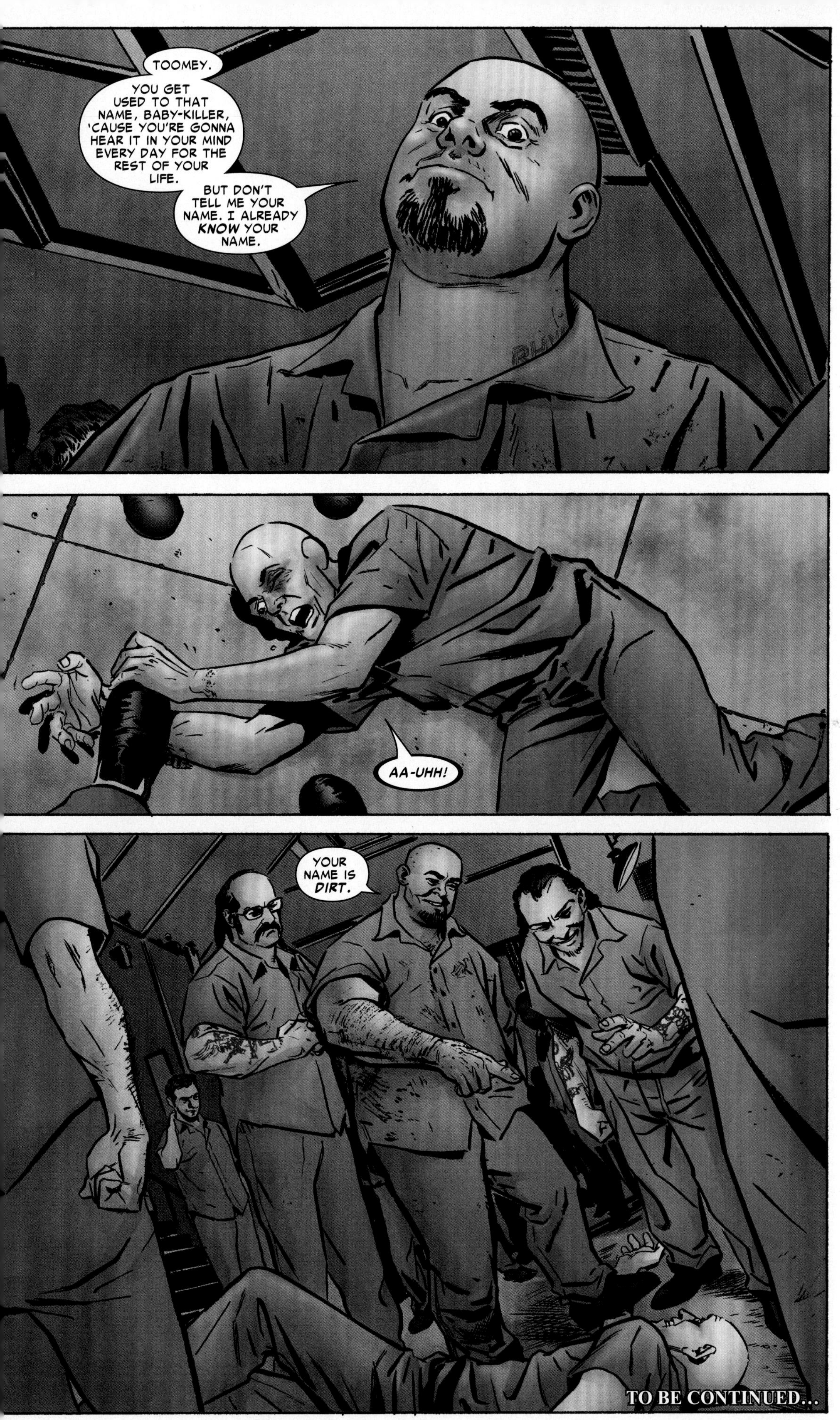
TOOMEY.
YOU GET USED TO THAT NAME, BABY-KILLER, 'CAUSE YOU'RE GONNA HEAR IT IN YOUR MIND EVERY DAY FOR THE REST OF YOUR LIFE.
BUT DON'T TELL ME YOUR NAME. I ALREADY KNOW YOUR NAME.
AA-UHH!
YOUR NAME IS DIRT.
TO BE CONTINUED...

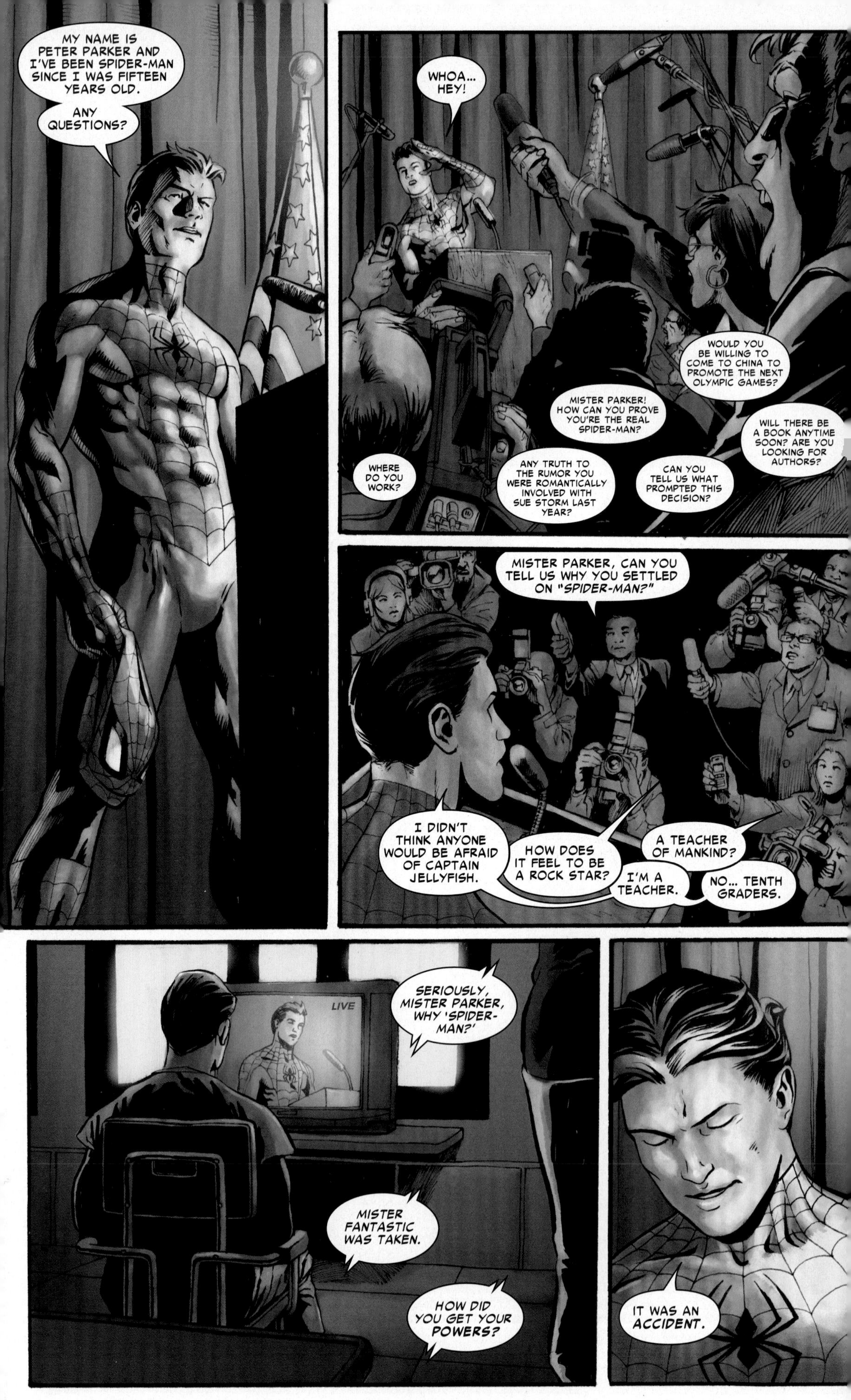
MY NAME IS PETER PARKER AND I'VE BEEN SPIDER-MAN SINCE I WAS FIFTEEN YEARS OLD.
ANY QUESTIONS?
WHOA... HEY!
WOULD YOU BE WILLING TO COME TO CHINA TO PROMOTE THE NEXT OLYMPIC GAMES?
MISTER PARKER! HOW CAN YOU PROVE YOU'RE THE REAL SPIDER-MAN?
WILL THERE BE A BOOK ANYTIME SOON? ARE YOU LOOKING FOR AUTHORS?
WHERE DO YOU WORK?
ANY TRUTH TO THE RUMOR YOU WERE ROMANTICALLY INVOLVED WITH SUE STORM LAST YEAR?
CAN YOU TELL US WHAT PROMPTED THIS DECISION?
MISTER PARKER, CAN YOU TELL US WHY YOU SETTLED ON "SPIDER-MAN?"
I DIDN'T THINK ANYONE WOULD BE AFRAID OF CAPTAIN JELLYFISH.
HOW DOES IT FEEL TO BE A ROCK STAR?
I'M A TEACHER.
A TEACHER OF MANKIND?
NO... TENTH GRADERS.
LIVE
SERIOUSLY, MISTER PARKER, WHY 'SPIDER-MAN?'
MISTER FANTASTIC WAS TAKEN.
HOW DID YOU GET YOUR POWERS?
IT WAS AN ACCIDENT.

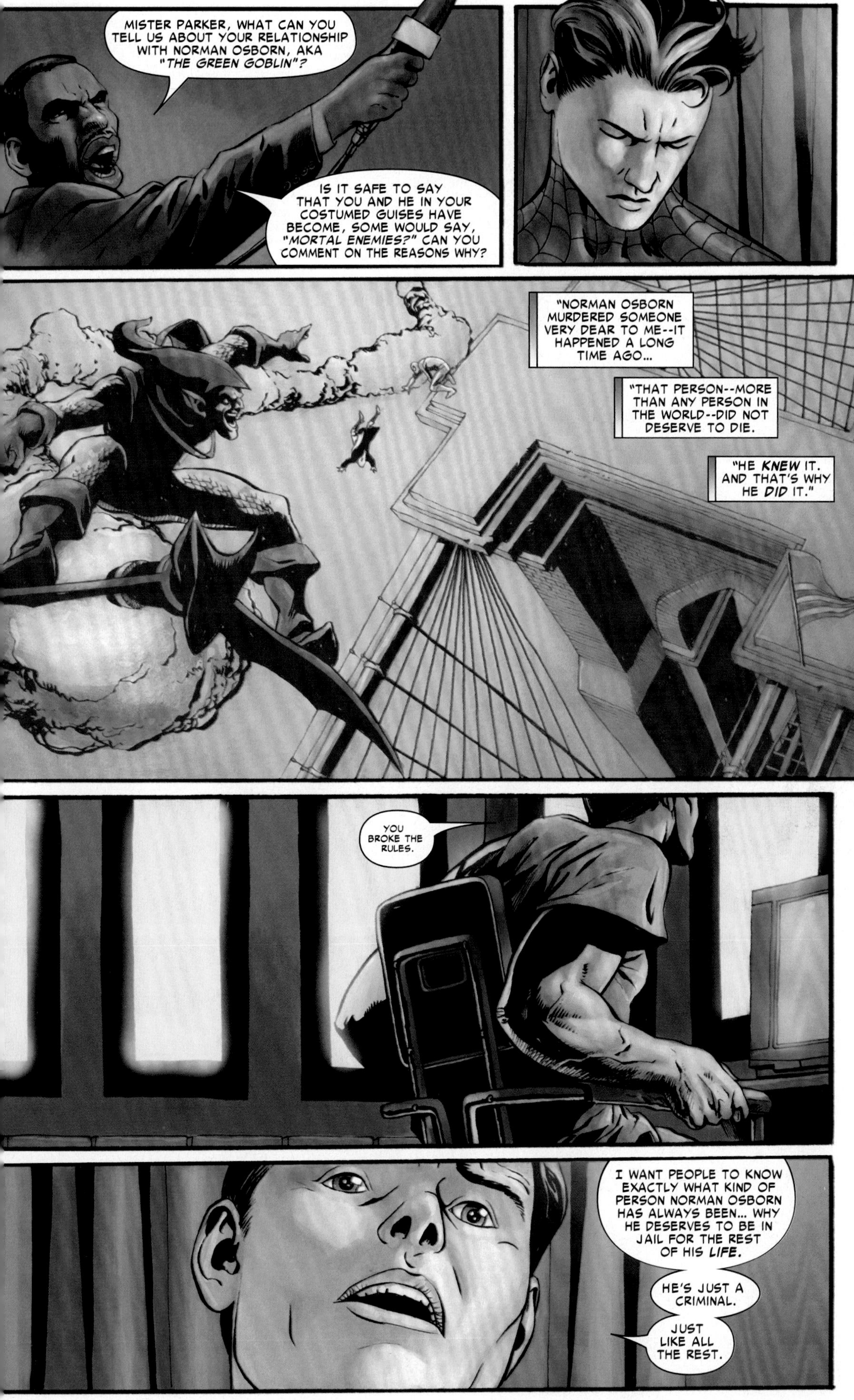
MISTER PARKER, WHAT CAN YOU TELL US ABOUT YOUR RELATIONSHIP WITH NORMAN OSBORN, AKA *"THE GREEN GOBLIN"?*
IS IT SAFE TO SAY THAT YOU AND HE IN YOUR COSTUMED GUISES HAVE BECOME, SOME WOULD SAY, *"MORTAL ENEMIES?"* CAN YOU COMMENT ON THE REASONS WHY?
"NORMAN OSBORN MURDERED SOMEONE VERY DEAR TO ME--IT HAPPENED A LONG TIME AGO...
"THAT PERSON--MORE THAN ANY PERSON IN THE WORLD--DID NOT DESERVE TO DIE.
"HE ***KNEW*** IT. AND THAT'S WHY HE ***DID*** IT."
YOU BROKE THE RULES.
I WANT PEOPLE TO KNOW EXACTLY WHAT KIND OF PERSON NORMAN OSBORN HAS ALWAYS BEEN... WHY HE DESERVES TO BE IN JAIL FOR THE REST OF HIS ***LIFE.***
HE'S JUST A CRIMINAL.
JUST LIKE ALL THE REST.

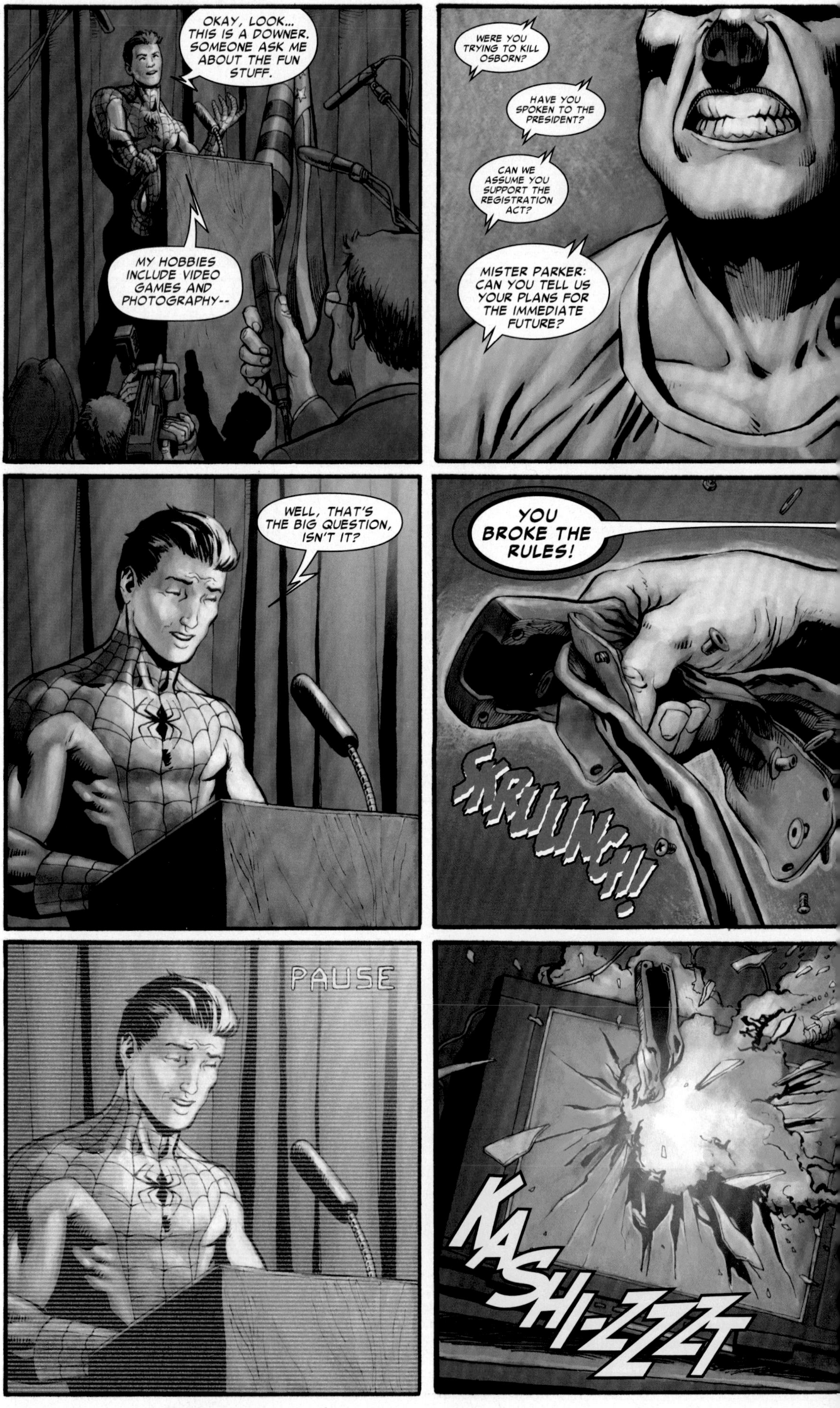
OKAY, LOOK... THIS IS A DOWNER. SOMEONE ASK ME ABOUT THE FUN STUFF.
MY HOBBIES INCLUDE VIDEO GAMES AND PHOTOGRAPHY--
WERE YOU TRYING TO KILL OSBORN?
HAVE YOU SPOKEN TO THE PRESIDENT?
CAN WE ASSUME YOU SUPPORT THE REGISTRATION ACT?
MISTER PARKER: CAN YOU TELL US YOUR PLANS FOR THE IMMEDIATE FUTURE?
WELL, THAT'S THE BIG QUESTION, ISN'T IT?
YOU BROKE THE RULES!
SKRUUNCH!
PAUSE
KASHI-ZZZT

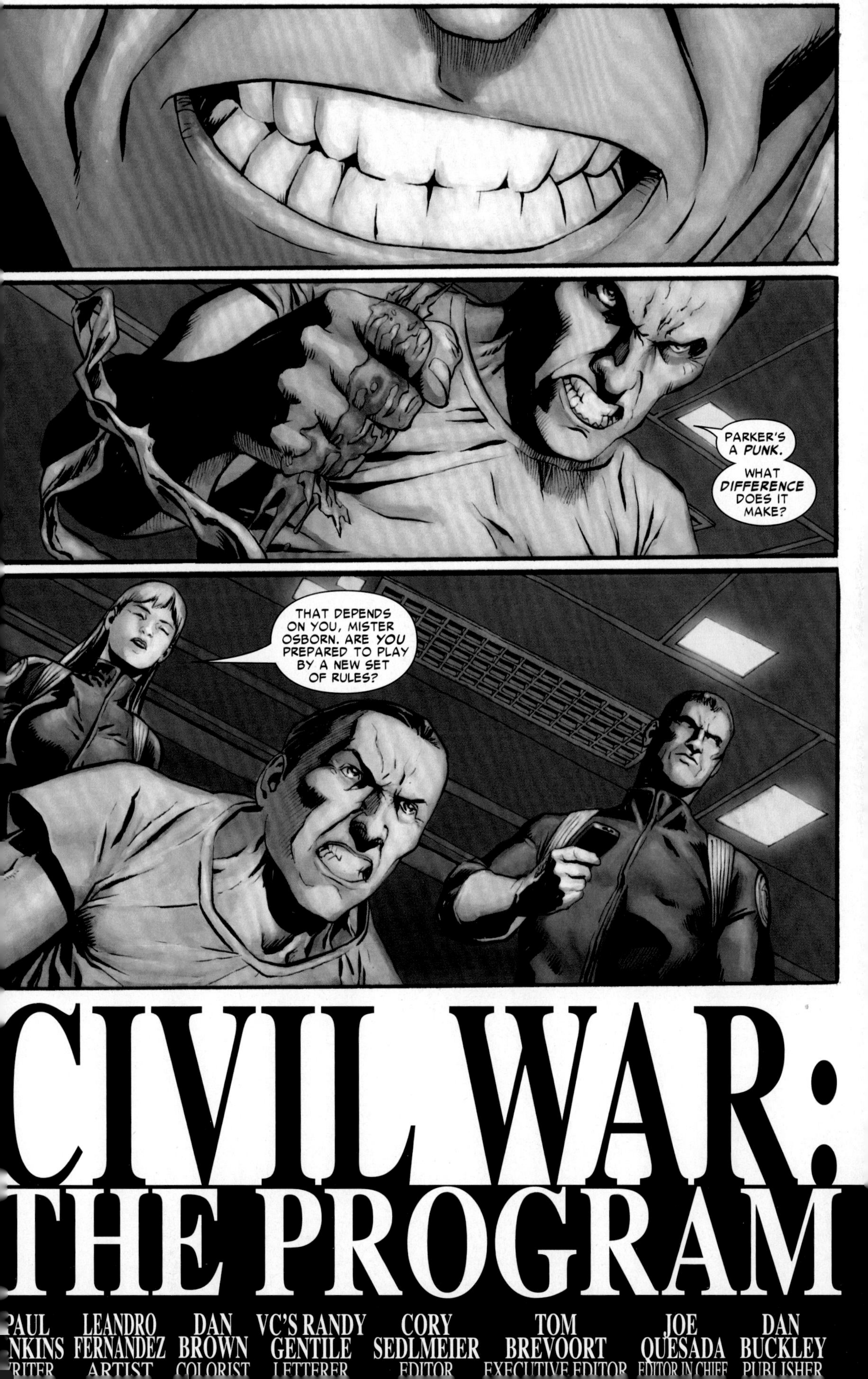
PARKER'S A PUNK. WHAT DIFFERENCE DOES IT MAKE?
THAT DEPENDS ON YOU, MISTER OSBORN. ARE YOU PREPARED TO PLAY BY A NEW SET OF RULES?

CIVIL WAR: THE PROGRAM

PAUL NKINS RITER
LEANDRO FERNANDEZ ARTIST
DAN BROWN COLORIST
VC'S RANDY GENTILE LETTERER
CORY SEDLMEIER EDITOR
TOM BREVOORT EXECUTIVE EDITOR
JOE QUESADA EDITOR IN CHIEF
DAN BUCKLEY PUBLISHER

By the year 59 B.C., Gaius Julius Caesar had become one of the most popular men in Rome. A veteran of numerous successful campaigns that extended the influence of Rome through Northern Europe, he was elected "Senior Consul of the Roman Republic" by the Centuriate Assembly.

Caesar shared the Consulate position with two men: Pompey the Great and Marcus Licinius Crassus, a millionaire of the day. Despite Caesar's obvious benefit to Rome, his moves were often blocked by a corrupt Roman senate. In 50 B.C., he was ordered to disband his legions and return to Rome.

To Caesar, this was an illegal act: his consulship was perfectly legitimate, and yet he had been forbidden to stand for a second term.

And so on January 10th in the year 49 B.C.—accused of insubordination and treason--Gaius Julius Caesar brought his single legion to the banks of the Rubicon river, a natural border that marked the edge of his territory. Neither he nor the Roman Senate wanted conflict, yet Caesar's hand had been forced, and he was not the kind of man to back down without a fight.

As described by the Greek historian, Plutarch, Julius Caesar knew that the very moment he crossed the Rubicon he would ignite a civil war.

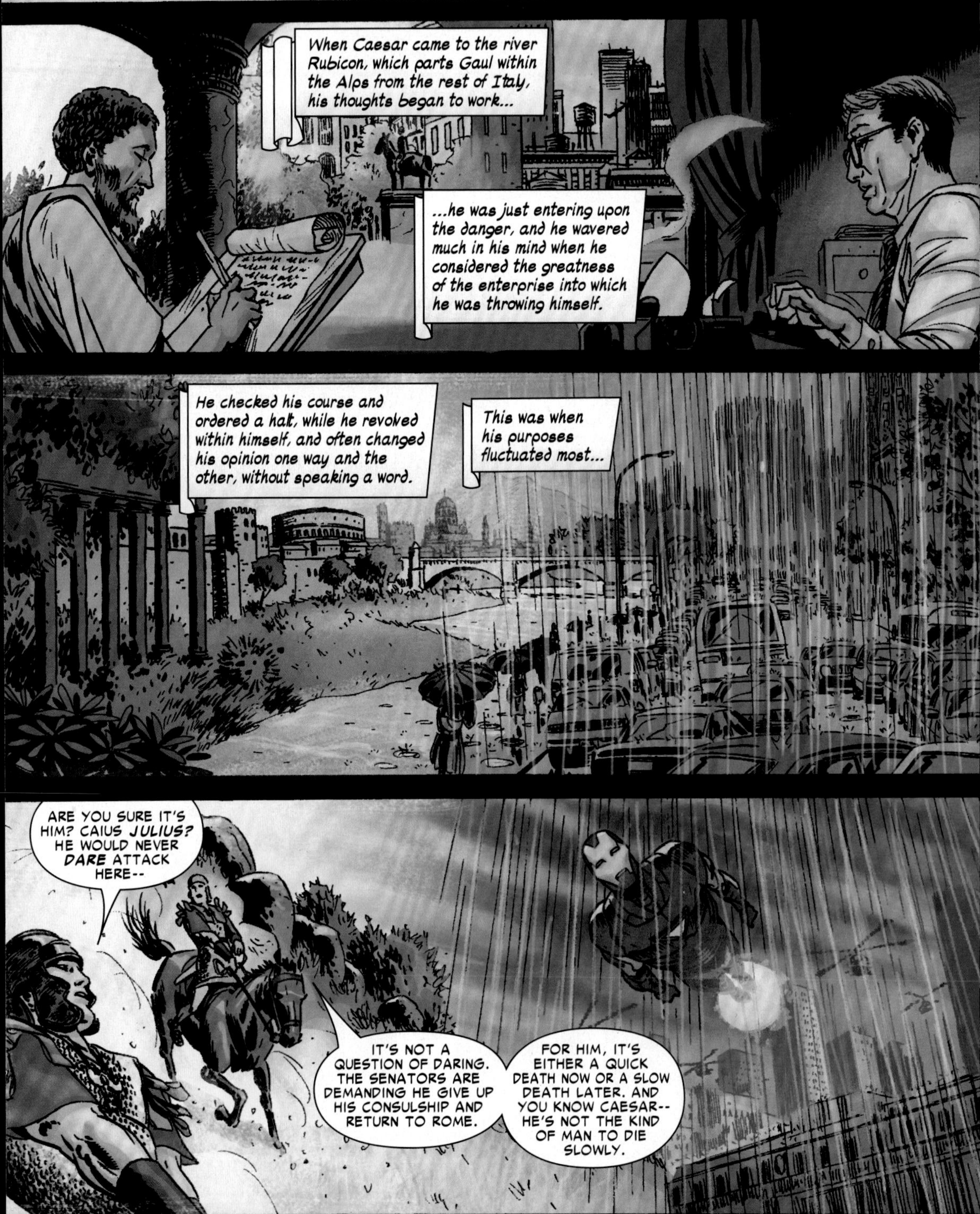
When Caesar came to the river Rubicon, which parts Gaul within the Alps from the rest of Italy, his thoughts began to work...
...he was just entering upon the danger, and he wavered much in his mind when he considered the greatness of the enterprise into which he was throwing himself.
He checked his course and ordered a halt, while he revolved within himself, and often changed his opinion one way and the other, without speaking a word.
This was when his purposes fluctuated most...
ARE YOU SURE IT'S HIM? CAIUS JULIUS? HE WOULD NEVER DARE ATTACK HERE--
IT'S NOT A QUESTION OF DARING. THE SENATORS ARE DEMANDING HE GIVE UP HIS CONSULSHIP AND RETURN TO ROME.
FOR HIM, IT'S EITHER A QUICK DEATH NOW OR A SLOW DEATH LATER. AND YOU KNOW CAESAR-- HE'S NOT THE KIND OF MAN TO DIE SLOWLY.

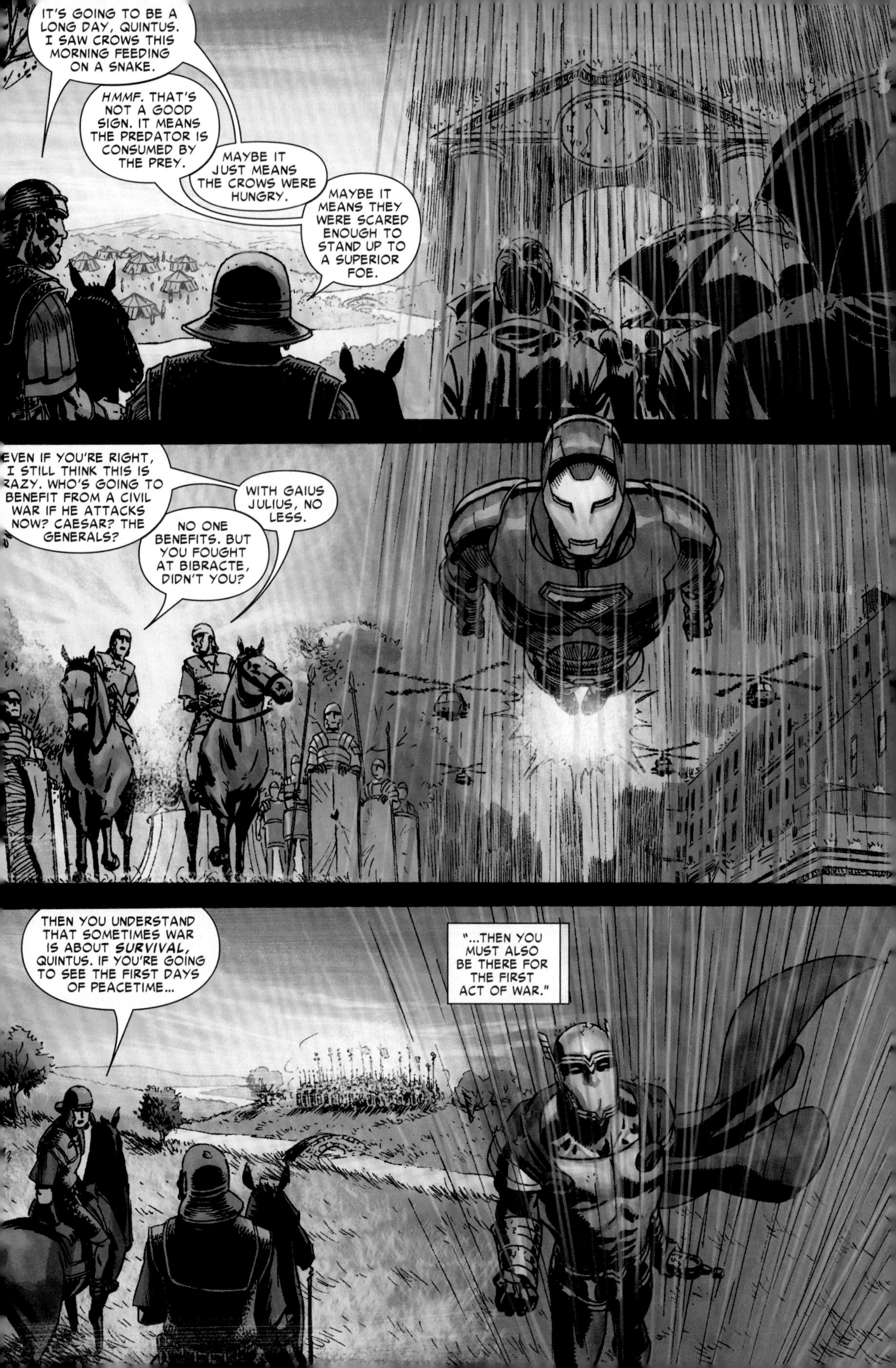

IT'S GOING TO BE A LONG DAY, QUINTUS. I SAW CROWS THIS MORNING FEEDING ON A SNAKE.
HMMF. THAT'S NOT A GOOD SIGN. IT MEANS THE PREDATOR IS CONSUMED BY THE PREY.
MAYBE IT JUST MEANS THE CROWS WERE HUNGRY.
MAYBE IT MEANS THEY WERE SCARED ENOUGH TO STAND UP TO A SUPERIOR FOE.
EVEN IF YOU'RE RIGHT, I STILL THINK THIS IS RAZY. WHO'S GOING TO BENEFIT FROM A CIVIL WAR IF HE ATTACKS NOW? CAESAR? THE GENERALS?
WITH GAIUS JULIUS, NO LESS.
NO ONE BENEFITS. BUT YOU FOUGHT AT BIBRACTE, DIDN'T YOU?
THEN YOU UNDERSTAND THAT SOMETIMES WAR IS ABOUT *SURVIVAL*, QUINTUS. IF YOU'RE GOING TO SEE THE FIRST DAYS OF PEACETIME...
"...THEN YOU MUST ALSO BE THERE FOR THE FIRST ACT OF WAR."

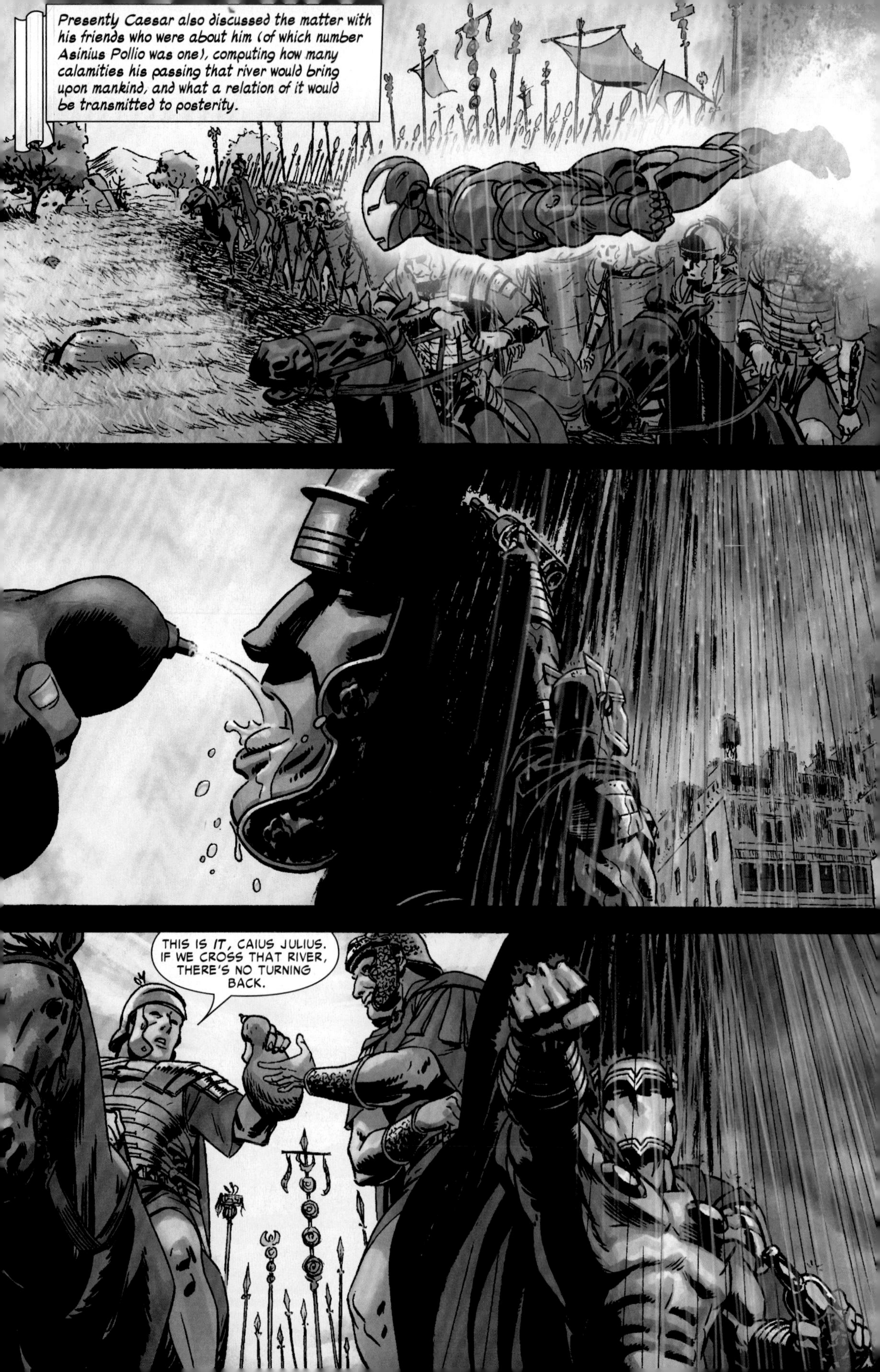
Presently Caesar also discussed the matter with his friends who were about him (of which number Asinius Pollio was one), computing how many calamities his passing that river would bring upon mankind, and what a relation of it would be transmitted to posterity.
THIS IS IT, CAIUS JULIUS. IF WE CROSS THAT RIVER, THERE'S NO TURNING BACK.

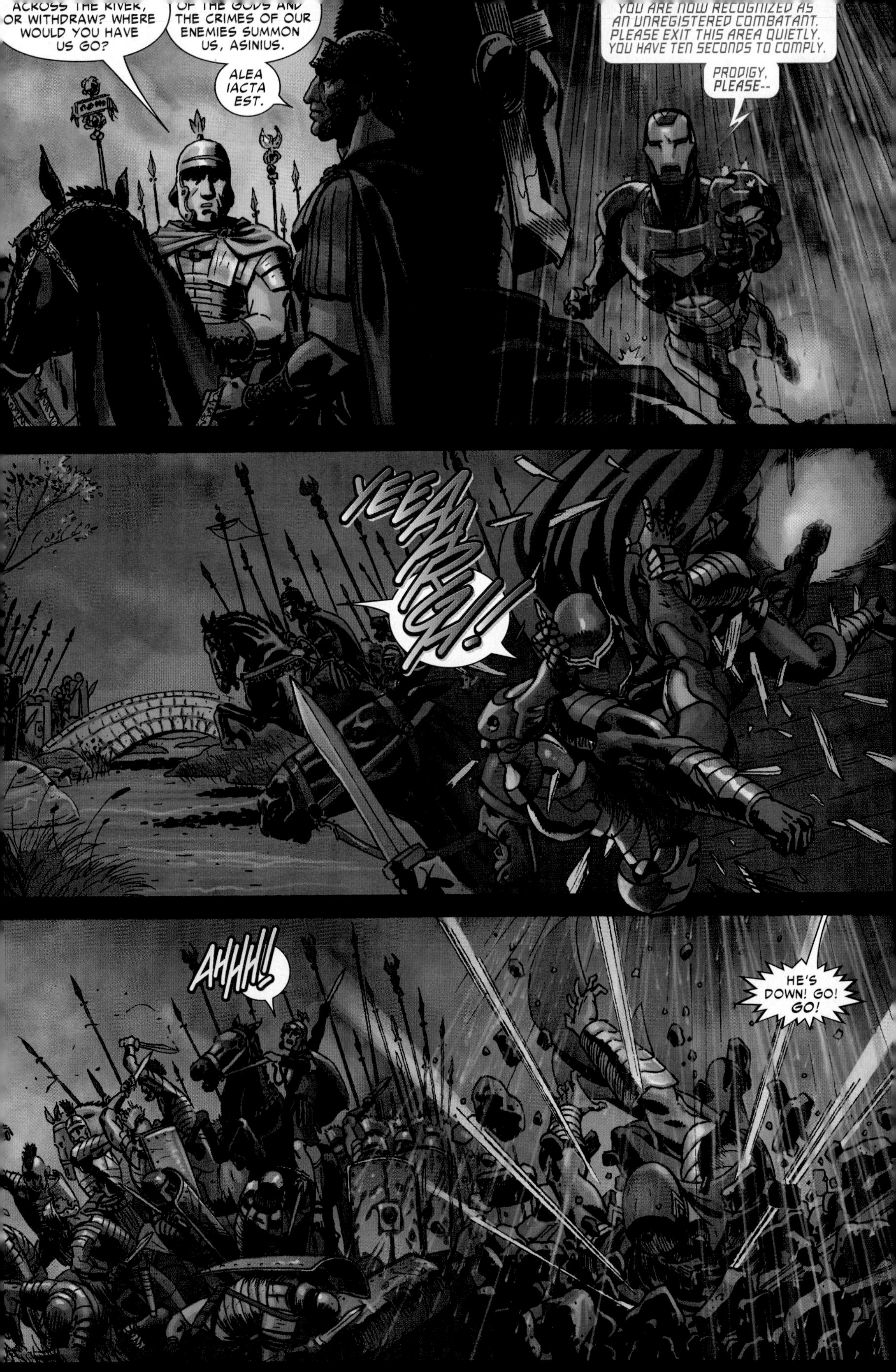
ACROSS THE RIVER, OR WITHDRAW? WHERE WOULD YOU HAVE US GO?
OF THE GODS AND THE CRIMES OF OUR ENEMIES SUMMON US, ASINIUS.
ALEA IACTA EST.
YOU ARE NOW RECOGNIZED AS AN UNREGISTERED COMBATANT. PLEASE EXIT THIS AREA QUIETLY. YOU HAVE TEN SECONDS TO COMPLY.
PRODIGY, PLEASE--
YEEAAARRGH!!
AHHH!!
HE'S DOWN! GO! GO!

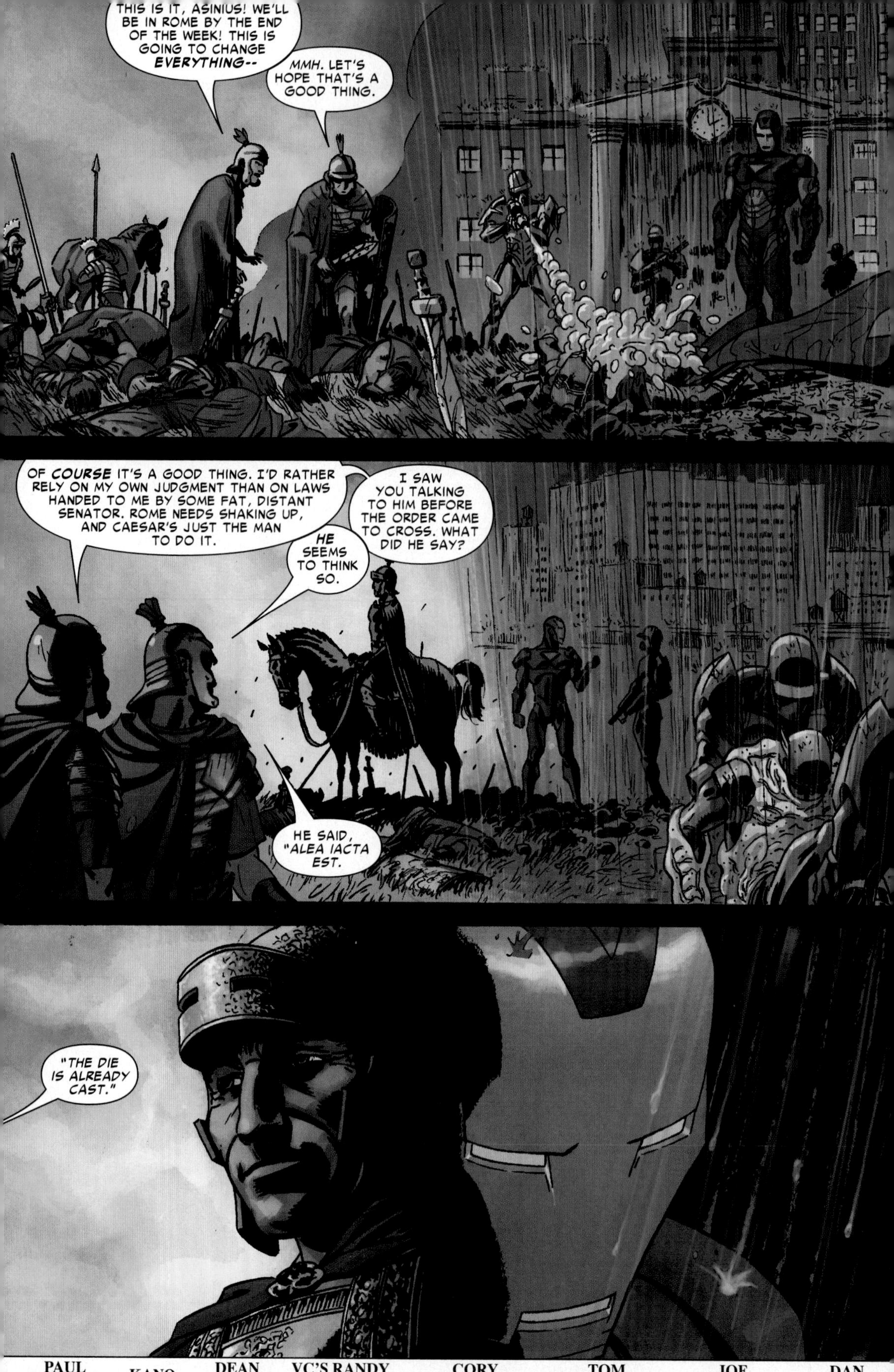
THIS IS IT, ASINIUS! WE'LL BE IN ROME BY THE END OF THE WEEK! THIS IS GOING TO CHANGE EVERYTHING--
MMH. LET'S HOPE THAT'S A GOOD THING.
OF COURSE IT'S A GOOD THING. I'D RATHER RELY ON MY OWN JUDGMENT THAN ON LAWS HANDED TO ME BY SOME FAT, DISTANT SENATOR. ROME NEEDS SHAKING UP, AND CAESAR'S JUST THE MAN TO DO IT.
HE SEEMS TO THINK SO.
I SAW YOU TALKING TO HIM BEFORE THE ORDER CAME TO CROSS. WHAT DID HE SAY?
HE SAID, "ALEA IACTA EST.
"THE DIE IS ALREADY CAST."

PAUL JENKINS WRITER | KANO ARTIST | DEAN WHITE COLORS | VC'S RANDY GENTILE LETTERS | CORY SEDLMEIER EDITOR | TOM BREVOORT EXECUTIVE EDITOR | JOE QUESADA EDITOR IN CHIEF | DAN BUCKLEY PUBLISHER

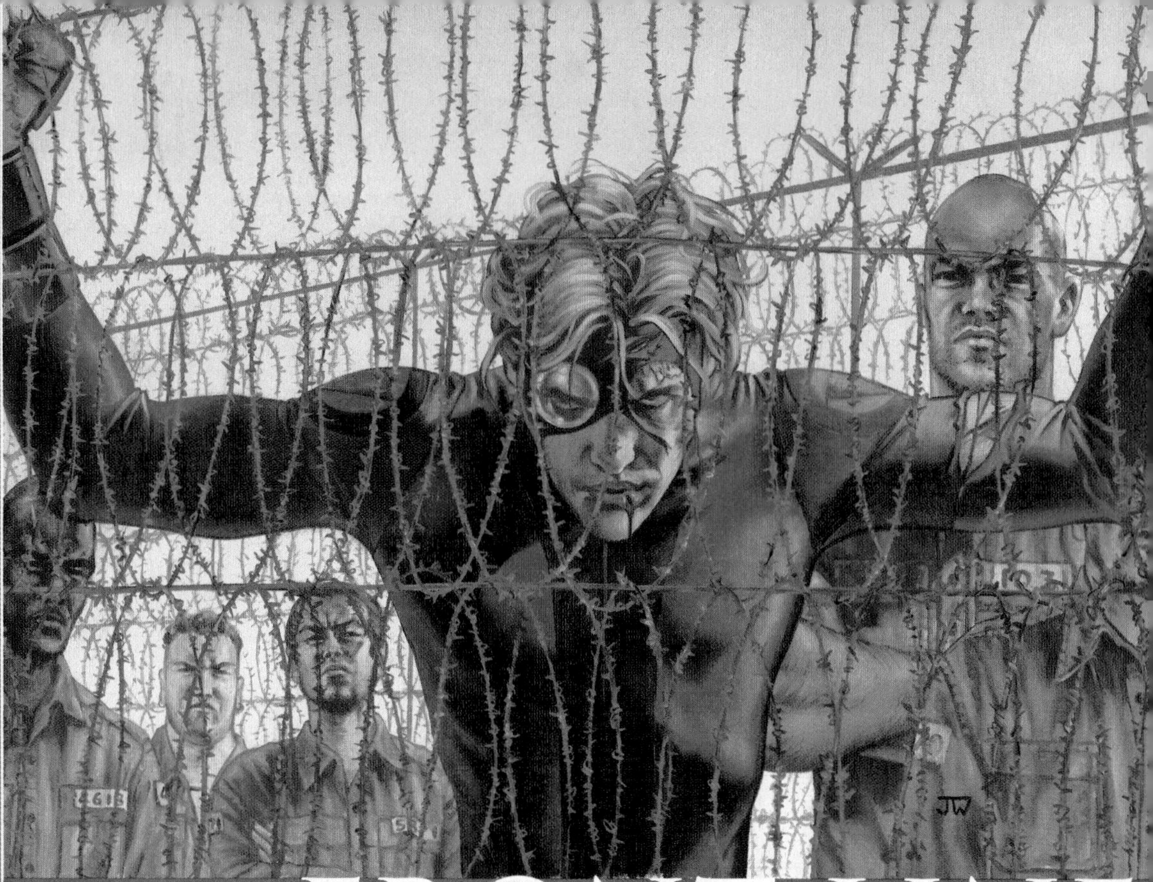

FRONT LINE

A MARVEL COMICS EVENT

CIVIL WAR

CIVIL WAR: FRONT LINE #3

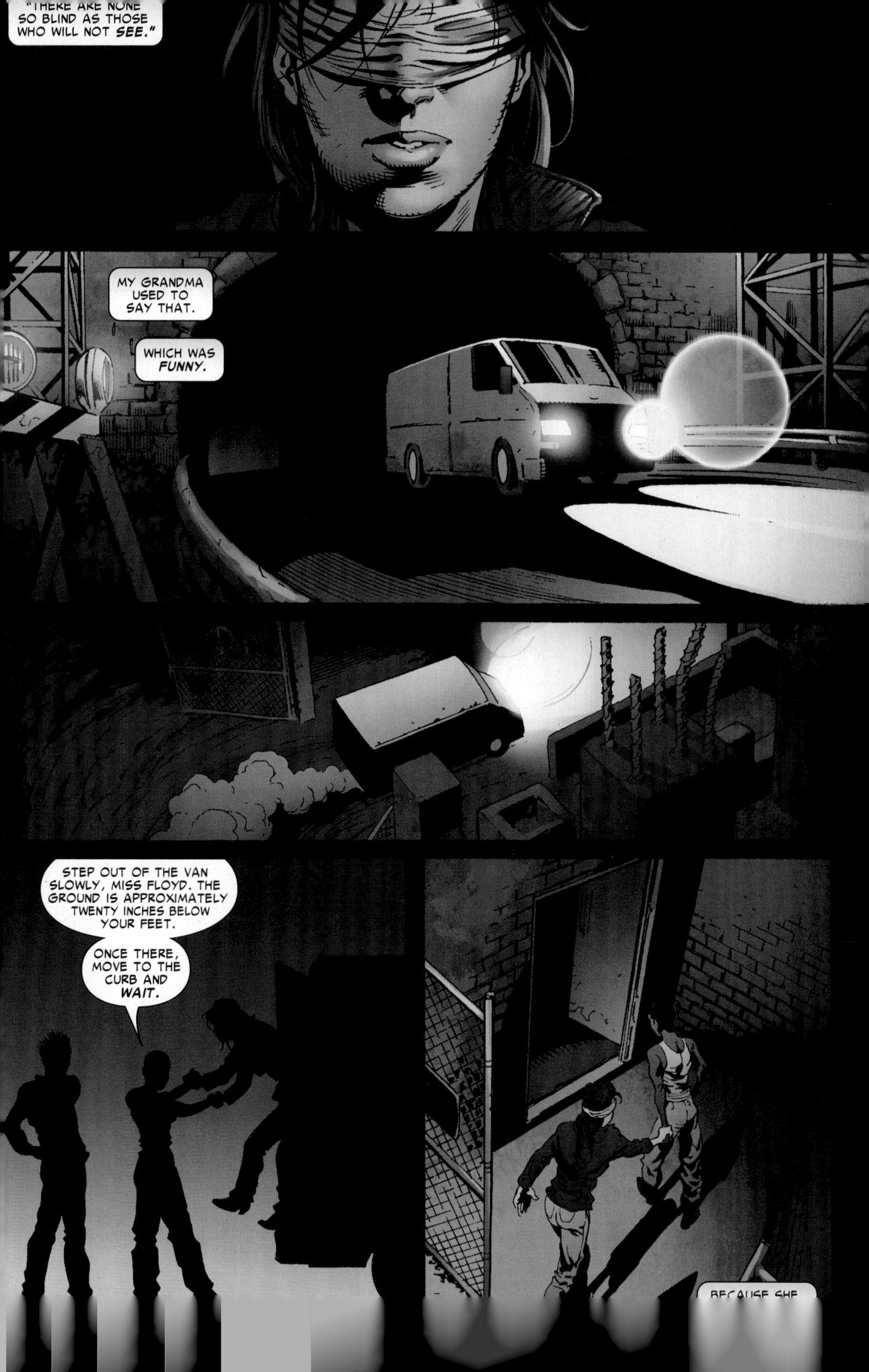
"THERE ARE NONE SO BLIND AS THOSE WHO WILL NOT SEE."
MY GRANDMA USED TO SAY THAT.
WHICH WAS FUNNY.
STEP OUT OF THE VAN SLOWLY, MISS FLOYD. THE GROUND IS APPROXIMATELY TWENTY INCHES BELOW YOUR FEET.
ONCE THERE, MOVE TO THE CURB AND WAIT.
BECAUSE SHE

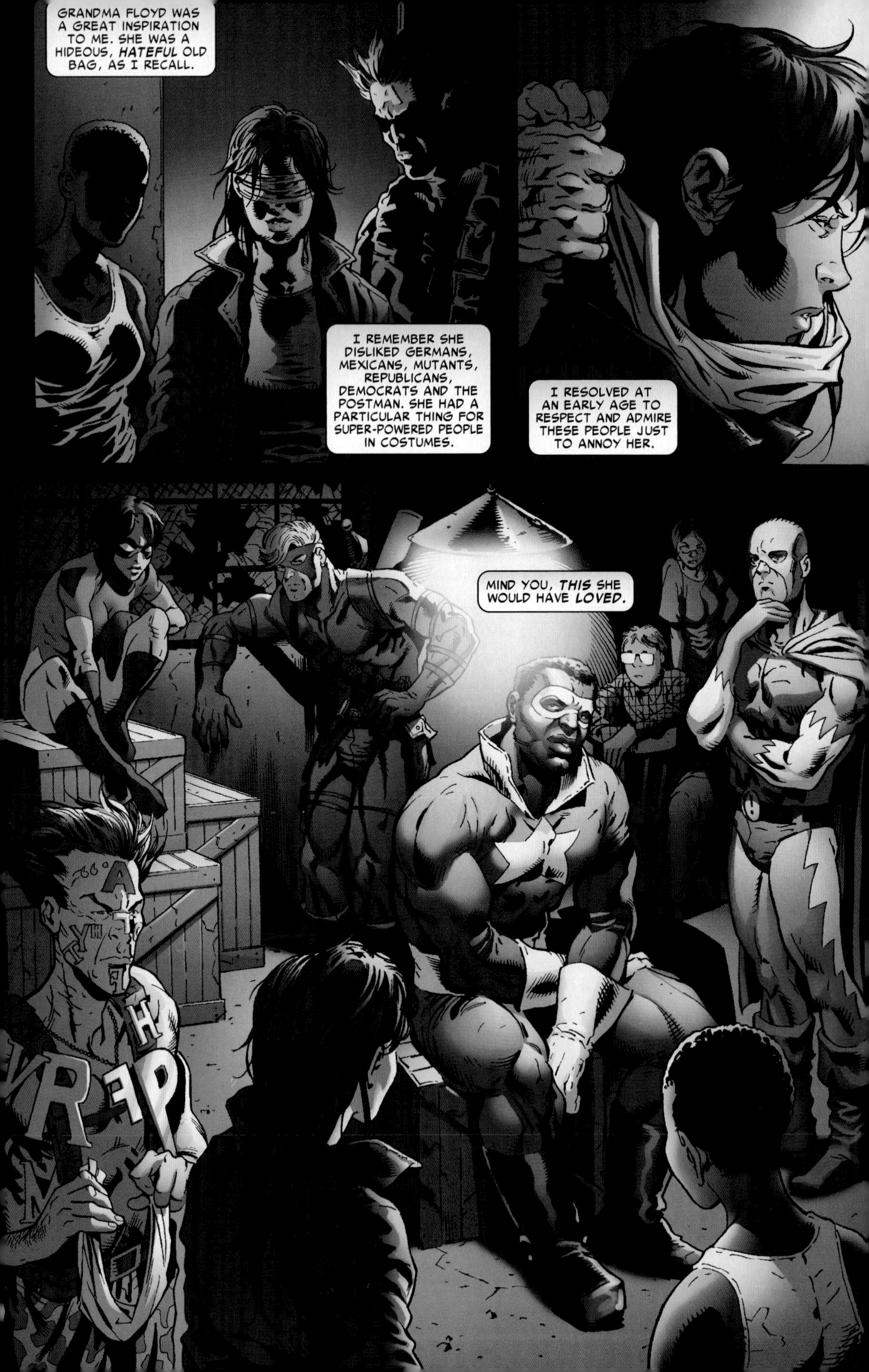
GRANDMA FLOYD WAS A GREAT INSPIRATION TO ME. SHE WAS A HIDEOUS, *HATEFUL* OLD BAG, AS I RECALL.
I REMEMBER SHE DISLIKED GERMANS, MEXICANS, MUTANTS, REPUBLICANS, DEMOCRATS AND THE POSTMAN. SHE HAD A PARTICULAR THING FOR SUPER-POWERED PEOPLE IN COSTUMES.
I RESOLVED AT AN EARLY AGE TO RESPECT AND ADMIRE THESE PEOPLE JUST TO ANNOY HER.
MIND YOU, *THIS* SHE WOULD HAVE *LOVED*.

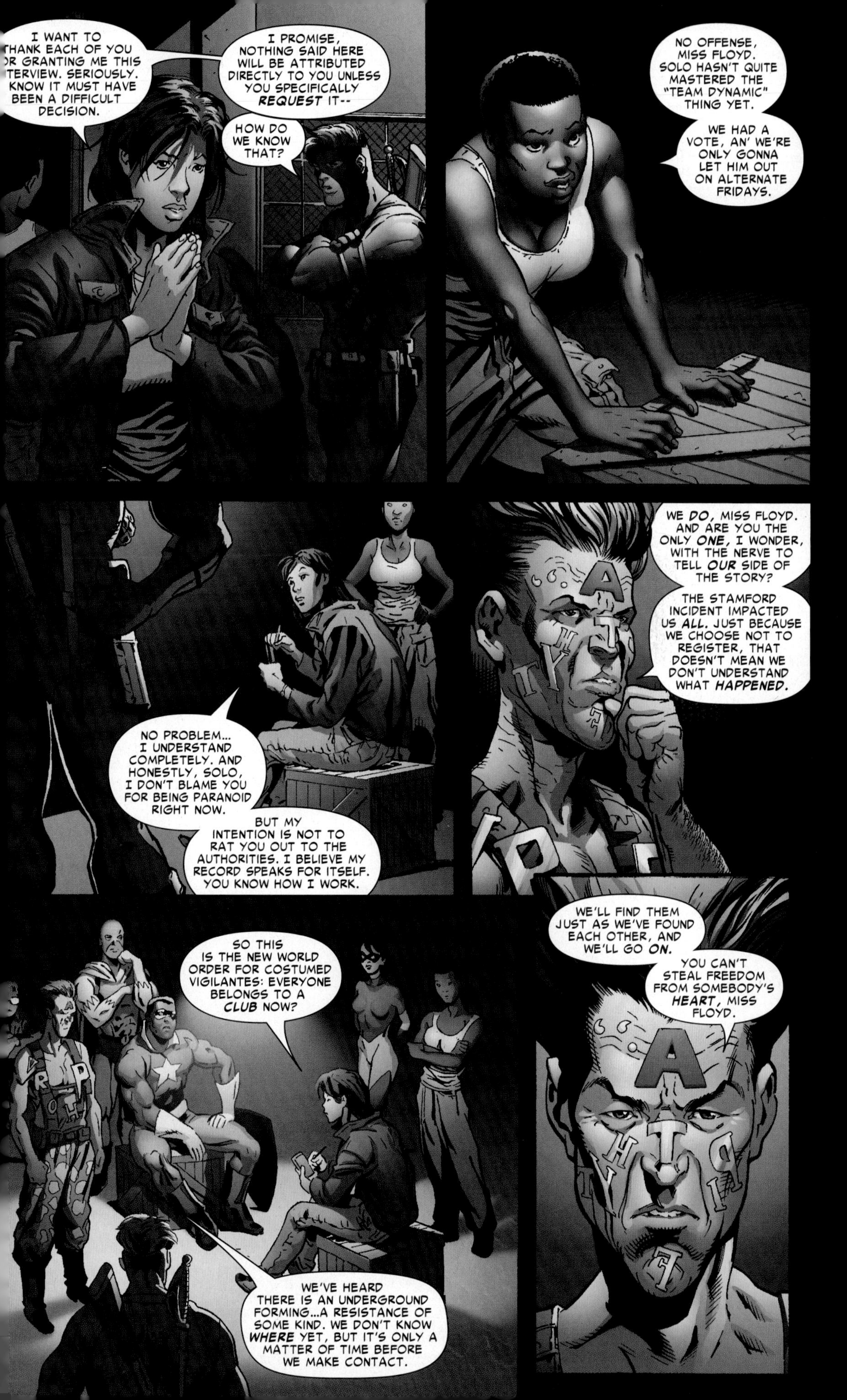

I WANT TO THANK EACH OF YOU OR GRANTING ME THIS TERVIEW. SERIOUSLY. KNOW IT MUST HAVE BEEN A DIFFICULT DECISION.
I PROMISE, NOTHING SAID HERE WILL BE ATTRIBUTED DIRECTLY TO YOU UNLESS YOU SPECIFICALLY REQUEST IT--
HOW DO WE KNOW THAT?
NO OFFENSE, MISS FLOYD. SOLO HASN'T QUITE MASTERED THE "TEAM DYNAMIC" THING YET.
WE HAD A VOTE, AN' WE'RE ONLY GONNA LET HIM OUT ON ALTERNATE FRIDAYS.
NO PROBLEM... I UNDERSTAND COMPLETELY. AND HONESTLY, SOLO, I DON'T BLAME YOU FOR BEING PARANOID RIGHT NOW.
BUT MY INTENTION IS NOT TO RAT YOU OUT TO THE AUTHORITIES. I BELIEVE MY RECORD SPEAKS FOR ITSELF. YOU KNOW HOW I WORK.
WE DO, MISS FLOYD. AND ARE YOU THE ONLY ONE, I WONDER, WITH THE NERVE TO TELL OUR SIDE OF THE STORY?
THE STAMFORD INCIDENT IMPACTED US ALL. JUST BECAUSE WE CHOOSE NOT TO REGISTER, THAT DOESN'T MEAN WE DON'T UNDERSTAND WHAT HAPPENED.
SO THIS IS THE NEW WORLD ORDER FOR COSTUMED VIGILANTES: EVERYONE BELONGS TO A CLUB NOW?
WE'VE HEARD THERE IS AN UNDERGROUND FORMING...A RESISTANCE OF SOME KIND. WE DON'T KNOW WHERE YET, BUT IT'S ONLY A MATTER OF TIME BEFORE WE MAKE CONTACT.
WE'LL FIND THEM JUST AS WE'VE FOUND EACH OTHER, AND WE'LL GO ON.
YOU CAN'T STEAL FREEDOM FROM SOMEBODY'S HEART, MISS FLOYD.

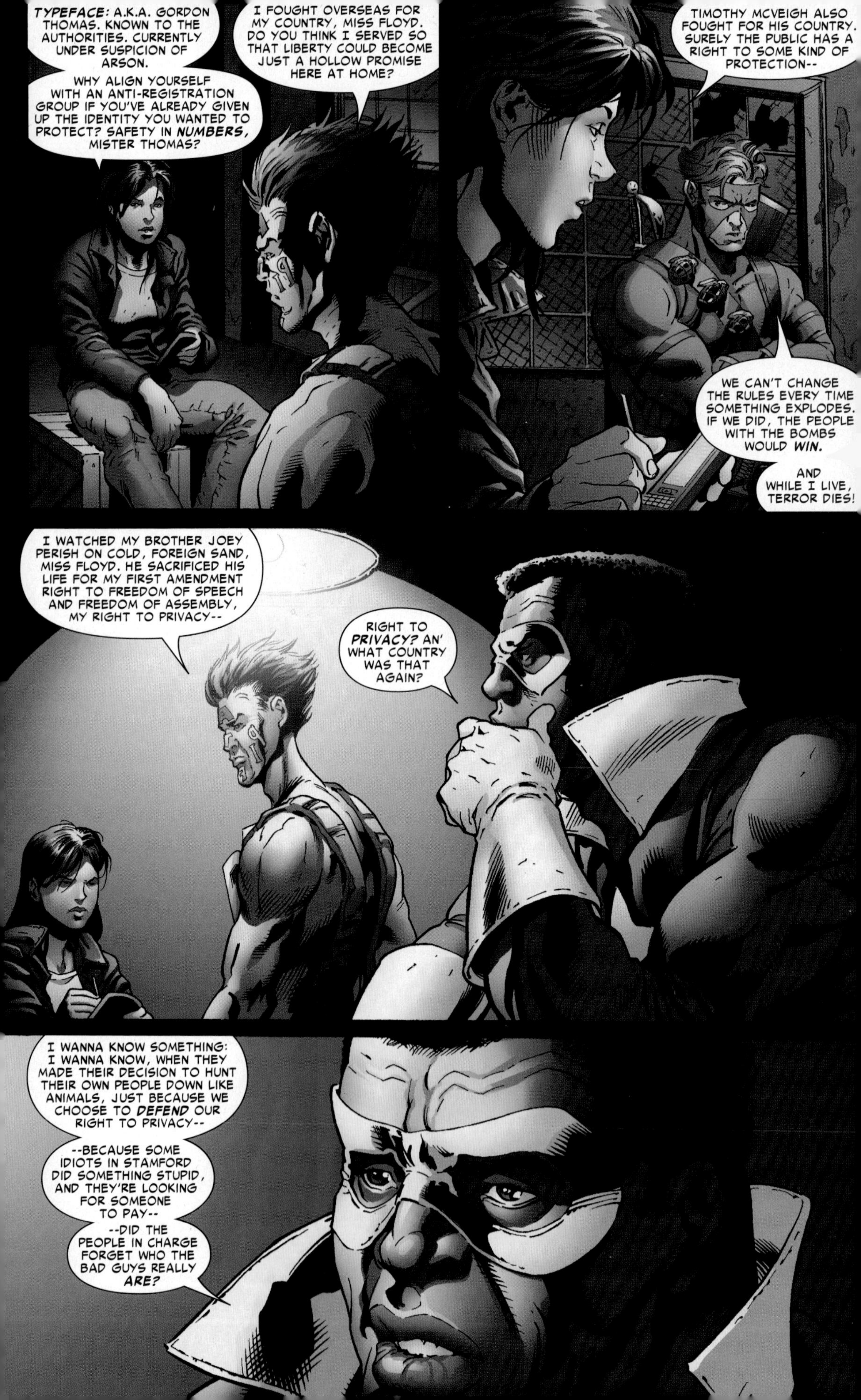
TYPEFACE: A.K.A. GORDON THOMAS. KNOWN TO THE AUTHORITIES. CURRENTLY UNDER SUSPICION OF ARSON.
WHY ALIGN YOURSELF WITH AN ANTI-REGISTRATION GROUP IF YOU'VE ALREADY GIVEN UP THE IDENTITY YOU WANTED TO PROTECT? SAFETY IN NUMBERS, MISTER THOMAS?
I FOUGHT OVERSEAS FOR MY COUNTRY, MISS FLOYD. DO YOU THINK I SERVED SO THAT LIBERTY COULD BECOME JUST A HOLLOW PROMISE HERE AT HOME?
TIMOTHY MCVEIGH ALSO FOUGHT FOR HIS COUNTRY. SURELY THE PUBLIC HAS A RIGHT TO SOME KIND OF PROTECTION--
WE CAN'T CHANGE THE RULES EVERY TIME SOMETHING EXPLODES. IF WE DID, THE PEOPLE WITH THE BOMBS WOULD WIN.
AND WHILE I LIVE, TERROR DIES!
I WATCHED MY BROTHER JOEY PERISH ON COLD, FOREIGN SAND, MISS FLOYD. HE SACRIFICED HIS LIFE FOR MY FIRST AMENDMENT RIGHT TO FREEDOM OF SPEECH AND FREEDOM OF ASSEMBLY, MY RIGHT TO PRIVACY--
RIGHT TO PRIVACY? AN' WHAT COUNTRY WAS THAT AGAIN?
I WANNA KNOW SOMETHING: I WANNA KNOW, WHEN THEY MADE THEIR DECISION TO HUNT THEIR OWN PEOPLE DOWN LIKE ANIMALS, JUST BECAUSE WE CHOOSE TO DEFEND OUR RIGHT TO PRIVACY--
--BECAUSE SOME IDIOTS IN STAMFORD DID SOMETHING STUPID, AND THEY'RE LOOKING FOR SOMEONE TO PAY--
--DID THE PEOPLE IN CHARGE FORGET WHO THE BAD GUYS REALLY ARE?

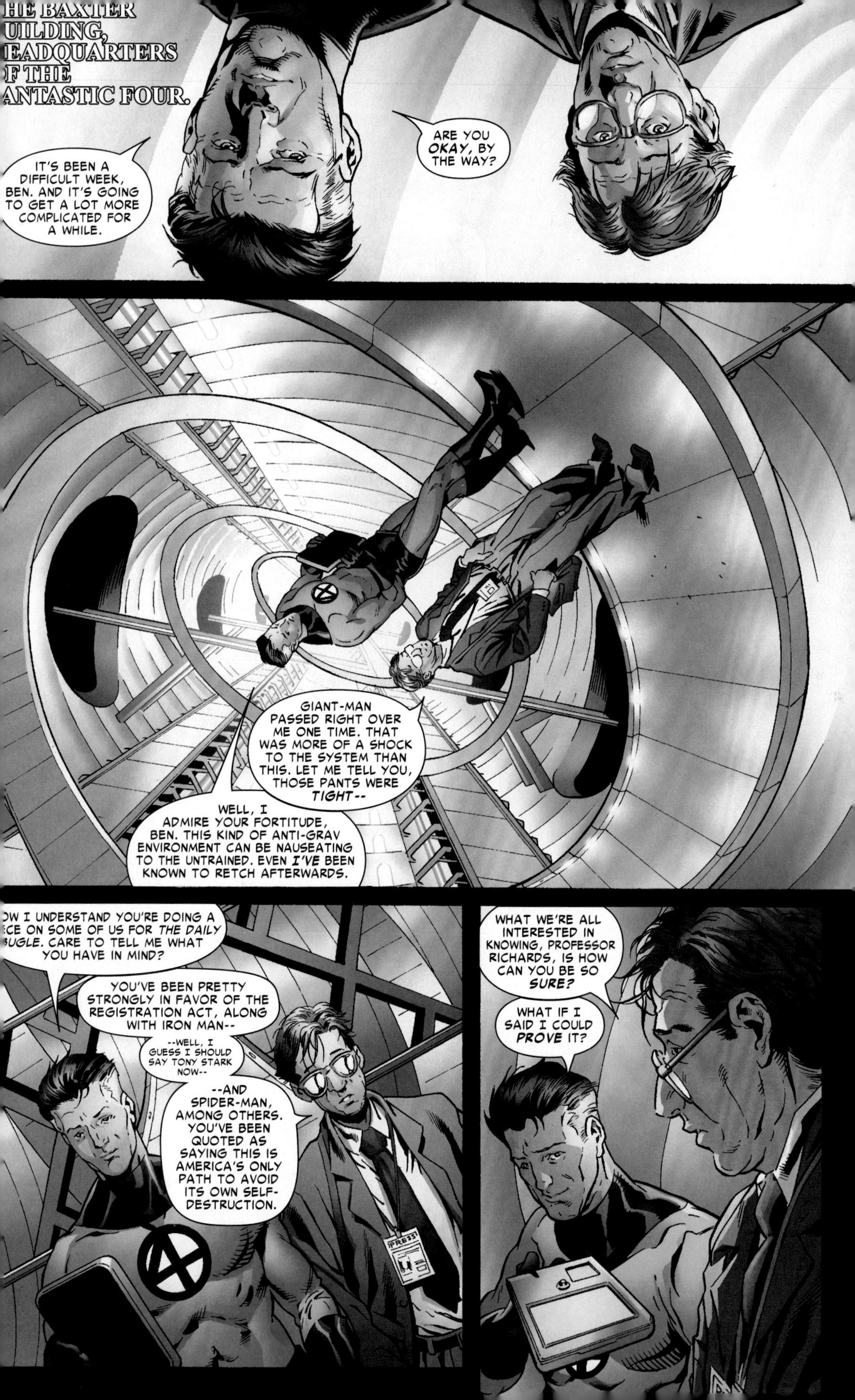
HE BAXTER UILDING, EADQUARTERS F THE ANTASTIC FOUR.
IT'S BEEN A DIFFICULT WEEK, BEN. AND IT'S GOING TO GET A LOT MORE COMPLICATED FOR A WHILE.
ARE YOU OKAY, BY THE WAY?
GIANT-MAN PASSED RIGHT OVER ME ONE TIME. THAT WAS MORE OF A SHOCK TO THE SYSTEM THAN THIS. LET ME TELL YOU, THOSE PANTS WERE TIGHT--
WELL, I ADMIRE YOUR FORTITUDE, BEN. THIS KIND OF ANTI-GRAV ENVIRONMENT CAN BE NAUSEATING TO THE UNTRAINED. EVEN I'VE BEEN KNOWN TO RETCH AFTERWARDS.
OW I UNDERSTAND YOU'RE DOING A ECE ON SOME OF US FOR THE DAILY UGLE. CARE TO TELL ME WHAT YOU HAVE IN MIND?
YOU'VE BEEN PRETTY STRONGLY IN FAVOR OF THE REGISTRATION ACT, ALONG WITH IRON MAN--
--WELL, I GUESS I SHOULD SAY TONY STARK NOW--
--AND SPIDER-MAN, AMONG OTHERS. YOU'VE BEEN QUOTED AS SAYING THIS IS AMERICA'S ONLY PATH TO AVOID ITS OWN SELF-DESTRUCTION.
PRESS
WHAT WE'RE ALL INTERESTED IN KNOWING, PROFESSOR RICHARDS, IS HOW CAN YOU BE SO SURE?
WHAT IF I SAID I COULD PROVE IT?

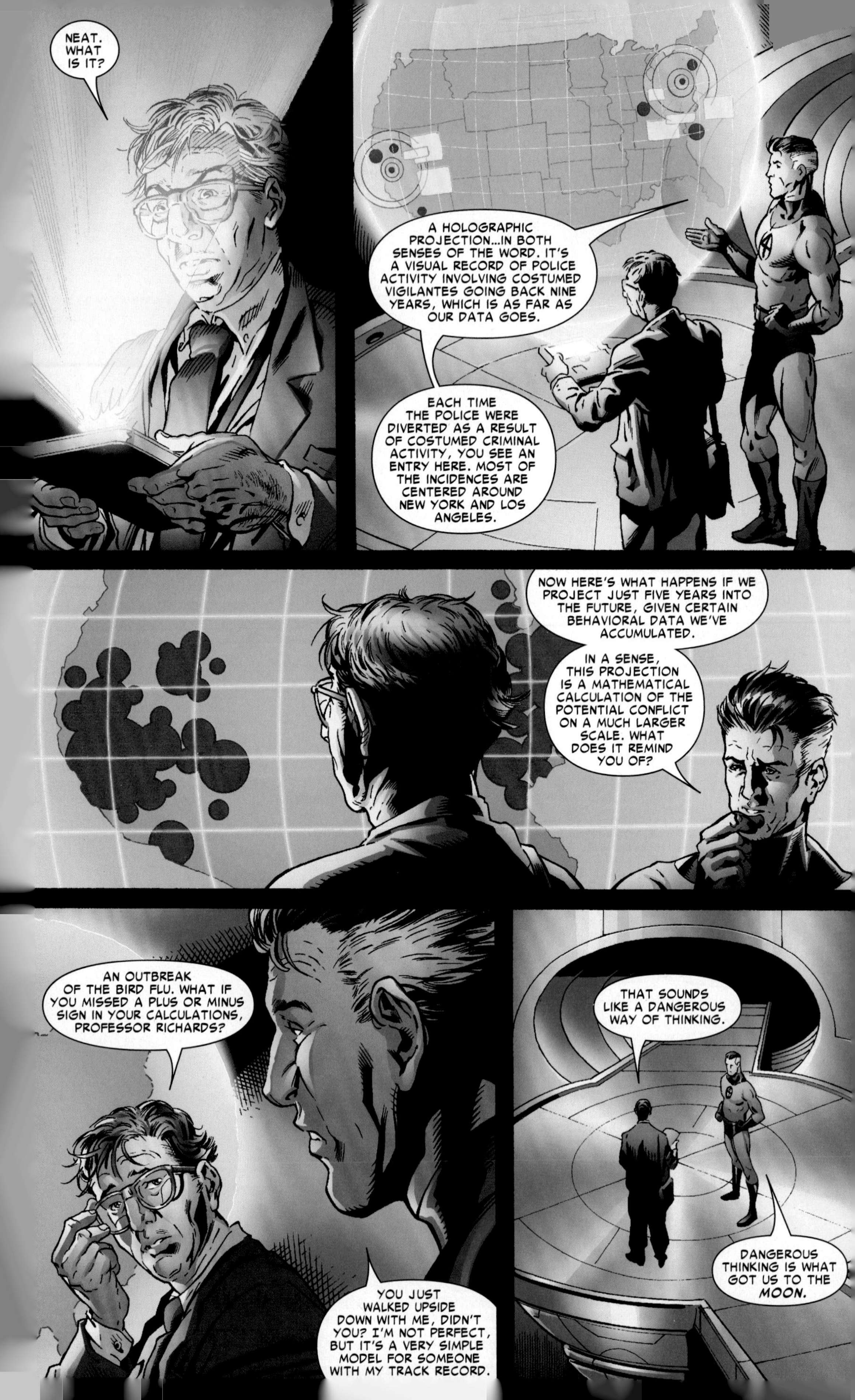
NEAT. WHAT IS IT?
A HOLOGRAPHIC PROJECTION...IN BOTH SENSES OF THE WORD. IT'S A VISUAL RECORD OF POLICE ACTIVITY INVOLVING COSTUMED VIGILANTES GOING BACK NINE YEARS, WHICH IS AS FAR AS OUR DATA GOES.
EACH TIME THE POLICE WERE DIVERTED AS A RESULT OF COSTUMED CRIMINAL ACTIVITY, YOU SEE AN ENTRY HERE. MOST OF THE INCIDENCES ARE CENTERED AROUND NEW YORK AND LOS ANGELES.
NOW HERE'S WHAT HAPPENS IF WE PROJECT JUST FIVE YEARS INTO THE FUTURE, GIVEN CERTAIN BEHAVIORAL DATA WE'VE ACCUMULATED.
IN A SENSE, THIS PROJECTION IS A MATHEMATICAL CALCULATION OF THE POTENTIAL CONFLICT ON A MUCH LARGER SCALE. WHAT DOES IT REMIND YOU OF?
AN OUTBREAK OF THE BIRD FLU. WHAT IF YOU MISSED A PLUS OR MINUS SIGN IN YOUR CALCULATIONS, PROFESSOR RICHARDS?
YOU JUST WALKED UPSIDE DOWN WITH ME, DIDN'T YOU? I'M NOT PERFECT, BUT IT'S A VERY SIMPLE MODEL FOR SOMEONE WITH MY TRACK RECORD.
THAT SOUNDS LIKE A DANGEROUS WAY OF THINKING.
DANGEROUS THINKING IS WHAT GOT US TO THE *MOON*.

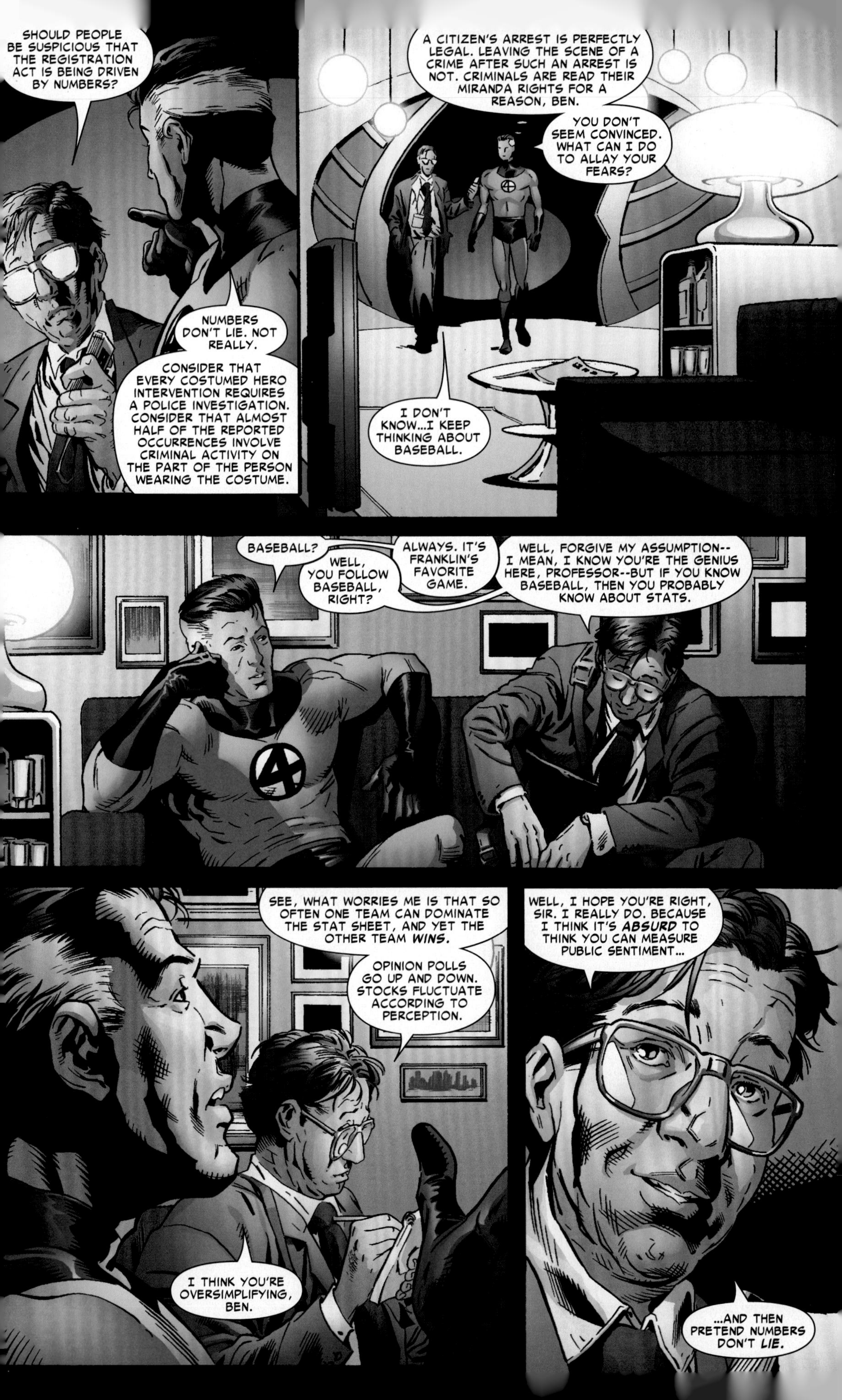
SHOULD PEOPLE BE SUSPICIOUS THAT THE REGISTRATION ACT IS BEING DRIVEN BY NUMBERS?
NUMBERS DON'T LIE. NOT REALLY.
CONSIDER THAT EVERY COSTUMED HERO INTERVENTION REQUIRES A POLICE INVESTIGATION. CONSIDER THAT ALMOST HALF OF THE REPORTED OCCURRENCES INVOLVE CRIMINAL ACTIVITY ON THE PART OF THE PERSON WEARING THE COSTUME.
A CITIZEN'S ARREST IS PERFECTLY LEGAL. LEAVING THE SCENE OF A CRIME AFTER SUCH AN ARREST IS NOT. CRIMINALS ARE READ THEIR MIRANDA RIGHTS FOR A REASON, BEN.
YOU DON'T SEEM CONVINCED. WHAT CAN I DO TO ALLAY YOUR FEARS?
I DON'T KNOW...I KEEP THINKING ABOUT BASEBALL.
BASEBALL?
WELL, YOU FOLLOW BASEBALL, RIGHT?
ALWAYS. IT'S FRANKLIN'S FAVORITE GAME.
WELL, FORGIVE MY ASSUMPTION-- I MEAN, I KNOW YOU'RE THE GENIUS HERE, PROFESSOR--BUT IF YOU KNOW BASEBALL, THEN YOU PROBABLY KNOW ABOUT STATS.
SEE, WHAT WORRIES ME IS THAT SO OFTEN ONE TEAM CAN DOMINATE THE STAT SHEET, AND YET THE OTHER TEAM WINS.
OPINION POLLS GO UP AND DOWN. STOCKS FLUCTUATE ACCORDING TO PERCEPTION.
I THINK YOU'RE OVERSIMPLIFYING, BEN.
WELL, I HOPE YOU'RE RIGHT, SIR. I REALLY DO. BECAUSE I THINK IT'S ABSURD TO THINK YOU CAN MEASURE PUBLIC SENTIMENT...
...AND THEN PRETEND NUMBERS DON'T LIE.

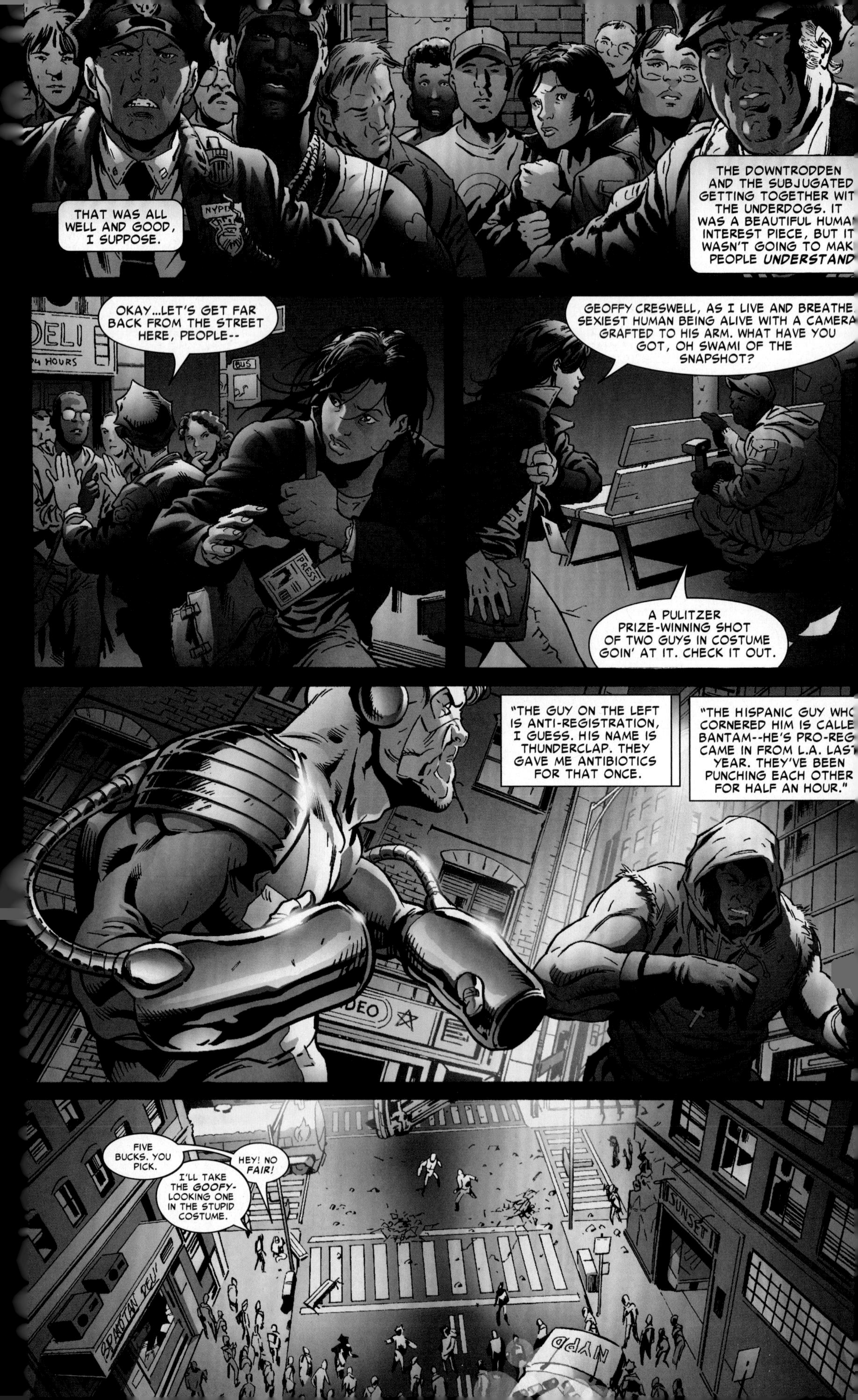
THAT WAS ALL WELL AND GOOD, I SUPPOSE.
THE DOWNTRODDEN AND THE SUBJUGATED GETTING TOGETHER WIT THE UNDERDOGS. IT WAS A BEAUTIFUL HUMA INTEREST PIECE, BUT IT WASN'T GOING TO MAK PEOPLE *UNDERSTAND*
DELI
24 HOURS
BUS
OKAY...LET'S GET FAR BACK FROM THE STREET HERE, PEOPLE--
PRESS
GEOFFY CRESWELL, AS I LIVE AND BREATHE. SEXIEST HUMAN BEING ALIVE WITH A CAMERA GRAFTED TO HIS ARM. WHAT HAVE YOU GOT, OH SWAMI OF THE SNAPSHOT?
A PULITZER PRIZE-WINNING SHOT OF TWO GUYS IN COSTUME GOIN' AT IT. CHECK IT OUT.
"THE GUY ON THE LEFT IS ANTI-REGISTRATION, I GUESS. HIS NAME IS THUNDERCLAP. THEY GAVE ME ANTIBIOTICS FOR THAT ONCE.
"THE HISPANIC GUY WHO CORNERED HIM IS CALLE BANTAM--HE'S PRO-REG CAME IN FROM L.A. LAST YEAR. THEY'VE BEEN PUNCHING EACH OTHER FOR HALF AN HOUR."
FIVE BUCKS. YOU PICK.
I'LL TAKE THE *GOOFY*-LOOKING ONE IN THE STUPID COSTUME.
HEY! NO *FAIR!*
SUNSET
NYPD

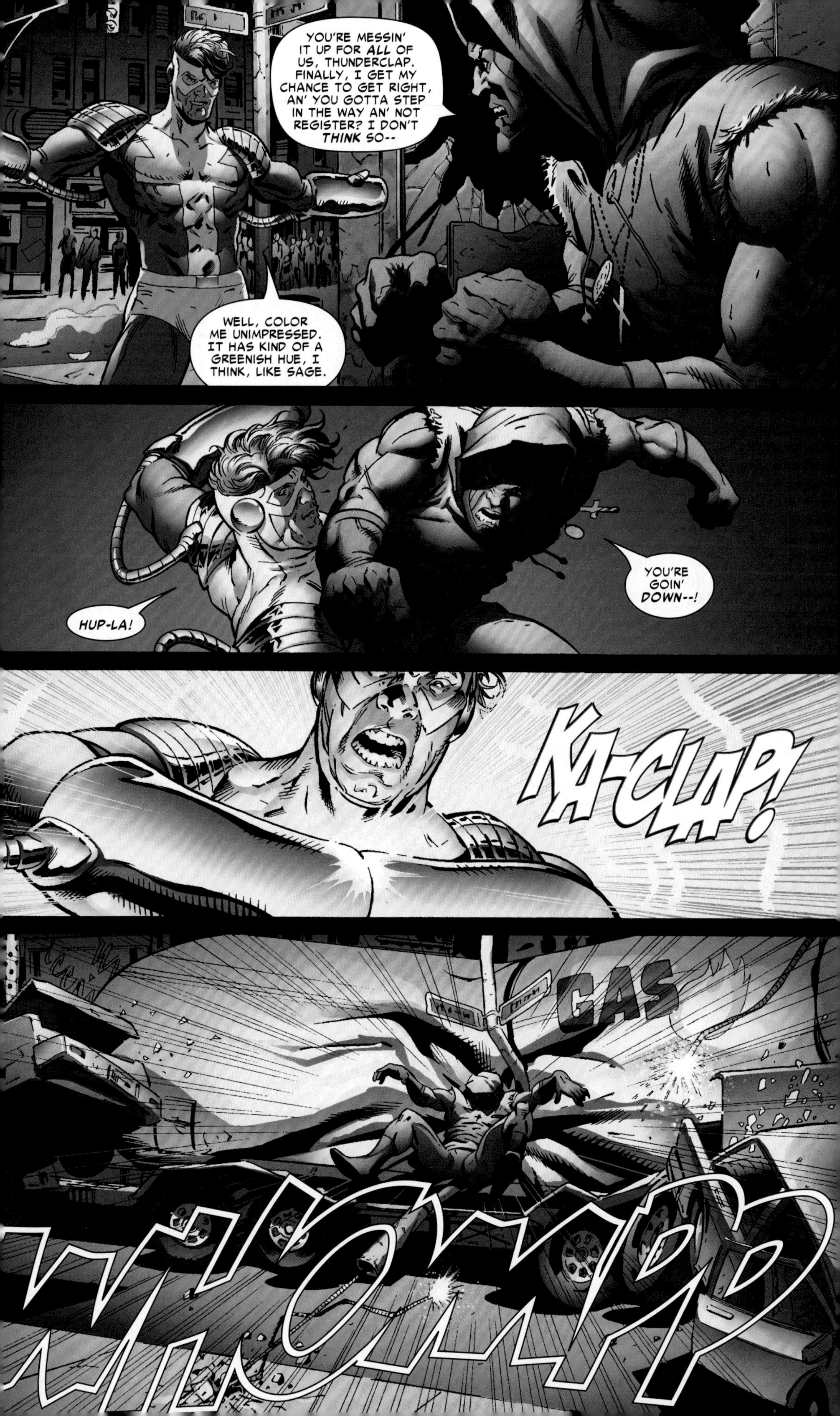
YOU'RE MESSIN' IT UP FOR ALL OF US, THUNDERCLAP. FINALLY, I GET MY CHANCE TO GET RIGHT, AN' YOU GOTTA STEP IN THE WAY AN' NOT REGISTER? I DON'T THINK SO--
WELL, COLOR ME UNIMPRESSED. IT HAS KIND OF A GREENISH HUE, I THINK, LIKE SAGE.
YOU'RE GOIN' DOWN--!
HUP-LA!
KA-CLAP!
GAS
WHOMP!

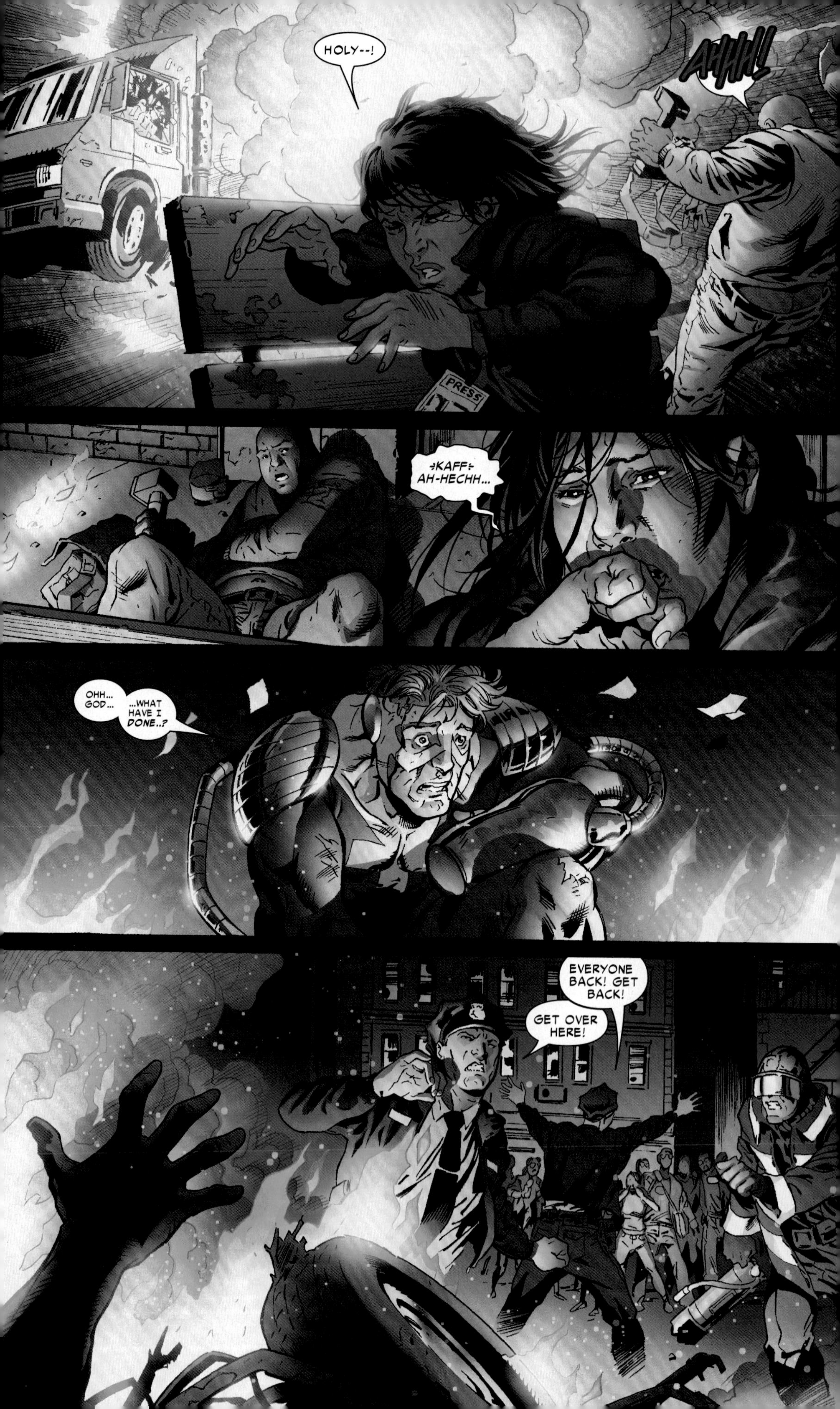
HOLY--!
AHHH!
=KAFF=
AH-HECHH...
OHH... GOD...
...WHAT HAVE I DONE..?
EVERYONE BACK! GET BACK!
GET OVER HERE!

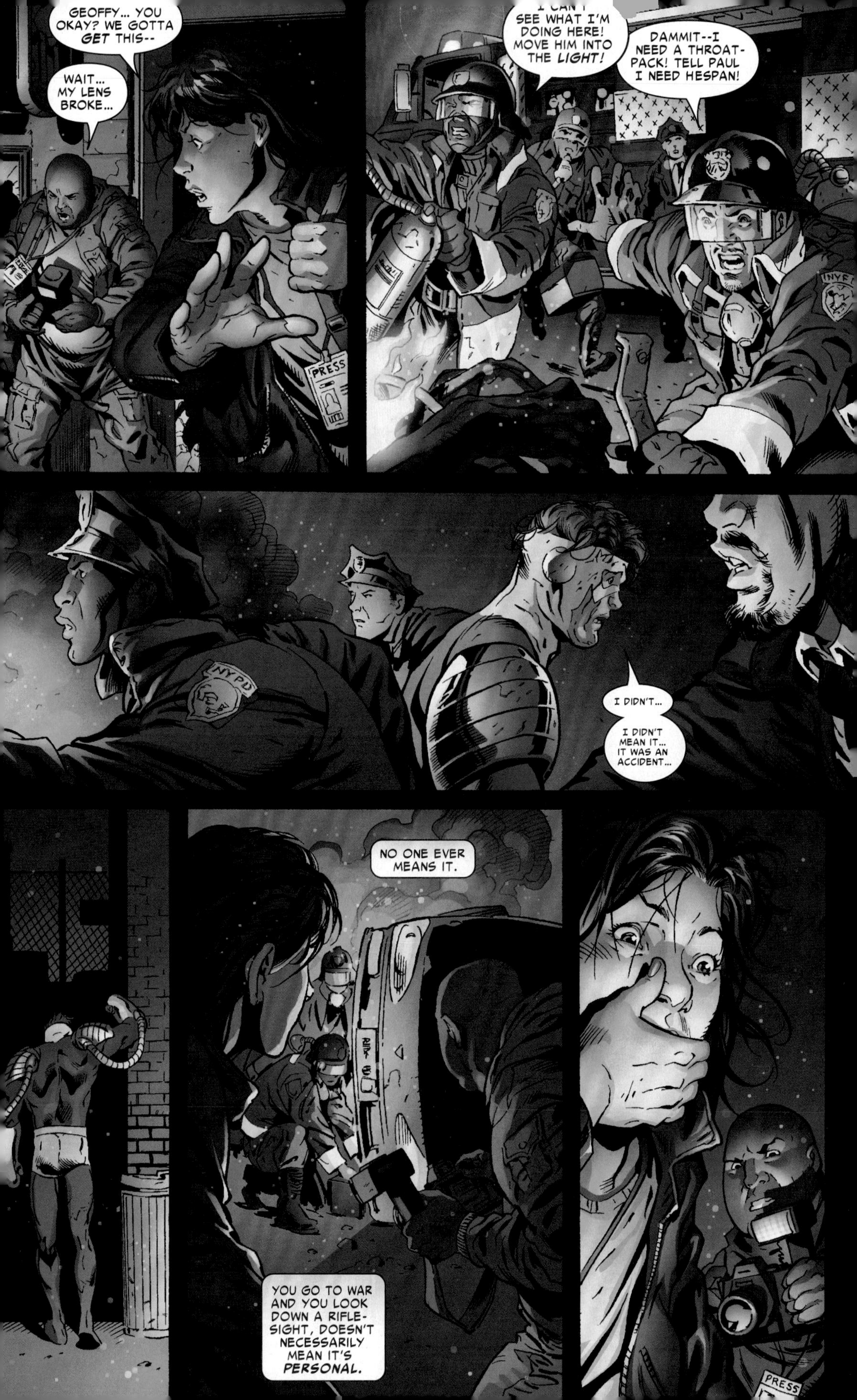
GEOFFY... YOU OKAY? WE GOTTA *GET* THIS--
WAIT... MY LENS BROKE...
PRESS
I CAN'T SEE WHAT I'M DOING HERE! MOVE HIM INTO THE *LIGHT!*
DAMMIT--I NEED A THROAT-PACK! TELL PAUL I NEED HESPAN!
NYPD
I DIDN'T...
I DIDN'T MEAN IT... IT WAS AN ACCIDENT...
NO ONE EVER MEANS IT.
YOU GO TO WAR AND YOU LOOK DOWN A RIFLE-SIGHT, DOESN'T NECESSARILY MEAN IT'S *PERSONAL.*
PRESS

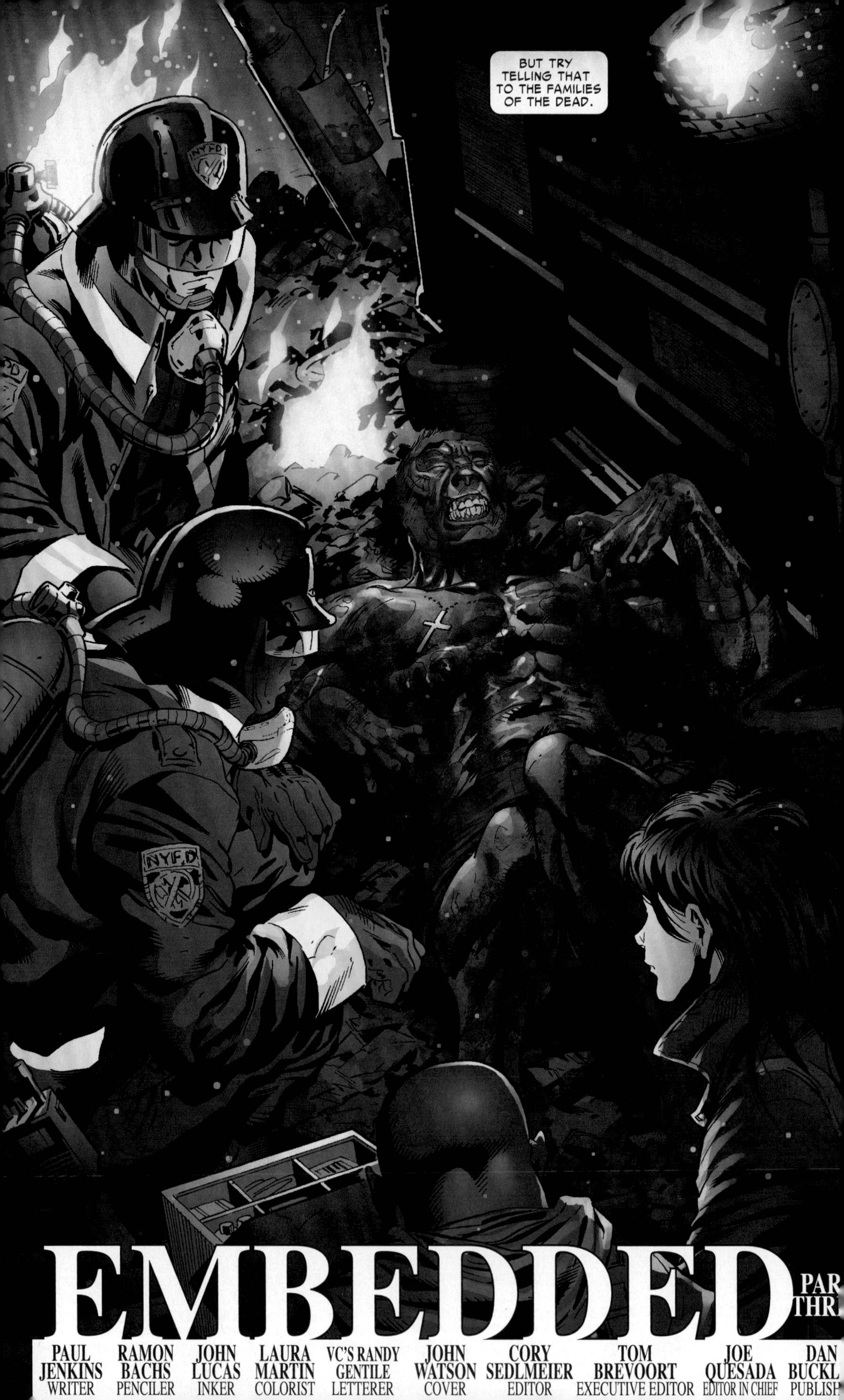
BUT TRY TELLING THAT TO THE FAMILIES OF THE DEAD.
NYFD
NYFD
EMBEDDED
PAR
THRI
PAUL JENKINS WRITER
RAMON BACHS PENCILER
JOHN LUCAS INKER
LAURA MARTIN COLORIST
VC'S RANDY GENTILE LETTERER
JOHN WATSON COVER
CORY SEDLMEIER EDITOR
TOM BREVOORT EXECUTIVE EDITOR
JOE QUESADA EDITOR IN CHIEF
DAN BUCKL PUBLISH

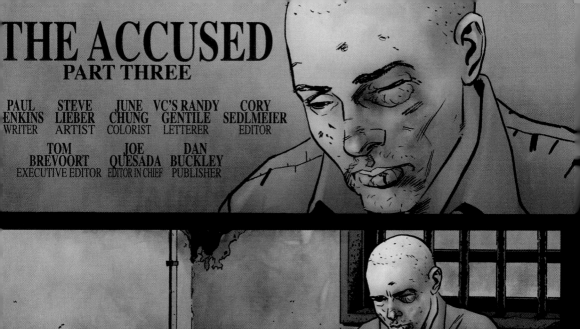

THE ACCUSED
PART THREE

PAUL
ENKINS
WRITER

STEVE
LIEBER
ARTIST

JUNE
CHUNG
COLORIST

VC'S RANDY
GENTILE
LETTERER

CORY
SEDLMEIER
EDITOR

TOM
BREVOORT
EXECUTIVE EDITOR

JOE
QUESADA
EDITOR IN CHIEF

DAN
BUCKLEY
PUBLISHER

YOU THINK I'VE LOST WEIGHT, JEN?

ONLY BECAUSE SOMEONE BIT A TWO-OUNCE CHUNK OUT OF MY ARM.

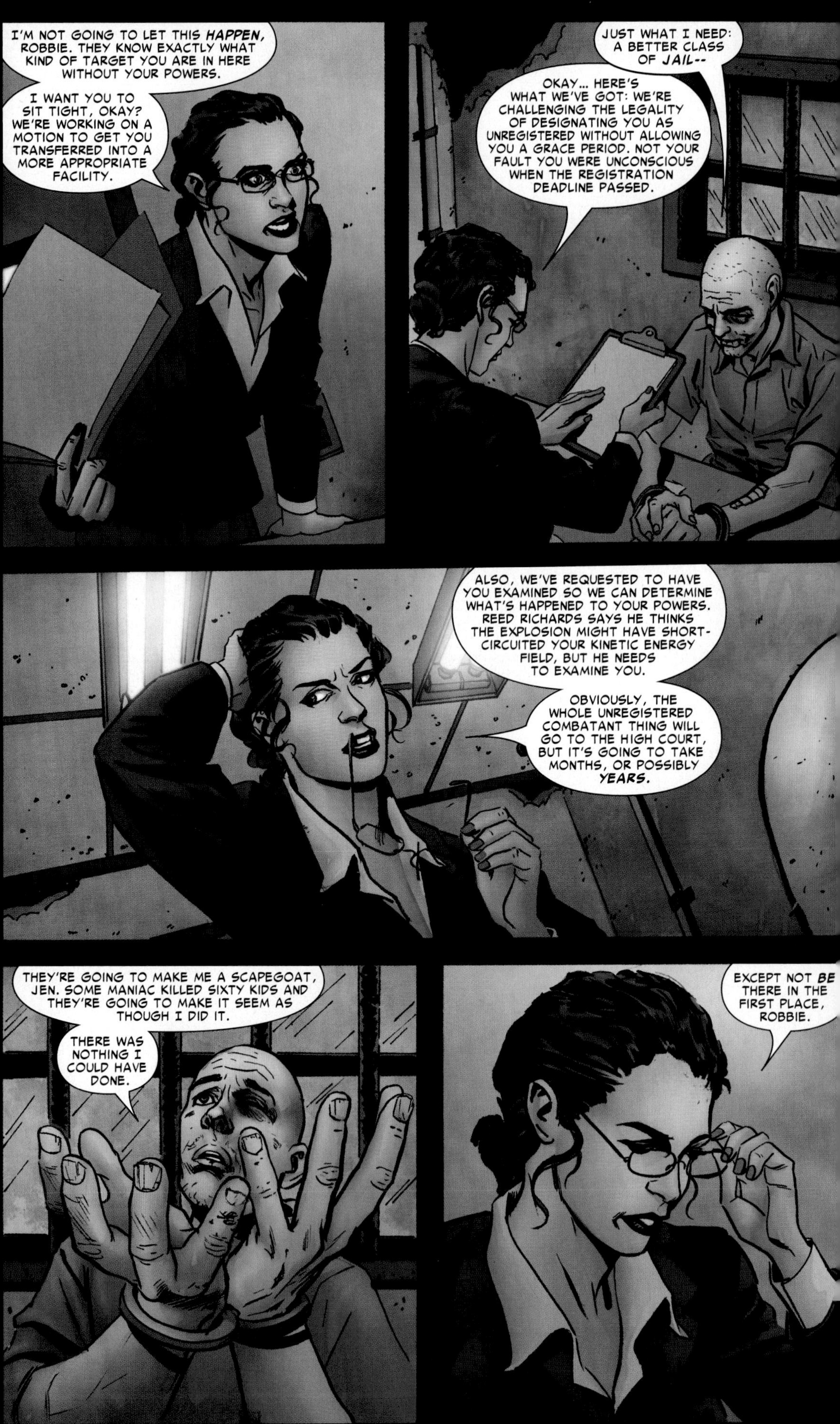
I'M NOT GOING TO LET THIS HAPPEN, ROBBIE. THEY KNOW EXACTLY WHAT KIND OF TARGET YOU ARE IN HERE WITHOUT YOUR POWERS.
I WANT YOU TO SIT TIGHT, OKAY? WE'RE WORKING ON A MOTION TO GET YOU TRANSFERRED INTO A MORE APPROPRIATE FACILITY.
JUST WHAT I NEED: A BETTER CLASS OF JAIL--
OKAY... HERE'S WHAT WE'VE GOT: WE'RE CHALLENGING THE LEGALITY OF DESIGNATING YOU AS UNREGISTERED WITHOUT ALLOWING YOU A GRACE PERIOD. NOT YOUR FAULT YOU WERE UNCONSCIOUS WHEN THE REGISTRATION DEADLINE PASSED.
ALSO, WE'VE REQUESTED TO HAVE YOU EXAMINED SO WE CAN DETERMINE WHAT'S HAPPENED TO YOUR POWERS. REED RICHARDS SAYS HE THINKS THE EXPLOSION MIGHT HAVE SHORT-CIRCUITED YOUR KINETIC ENERGY FIELD, BUT HE NEEDS TO EXAMINE YOU.
OBVIOUSLY, THE WHOLE UNREGISTERED COMBATANT THING WILL GO TO THE HIGH COURT, BUT IT'S GOING TO TAKE MONTHS, OR POSSIBLY YEARS.
THEY'RE GOING TO MAKE ME A SCAPEGOAT, JEN. SOME MANIAC KILLED SIXTY KIDS AND THEY'RE GOING TO MAKE IT SEEM AS THOUGH I DID IT.
THERE WAS NOTHING I COULD HAVE DONE.
EXCEPT NOT BE THERE IN THE FIRST PLACE, ROBBIE.

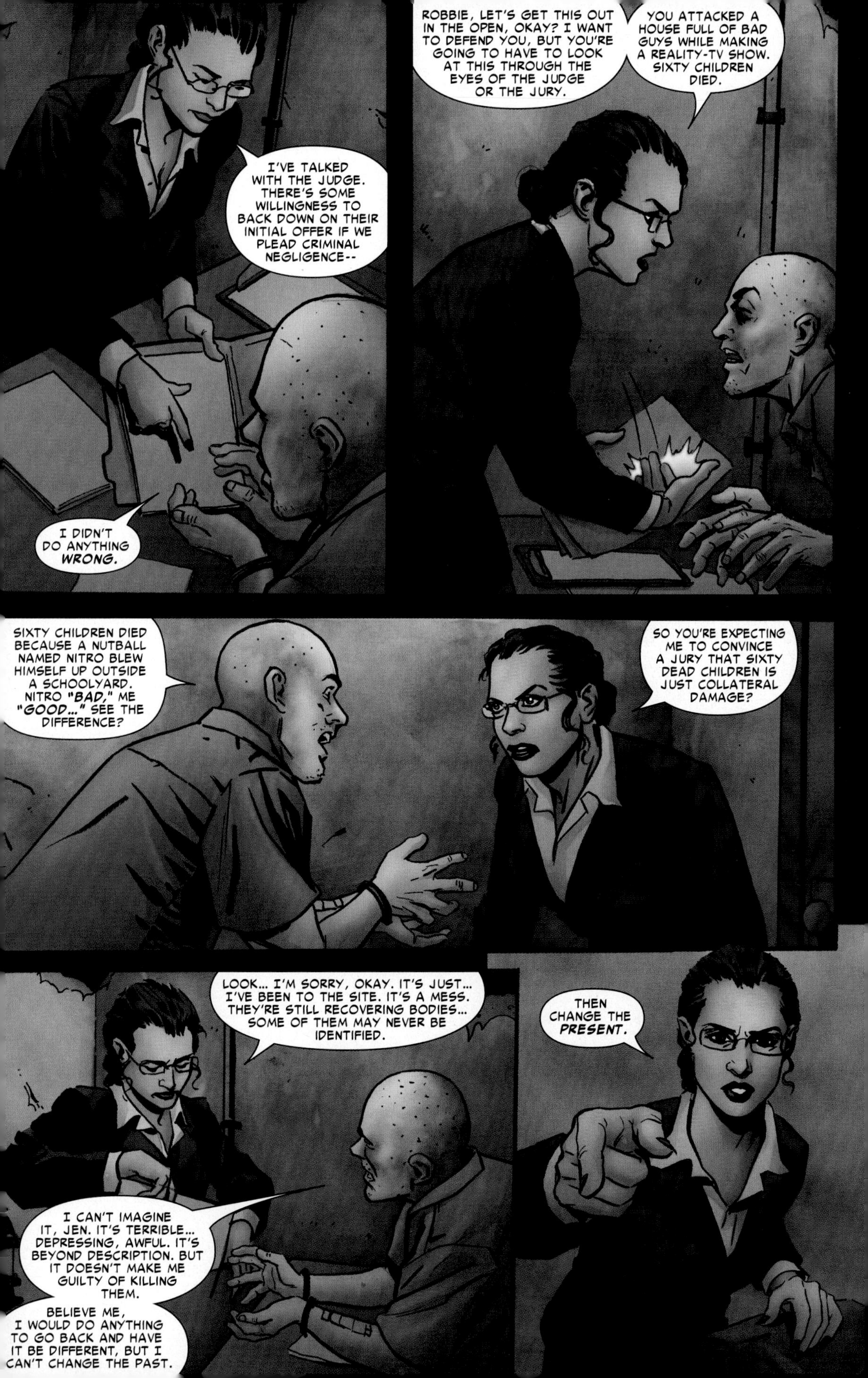
I'VE TALKED WITH THE JUDGE. THERE'S SOME WILLINGNESS TO BACK DOWN ON THEIR INITIAL OFFER IF WE PLEAD CRIMINAL NEGLIGENCE--
I DIDN'T DO ANYTHING *WRONG.*
ROBBIE, LET'S GET THIS OUT IN THE OPEN, OKAY? I WANT TO DEFEND YOU, BUT YOU'RE GOING TO HAVE TO LOOK AT THIS THROUGH THE EYES OF THE JUDGE OR THE JURY.
YOU ATTACKED A HOUSE FULL OF BAD GUYS WHILE MAKING A REALITY-TV SHOW. SIXTY CHILDREN DIED.
SIXTY CHILDREN DIED BECAUSE A NUTBALL NAMED NITRO BLEW HIMSELF UP OUTSIDE A SCHOOLYARD. NITRO "*BAD*," ME "*GOOD*..." SEE THE DIFFERENCE?
SO YOU'RE EXPECTING ME TO CONVINCE A JURY THAT SIXTY DEAD CHILDREN IS JUST COLLATERAL DAMAGE?
LOOK... I'M SORRY, OKAY. IT'S JUST... I'VE BEEN TO THE SITE. IT'S A MESS. THEY'RE STILL RECOVERING BODIES... SOME OF THEM MAY NEVER BE IDENTIFIED.
I CAN'T IMAGINE IT, JEN. IT'S TERRIBLE... DEPRESSING, AWFUL. IT'S BEYOND DESCRIPTION. BUT IT DOESN'T MAKE ME GUILTY OF KILLING THEM.
BELIEVE ME, I WOULD DO ANYTHING TO GO BACK AND HAVE IT BE DIFFERENT, BUT I CAN'T CHANGE THE PAST.
THEN CHANGE THE *PRESENT*.

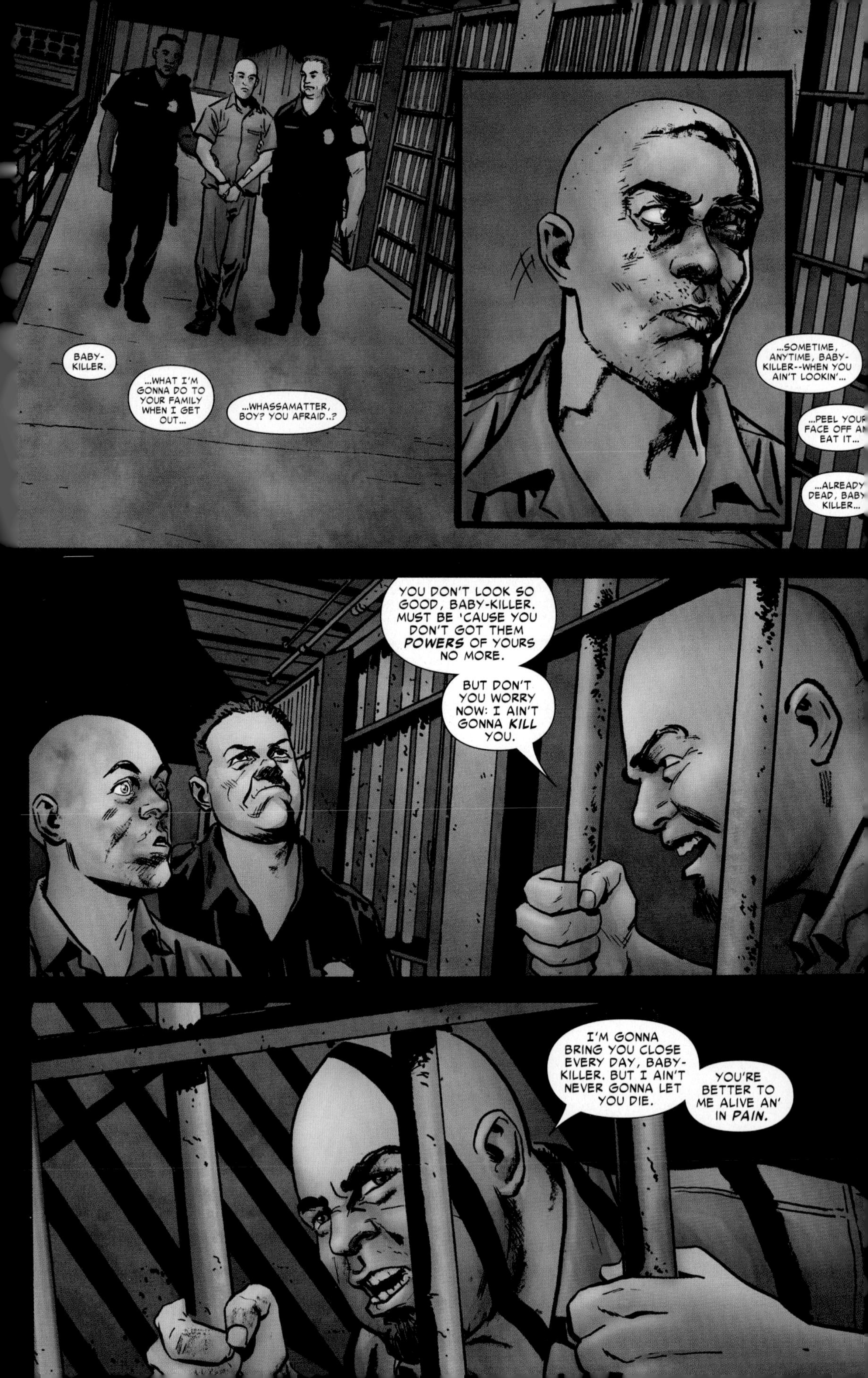
BABY-KILLER.
...WHAT I'M GONNA DO TO YOUR FAMILY WHEN I GET OUT...
...WHASSAMATTER, BOY? YOU AFRAID..?
...SOMETIME, ANYTIME, BABY-KILLER--WHEN YOU AIN'T LOOKIN'...
...PEEL YOUR FACE OFF AN EAT IT...
...ALREADY DEAD, BABY KILLER...
YOU DON'T LOOK SO GOOD, BABY-KILLER. MUST BE 'CAUSE YOU DON'T GOT THEM POWERS OF YOURS NO MORE.
BUT DON'T YOU WORRY NOW: I AIN'T GONNA KILL YOU.
I'M GONNA BRING YOU CLOSE EVERY DAY, BABY-KILLER. BUT I AIN'T NEVER GONNA LET YOU DIE.
YOU'RE BETTER TO ME ALIVE AN' IN PAIN.

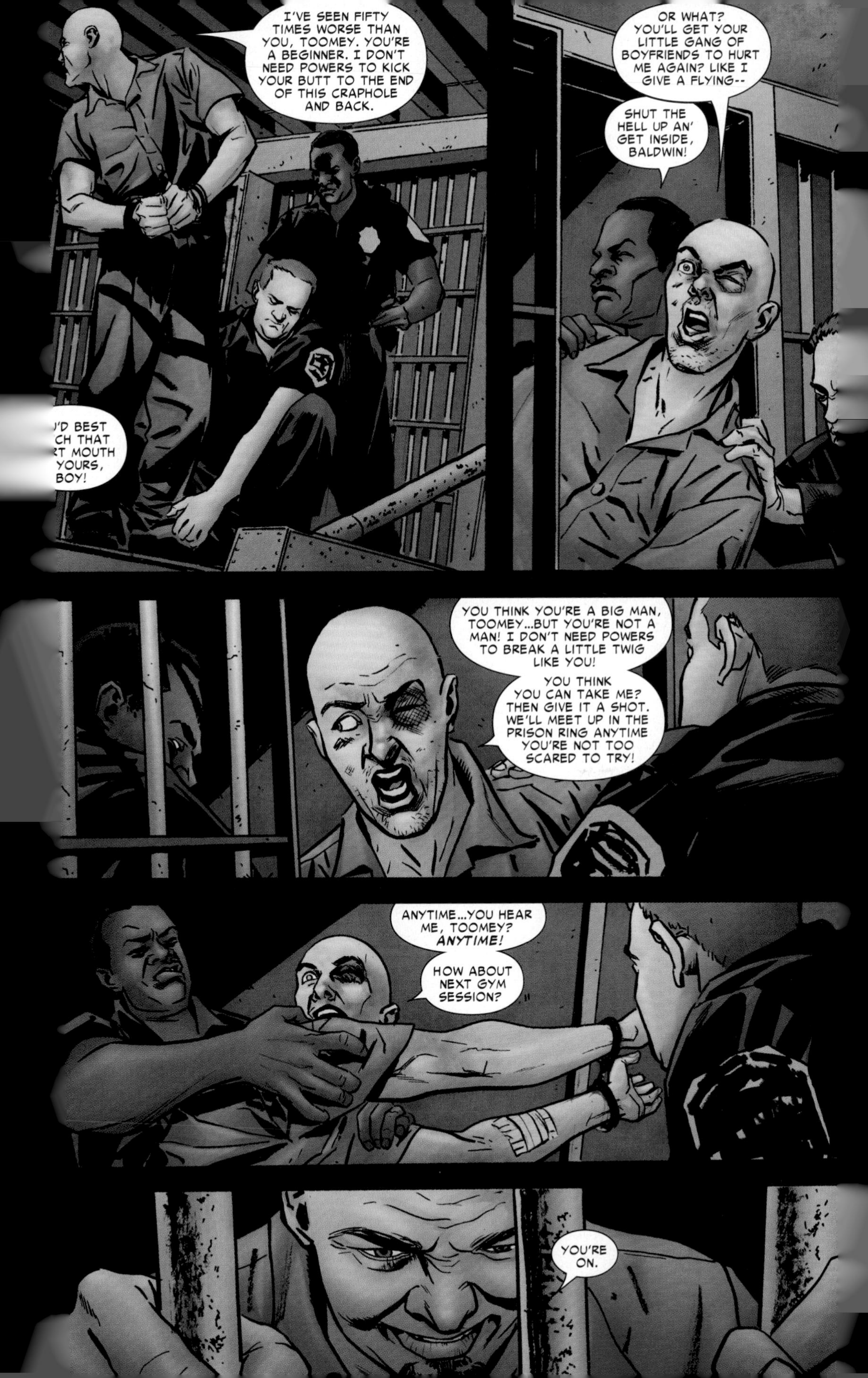
I'VE SEEN FIFTY TIMES WORSE THAN YOU, TOOMEY. YOU'RE A BEGINNER. I DON'T NEED POWERS TO KICK YOUR BUTT TO THE END OF THIS CRAPHOLE AND BACK.
'D BEST CH THAT T MOUTH YOURS, BOY!
OR WHAT? YOU'LL GET YOUR LITTLE GANG OF BOYFRIENDS TO HURT ME AGAIN? LIKE I GIVE A FLYING--
SHUT THE HELL UP AN' GET INSIDE, BALDWIN!
YOU THINK YOU'RE A BIG MAN, TOOMEY...BUT YOU'RE NOT A MAN! I DON'T NEED POWERS TO BREAK A LITTLE TWIG LIKE YOU!
YOU THINK YOU CAN TAKE ME? THEN GIVE IT A SHOT. WE'LL MEET UP IN THE PRISON RING ANYTIME YOU'RE NOT TOO SCARED TO TRY!
ANYTIME...YOU HEAR ME, TOOMEY? *ANYTIME!*
HOW ABOUT NEXT GYM SESSION?
YOU'RE ON.

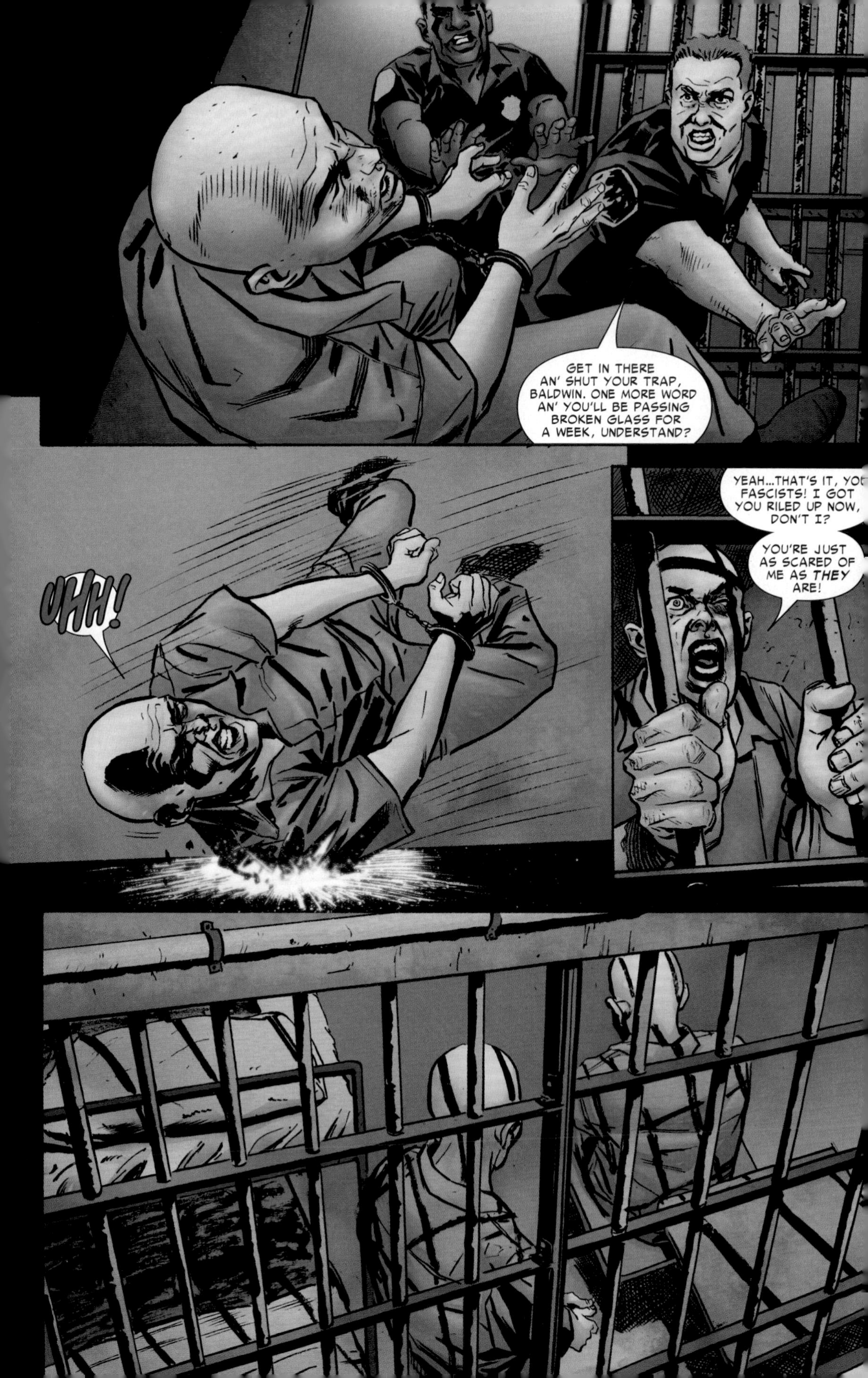
GET IN THERE AN' SHUT YOUR TRAP, BALDWIN. ONE MORE WORD AN' YOU'LL BE PASSING BROKEN GLASS FOR A WEEK, UNDERSTAND?
UHH!
YEAH...THAT'S IT, YOU FASCISTS! I GOT YOU RILED UP NOW, DON'T I?
YOU'RE JUST AS SCARED OF ME AS *THEY* ARE!

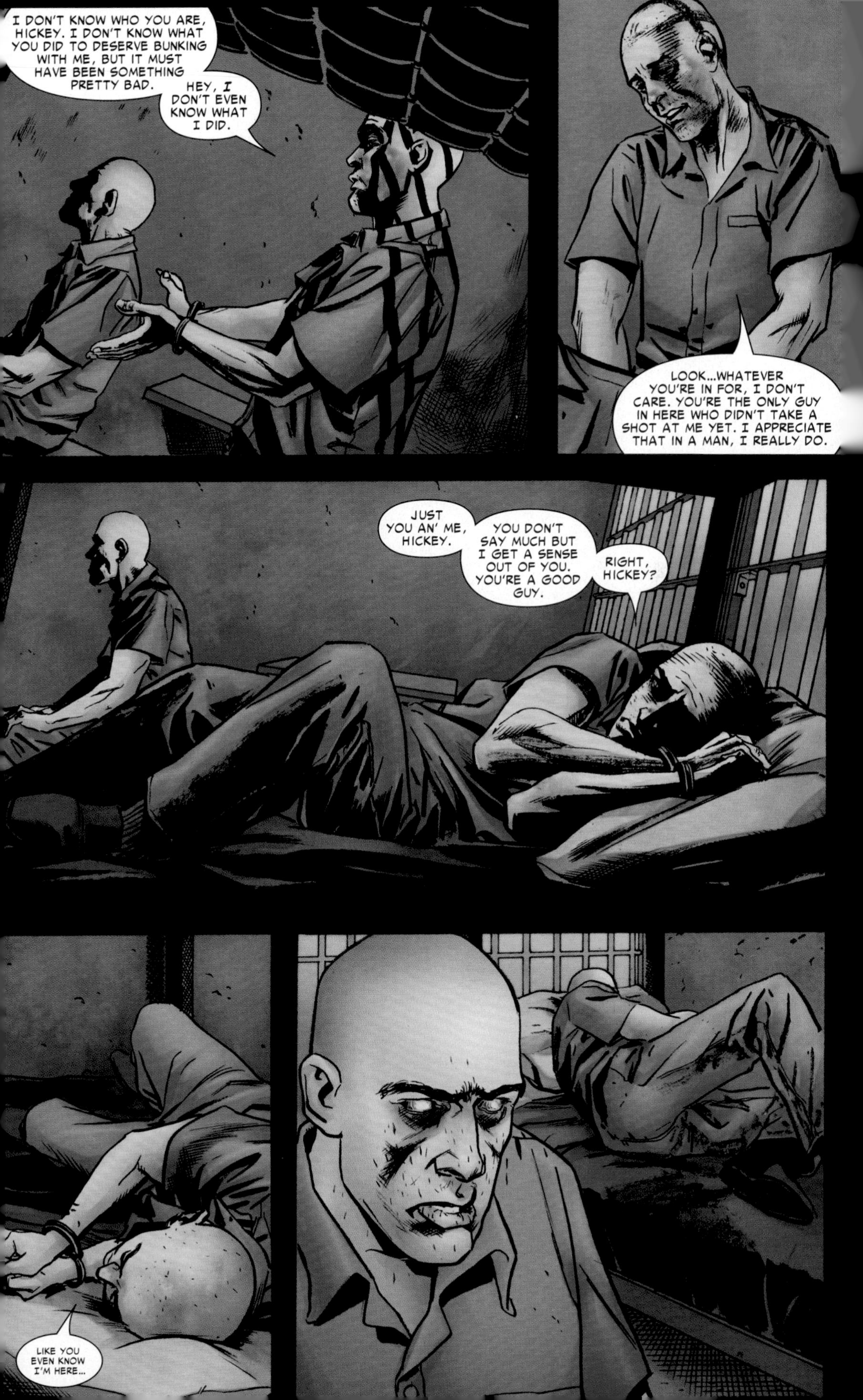
I DON'T KNOW WHO YOU ARE, HICKEY. I DON'T KNOW WHAT YOU DID TO DESERVE BUNKING WITH ME, BUT IT MUST HAVE BEEN SOMETHING PRETTY BAD.
HEY, I DON'T EVEN KNOW WHAT I DID.
LOOK...WHATEVER YOU'RE IN FOR, I DON'T CARE. YOU'RE THE ONLY GUY IN HERE WHO DIDN'T TAKE A SHOT AT ME YET. I APPRECIATE THAT IN A MAN, I REALLY DO.
JUST YOU AN' ME, HICKEY.
YOU DON'T SAY MUCH BUT I GET A SENSE OUT OF YOU. YOU'RE A GOOD GUY.
RIGHT, HICKEY?
LIKE YOU EVEN KNOW I'M HERE...

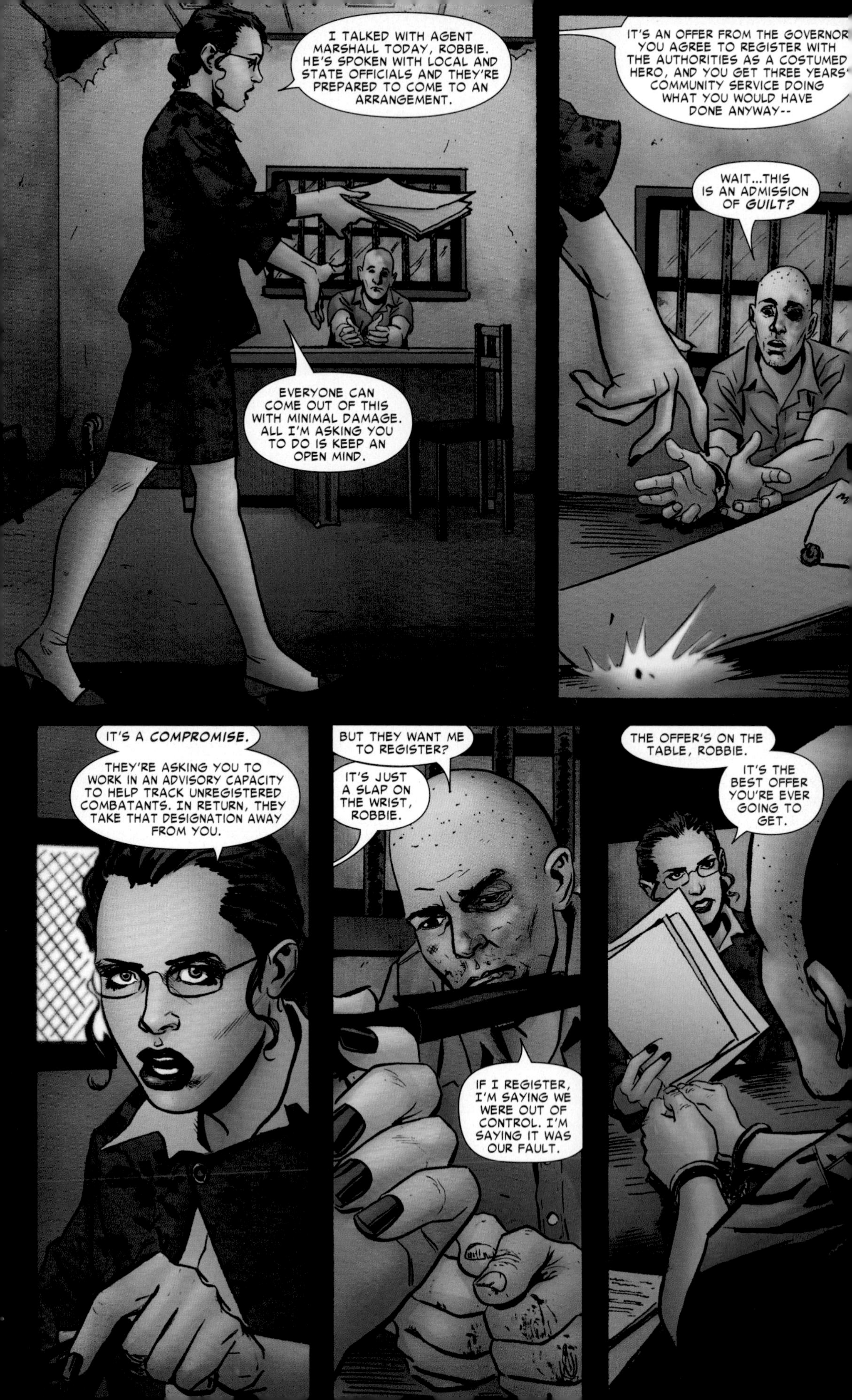
I TALKED WITH AGENT MARSHALL TODAY, ROBBIE. HE'S SPOKEN WITH LOCAL AND STATE OFFICIALS AND THEY'RE PREPARED TO COME TO AN ARRANGEMENT.
EVERYONE CAN COME OUT OF THIS WITH MINIMAL DAMAGE. ALL I'M ASKING YOU TO DO IS KEEP AN OPEN MIND.
IT'S AN OFFER FROM THE GOVERNOR. YOU AGREE TO REGISTER WITH THE AUTHORITIES AS A COSTUMED HERO, AND YOU GET THREE YEARS' COMMUNITY SERVICE DOING WHAT YOU WOULD HAVE DONE ANYWAY--
WAIT...THIS IS AN ADMISSION OF *GUILT?*
IT'S A *COMPROMISE.*
THEY'RE ASKING YOU TO WORK IN AN ADVISORY CAPACITY TO HELP TRACK UNREGISTERED COMBATANTS. IN RETURN, THEY TAKE THAT DESIGNATION AWAY FROM YOU.
BUT THEY WANT ME TO REGISTER?
IT'S JUST A SLAP ON THE WRIST, ROBBIE.
IF I REGISTER, I'M SAYING WE WERE OUT OF CONTROL. I'M SAYING IT WAS OUR FAULT.
THE OFFER'S ON THE TABLE, ROBBIE.
IT'S THE BEST OFFER YOU'RE EVER GOING TO GET.

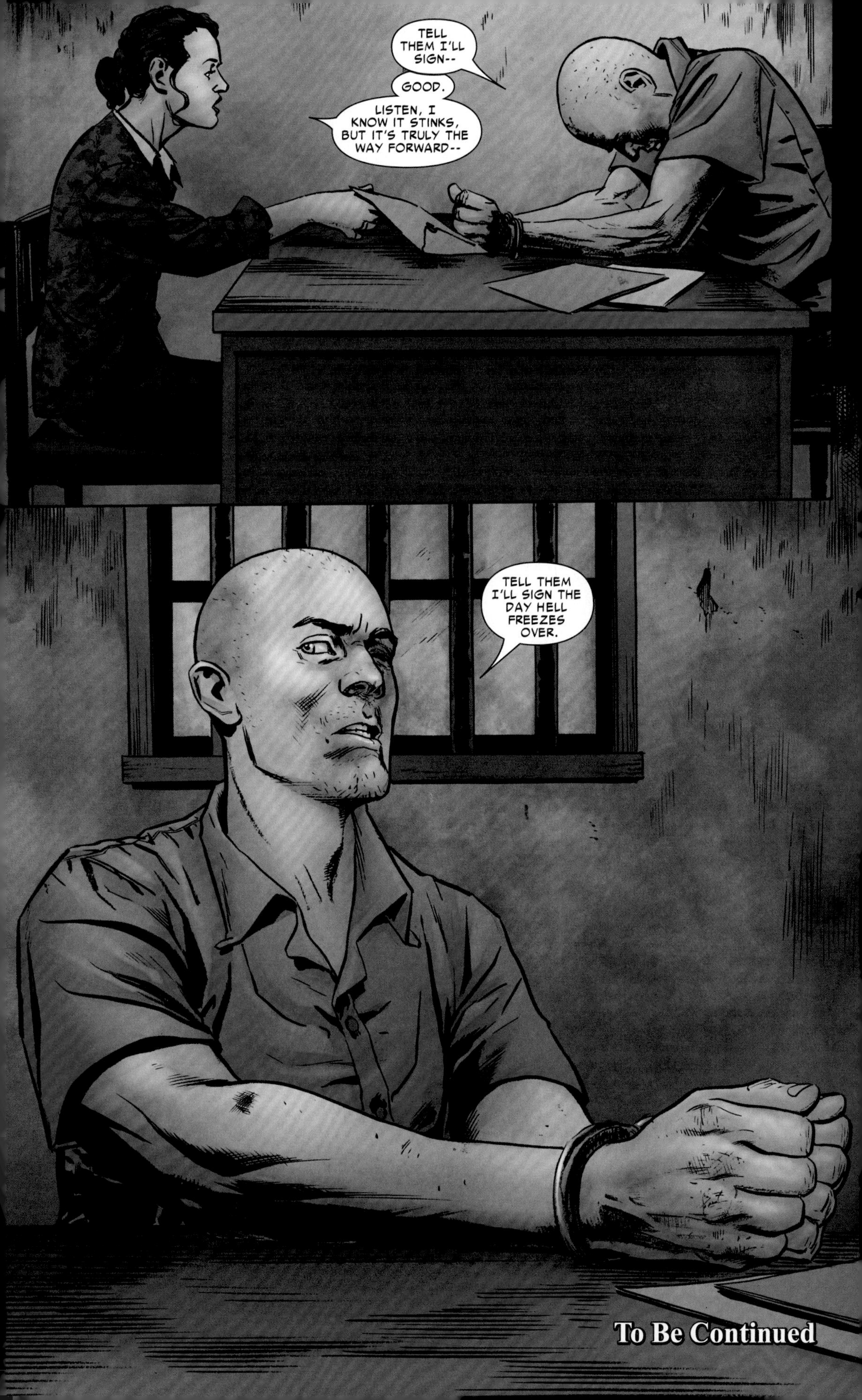
TELL THEM I'LL SIGN--
GOOD.
LISTEN, I KNOW IT STINKS, BUT IT'S TRULY THE WAY FORWARD--
TELL THEM I'LL SIGN THE DAY HELL FREEZES OVER.
To Be Continued

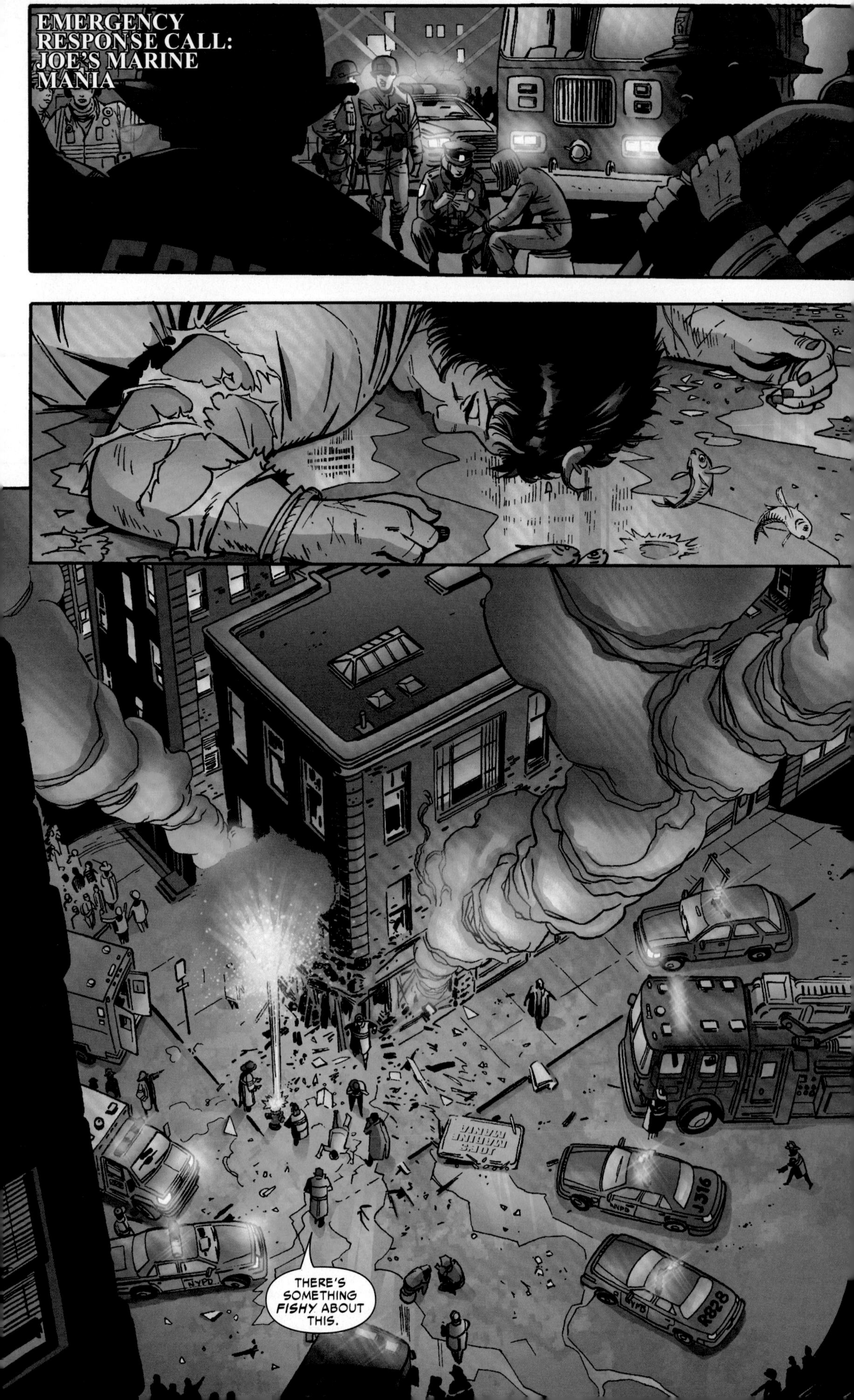
EMERGENCY RESPONSE CALL: JOE'S MARINE MANIA
JOE'S MARINE MANIA
NYPD
J316
R828
THERE'S SOMETHING *FISHY* ABOUT THIS.

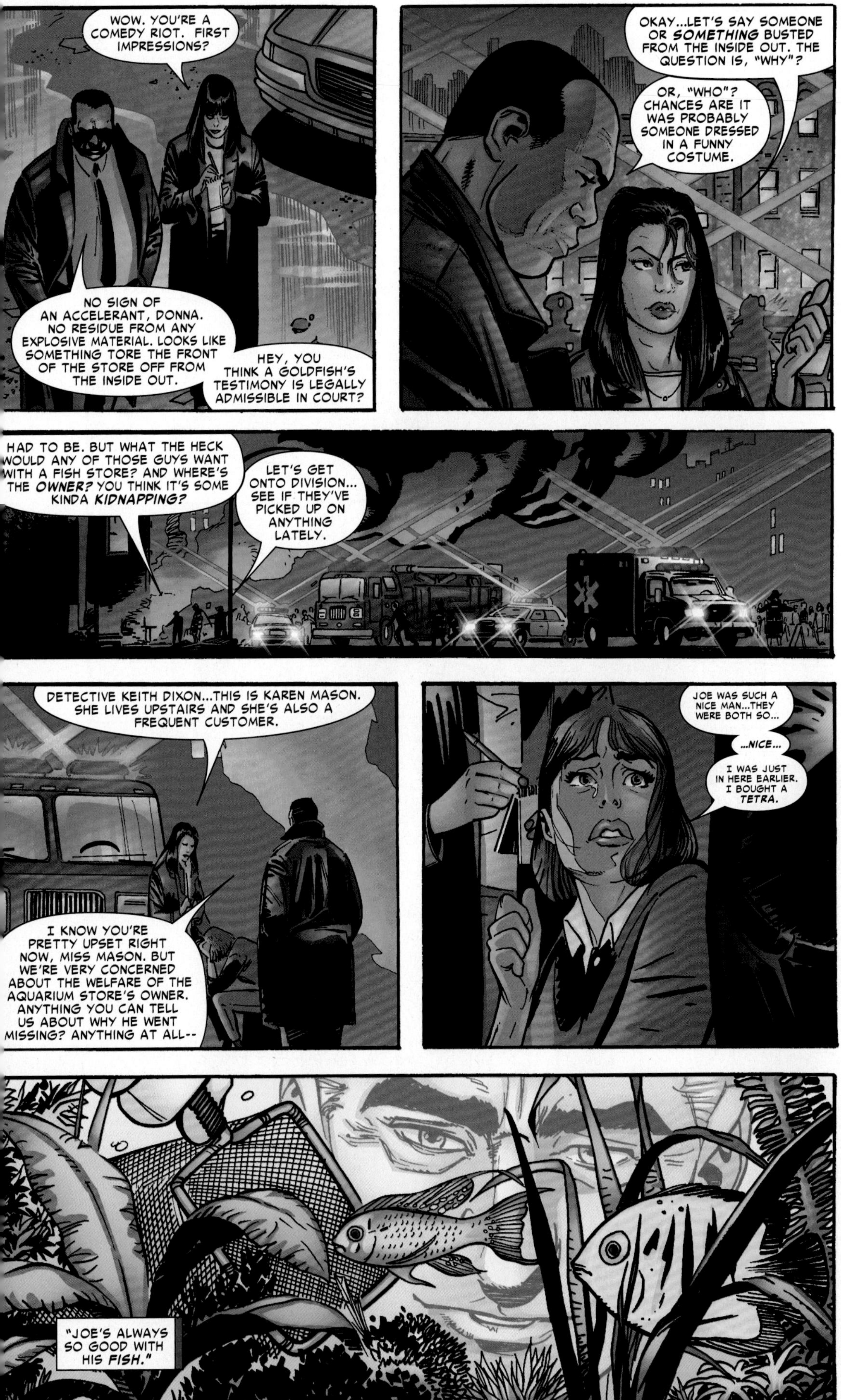
WOW. YOU'RE A COMEDY RIOT. FIRST IMPRESSIONS?
NO SIGN OF AN ACCELERANT, DONNA. NO RESIDUE FROM ANY EXPLOSIVE MATERIAL. LOOKS LIKE SOMETHING TORE THE FRONT OF THE STORE OFF FROM THE INSIDE OUT.
HEY, YOU THINK A GOLDFISH'S TESTIMONY IS LEGALLY ADMISSIBLE IN COURT?
OKAY...LET'S SAY SOMEONE OR SOMETHING BUSTED FROM THE INSIDE OUT. THE QUESTION IS, "WHY"?
OR, "WHO"? CHANCES ARE IT WAS PROBABLY SOMEONE DRESSED IN A FUNNY COSTUME.
HAD TO BE. BUT WHAT THE HECK WOULD ANY OF THOSE GUYS WANT WITH A FISH STORE? AND WHERE'S THE OWNER? YOU THINK IT'S SOME KINDA KIDNAPPING?
LET'S GET ONTO DIVISION... SEE IF THEY'VE PICKED UP ON ANYTHING LATELY.
DETECTIVE KEITH DIXON...THIS IS KAREN MASON. SHE LIVES UPSTAIRS AND SHE'S ALSO A FREQUENT CUSTOMER.
I KNOW YOU'RE PRETTY UPSET RIGHT NOW, MISS MASON. BUT WE'RE VERY CONCERNED ABOUT THE WELFARE OF THE AQUARIUM STORE'S OWNER. ANYTHING YOU CAN TELL US ABOUT WHY HE WENT MISSING? ANYTHING AT ALL--
JOE WAS SUCH A NICE MAN...THEY WERE BOTH SO...
...NICE...
I WAS JUST IN HERE EARLIER. I BOUGHT A TETRA.
"JOE'S ALWAYS SO GOOD WITH HIS FISH."

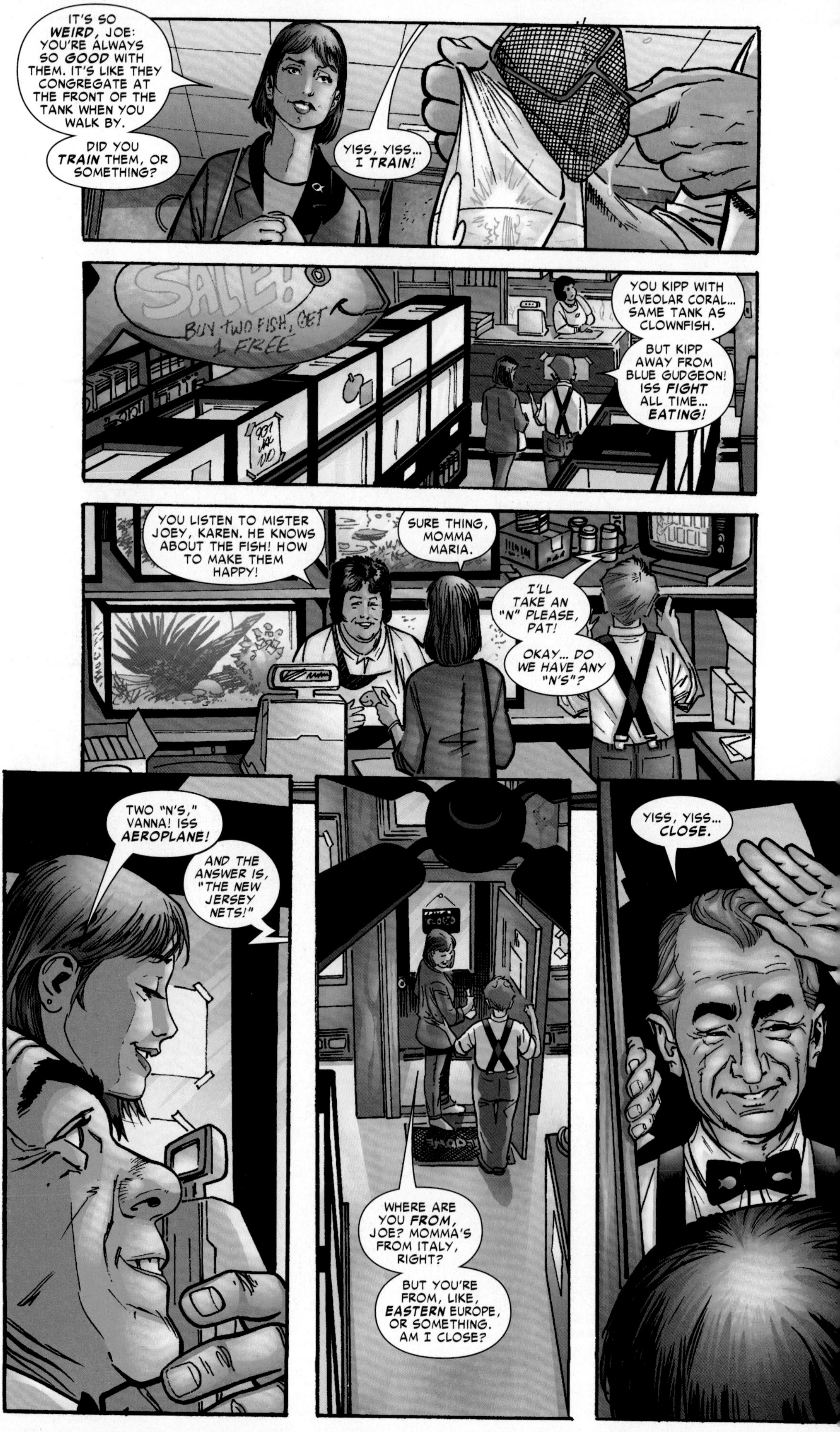
IT'S SO WEIRD, JOE: YOU'RE ALWAYS SO GOOD WITH THEM. IT'S LIKE THEY CONGREGATE AT THE FRONT OF THE TANK WHEN YOU WALK BY.
DID YOU TRAIN THEM, OR SOMETHING?
YISS, YISS... I TRAIN!
SALE! BUY TWO FISH, GET 1 FREE
YOU KIPP WITH ALVEOLAR CORAL... SAME TANK AS CLOWNFISH.
BUT KIPP AWAY FROM BLUE GUDGEON! ISS FIGHT ALL TIME... EATING!
YOU LISTEN TO MISTER JOEY, KAREN. HE KNOWS ABOUT THE FISH! HOW TO MAKE THEM HAPPY!
SURE THING, MOMMA MARIA.
I'LL TAKE AN "N" PLEASE, PAT!
OKAY... DO WE HAVE ANY "N'S"?
TWO "N'S," VANNA! ISS AEROPLANE!
AND THE ANSWER IS, "THE NEW JERSEY NETS!"
WHERE ARE YOU FROM, JOE? MOMMA'S FROM ITALY, RIGHT?
BUT YOU'RE FROM, LIKE, EASTERN EUROPE, OR SOMETHING. AM I CLOSE?
YISS, YISS... CLOSE.

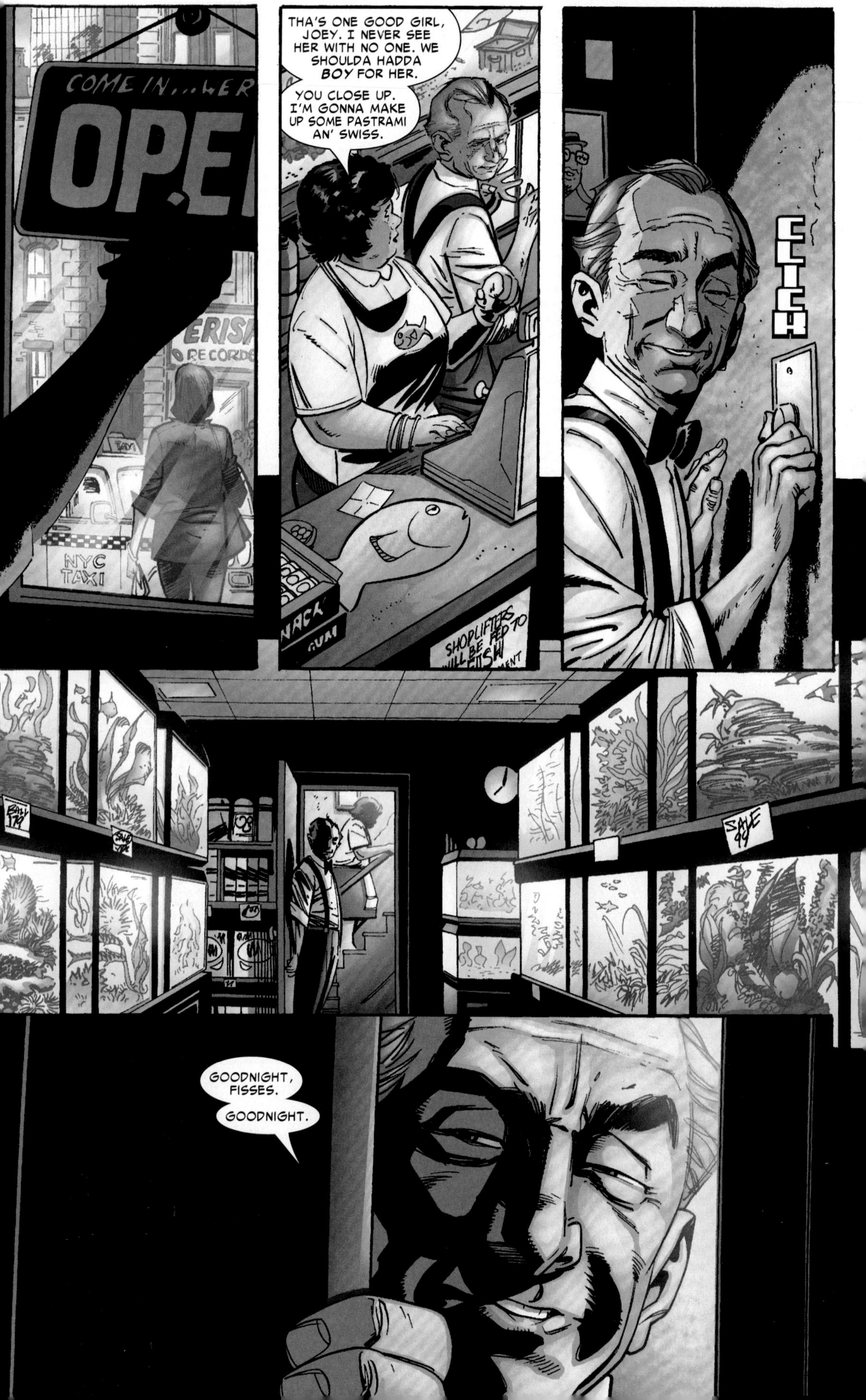
COME IN...WER
OPE
NYC TAXI
THA'S ONE GOOD GIRL, JOEY. I NEVER SEE HER WITH NO ONE. WE SHOULDA HADDA *BOY* FOR HER.
YOU CLOSE UP. I'M GONNA MAKE UP SOME PASTRAMI AN' SWISS.
SHOPLIFTERS WILL BE FED TO FISH
CLICK
SALE 99
GOODNIGHT, FISSES.
GOODNIGHT.

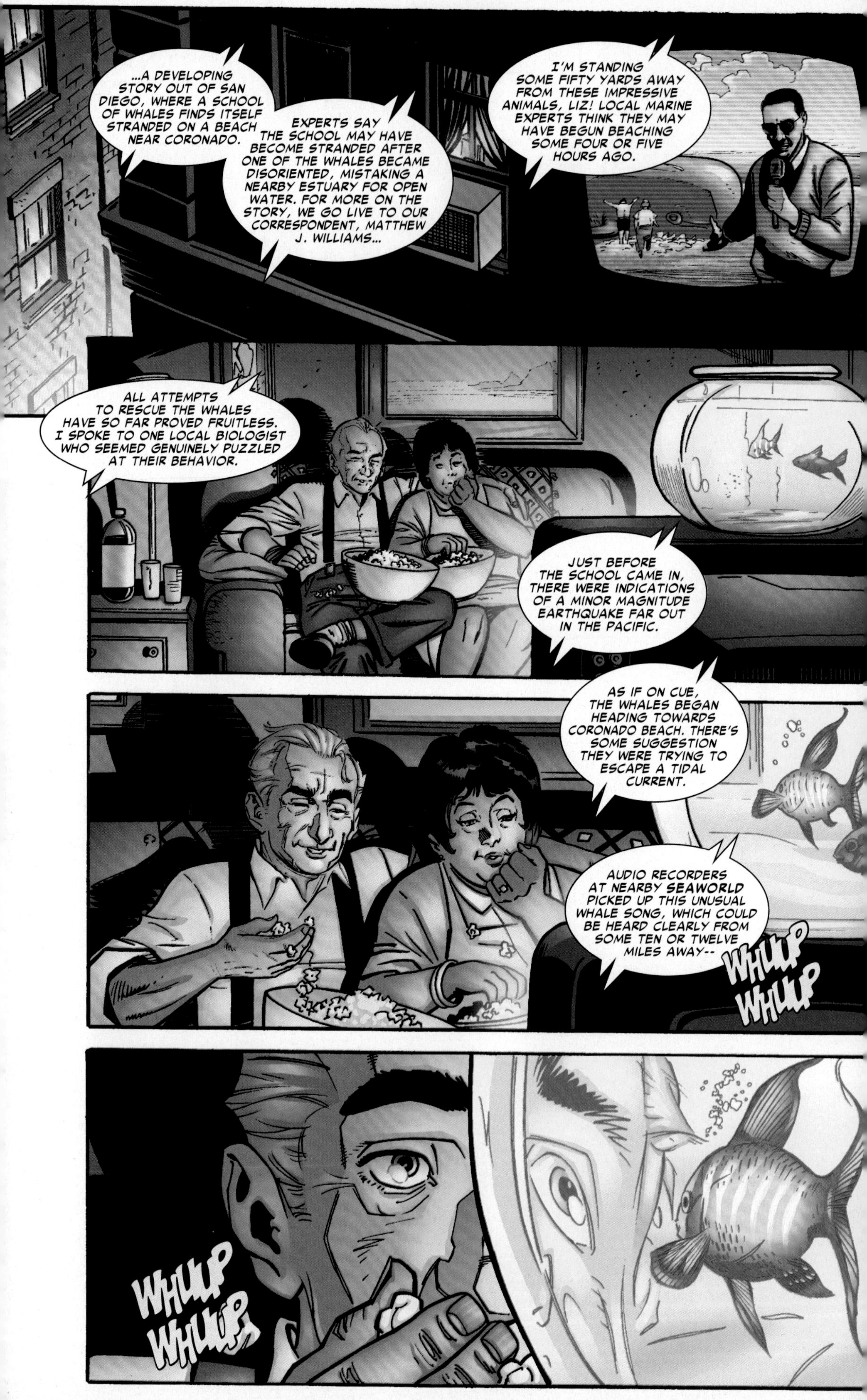

...A DEVELOPING STORY OUT OF SAN DIEGO, WHERE A SCHOOL OF WHALES FINDS ITSELF STRANDED ON A BEACH NEAR CORONADO.
EXPERTS SAY THE SCHOOL MAY HAVE BECOME STRANDED AFTER ONE OF THE WHALES BECAME DISORIENTED, MISTAKING A NEARBY ESTUARY FOR OPEN WATER. FOR MORE ON THE STORY, WE GO LIVE TO OUR CORRESPONDENT, MATTHEW J. WILLIAMS...
I'M STANDING SOME FIFTY YARDS AWAY FROM THESE IMPRESSIVE ANIMALS, LIZ! LOCAL MARINE EXPERTS THINK THEY MAY HAVE BEGUN BEACHING SOME FOUR OR FIVE HOURS AGO.
ALL ATTEMPTS TO RESCUE THE WHALES HAVE SO FAR PROVED FRUITLESS. I SPOKE TO ONE LOCAL BIOLOGIST WHO SEEMED GENUINELY PUZZLED AT THEIR BEHAVIOR.
JUST BEFORE THE SCHOOL CAME IN, THERE WERE INDICATIONS OF A MINOR MAGNITUDE EARTHQUAKE FAR OUT IN THE PACIFIC.
AS IF ON CUE, THE WHALES BEGAN HEADING TOWARDS CORONADO BEACH. THERE'S SOME SUGGESTION THEY WERE TRYING TO ESCAPE A TIDAL CURRENT.
AUDIO RECORDERS AT NEARBY SEAWORLD PICKED UP THIS UNUSUAL WHALE SONG, WHICH COULD BE HEARD CLEARLY FROM SOME TEN OR TWELVE MILES AWAY--
WHUUP WHUUP
WHUUP WHUUP

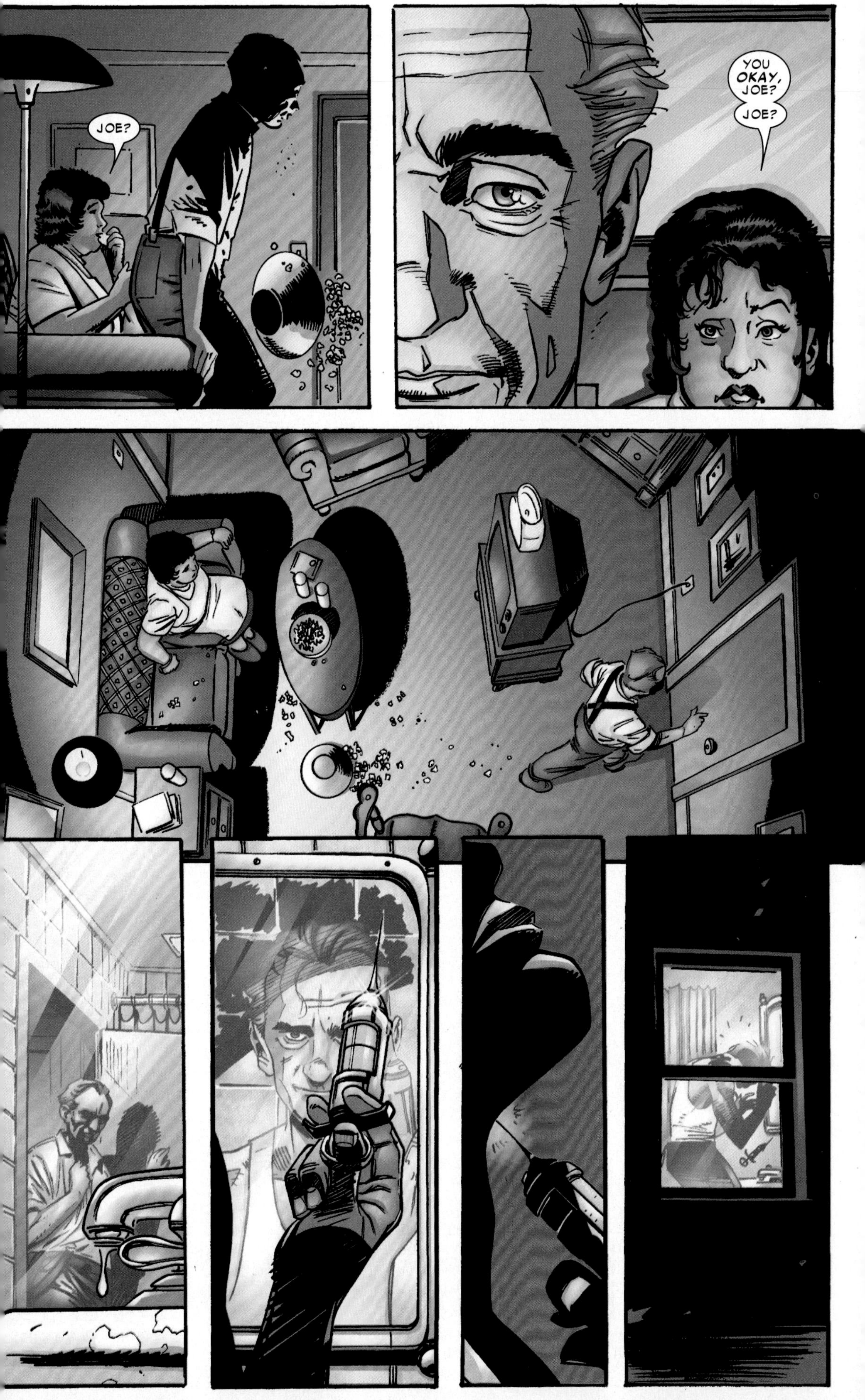
JOE?
YOU OKAY, JOE?
JOE?

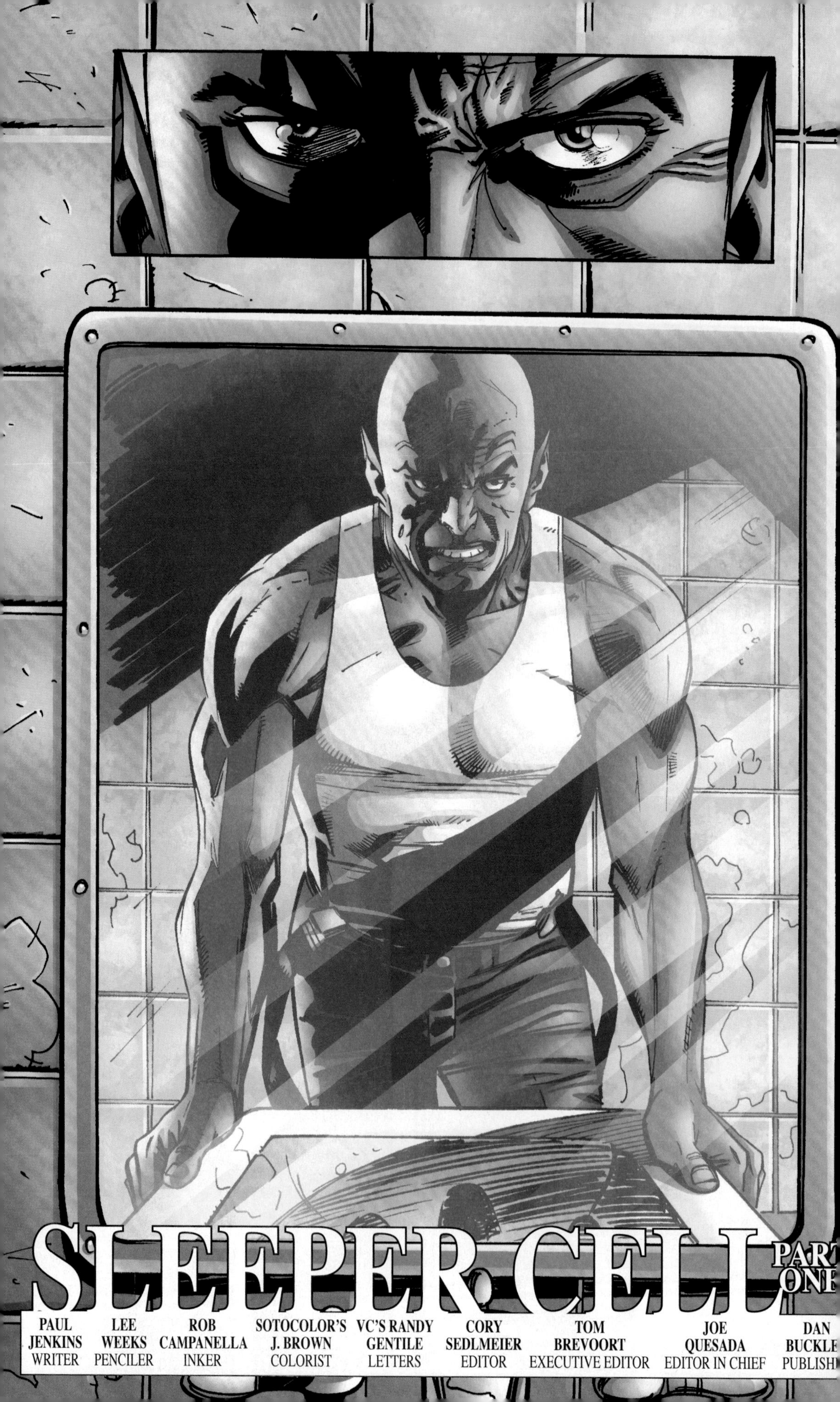
SLEEPER CELL PART ONE
PAUL JENKINS WRITER
LEE WEEKS PENCILER
ROB CAMPANELLA INKER
SOTOCOLOR'S J. BROWN COLORIST
VC'S RANDY GENTILE LETTERS
CORY SEDLMEIER EDITOR
TOM BREVOORT EXECUTIVE EDITOR
JOE QUESADA EDITOR IN CHIEF

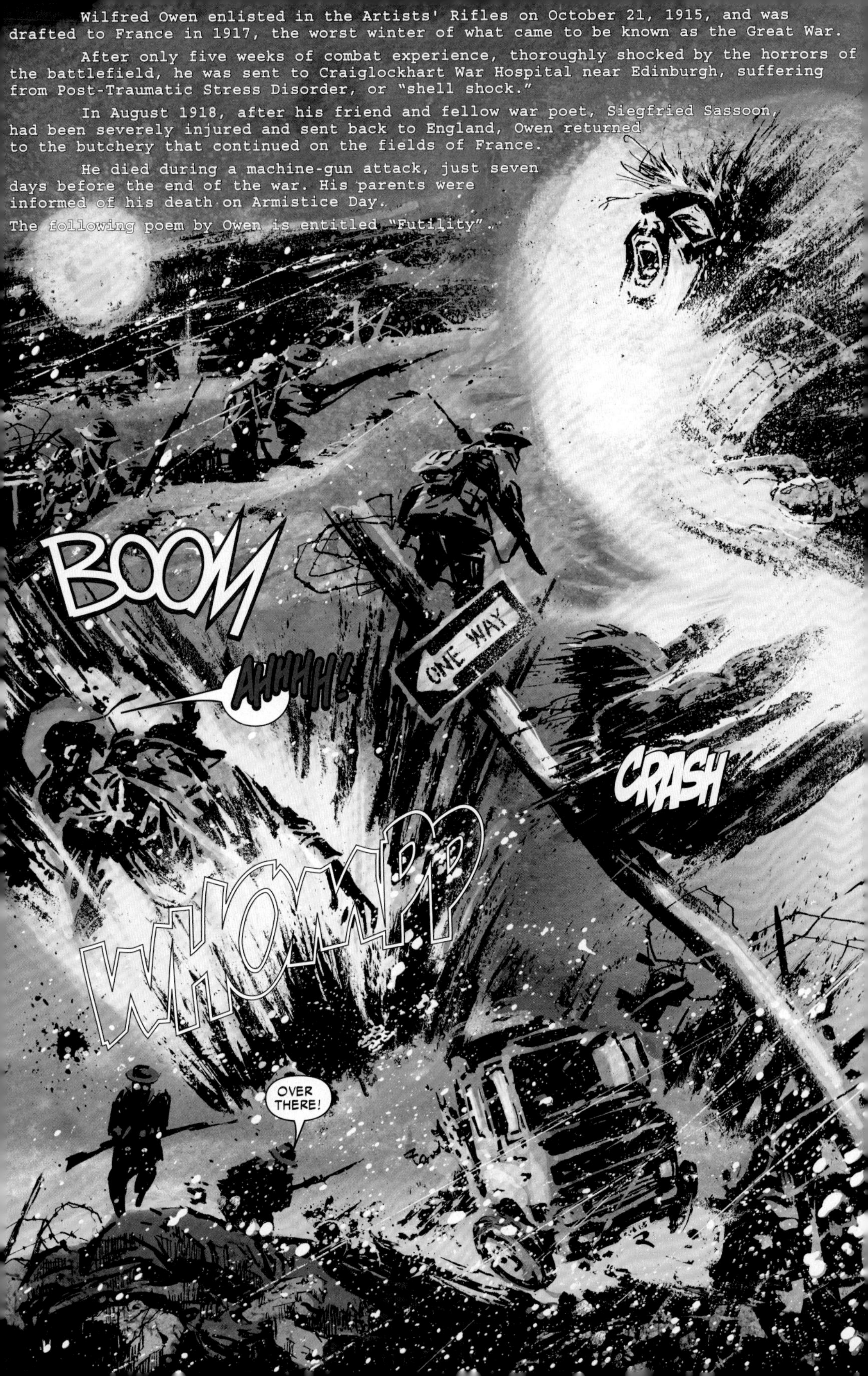
Wilfred Owen enlisted in the Artists' Rifles on October 21, 1915, and was drafted to France in 1917, the worst winter of what came to be known as the Great War.
After only five weeks of combat experience, thoroughly shocked by the horrors of the battlefield, he was sent to Craiglockhart War Hospital near Edinburgh, suffering from Post-Traumatic Stress Disorder, or "shell shock."
In August 1918, after his friend and fellow war poet, Siegfried Sassoon, had been severely injured and sent back to England, Owen returned to the butchery that continued on the fields of France.
He died during a machine-gun attack, just seven days before the end of the war. His parents were informed of his death on Armistice Day.
The following poem by Owen is entitled "Futility".
BOOM
AHHHH!
ONE WAY
CRASH
WHOMPP
OVER THERE!

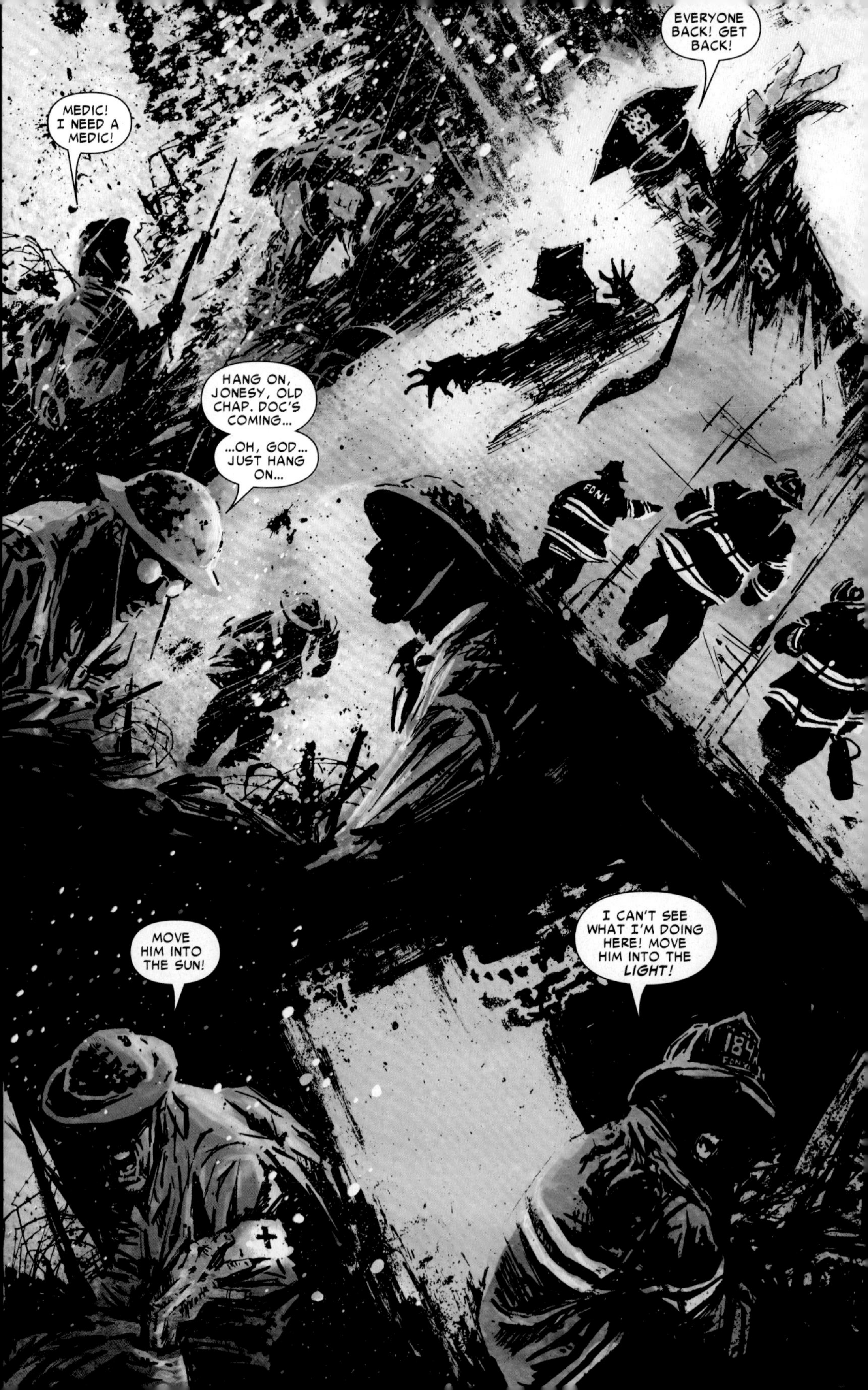
MEDIC! I NEED A MEDIC!
EVERYONE BACK! GET BACK!
HANG ON, JONESY, OLD CHAP. DOC'S COMING...
...OH, GOD... JUST HANG ON...
FDNY
MOVE HIM INTO THE SUN!
I CAN'T SEE WHAT I'M DOING HERE! MOVE HIM INTO THE *LIGHT!*
184
FDNY

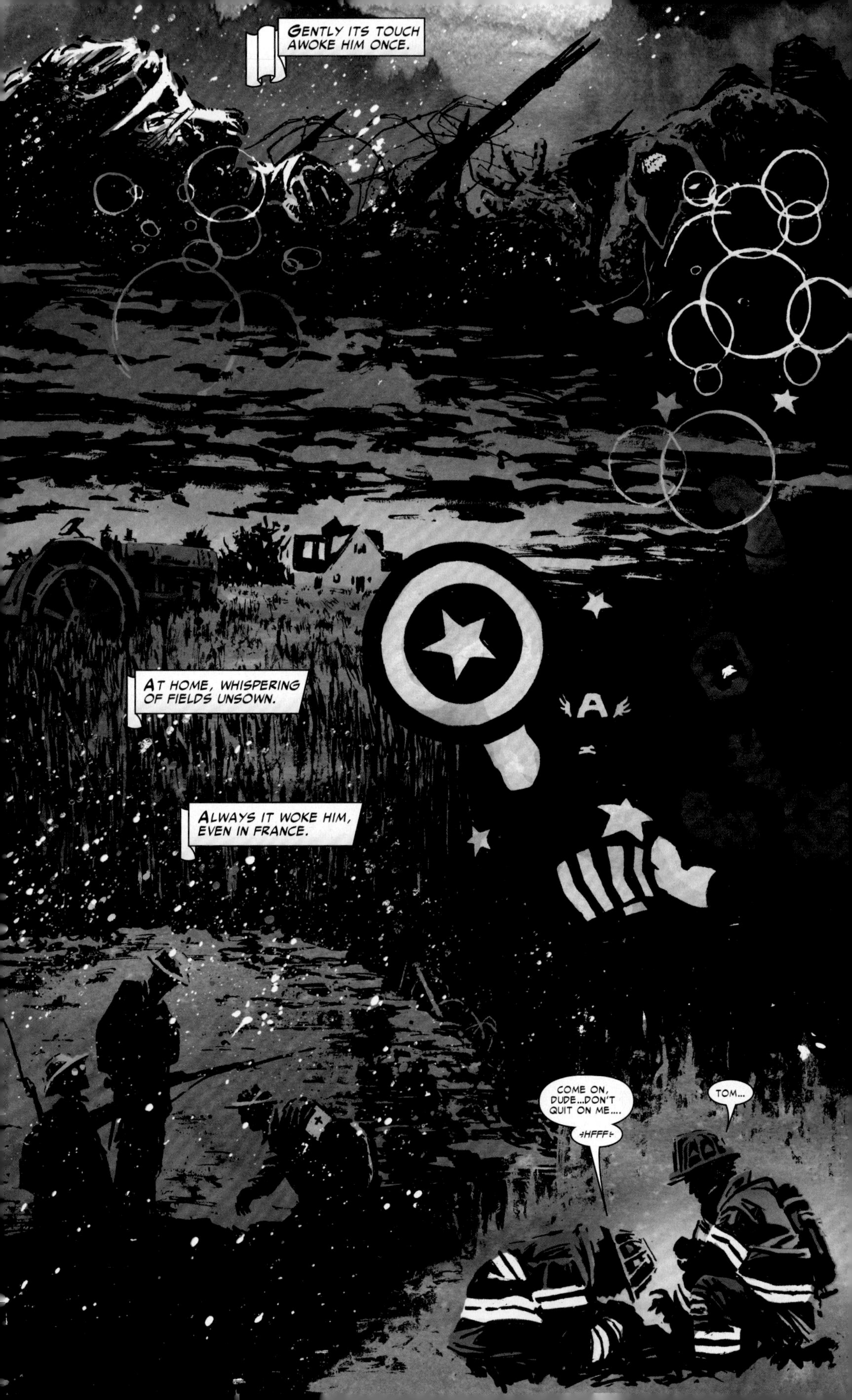
GENTLY ITS TOUCH AWOKE HIM ONCE.
AT HOME, WHISPERING OF FIELDS UNSOWN.
ALWAYS IT WOKE HIM, EVEN IN FRANCE.
COME ON, DUDE...DON'T QUIT ON ME....
HFFF
TOM...

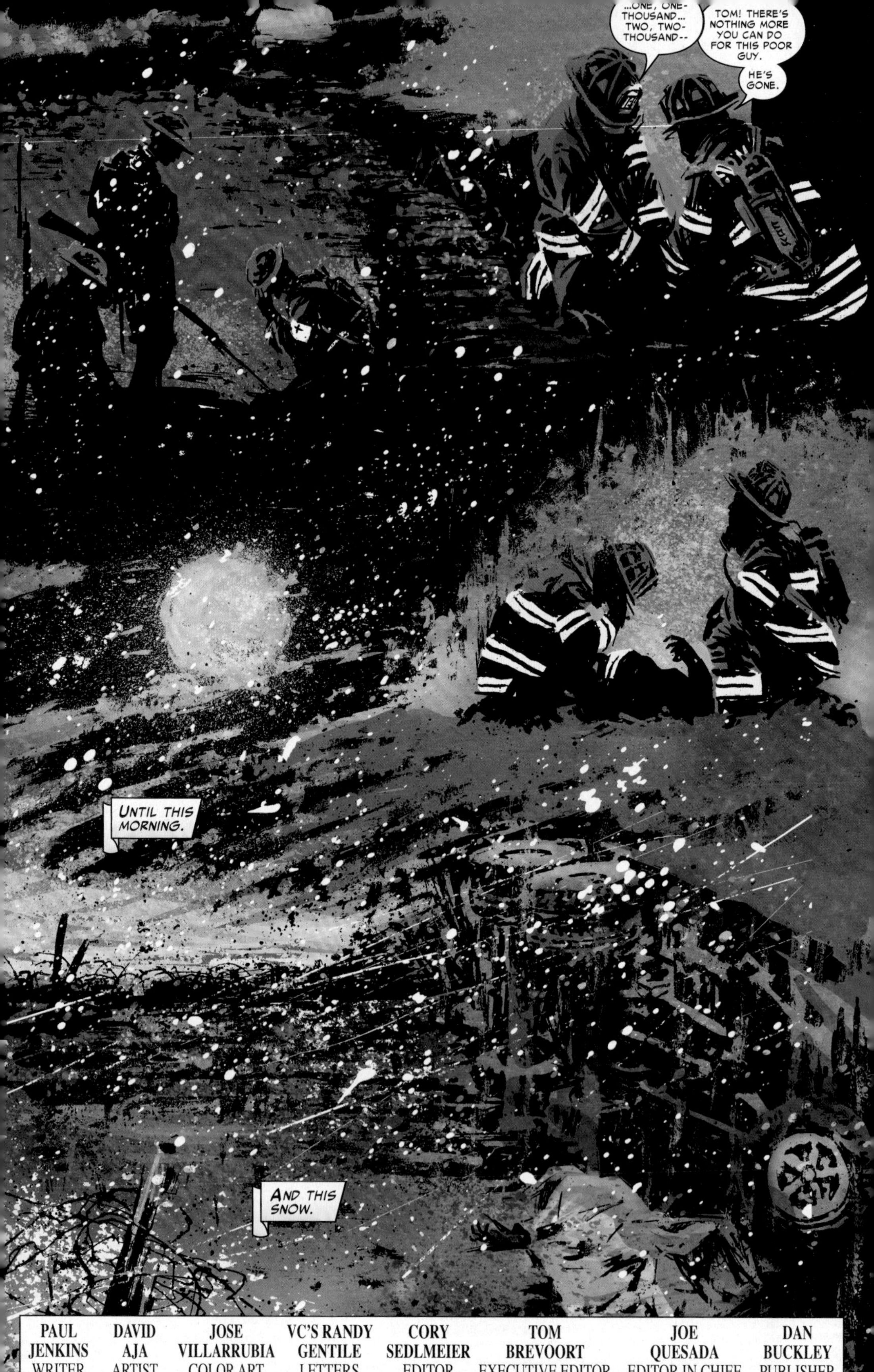
...ONE, ONE-THOUSAND... TWO, TWO-THOUSAND--
TOM! THERE'S NOTHING MORE YOU CAN DO FOR THIS POOR GUY.
HE'S GONE.
UNTIL THIS MORNING.
AND THIS SNOW.

PAUL JENKINS WRITER	DAVID AJA ARTIST	JOSE VILLARRUBIA COLOR ART	VC'S RANDY GENTILE LETTERS	CORY SEDLMEIER EDITOR	TOM BREVOORT EXECUTIVE EDITOR	JOE QUESADA EDITOR IN CHIEF	DAN BUCKLEY PUBLISHER

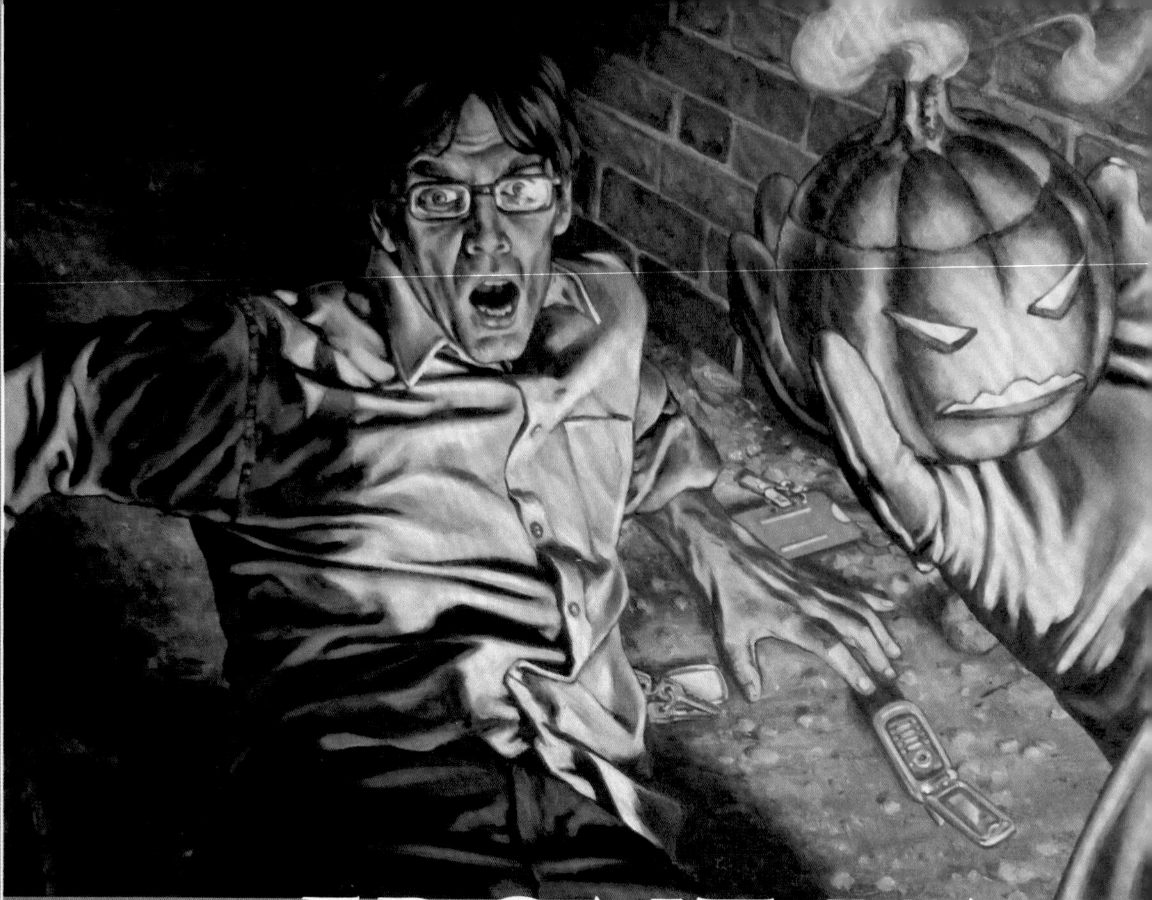

FRONT LINE
A MARVEL COMICS EVENT

CIVIL WAR

CIVIL WAR: FRONT LINE #4

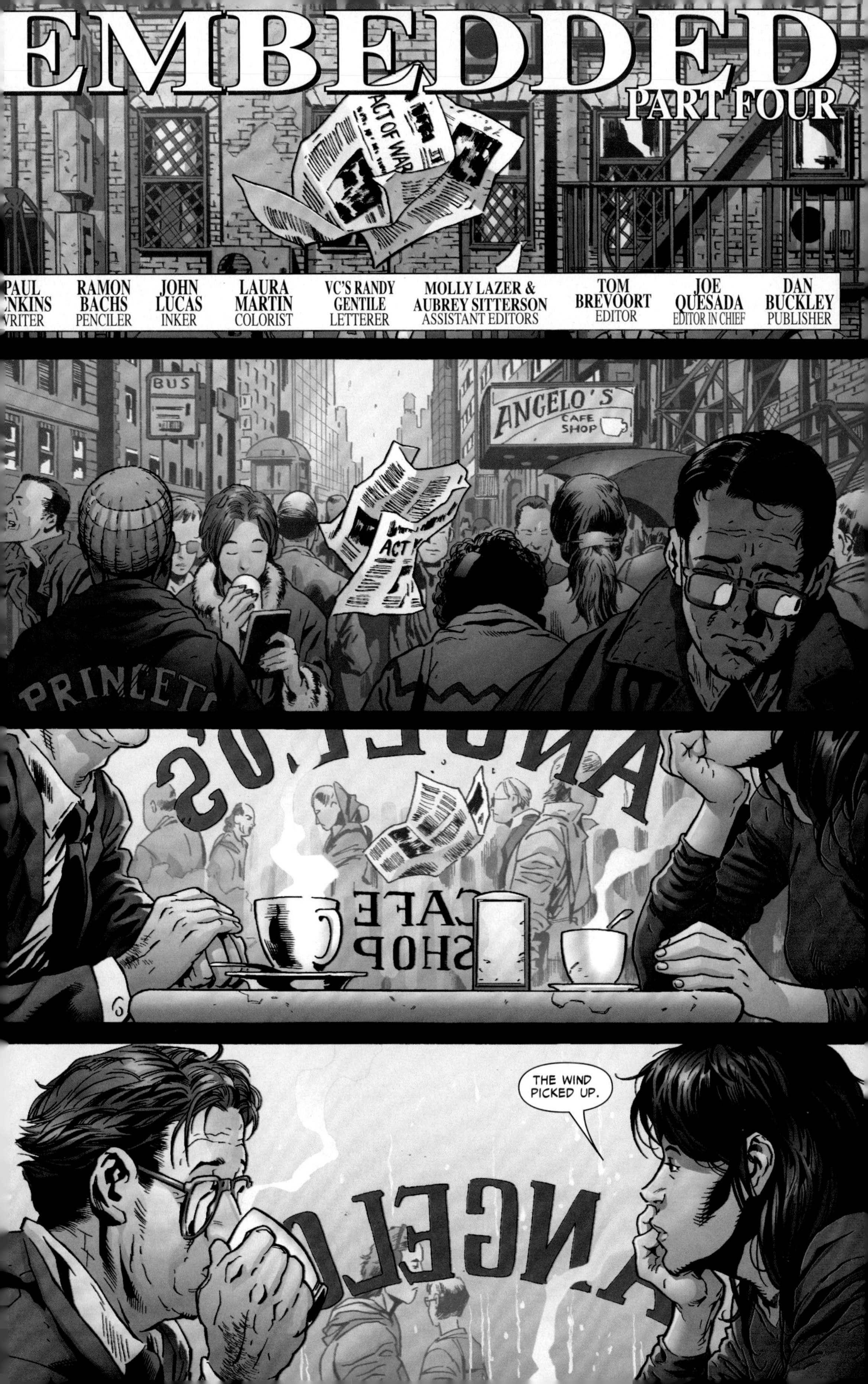
EMBEDDED
PART FOUR
ACT OF WAR
PAUL
RAMON BACHS PENCILER
JOHN LUCAS INKER
LAURA MARTIN COLORIST
VC'S RANDY GENTILE LETTERER
MOLLY LAZER & AUBREY SITTERSON ASSISTANT EDITORS
TOM BREVOORT EDITOR
JOE QUESADA EDITOR IN CHIEF
DAN BUCKLEY PUBLISHER
BUS
ANGELO'S CAFE SHOP
ACT
THE WIND PICKED UP.

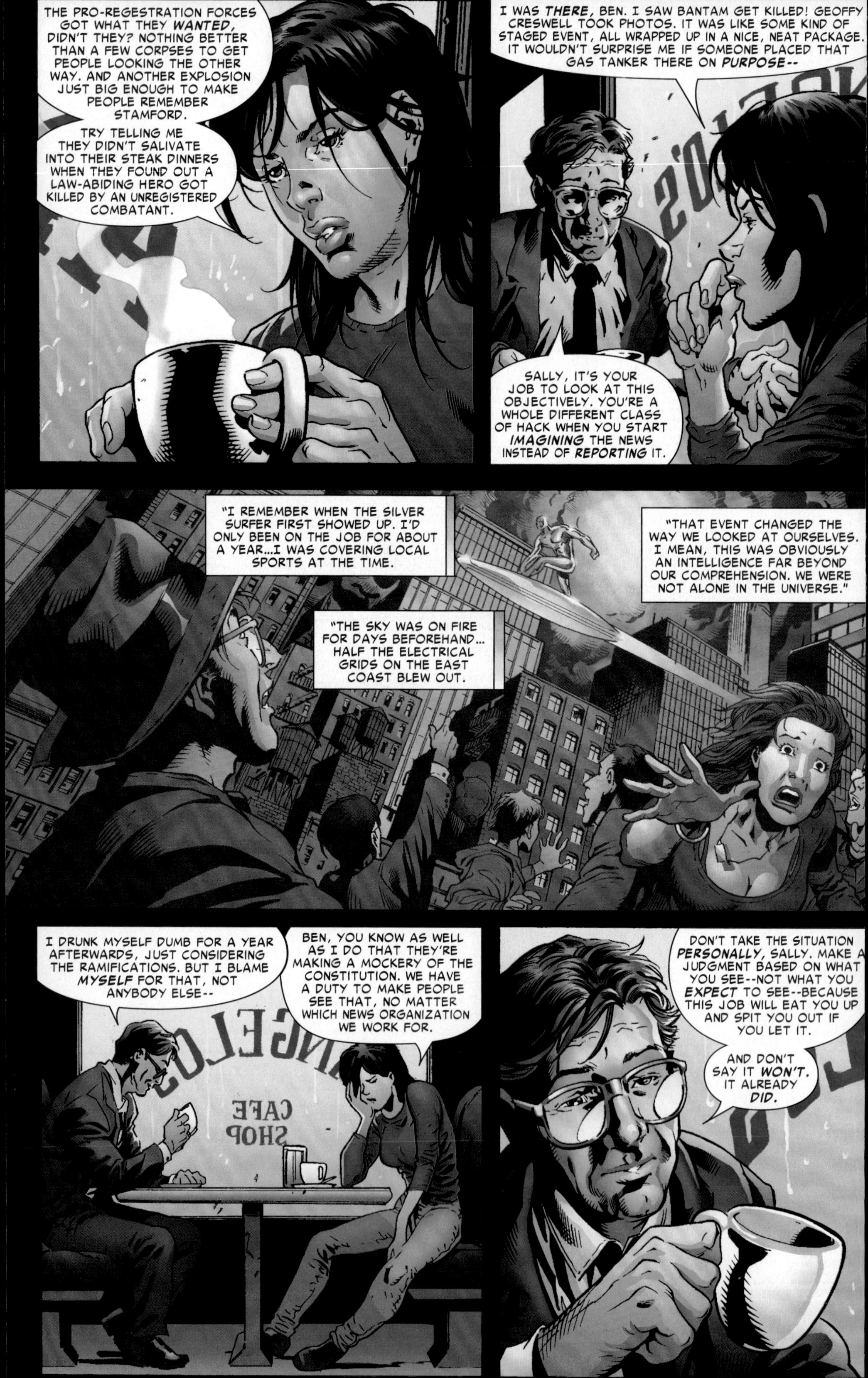
THE PRO-REGESTRATION FORCES GOT WHAT THEY *WANTED*, DIDN'T THEY? NOTHING BETTER THAN A FEW CORPSES TO GET PEOPLE LOOKING THE OTHER WAY. AND ANOTHER EXPLOSION JUST BIG ENOUGH TO MAKE PEOPLE REMEMBER STAMFORD.
TRY TELLING ME THEY DIDN'T SALIVATE INTO THEIR STEAK DINNERS WHEN THEY FOUND OUT A LAW-ABIDING HERO GOT KILLED BY AN UNREGISTERED COMBATANT.
I WAS *THERE*, BEN. I SAW BANTAM GET KILLED! GEOFFY CRESWELL TOOK PHOTOS. IT WAS LIKE SOME KIND OF STAGED EVENT, ALL WRAPPED UP IN A NICE, NEAT PACKAGE. IT WOULDN'T SURPRISE ME IF SOMEONE PLACED THAT GAS TANKER THERE ON *PURPOSE*--
SALLY, IT'S YOUR JOB TO LOOK AT THIS OBJECTIVELY. YOU'RE A WHOLE DIFFERENT CLASS OF HACK WHEN YOU START *IMAGINING* THE NEWS INSTEAD OF *REPORTING* IT.
"I REMEMBER WHEN THE SILVER SURFER FIRST SHOWED UP. I'D ONLY BEEN ON THE JOB FOR ABOUT A YEAR...I WAS COVERING LOCAL SPORTS AT THE TIME.
"THE SKY WAS ON FIRE FOR DAYS BEFOREHAND... HALF THE ELECTRICAL GRIDS ON THE EAST COAST BLEW OUT.
"THAT EVENT CHANGED THE WAY WE LOOKED AT OURSELVES. I MEAN, THIS WAS OBVIOUSLY AN INTELLIGENCE FAR BEYOND OUR COMPREHENSION. WE WERE NOT ALONE IN THE UNIVERSE."
I DRUNK MYSELF DUMB FOR A YEAR AFTERWARDS, JUST CONSIDERING THE RAMIFICATIONS. BUT I BLAME *MYSELF* FOR THAT, NOT ANYBODY ELSE--
BEN, YOU KNOW AS WELL AS I DO THAT THEY'RE MAKING A MOCKERY OF THE CONSTITUTION. WE HAVE A DUTY TO MAKE PEOPLE SEE THAT, NO MATTER WHICH NEWS ORGANIZATION WE WORK FOR.
CAFE
SHOP
DON'T TAKE THE SITUATION *PERSONALLY*, SALLY. MAKE A JUDGMENT BASED ON WHAT YOU SEE--NOT WHAT YOU *EXPECT* TO SEE--BECAUSE THIS JOB WILL EAT YOU UP AND SPIT YOU OUT IF YOU LET IT.
AND DON'T SAY IT *WON'T*. IT ALREADY *DID*.

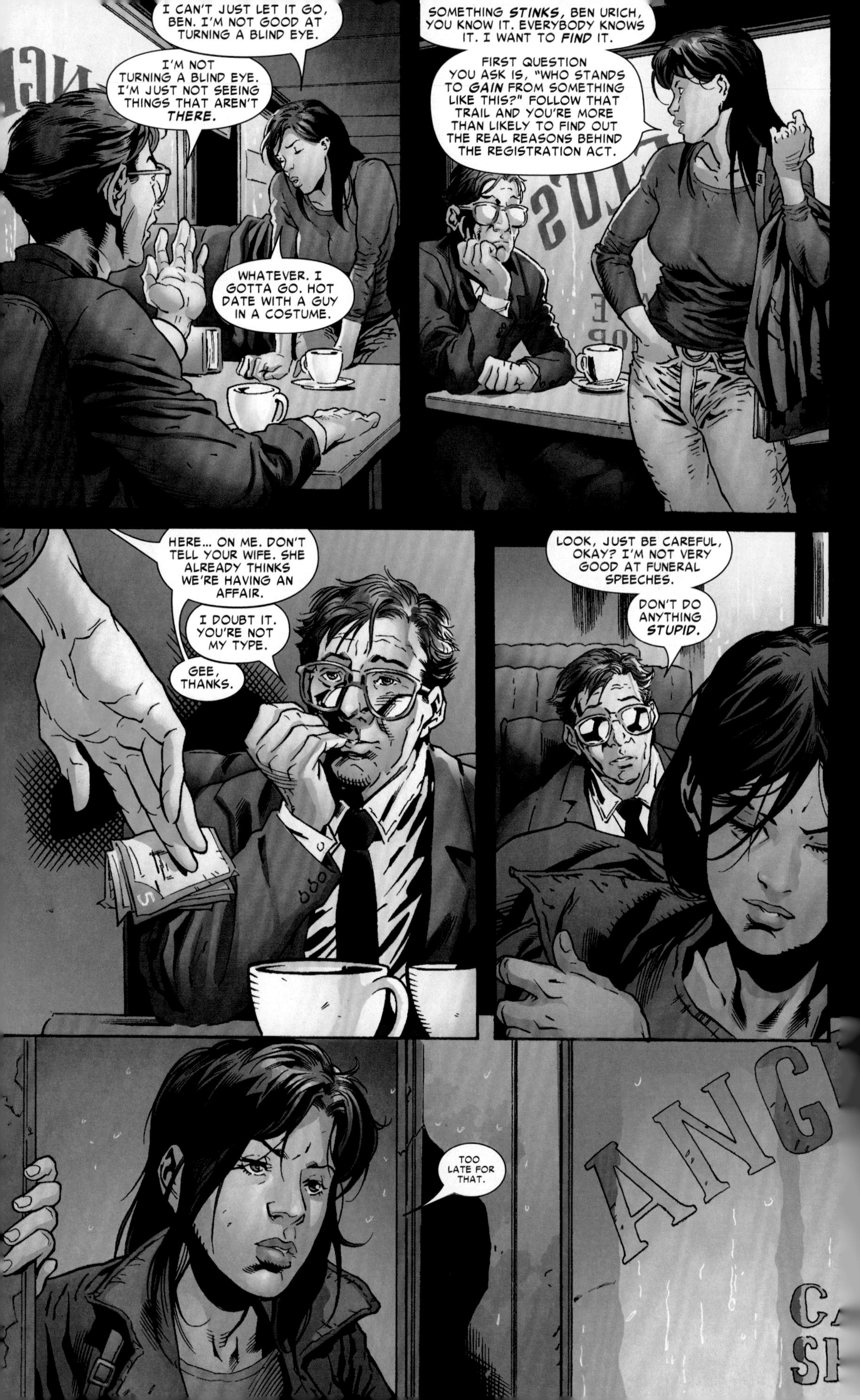
I CAN'T JUST LET IT GO, BEN. I'M NOT GOOD AT TURNING A BLIND EYE.
I'M NOT TURNING A BLIND EYE. I'M JUST NOT SEEING THINGS THAT AREN'T *THERE*.
WHATEVER. I GOTTA GO. HOT DATE WITH A GUY IN A COSTUME.
SOMETHING *STINKS*, BEN URICH, YOU KNOW IT. EVERYBODY KNOWS IT. I WANT TO *FIND* IT.
FIRST QUESTION YOU ASK IS, "WHO STANDS TO *GAIN* FROM SOMETHING LIKE THIS?" FOLLOW THAT TRAIL AND YOU'RE MORE THAN LIKELY TO FIND OUT THE REAL REASONS BEHIND THE REGISTRATION ACT.
HERE... ON ME. DON'T TELL YOUR WIFE. SHE ALREADY THINKS WE'RE HAVING AN AFFAIR.
I DOUBT IT. YOU'RE NOT MY TYPE.
GEE, THANKS.
LOOK, JUST BE CAREFUL, OKAY? I'M NOT VERY GOOD AT FUNERAL SPEECHES.
DON'T DO ANYTHING *STUPID*.
TOO LATE FOR THAT.

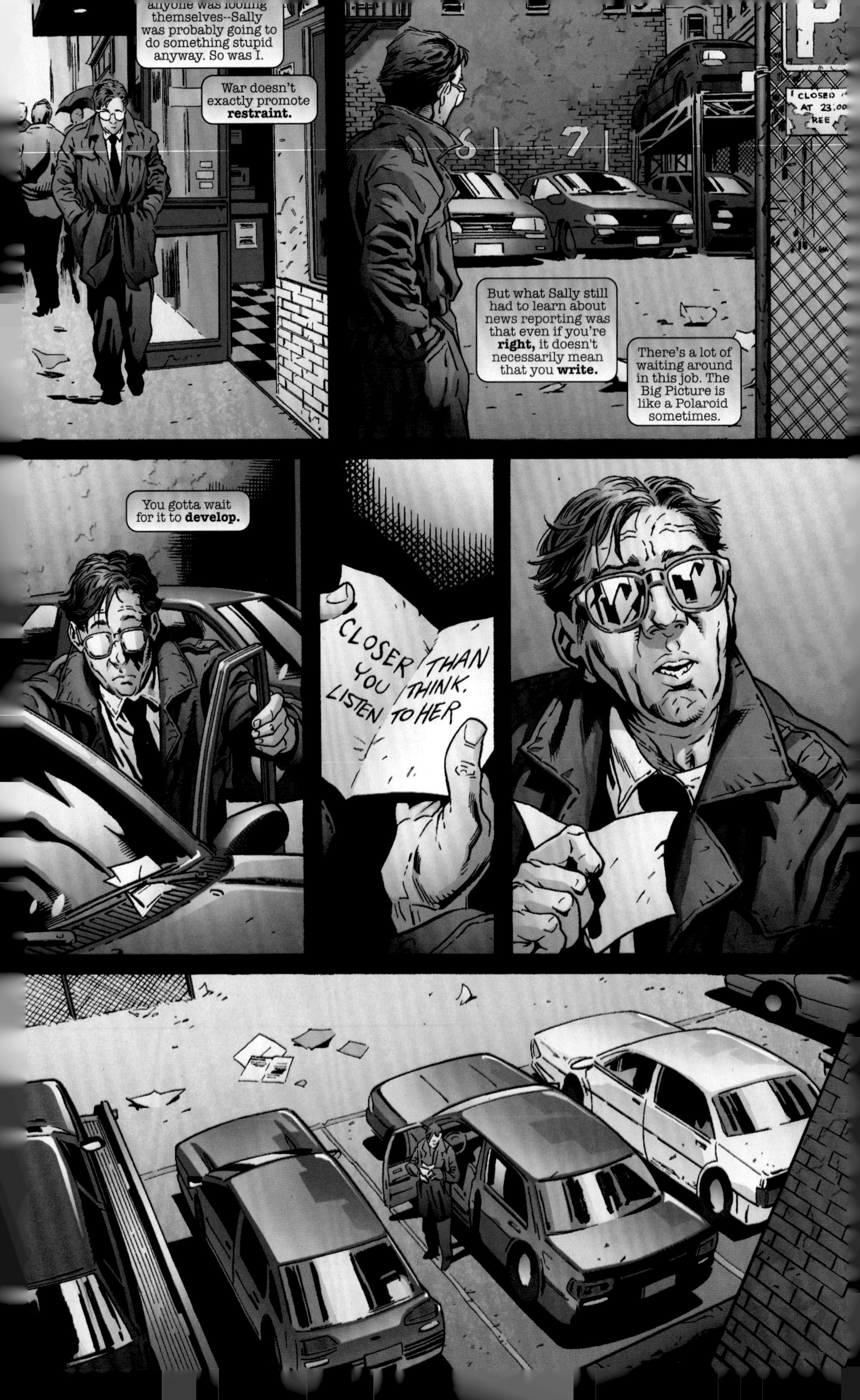
anyone was fooling themselves--Sally was probably going to do something stupid anyway. So was I.
War doesn't exactly promote **restraint.**
CLOSED AT 23:00
But what Sally still had to learn about news reporting was that even if you're **right,** it doesn't necessarily mean that you **write.**
There's a lot of waiting around in this job. The Big Picture is like a Polaroid sometimes.
You gotta wait for it to **develop.**
CLOSER THAN YOU THINK. LISTEN TO HER

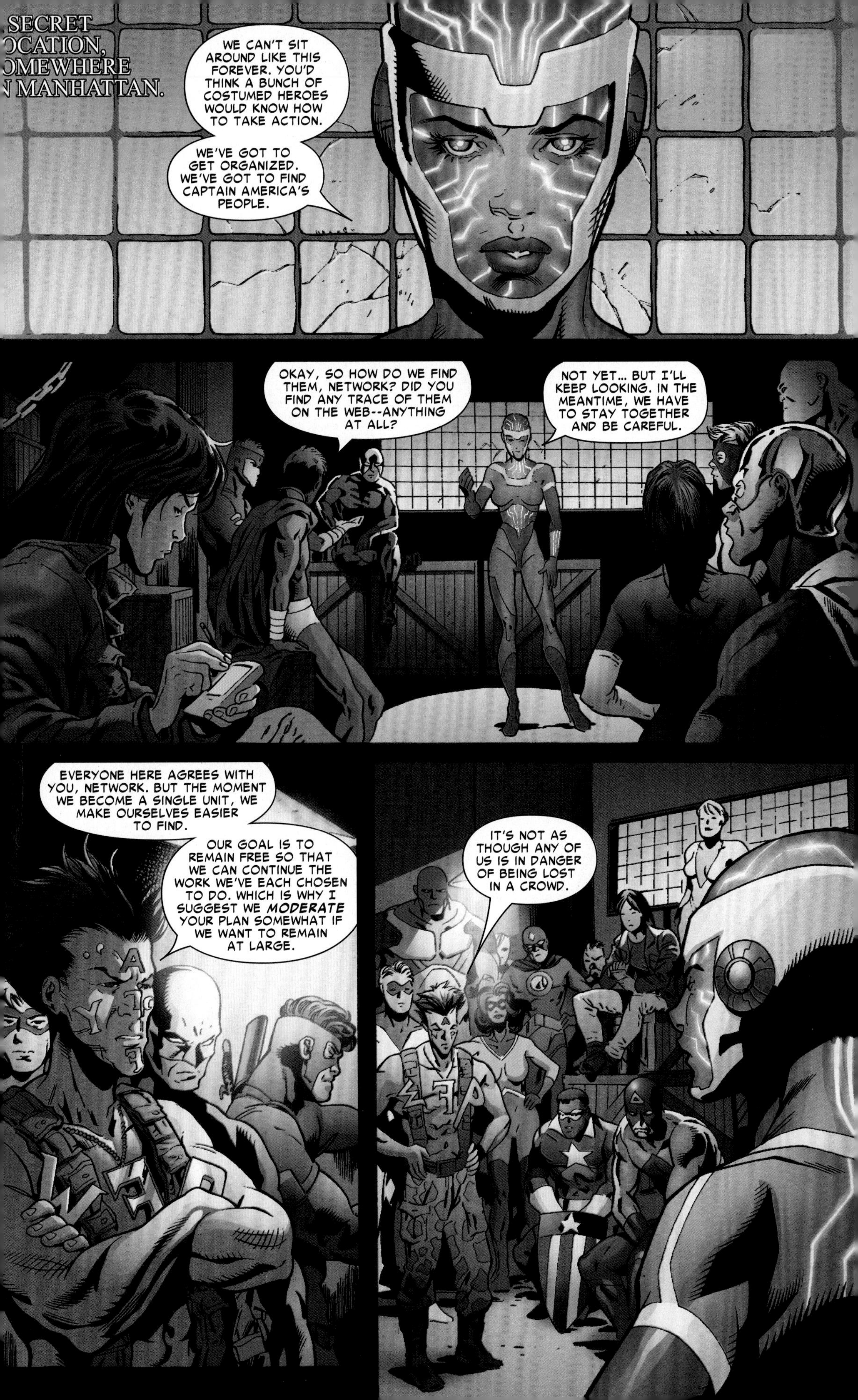
SECRET
OCATION,
OMEWHERE
N MANHATTAN.
WE CAN'T SIT AROUND LIKE THIS FOREVER. YOU'D THINK A BUNCH OF COSTUMED HEROES WOULD KNOW HOW TO TAKE ACTION.
WE'VE GOT TO GET ORGANIZED. WE'VE GOT TO FIND CAPTAIN AMERICA'S PEOPLE.
OKAY, SO HOW DO WE FIND THEM, NETWORK? DID YOU FIND ANY TRACE OF THEM ON THE WEB--ANYTHING AT ALL?
NOT YET... BUT I'LL KEEP LOOKING. IN THE MEANTIME, WE HAVE TO STAY TOGETHER AND BE CAREFUL.
EVERYONE HERE AGREES WITH YOU, NETWORK. BUT THE MOMENT WE BECOME A SINGLE UNIT, WE MAKE OURSELVES EASIER TO FIND.
OUR GOAL IS TO REMAIN FREE SO THAT WE CAN CONTINUE THE WORK WE'VE EACH CHOSEN TO DO. WHICH IS WHY I SUGGEST WE *MODERATE* YOUR PLAN SOMEWHAT IF WE WANT TO REMAIN AT LARGE.
IT'S NOT AS THOUGH ANY OF US IS IN DANGER OF BEING LOST IN A CROWD.

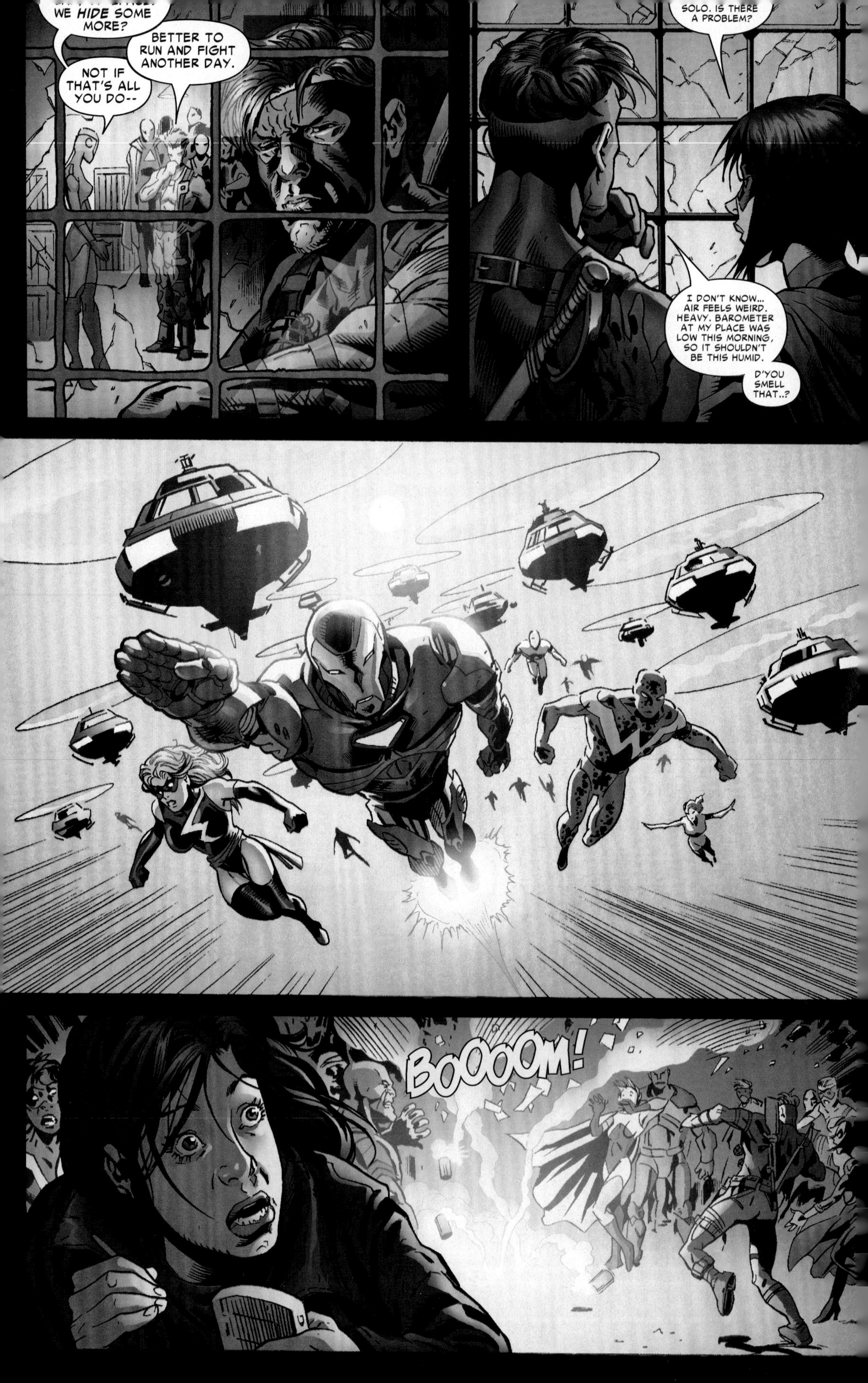
WE *HIDE* SOME MORE?
BETTER TO RUN AND FIGHT ANOTHER DAY.
NOT IF THAT'S ALL YOU DO--
SOLO. IS THERE A PROBLEM?
I DON'T KNOW... AIR FEELS WEIRD. HEAVY. BAROMETER AT MY PLACE WAS LOW THIS MORNING, SO IT SHOULDN'T BE THIS HUMID.
D'YOU SMELL THAT..?
BOOOOM!

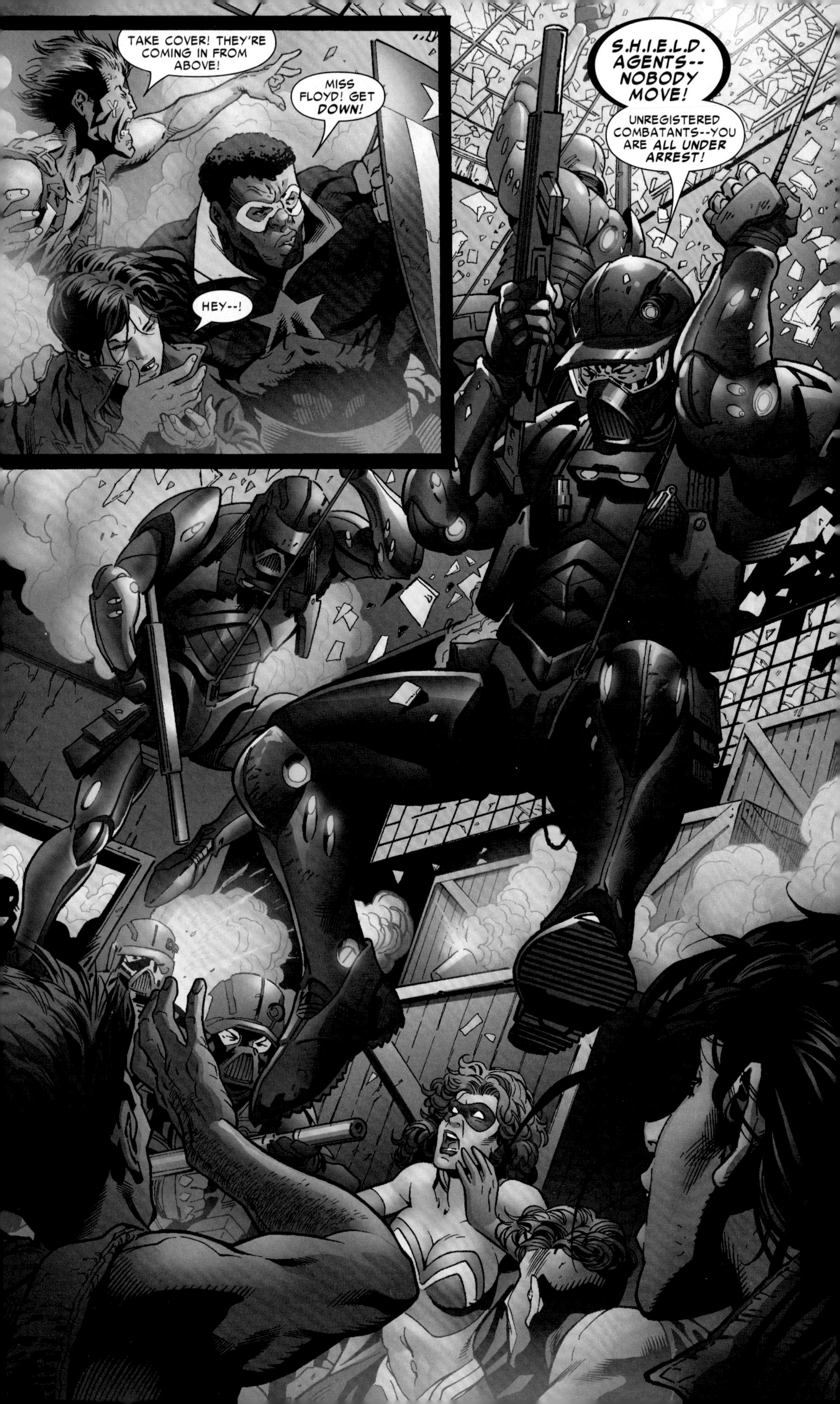
TAKE COVER! THEY'RE COMING IN FROM ABOVE!
MISS FLOYD! GET DOWN!
HEY--!
S.H.I.E.L.D. AGENTS-- NOBODY MOVE!
UNREGISTERED COMBATANTS--YOU ARE ALL UNDER ARREST!

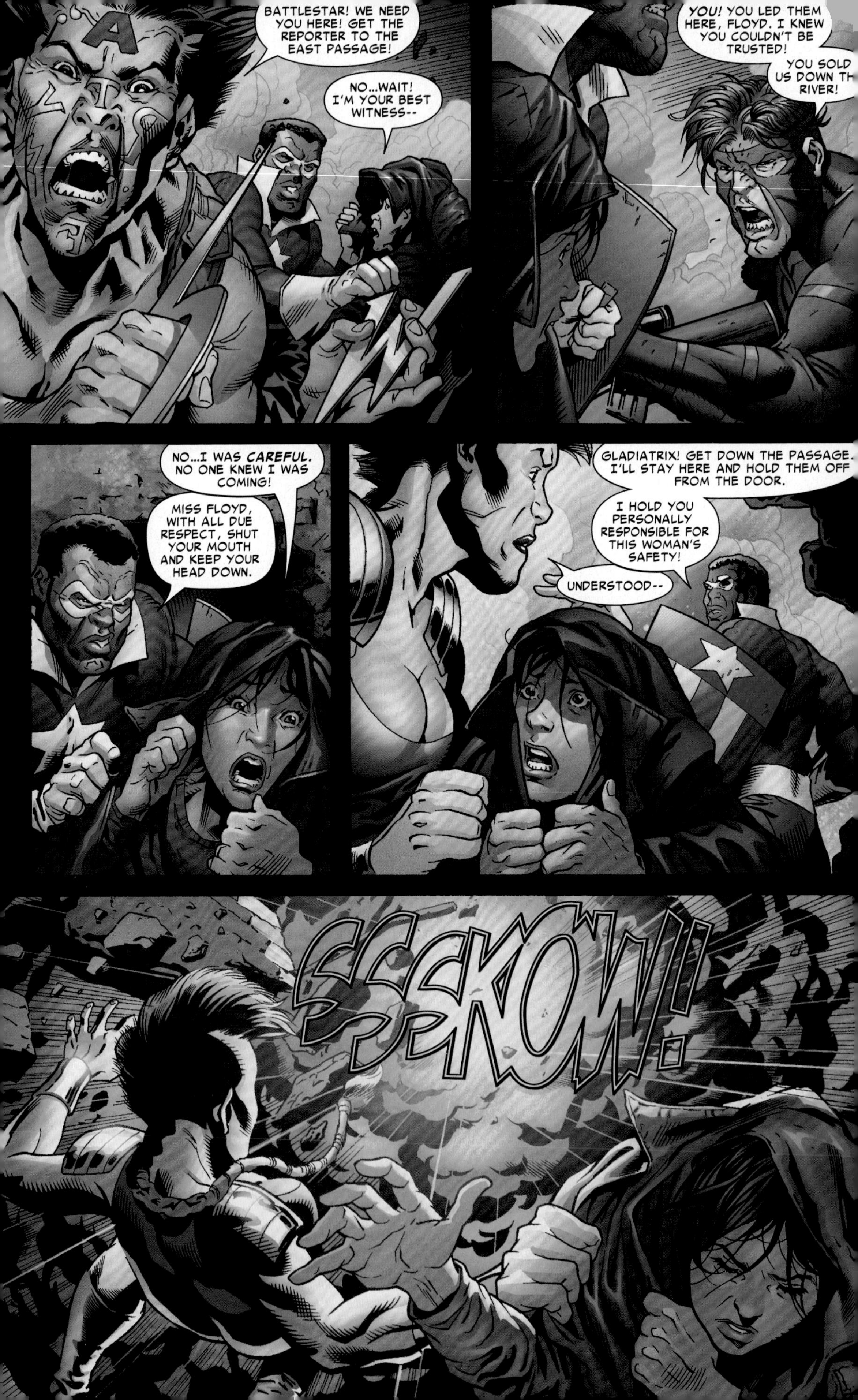

BATTLESTAR! WE NEED YOU HERE! GET THE REPORTER TO THE EAST PASSAGE!
NO...WAIT! I'M YOUR BEST WITNESS--
YOU! YOU LED THEM HERE, FLOYD. I KNEW YOU COULDN'T BE TRUSTED!
YOU SOLD US DOWN THE RIVER!
NO...I WAS CAREFUL. NO ONE KNEW I WAS COMING!
MISS FLOYD, WITH ALL DUE RESPECT, SHUT YOUR MOUTH AND KEEP YOUR HEAD DOWN.
GLADIATRIX! GET DOWN THE PASSAGE. I'LL STAY HERE AND HOLD THEM OFF FROM THE DOOR.
I HOLD YOU PERSONALLY RESPONSIBLE FOR THIS WOMAN'S SAFETY!
UNDERSTOOD--
SSSKOW!! SSPANOW!!

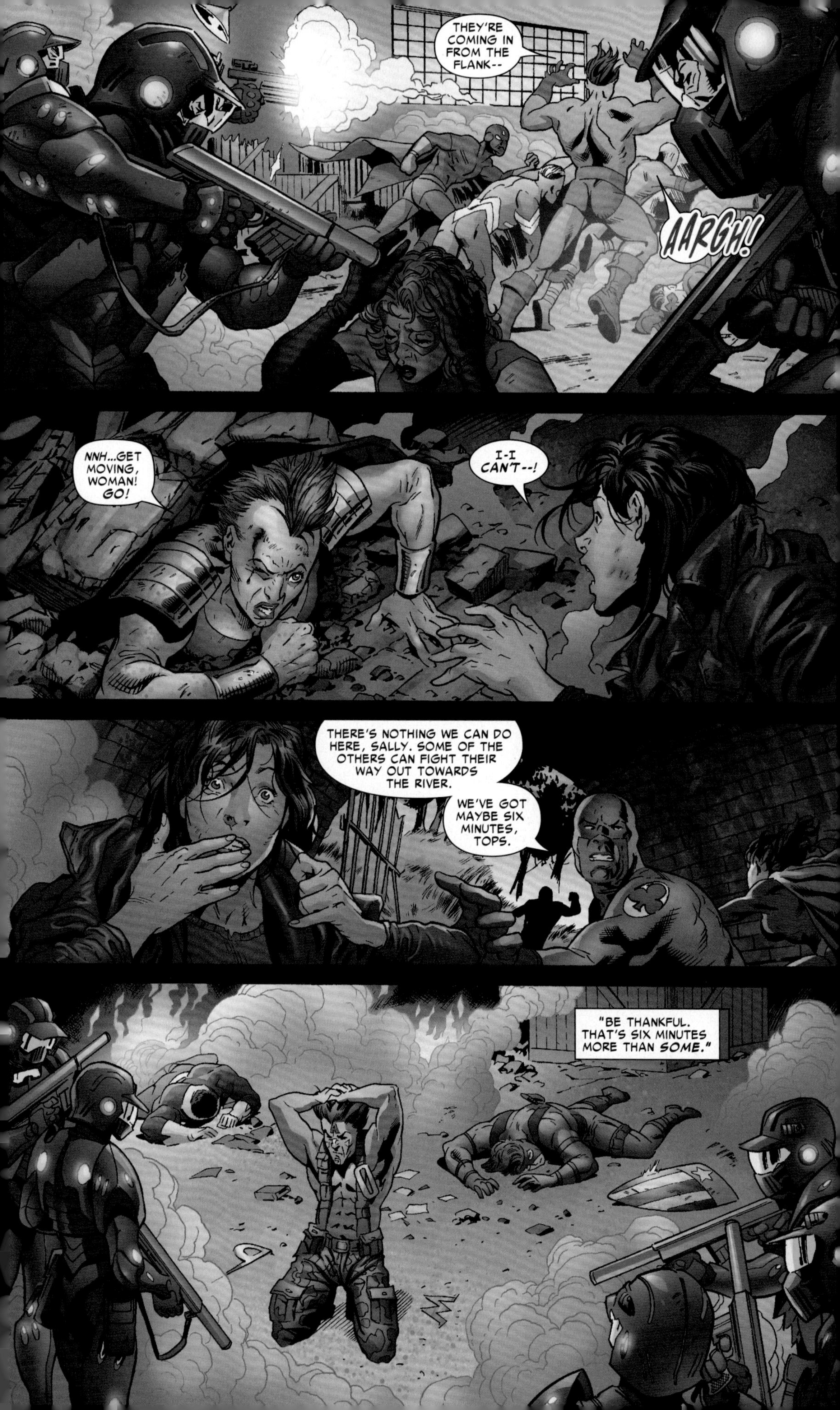
THEY'RE COMING IN FROM THE FLANK--
AARGH!
NNH...GET MOVING, WOMAN! GO!
I-I CAN'T--!
THERE'S NOTHING WE CAN DO HERE, SALLY. SOME OF THE OTHERS CAN FIGHT THEIR WAY OUT TOWARDS THE RIVER.
WE'VE GOT MAYBE SIX MINUTES, TOPS.
"BE THANKFUL. THAT'S SIX MINUTES MORE THAN SOME."

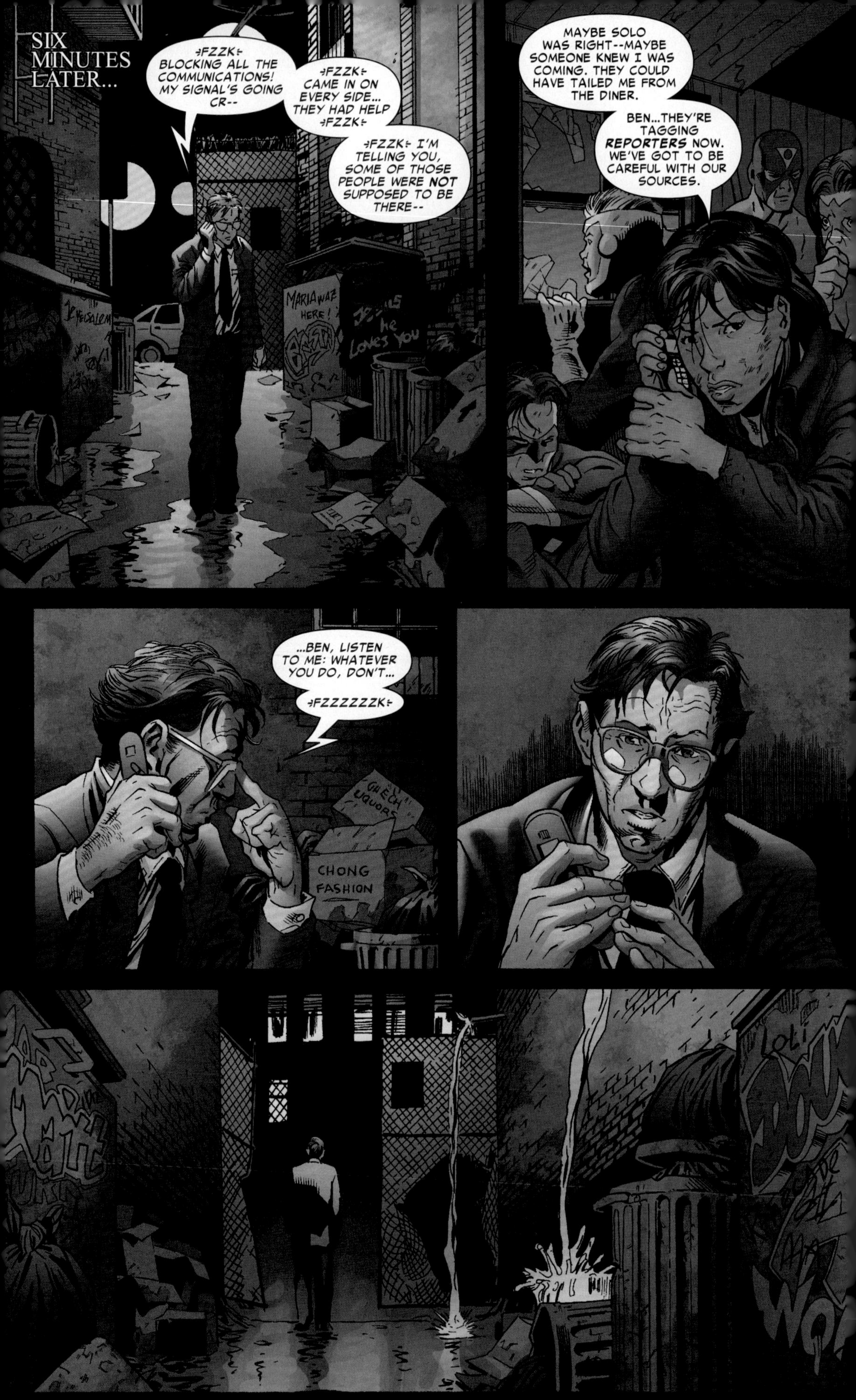
SIX MINUTES LATER...
⊰FZZK⊱ BLOCKING ALL THE COMMUNICATIONS! MY SIGNAL'S GOING CR--
⊰FZZK⊱ CAME IN ON EVERY SIDE... THEY HAD HELP ⊰FZZK⊱
⊰FZZK⊱ I'M TELLING YOU, SOME OF THOSE PEOPLE WERE **NOT** SUPPOSED TO BE THERE--
MARIA WAZ HERE!
JESUS he Loves You
MAYBE SOLO WAS RIGHT--MAYBE SOMEONE KNEW I WAS COMING. THEY COULD HAVE TAILED ME FROM THE DINER.
BEN...THEY'RE TAGGING **REPORTERS** NOW. WE'VE GOT TO BE CAREFUL WITH OUR SOURCES.
...BEN, LISTEN TO ME: WHATEVER YOU DO, DON'T...
⊰FZZZZZZK⊱
CHONG FASHION

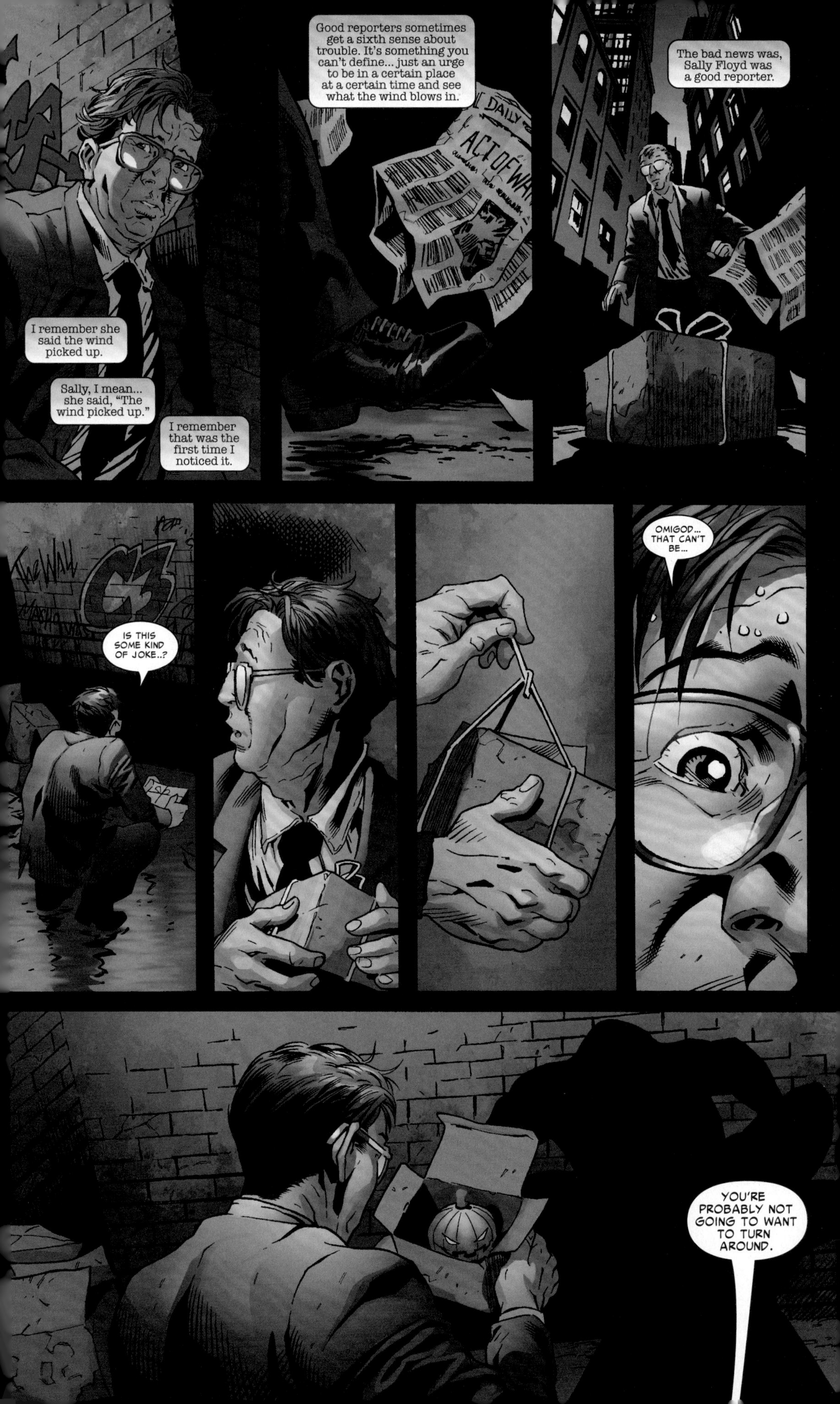
I remember she said the wind picked up.
Sally, I mean... she said, "The wind picked up."
I remember that was the first time I noticed it.
Good reporters sometimes get a sixth sense about trouble. It's something you can't define... just an urge to be in a certain place at a certain time and see what the wind blows in.
DAILY
ACT OF WA
The bad news was, Sally Floyd was a good reporter.
IS THIS SOME KIND OF JOKE..?
OMIGOD... THAT CAN'T BE...
YOU'RE PROBABLY NOT GOING TO WANT TO TURN AROUND.

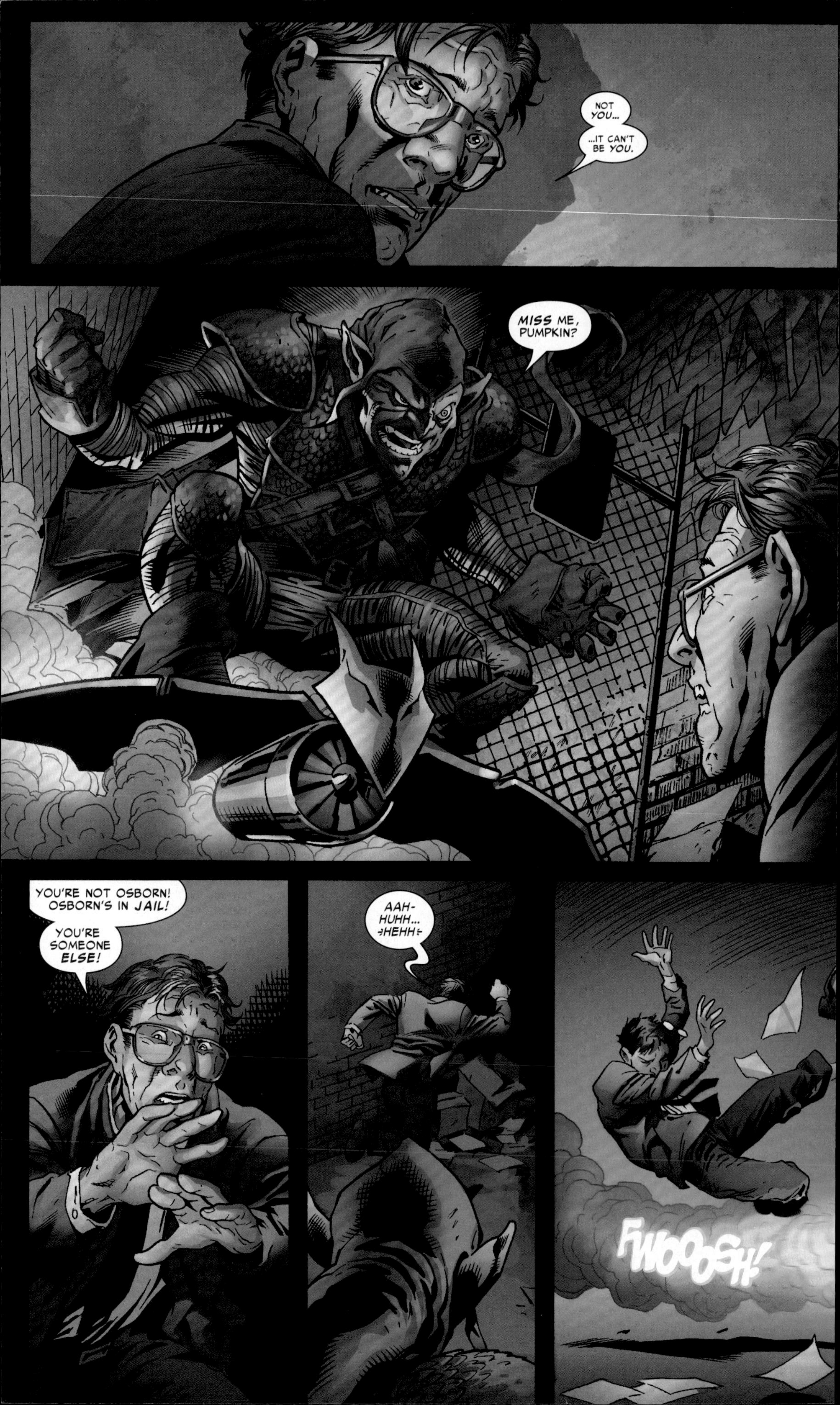
NOT YOU...
...IT CAN'T BE YOU.
MISS ME, PUMPKIN?
YOU'RE NOT OSBORN! OSBORN'S IN JAIL!
YOU'RE SOMEONE ELSE!
AAH-HUHH... HEHH
FWOOOSH!

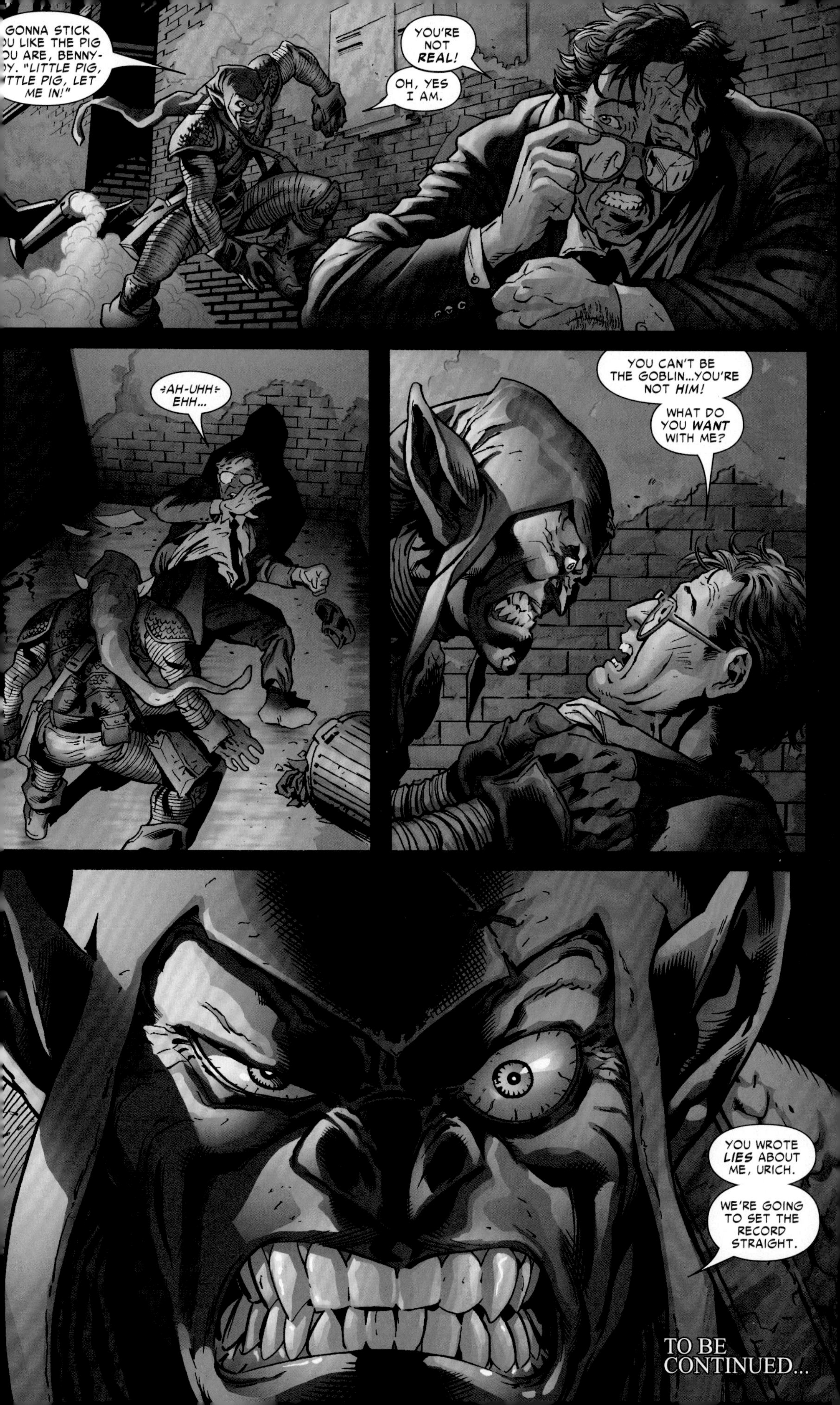

GONNA STICK OU LIKE THE PIG OU ARE, BENNY-OY. "LITTLE PIG, TTLE PIG, LET ME IN!"
YOU'RE NOT REAL!
OH, YES I AM.
=AH-UHH= EHH...
YOU CAN'T BE THE GOBLIN...YOU'RE NOT HIM!
WHAT DO YOU WANT WITH ME?
YOU WROTE LIES ABOUT ME, URICH.
WE'RE GOING TO SET THE RECORD STRAIGHT.
TO BE CONTINUED...

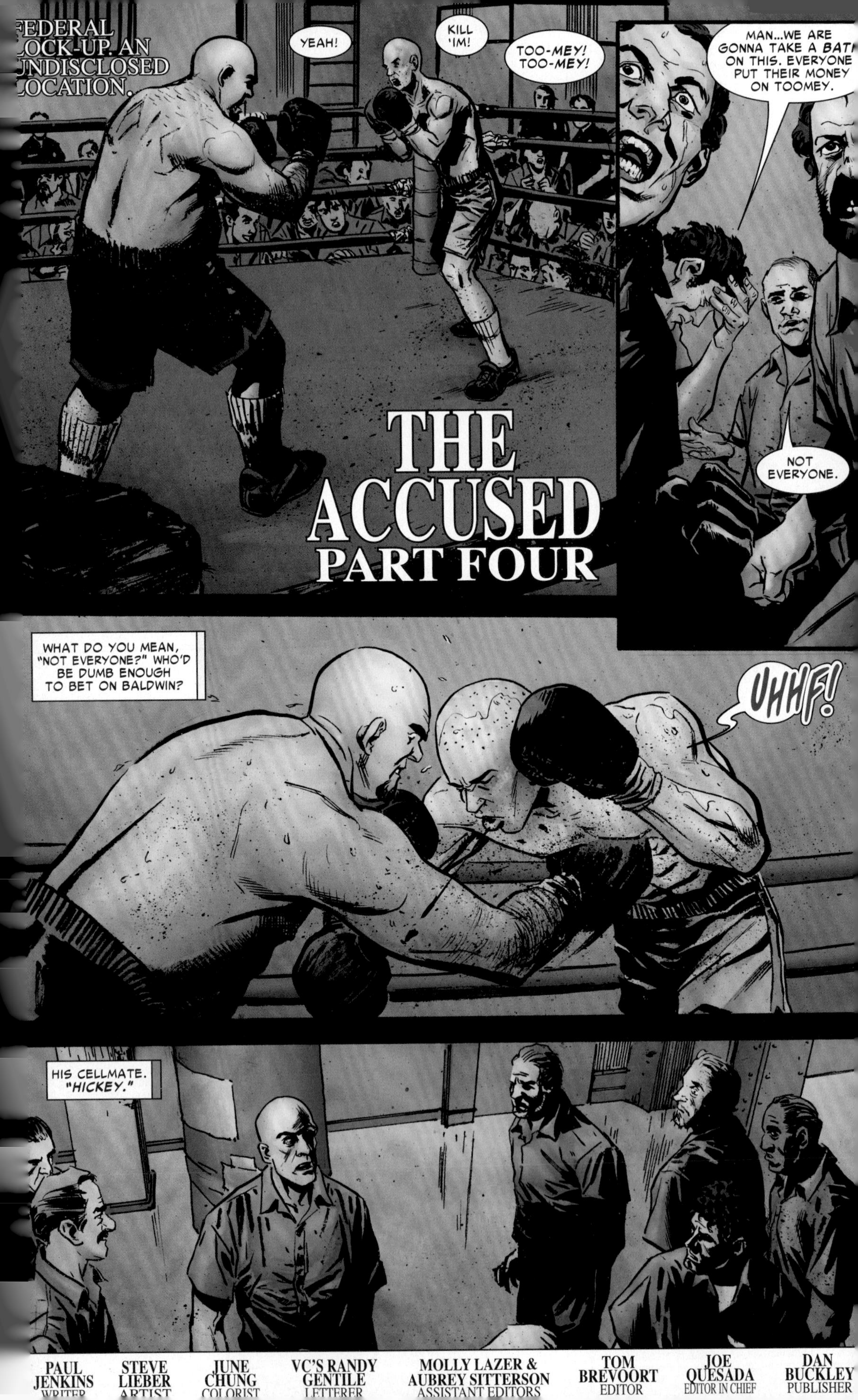
FEDERAL LOCK-UP. AN UNDISCLOSED LOCATION.
YEAH!
KILL 'IM!
TOO-MEY! TOO-MEY!
THE ACCUSED PART FOUR
MAN...WE ARE GONNA TAKE A BAT ON THIS. EVERYONE PUT THEIR MONEY ON TOOMEY.
NOT EVERYONE.
WHAT DO YOU MEAN, "NOT EVERYONE?" WHO'D BE DUMB ENOUGH TO BET ON BALDWIN?
UHHF!
HIS CELLMATE. "HICKEY."
PAUL JENKINS WRITER
STEVE LIEBER ARTIST
JUNE CHUNG COLORIST
VC'S RANDY GENTILE LETTERER
MOLLY LAZER & AUBREY SITTERSON ASSISTANT EDITORS
TOM BREVOORT EDITOR
JOE QUESADA EDITOR IN CHIEF
DAN BUCKLEY PUBLISHER

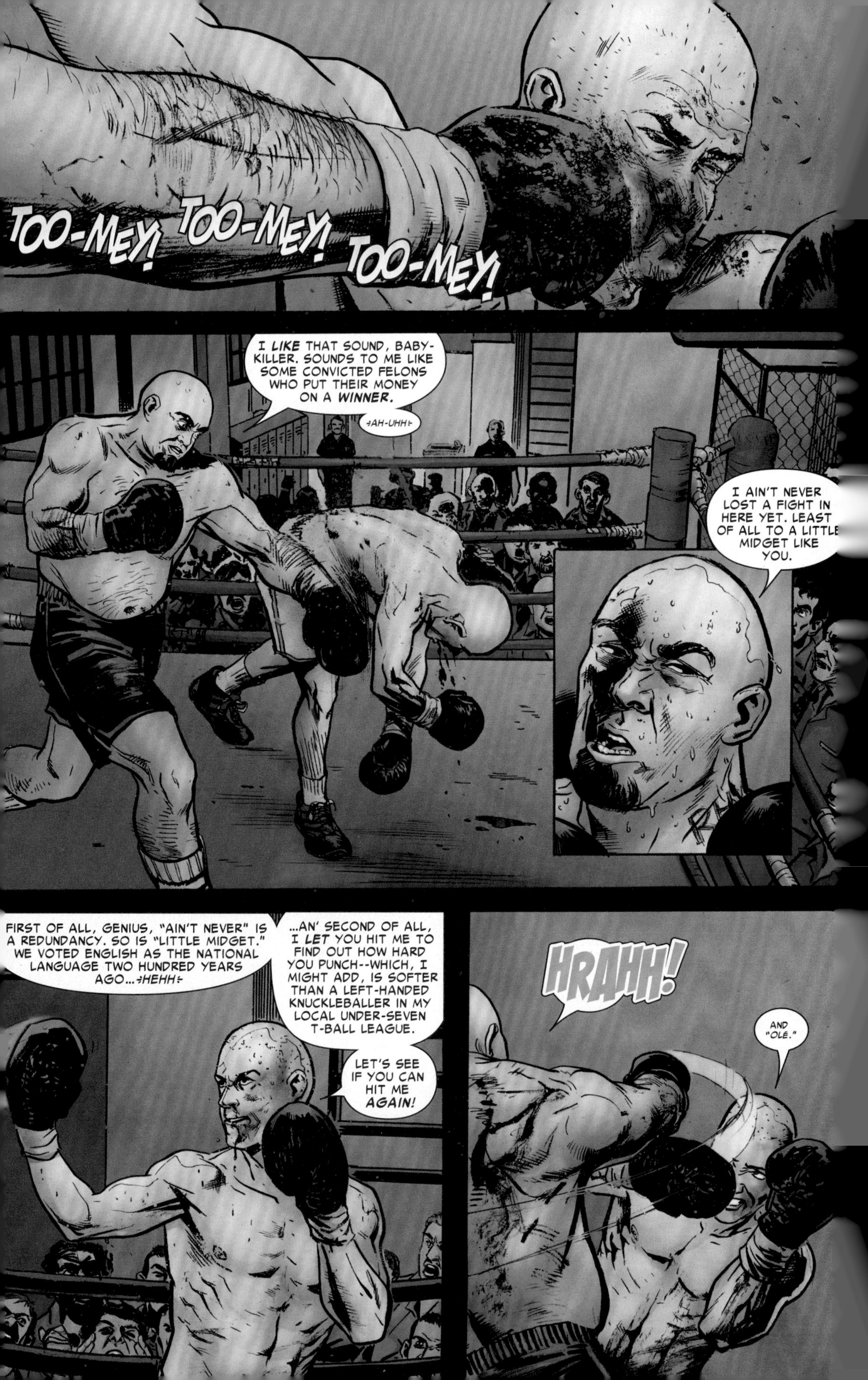
TOO-MEY! TOO-MEY! TOO-MEY!
I LIKE THAT SOUND, BABY-KILLER. SOUNDS TO ME LIKE SOME CONVICTED FELONS WHO PUT THEIR MONEY ON A WINNER.
AH-UHH
I AIN'T NEVER LOST A FIGHT IN HERE YET. LEAST OF ALL TO A LITTLE MIDGET LIKE YOU.
FIRST OF ALL, GENIUS, "AIN'T NEVER" IS A REDUNDANCY. SO IS "LITTLE MIDGET." WE VOTED ENGLISH AS THE NATIONAL LANGUAGE TWO HUNDRED YEARS AGO... HEHH
...AN' SECOND OF ALL, I LET YOU HIT ME TO FIND OUT HOW HARD YOU PUNCH--WHICH, I MIGHT ADD, IS SOFTER THAN A LEFT-HANDED KNUCKLEBALLER IN MY LOCAL UNDER-SEVEN T-BALL LEAGUE.
LET'S SEE IF YOU CAN HIT ME AGAIN!
HRAHH!
AND "OLÉ."

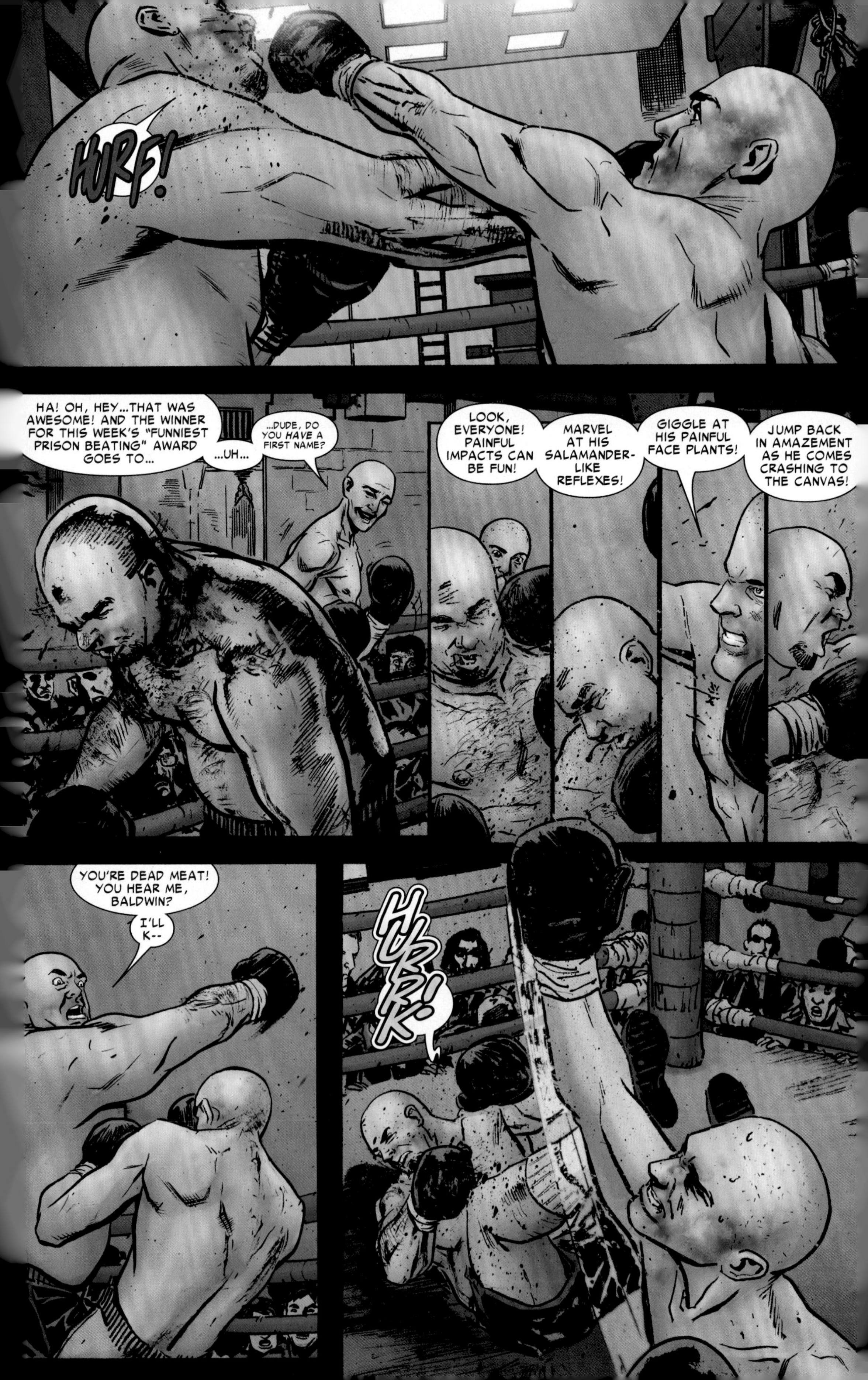
HURF!
HA! OH, HEY...THAT WAS AWESOME! AND THE WINNER FOR THIS WEEK'S "FUNNIEST PRISON BEATING" AWARD GOES TO...
...UH...
...DUDE, DO YOU *HAVE* A FIRST NAME?
LOOK, EVERYONE! PAINFUL IMPACTS CAN BE FUN!
MARVEL AT HIS SALAMANDER-LIKE REFLEXES!
GIGGLE AT HIS PAINFUL FACE PLANTS!
JUMP BACK IN AMAZEMENT AS HE COMES CRASHING TO THE CANVAS!
YOU'RE DEAD MEAT! YOU HEAR ME, BALDWIN?
I'LL K--
HURRK!

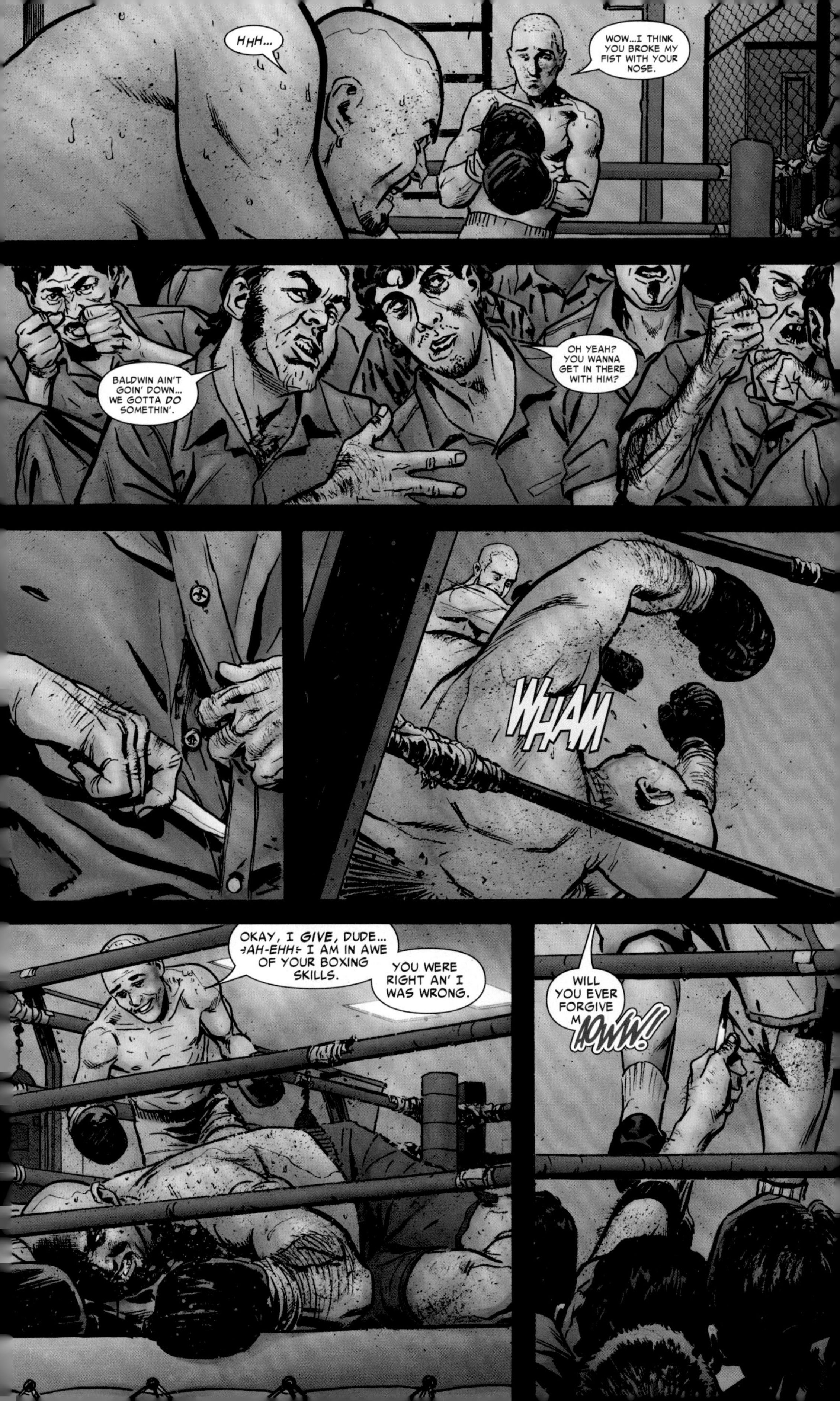
HHH...
WOW...I THINK YOU BROKE MY FIST WITH YOUR NOSE.
BALDWIN AIN'T GOIN' DOWN... WE GOTTA DO SOMETHIN'.
OH YEAH? YOU WANNA GET IN THERE WITH HIM?
WHAM
OKAY, I GIVE, DUDE... ÷AH-EHH÷ I AM IN AWE OF YOUR BOXING SKILLS.
YOU WERE RIGHT AN' I WAS WRONG.
WILL YOU EVER FORGIVE M
AOWW!!

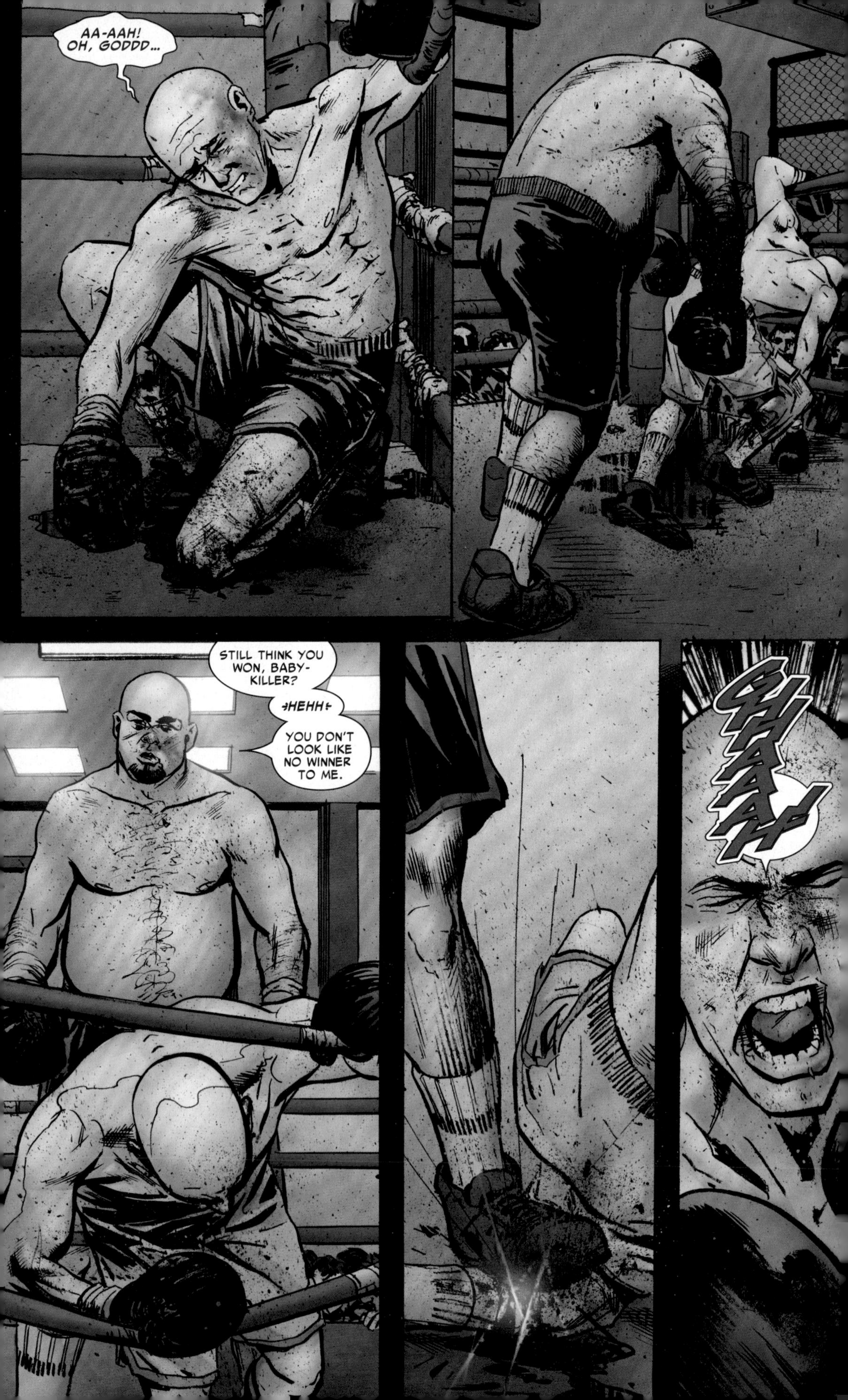
AA-AAH! OH, GODDD...
STILL THINK YOU WON, BABY-KILLER?
-HEHH-
YOU DON'T LOOK LIKE NO WINNER TO ME.
GHAAAH!

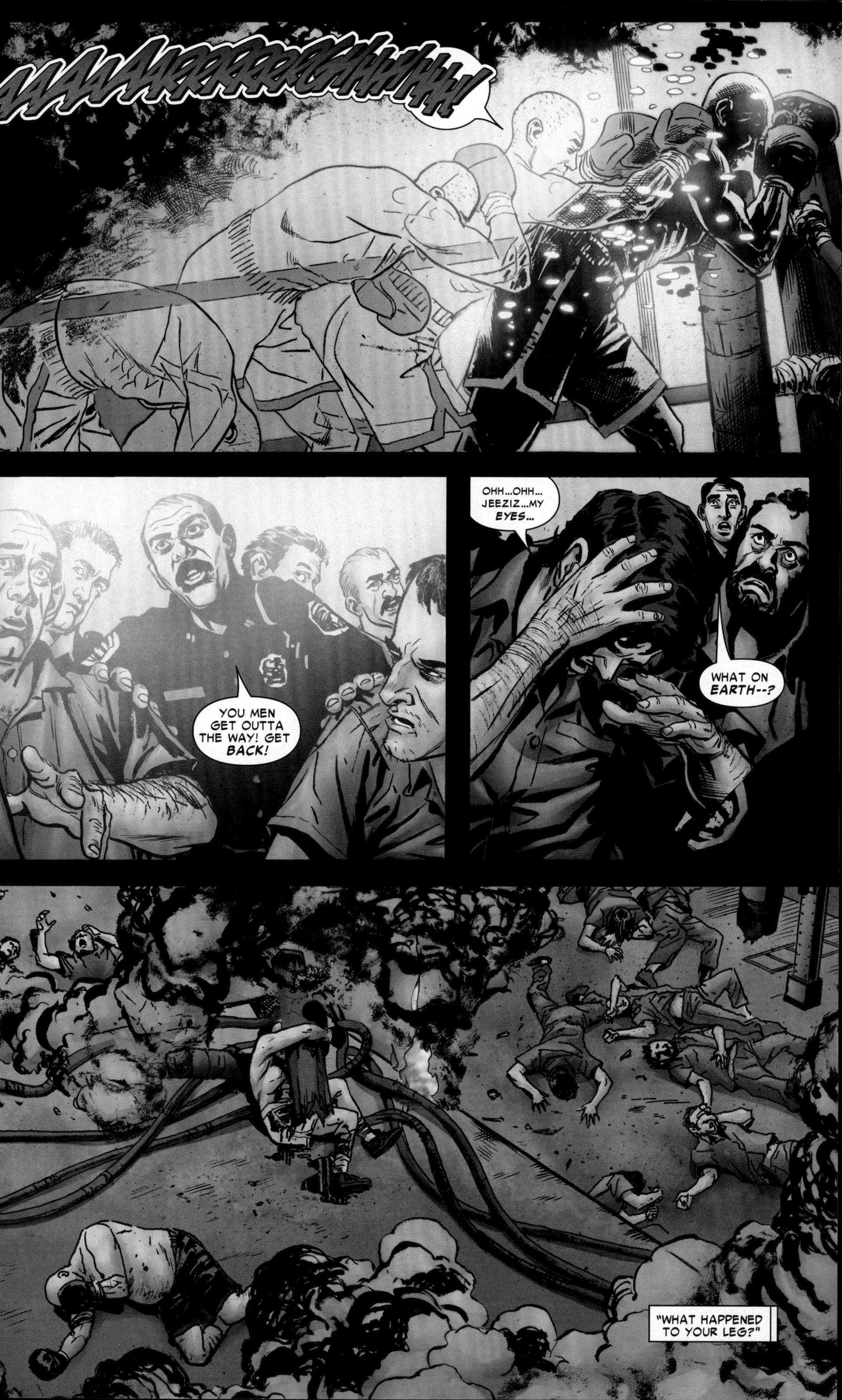

AAAWAARRRRRRGHHHHH!
YOU MEN GET OUTTA THE WAY! GET BACK!
OHH...OHH... JEEZIZ...MY EYES...
WHAT ON EARTH--?
"WHAT HAPPENED TO YOUR LEG?"

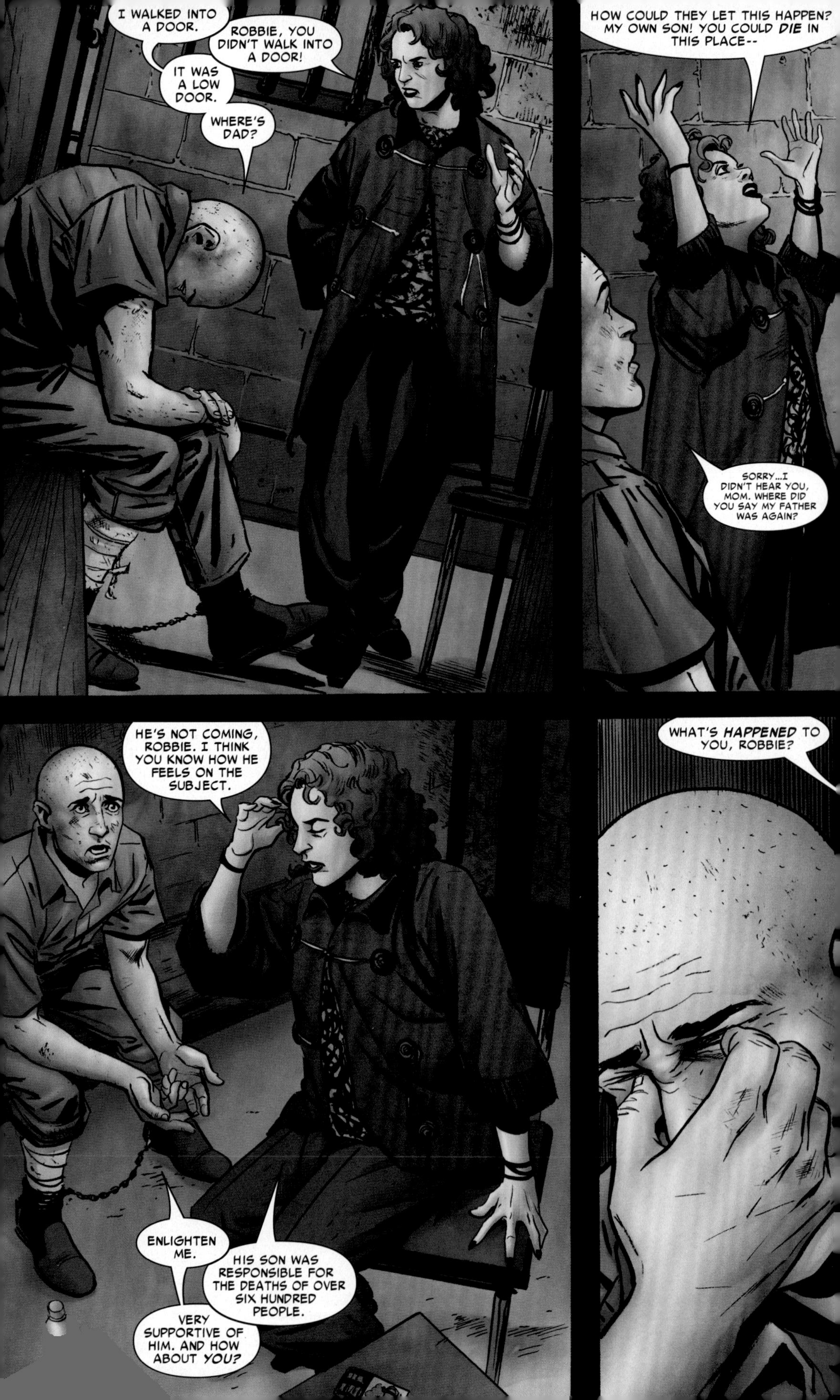

I WALKED INTO A DOOR.
ROBBIE, YOU DIDN'T WALK INTO A DOOR!
IT WAS A LOW DOOR.
WHERE'S DAD?
HOW COULD THEY LET THIS HAPPEN? MY OWN SON! YOU COULD DIE IN THIS PLACE--
SORRY...I DIDN'T HEAR YOU, MOM. WHERE DID YOU SAY MY FATHER WAS AGAIN?
HE'S NOT COMING, ROBBIE. I THINK YOU KNOW HOW HE FEELS ON THE SUBJECT.
ENLIGHTEN ME.
HIS SON WAS RESPONSIBLE FOR THE DEATHS OF OVER SIX HUNDRED PEOPLE.
VERY SUPPORTIVE OF HIM. AND HOW ABOUT YOU?
WHAT'S HAPPENED TO YOU, ROBBIE?

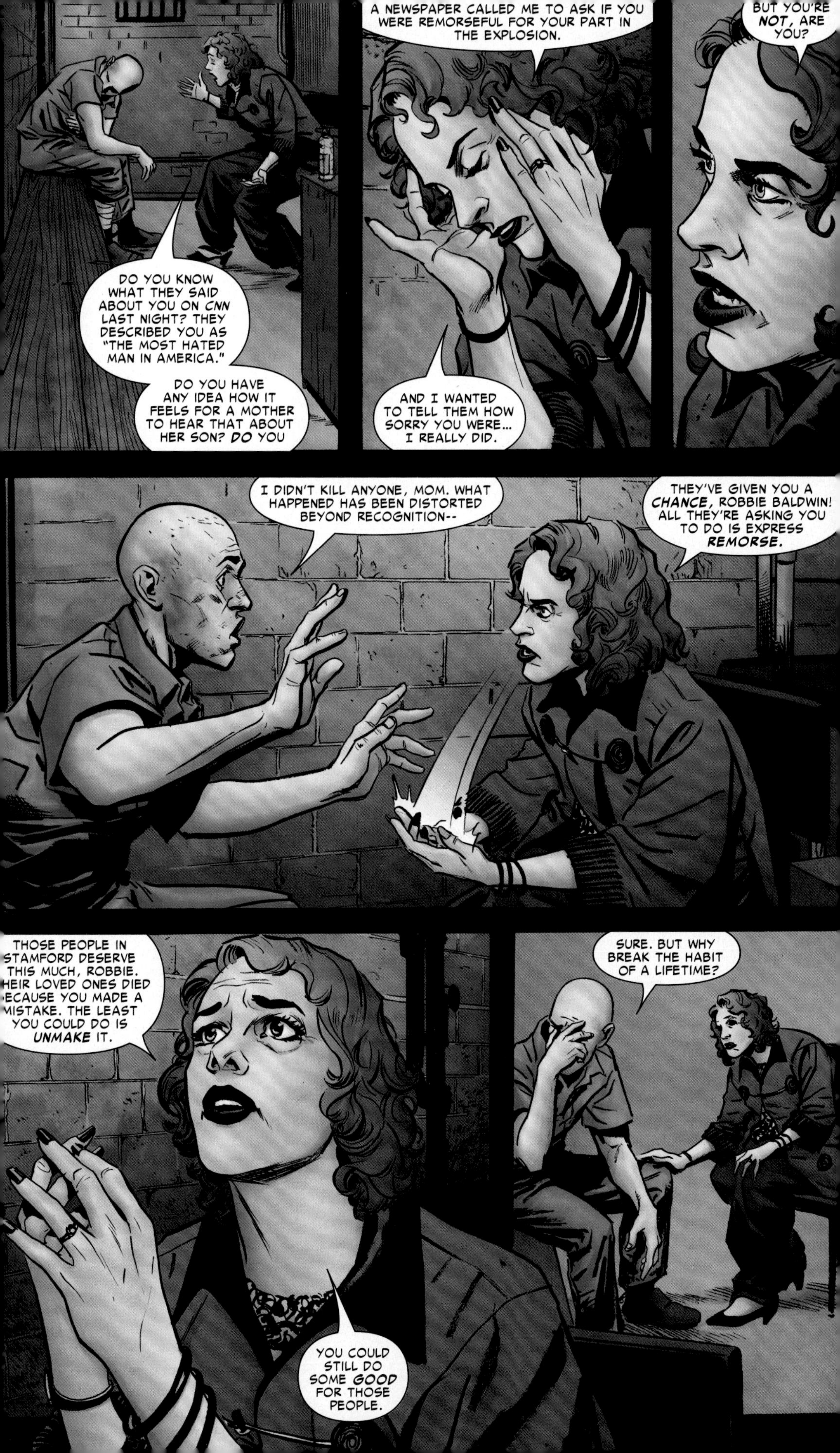
DO YOU KNOW WHAT THEY SAID ABOUT YOU ON CNN LAST NIGHT? THEY DESCRIBED YOU AS "THE MOST HATED MAN IN AMERICA."
DO YOU HAVE ANY IDEA HOW IT FEELS FOR A MOTHER TO HEAR THAT ABOUT HER SON? DO YOU
A NEWSPAPER CALLED ME TO ASK IF YOU WERE REMORSEFUL FOR YOUR PART IN THE EXPLOSION.
AND I WANTED TO TELL THEM HOW SORRY YOU WERE... I REALLY DID.
BUT YOU'RE NOT, ARE YOU?
I DIDN'T KILL ANYONE, MOM. WHAT HAPPENED HAS BEEN DISTORTED BEYOND RECOGNITION--
THEY'VE GIVEN YOU A CHANCE, ROBBIE BALDWIN! ALL THEY'RE ASKING YOU TO DO IS EXPRESS REMORSE.
THOSE PEOPLE IN STAMFORD DESERVE THIS MUCH, ROBBIE. HEIR LOVED ONES DIED ECAUSE YOU MADE A MISTAKE. THE LEAST YOU COULD DO IS UNMAKE IT.
YOU COULD STILL DO SOME GOOD FOR THOSE PEOPLE.
SURE. BUT WHY BREAK THE HABIT OF A LIFETIME?

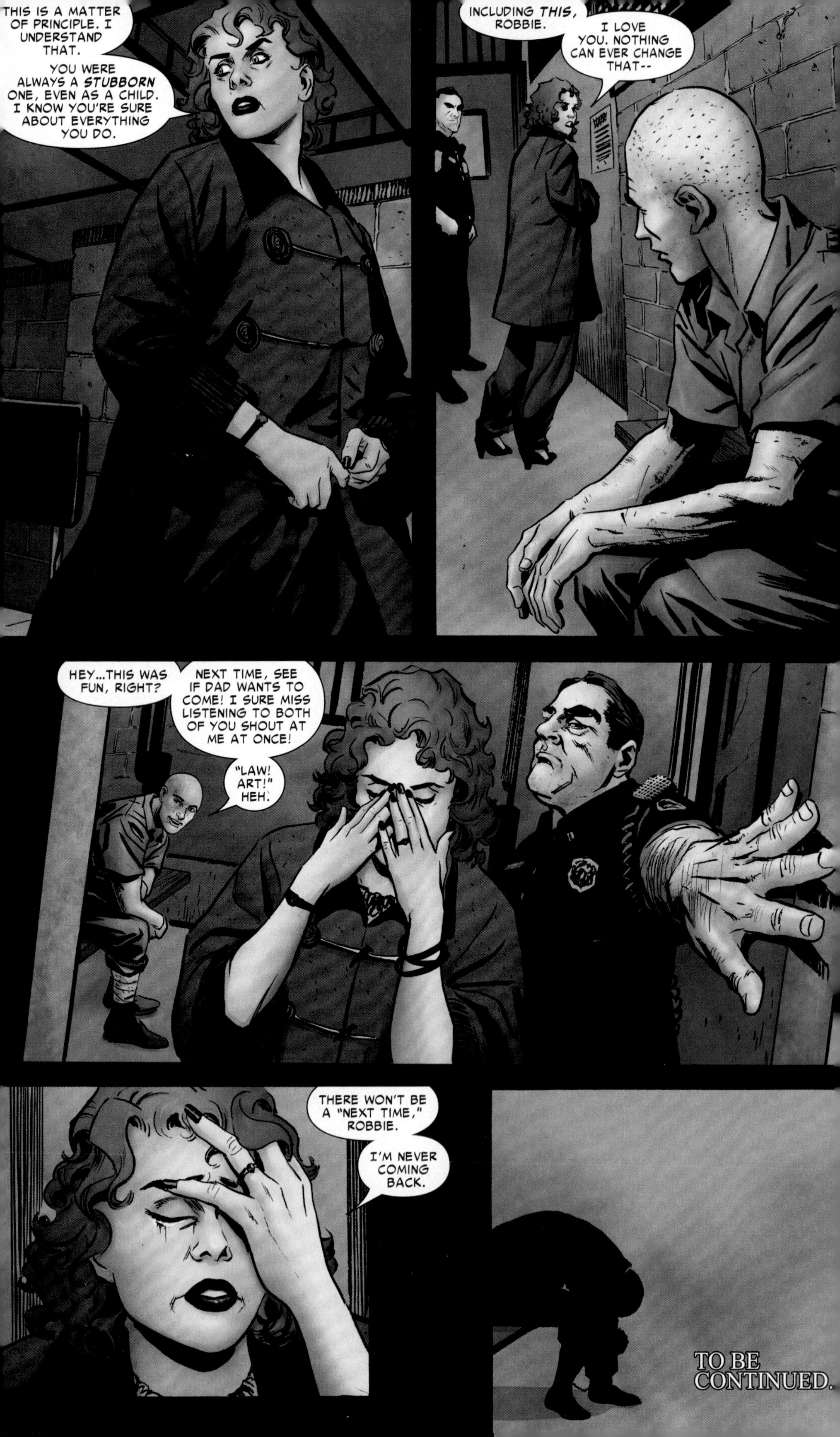
THIS IS A MATTER OF PRINCIPLE. I UNDERSTAND THAT.
YOU WERE ALWAYS A STUBBORN ONE, EVEN AS A CHILD. I KNOW YOU'RE SURE ABOUT EVERYTHING YOU DO.
INCLUDING THIS, ROBBIE.
I LOVE YOU. NOTHING CAN EVER CHANGE THAT--
HEY...THIS WAS FUN, RIGHT?
NEXT TIME, SEE IF DAD WANTS TO COME! I SURE MISS LISTENING TO BOTH OF YOU SHOUT AT ME AT ONCE!
"LAW! ART!" HEH.
THERE WON'T BE A "NEXT TIME," ROBBIE.
I'M NEVER COMING BACK.
TO BE CONTINUED.

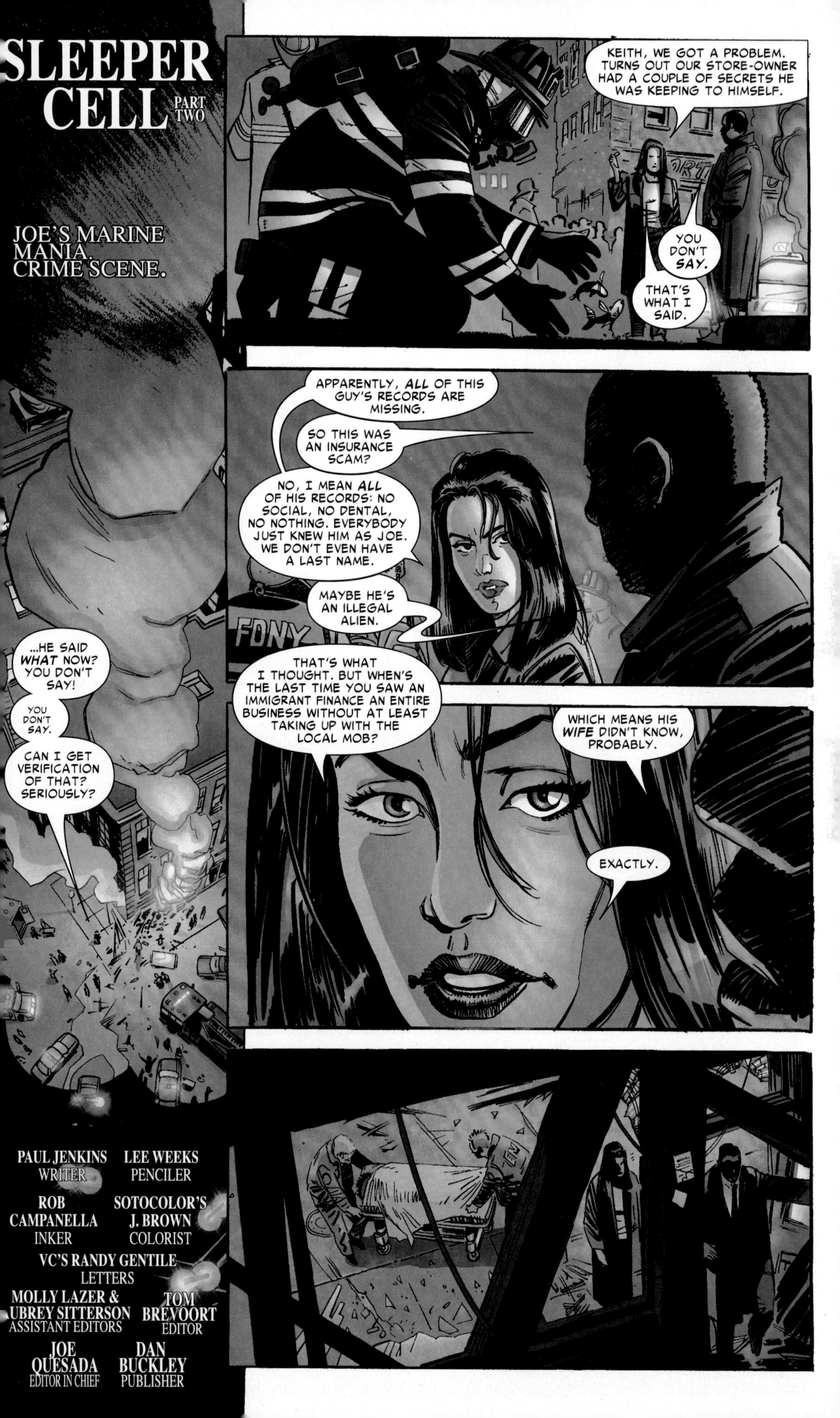
SLEEPER CELL PART TWO
JOE'S MARINE MANIA. CRIME SCENE.
KEITH, WE GOT A PROBLEM. TURNS OUT OUR STORE-OWNER HAD A COUPLE OF SECRETS HE WAS KEEPING TO HIMSELF.
YOU DON'T SAY.
THAT'S WHAT I SAID.
...HE SAID WHAT NOW? YOU DON'T SAY!
YOU DON'T SAY.
CAN I GET VERIFICATION OF THAT? SERIOUSLY?
APPARENTLY, ALL OF THIS GUY'S RECORDS ARE MISSING.
SO THIS WAS AN INSURANCE SCAM?
NO, I MEAN ALL OF HIS RECORDS: NO SOCIAL, NO DENTAL, NO NOTHING. EVERYBODY JUST KNEW HIM AS JOE. WE DON'T EVEN HAVE A LAST NAME.
MAYBE HE'S AN ILLEGAL ALIEN.
FDNY
THAT'S WHAT I THOUGHT. BUT WHEN'S THE LAST TIME YOU SAW AN IMMIGRANT FINANCE AN ENTIRE BUSINESS WITHOUT AT LEAST TAKING UP WITH THE LOCAL MOB?
WHICH MEANS HIS WIFE DIDN'T KNOW, PROBABLY.
EXACTLY.
PAUL JENKINS WRITER
LEE WEEKS PENCILER
ROB CAMPANELLA INKER
SOTOCOLOR'S J. BROWN COLORIST
VC'S RANDY GENTILE LETTERS
MOLLY LAZER & UBREY SITTERSON ASSISTANT EDITORS
TOM BREVOORT EDITOR
JOE QUESADA EDITOR IN CHIEF
DAN BUCKLEY PUBLISHER

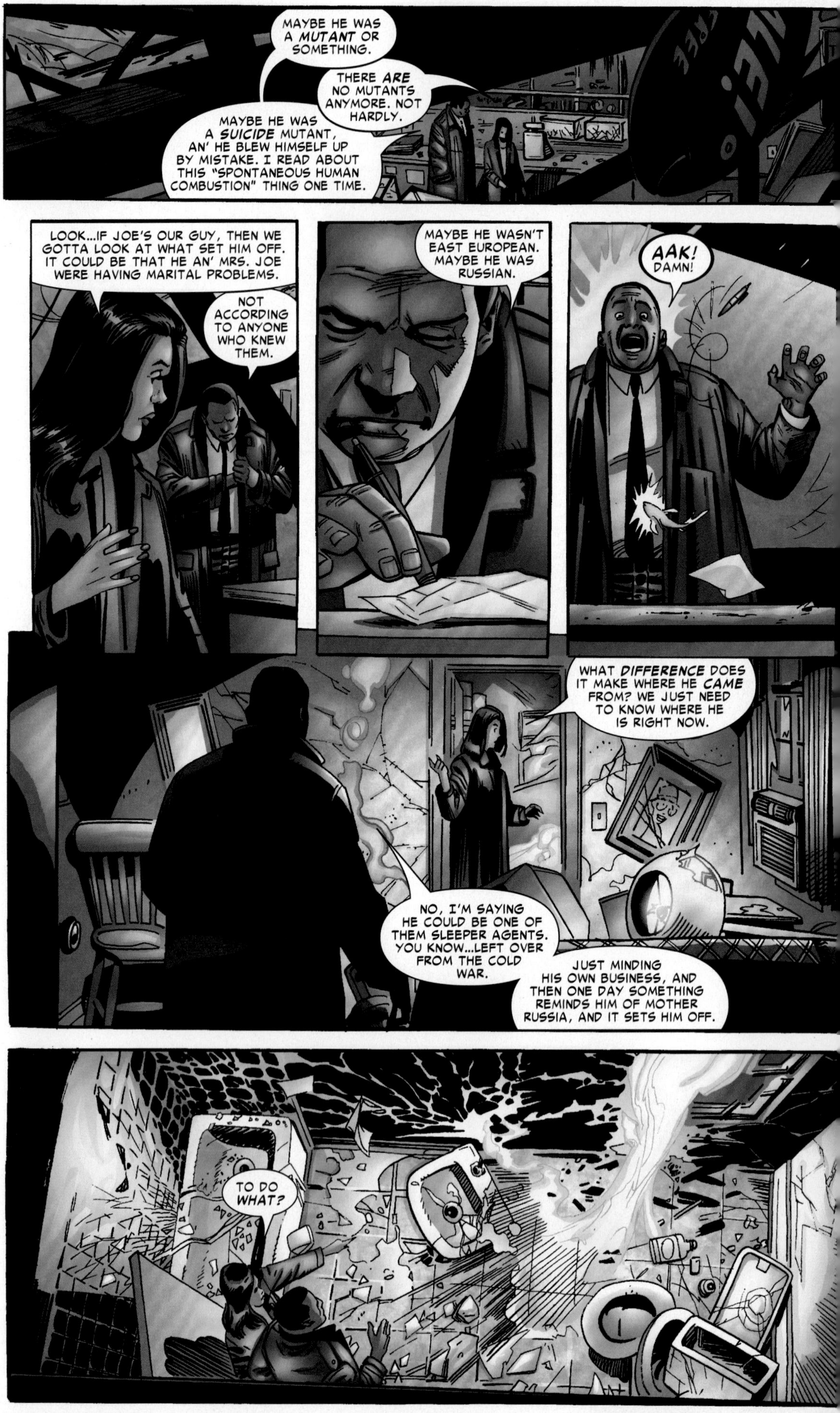
MAYBE HE WAS A *MUTANT* OR SOMETHING.
THERE *ARE* NO MUTANTS ANYMORE. NOT HARDLY.
MAYBE HE WAS A *SUICIDE* MUTANT, AN' HE BLEW HIMSELF UP BY MISTAKE. I READ ABOUT THIS "SPONTANEOUS HUMAN COMBUSTION" THING ONE TIME.
LOOK...IF JOE'S OUR GUY, THEN WE GOTTA LOOK AT WHAT SET HIM OFF. IT COULD BE THAT HE AN' MRS. JOE WERE HAVING MARITAL PROBLEMS.
NOT ACCORDING TO ANYONE WHO KNEW THEM.
MAYBE HE WASN'T EAST EUROPEAN. MAYBE HE WAS RUSSIAN.
AAK! DAMN!
WHAT *DIFFERENCE* DOES IT MAKE WHERE HE *CAME* FROM? WE JUST NEED TO KNOW WHERE HE IS RIGHT NOW.
NO, I'M SAYING HE COULD BE ONE OF THEM SLEEPER AGENTS. YOU KNOW...LEFT OVER FROM THE COLD WAR.
JUST MINDING HIS OWN BUSINESS, AND THEN ONE DAY SOMETHING REMINDS HIM OF MOTHER RUSSIA, AND IT SETS HIM OFF.
TO DO *WHAT?*

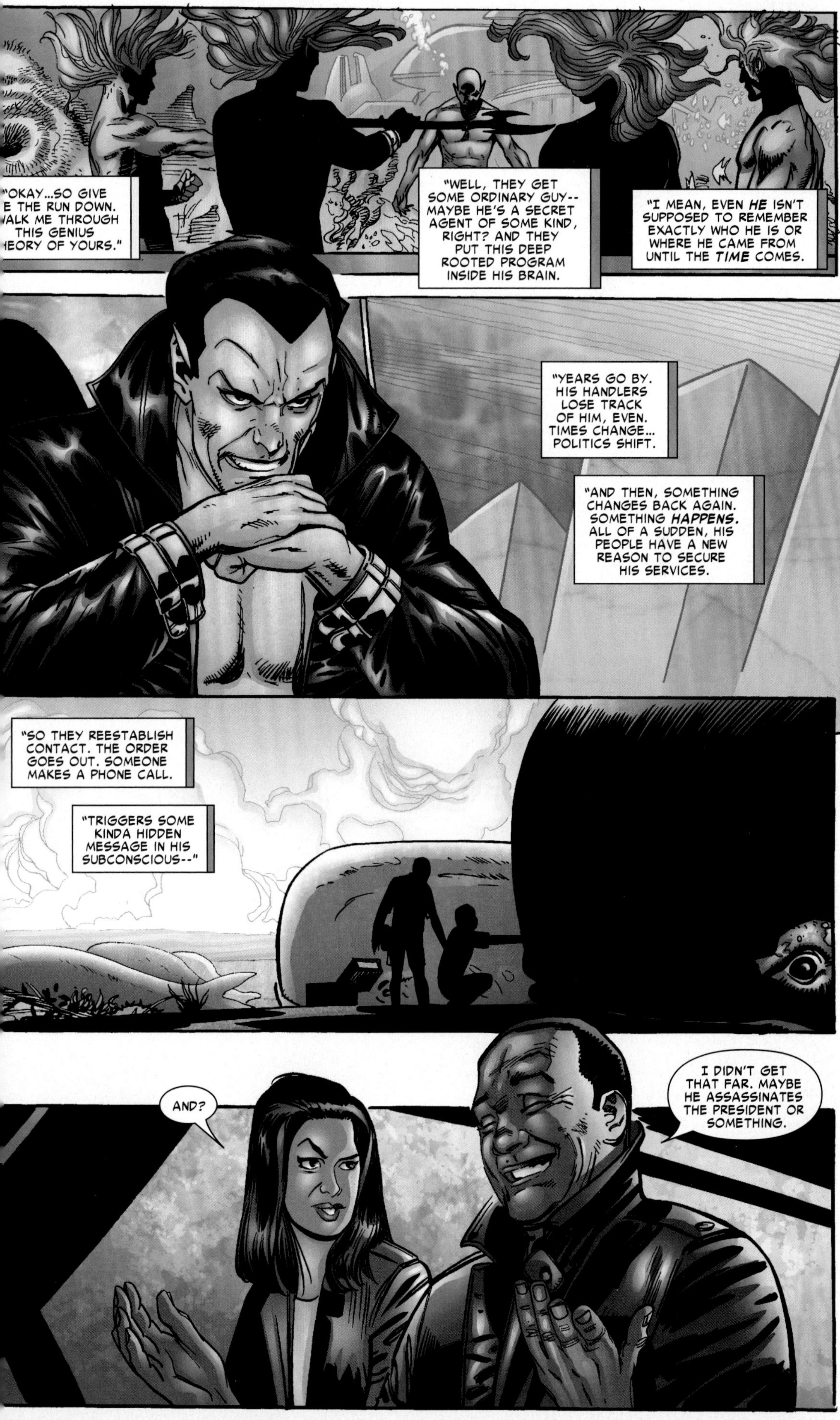
"OKAY...SO GIVE
E THE RUN DOWN.
ALK ME THROUGH
THIS GENIUS
HEORY OF YOURS."
"WELL, THEY GET SOME ORDINARY GUY-- MAYBE HE'S A SECRET AGENT OF SOME KIND, RIGHT? AND THEY PUT THIS DEEP ROOTED PROGRAM INSIDE HIS BRAIN.
"I MEAN, EVEN HE ISN'T SUPPOSED TO REMEMBER EXACTLY WHO HE IS OR WHERE HE CAME FROM UNTIL THE TIME COMES.
"YEARS GO BY. HIS HANDLERS LOSE TRACK OF HIM, EVEN. TIMES CHANGE... POLITICS SHIFT.
"AND THEN, SOMETHING CHANGES BACK AGAIN. SOMETHING HAPPENS. ALL OF A SUDDEN, HIS PEOPLE HAVE A NEW REASON TO SECURE HIS SERVICES.
"SO THEY REESTABLISH CONTACT. THE ORDER GOES OUT. SOMEONE MAKES A PHONE CALL.
"TRIGGERS SOME KINDA HIDDEN MESSAGE IN HIS SUBCONSCIOUS--"
AND?
I DIDN'T GET THAT FAR. MAYBE HE ASSASSINATES THE PRESIDENT OR SOMETHING.

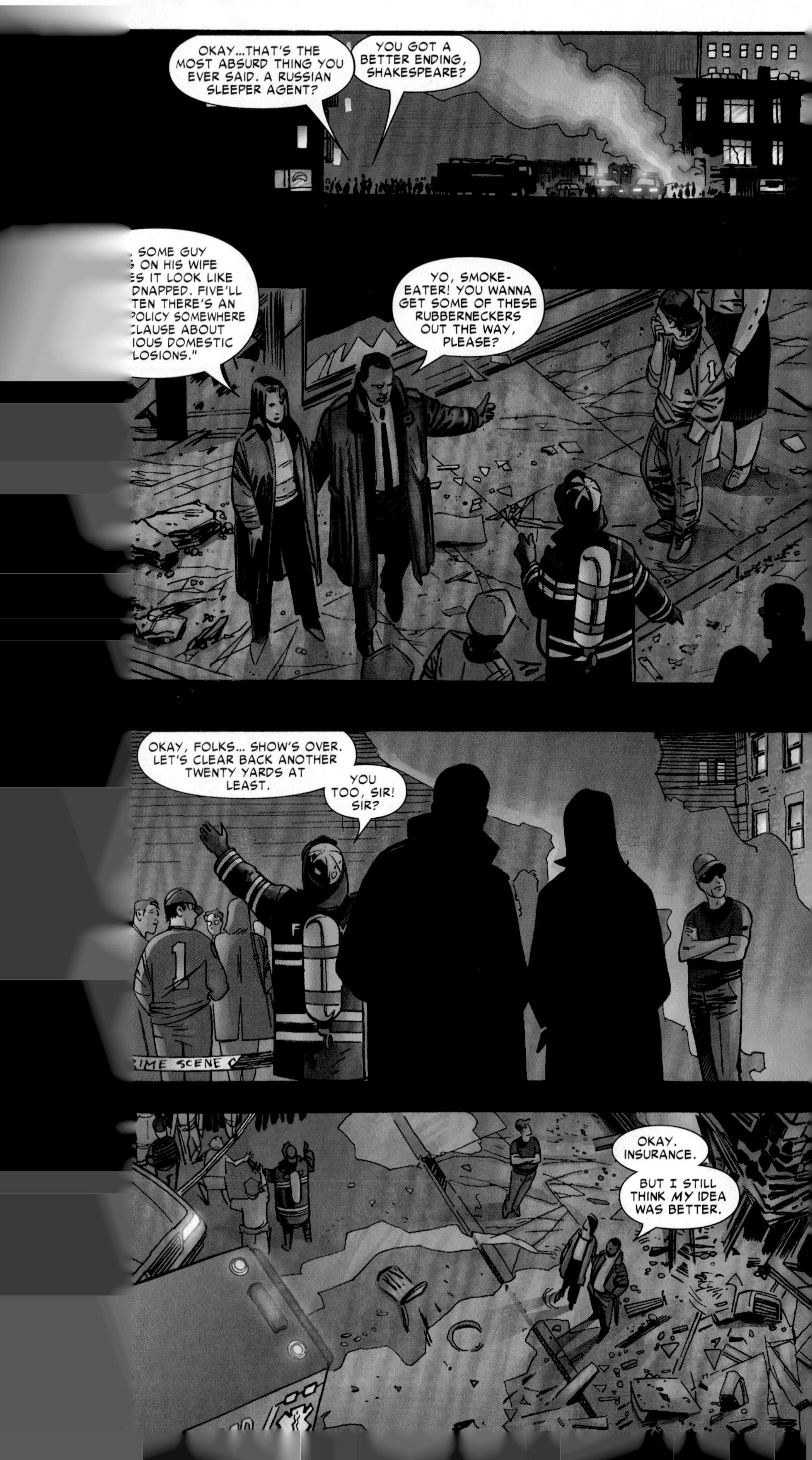
OKAY...THAT'S THE MOST ABSURD THING YOU EVER SAID. A RUSSIAN SLEEPER AGENT?
YOU GOT A BETTER ENDING, SHAKESPEARE?
SOME GUY ON HIS WIFE IT LOOK LIKE FIVE'LL THERE'S AN POLICY SOMEWHERE CLAUSE ABOUT DOMESTIC
YO, SMOKE-EATER! YOU WANNA GET SOME OF THESE RUBBERNECKERS OUT THE WAY, PLEASE?
OKAY, FOLKS... SHOW'S OVER. LET'S CLEAR BACK ANOTHER TWENTY YARDS AT LEAST.
YOU TOO, SIR! SIR?
SCENE
OKAY. INSURANCE.
BUT I STILL THINK MY IDEA WAS BETTER.

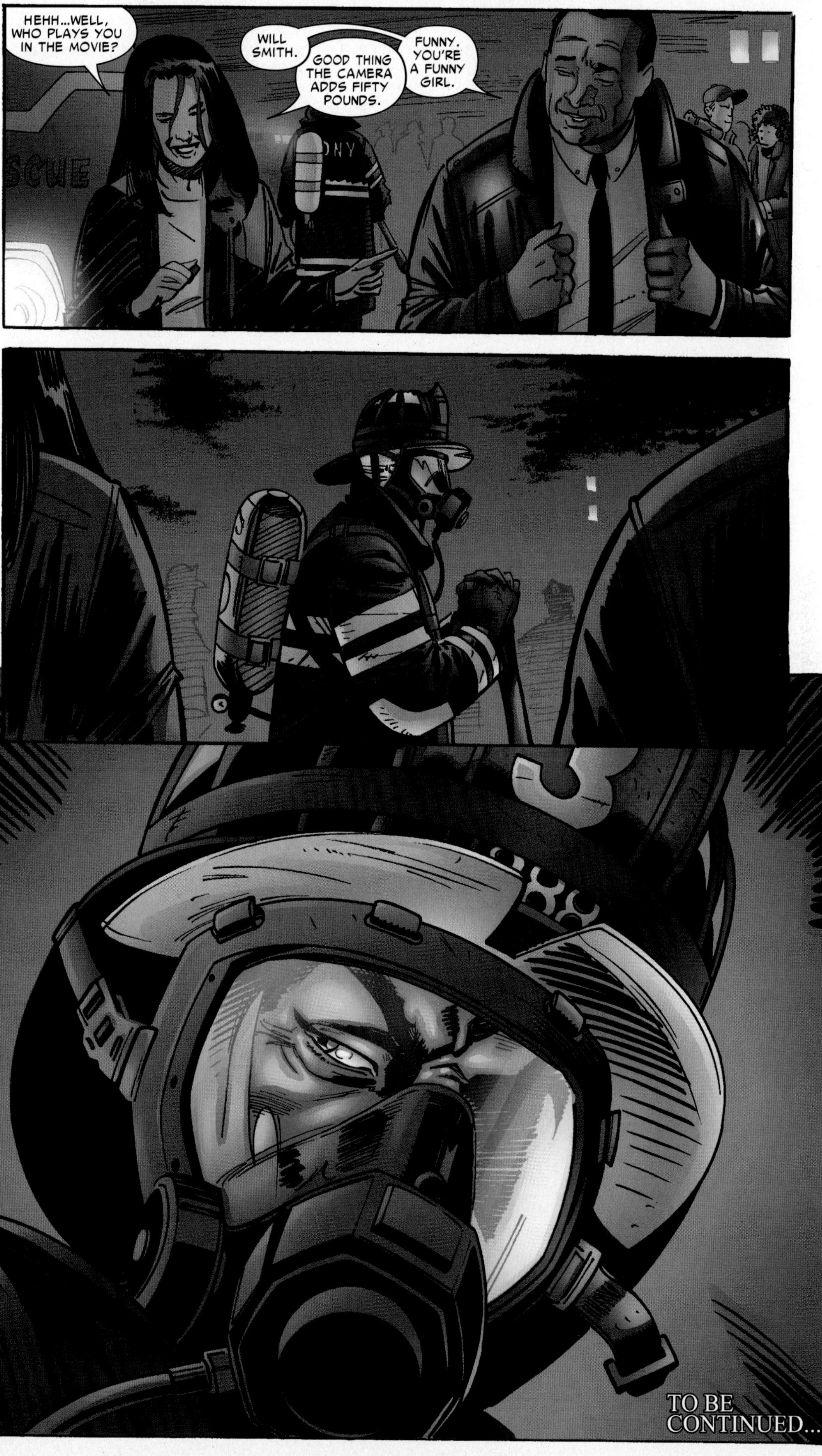
HEHH...WELL, WHO PLAYS YOU IN THE MOVIE?
WILL SMITH.
GOOD THING THE CAMERA ADDS FIFTY POUNDS.
FUNNY. YOU'RE A FUNNY GIRL.
RESCUE
FDNY
TO BE CONTINUED...

The Vietnam War

According to the Adjutant General's Center (TACGEN) file dated 1981, the United States suffered over 50,000 fatalities, including over 3000 military personnel who either died in captivity or were MIA. Over 300,000 were wounded.

In 1995, on the twentieth anniversary of the ending of the war, North Vietnam supplied the Agence France Presse with fatality figures of their own: over 1,100,000 KIA, and over 600,000 wounded.

Sometimes the numbers speak for themselves.

The words here are adapted from the song Goodnight Saigon by Billy Joel.
While they reflect the thoughts of a US Marine Corps recruit, it can be said that they reflect the thoughts of every soldier from every war in history...

PAUL JENKINS WRITER · SEAN CHEN PENCILER · RICK MAGYAR INKER · SOTOCOLOR'S A. CROSSLEY COLORIST · VC'S RANDY GENTILE LETTERER · MOLLY LAZER AND AUBREY SITTERSON ASSISTANT EDITORS · TOM BREVOORT EDITOR · JOE QUESADA EDITOR IN CHIEF · DAN BUCKLEY PUBLISHER

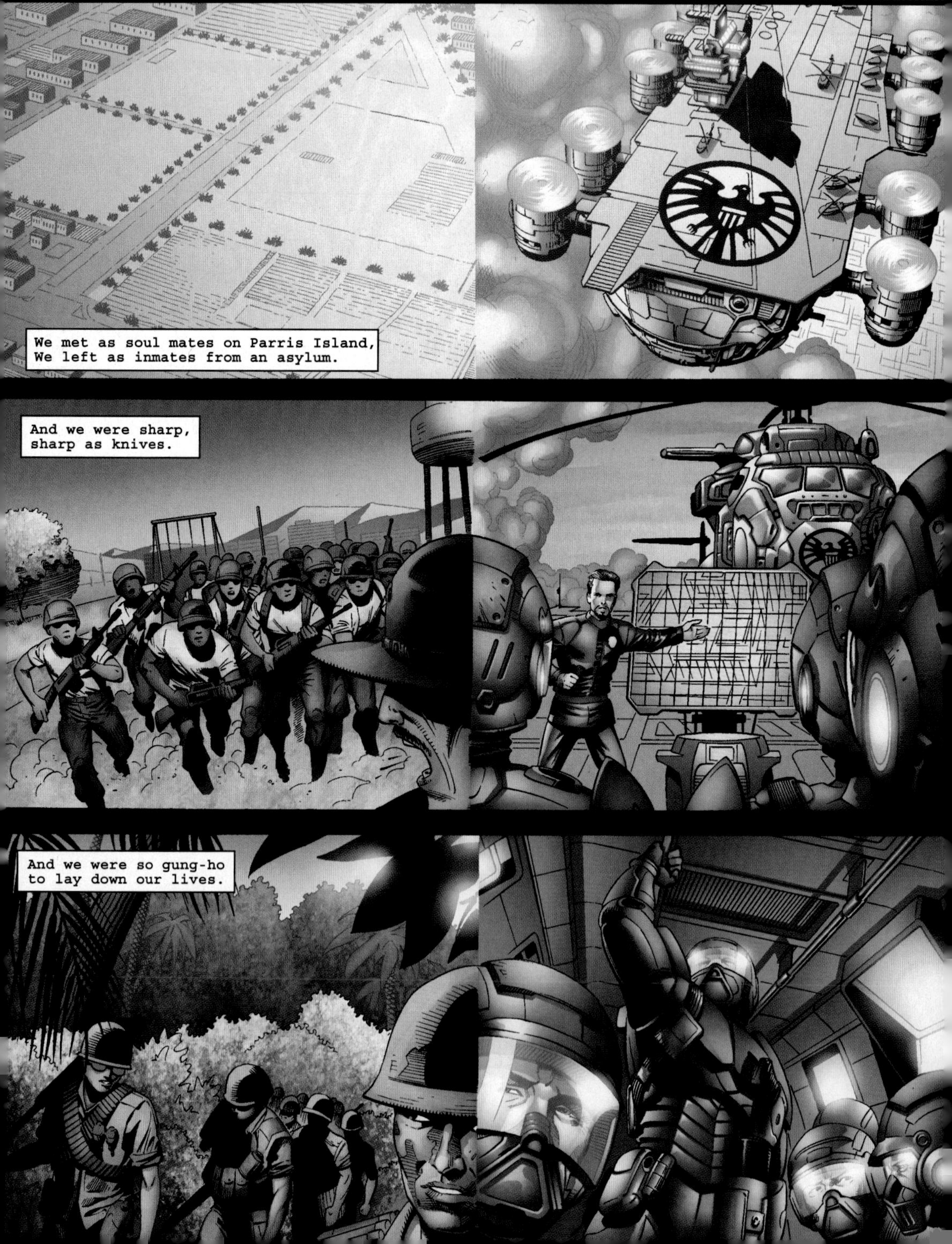
We met as soul mates on Parris Island,
We left as inmates from an asylum.
And we were sharp, sharp as knives.
And we were so gung-ho to lay down our lives.

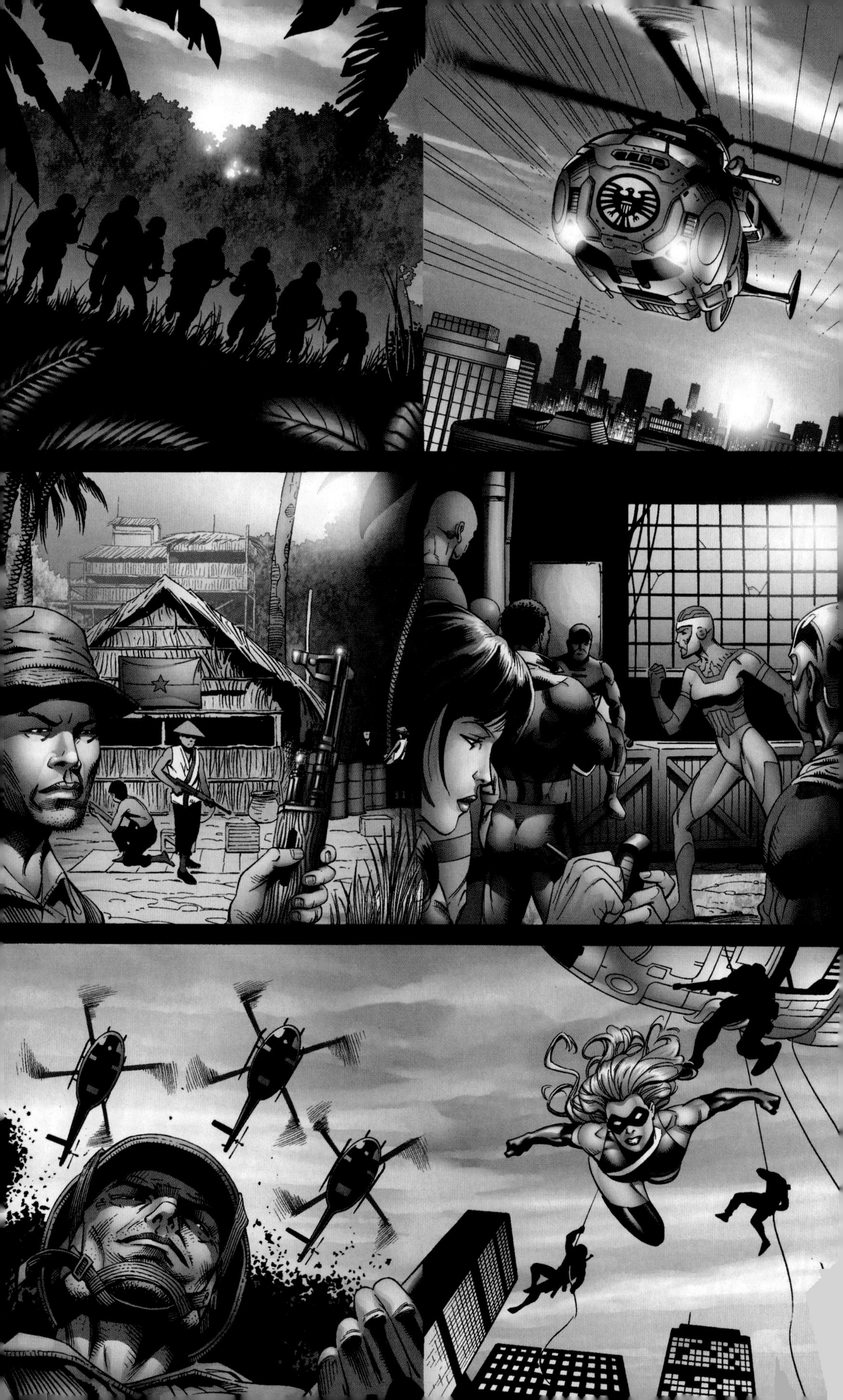

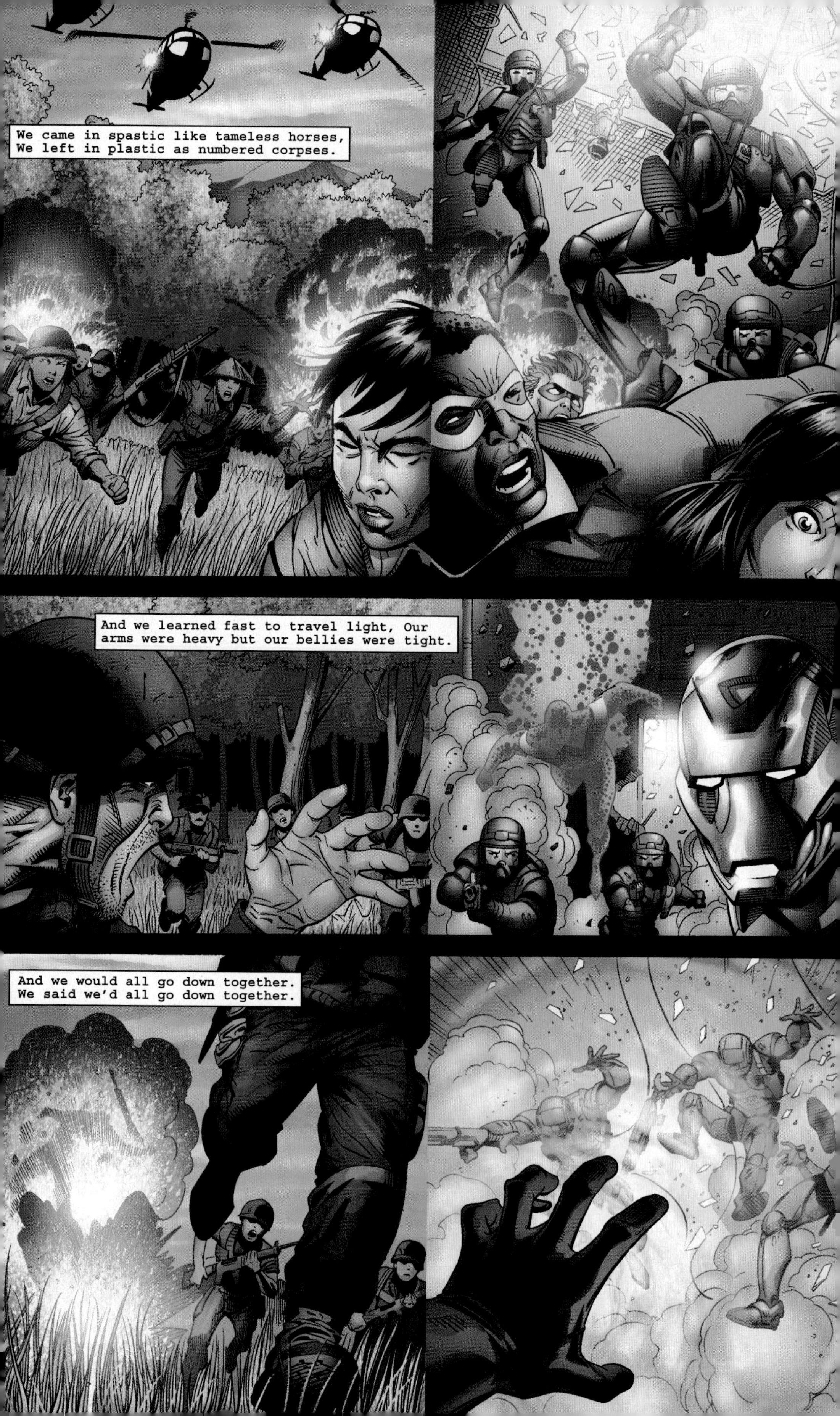
We came in spastic like tameless horses,
We left in plastic as numbered corpses.
And we learned fast to travel light, Our arms were heavy but our bellies were tight.
And we would all go down together.
We said we'd all go down together.

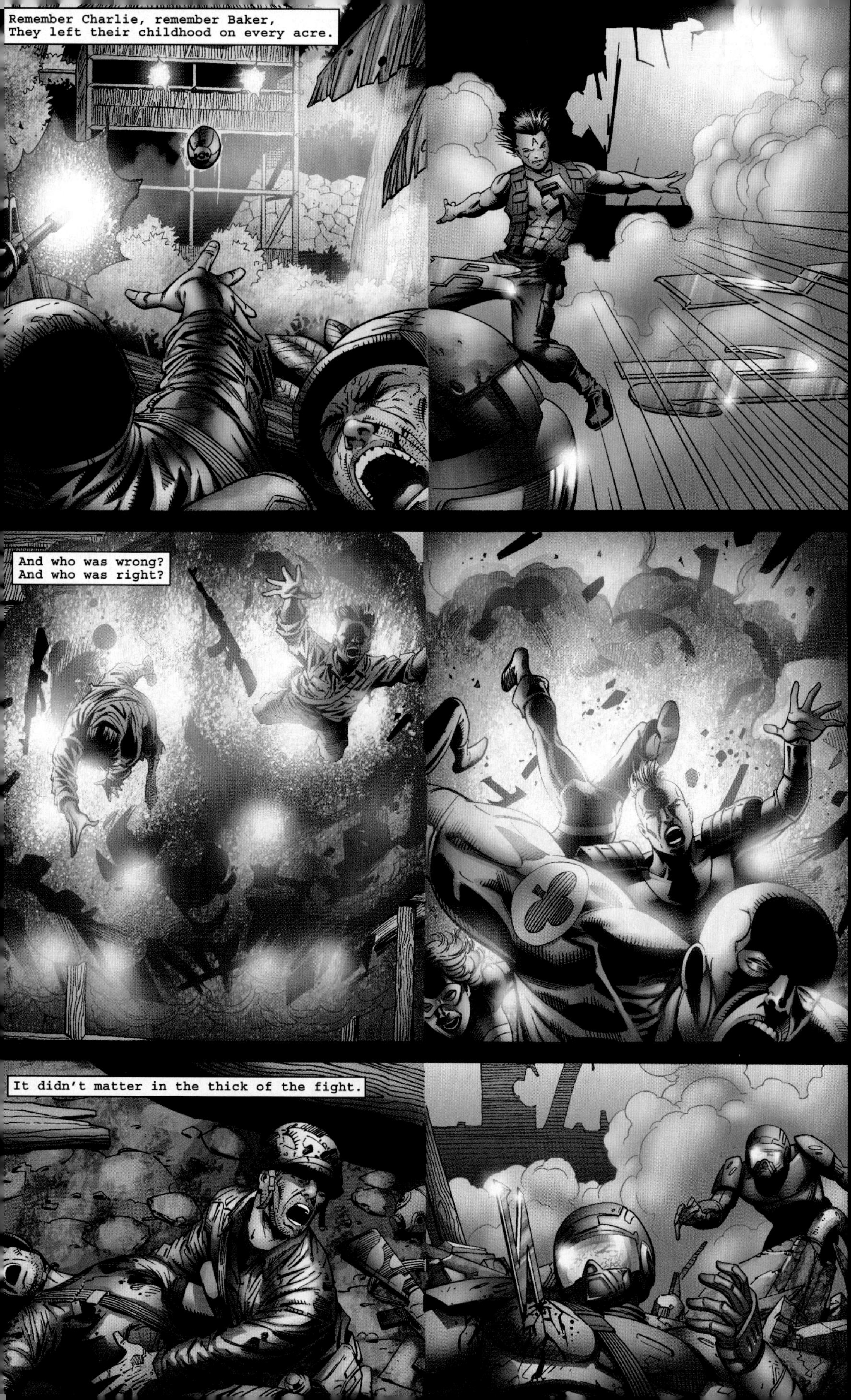
Remember Charlie, remember Baker,
They left their childhood on every acre.
And who was wrong?
And who was right?
It didn't matter in the thick of the fight.

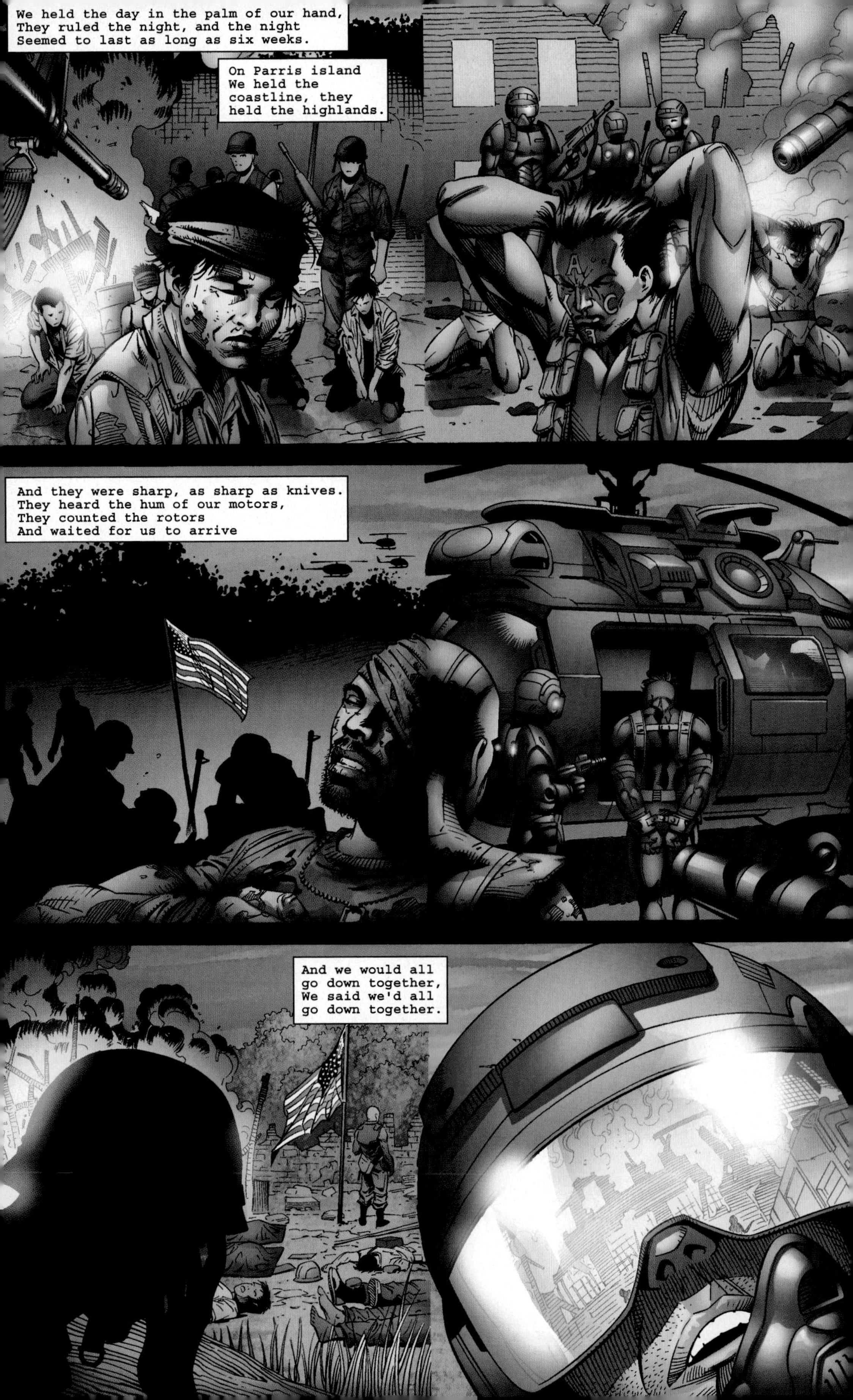
We held the day in the palm of our hand,
They ruled the night, and the night
Seemed to last as long as six weeks.
On Parris island
We held the
coastline, they
held the highlands.
And they were sharp, as sharp as knives.
They heard the hum of our motors,
They counted the rotors
And waited for us to arrive
And we would all
go down together,
We said we'd all
go down together.

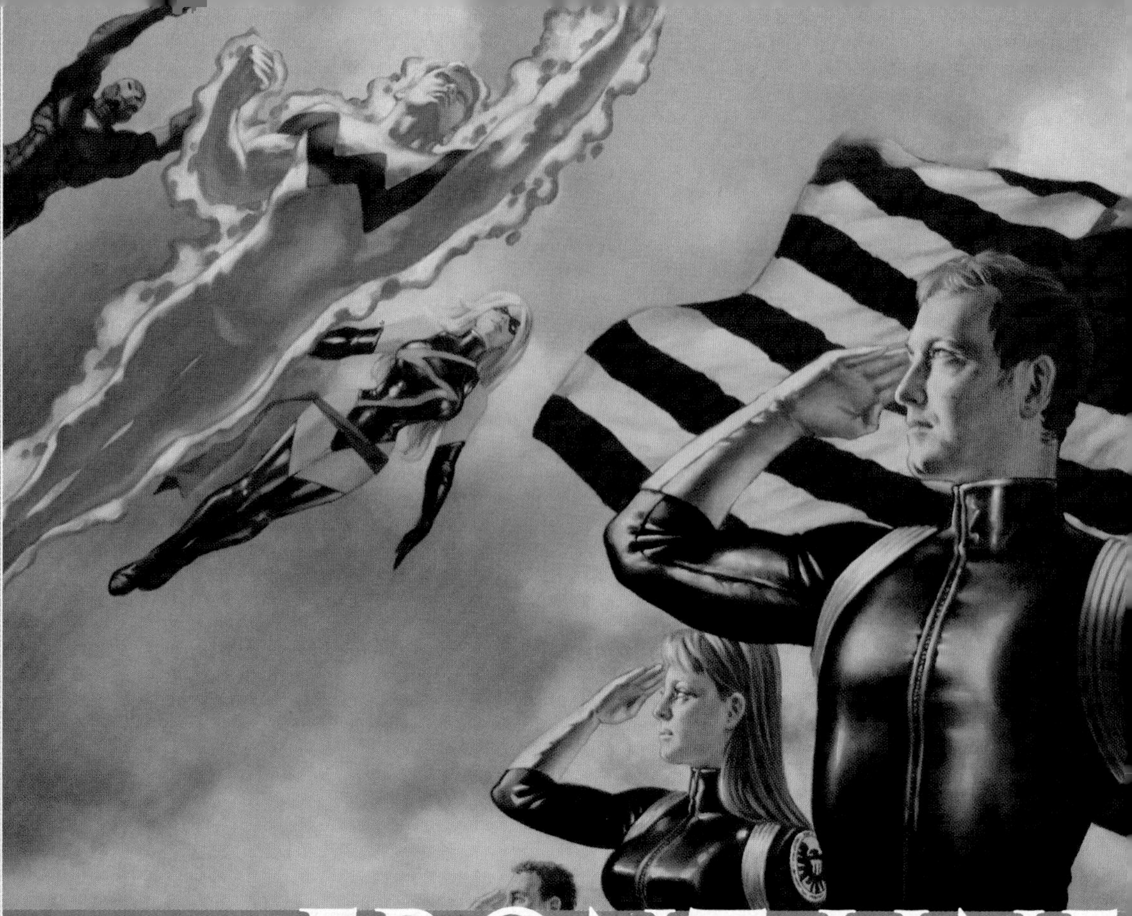

FRONT LINE
A MARVEL COMICS EVENT

CIVIL WAR

CIVIL WAR: FRONT LINE #5

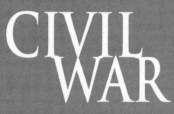

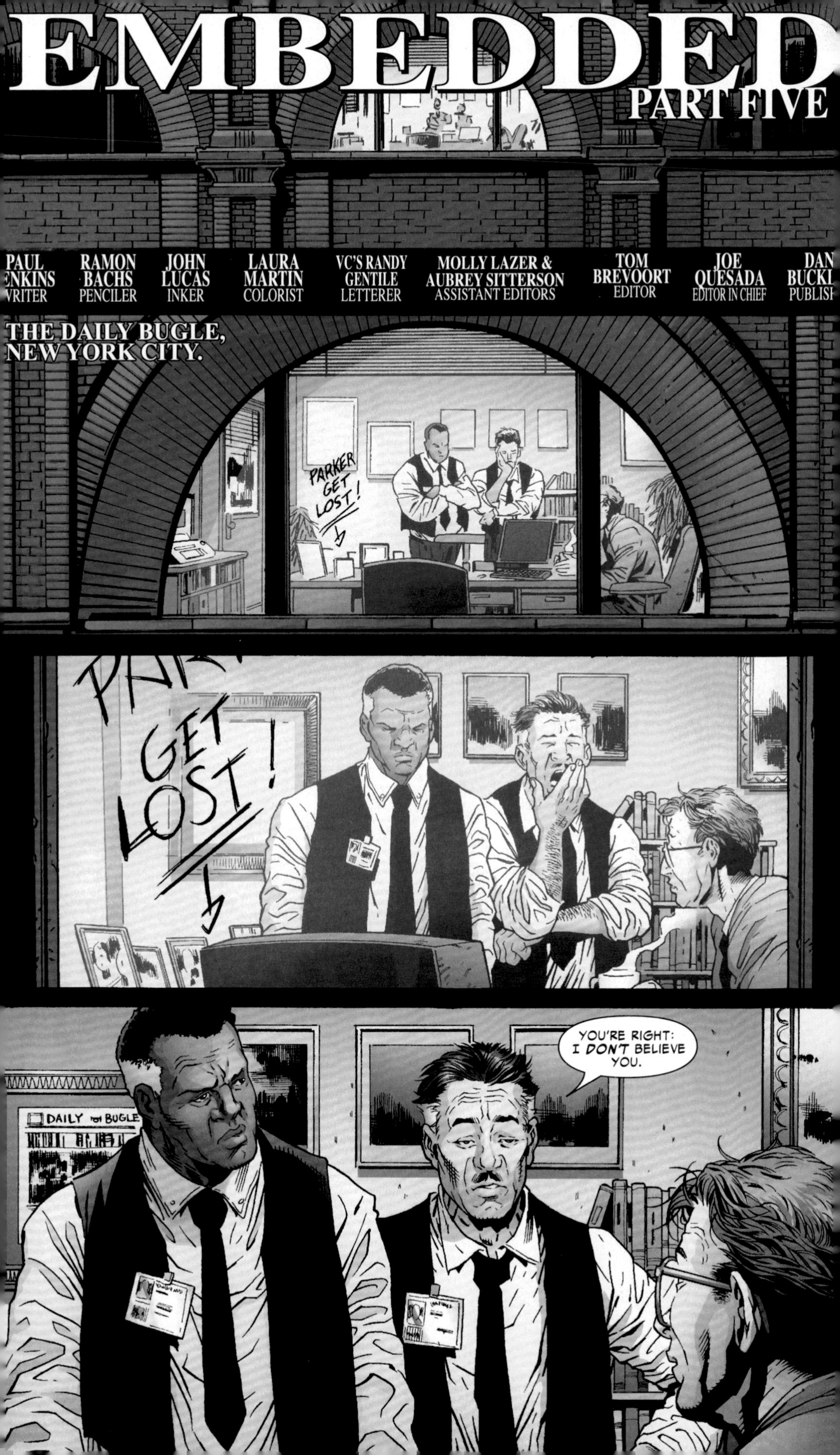
EMBEDDED
PART FIVE
PAUL JENKINS WRITER
RAMON BACHS PENCILER
JOHN LUCAS INKER
LAURA MARTIN COLORIST
VC'S RANDY GENTILE LETTERER
MOLLY LAZER & AUBREY SITTERSON ASSISTANT EDITORS
TOM BREVOORT EDITOR
JOE QUESADA EDITOR IN CHIEF
DAN BUCKLEY PUBLISHER
THE DAILY BUGLE, NEW YORK CITY.
PARKER GET LOST!
GET LOST!
DAILY BUGLE
YOU'RE RIGHT: I *DON'T* BELIEVE YOU.

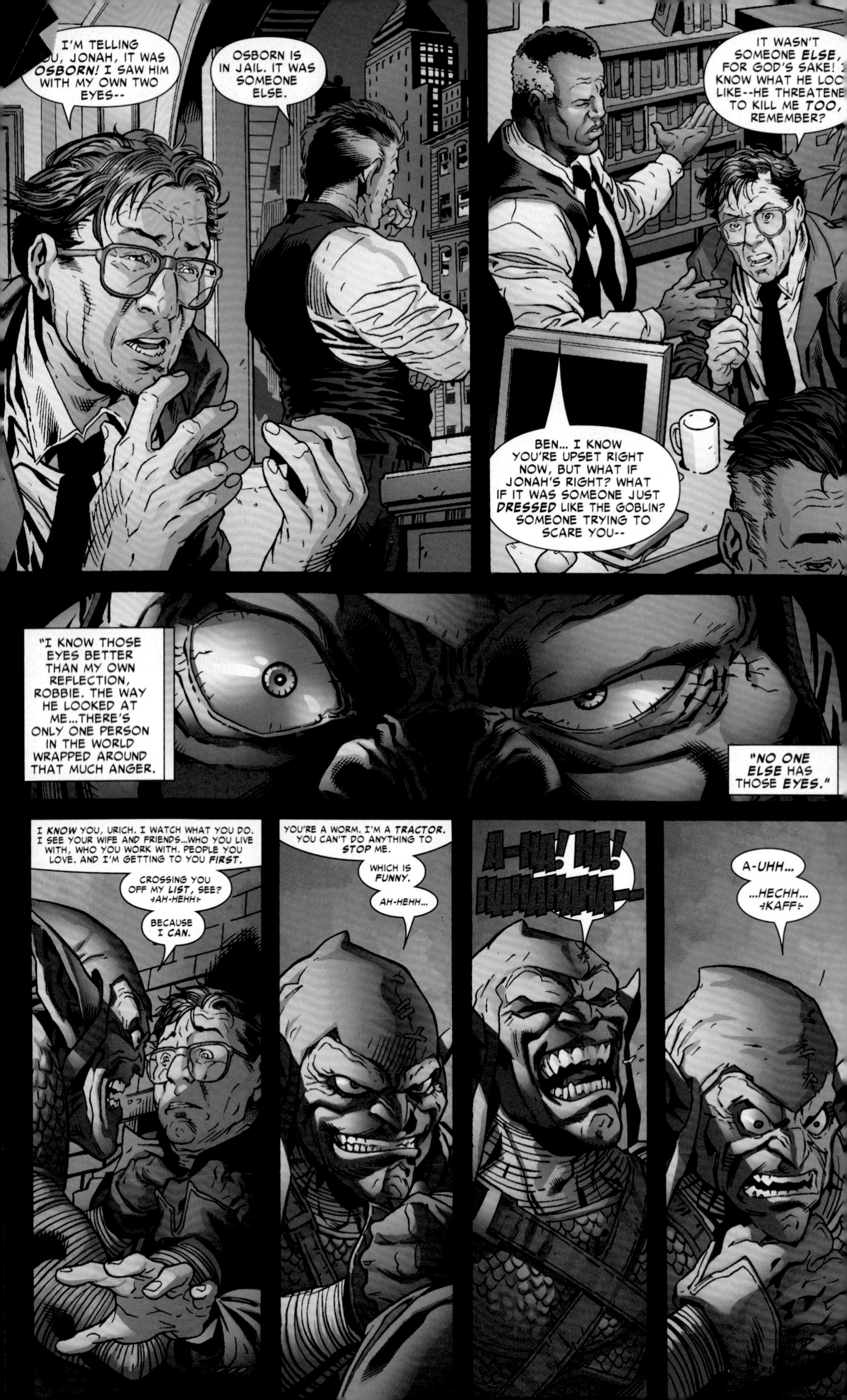

I'M TELLING YOU, JONAH, IT WAS OSBORN! I SAW HIM WITH MY OWN TWO EYES--
OSBORN IS IN JAIL. IT WAS SOMEONE ELSE.
IT WASN'T SOMEONE ELSE, FOR GOD'S SAKE! I KNOW WHAT HE LOOKS LIKE--HE THREATENED TO KILL ME TOO, REMEMBER?
BEN... I KNOW YOU'RE UPSET RIGHT NOW, BUT WHAT IF JONAH'S RIGHT? WHAT IF IT WAS SOMEONE JUST DRESSED LIKE THE GOBLIN? SOMEONE TRYING TO SCARE YOU--
"I KNOW THOSE EYES BETTER THAN MY OWN REFLECTION, ROBBIE. THE WAY HE LOOKED AT ME...THERE'S ONLY ONE PERSON IN THE WORLD WRAPPED AROUND THAT MUCH ANGER.
"NO ONE ELSE HAS THOSE EYES."
I KNOW YOU, URICH. I WATCH WHAT YOU DO. I SEE YOUR WIFE AND FRIENDS...WHO YOU LIVE WITH, WHO YOU WORK WITH. PEOPLE YOU LOVE. AND I'M GETTING TO YOU FIRST.
CROSSING YOU OFF MY LIST, SEE? AH-HEHH
BECAUSE I CAN.
YOU'RE A WORM. I'M A TRACTOR. YOU CAN'T DO ANYTHING TO STOP ME.
WHICH IS FUNNY.
AH-HEHH...
A-HA! HA! HAHAHAHA--
A-UHH...
...HECHH... KAFF

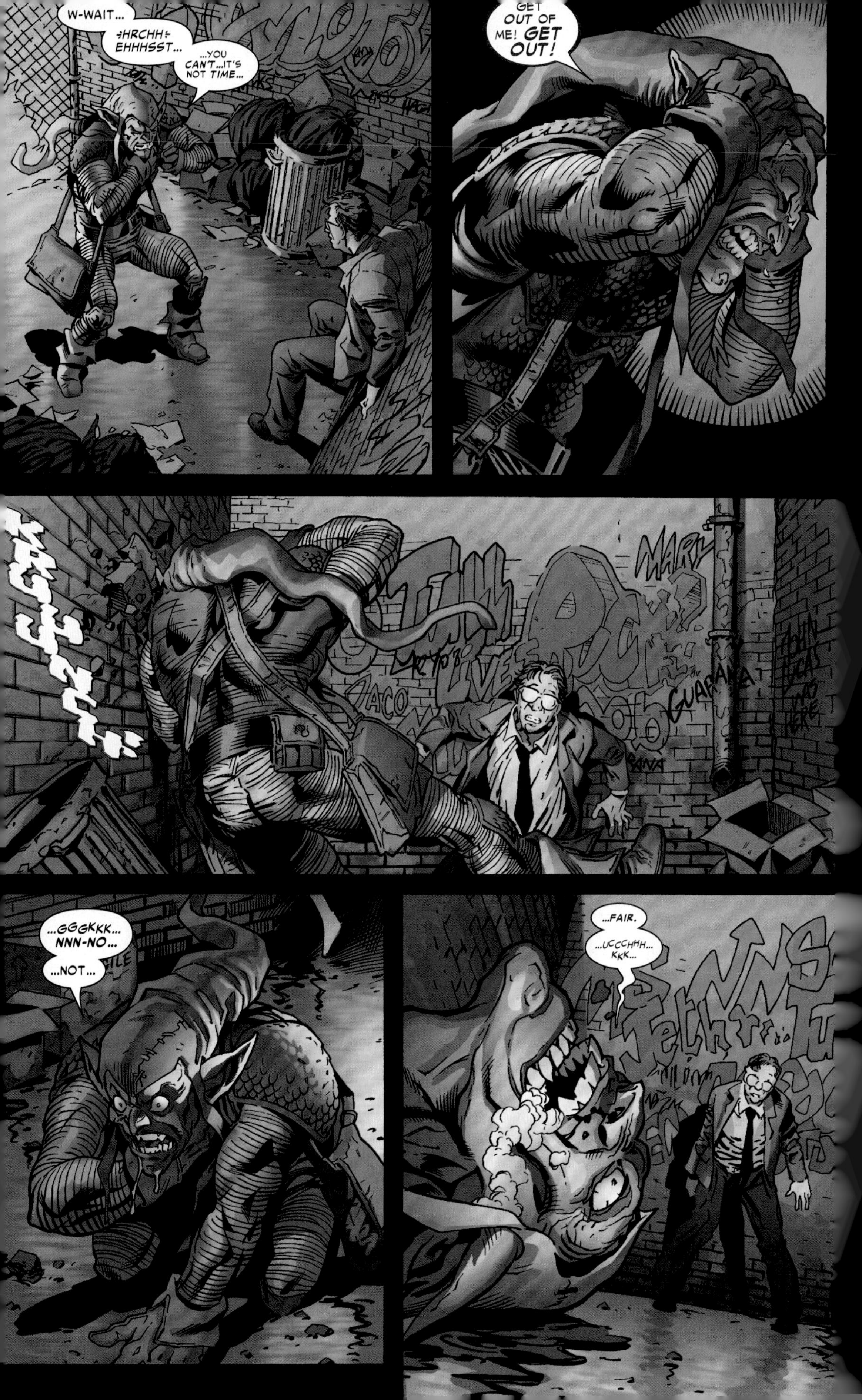
W-WAIT...
HRCHH EHHHSST...
...YOU CAN'T...IT'S NOT TIME...
GET OUT OF ME! GET OUT!
...GGGKKK... NNN-NO...
...NOT...
...FAIR.
...UCCCHHH... KKK...

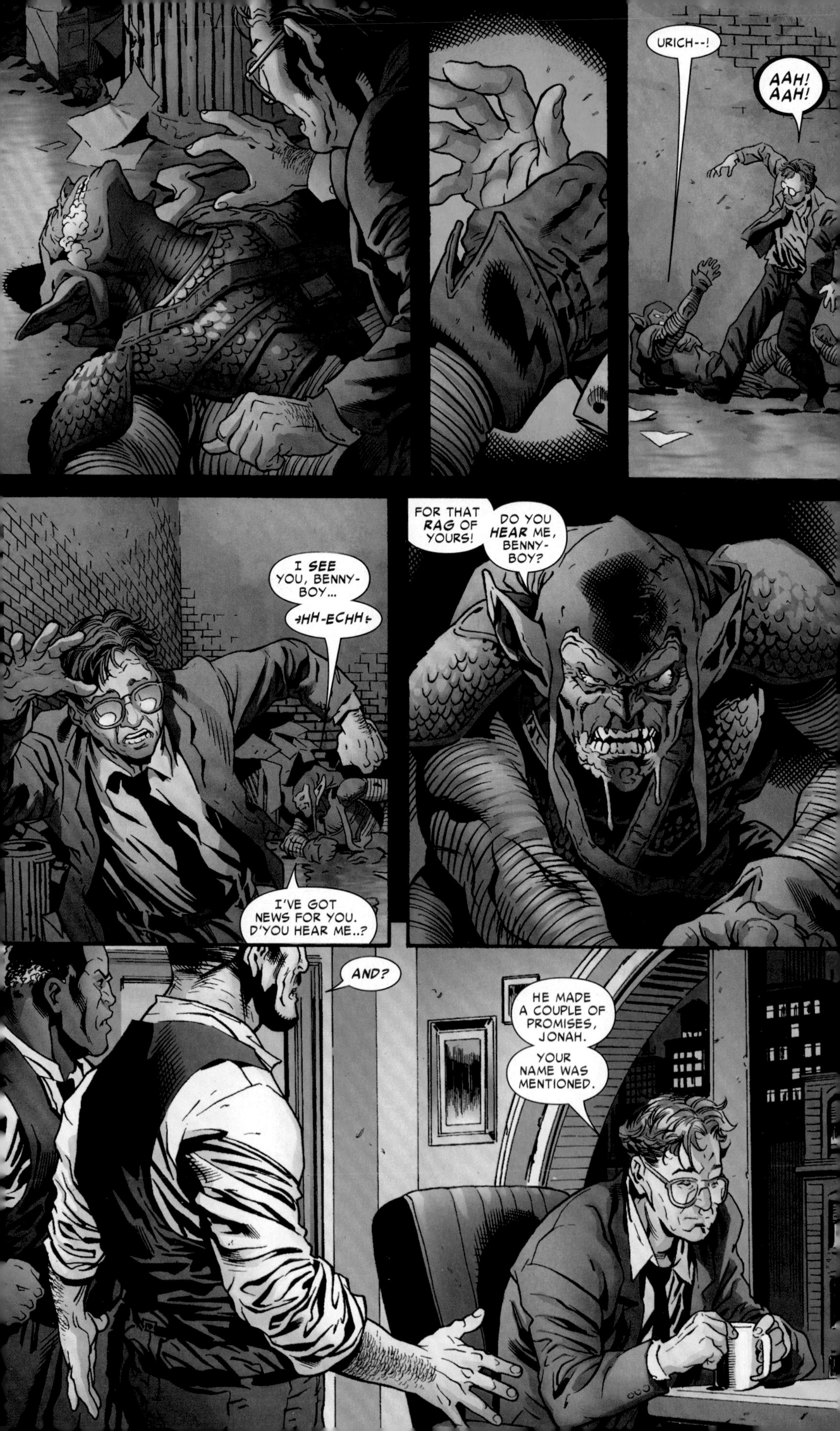
URICH--!
AAH! AAH!
I SEE YOU, BENNY-BOY...
-HH-ECHH-
I'VE GOT NEWS FOR YOU. D'YOU HEAR ME..?
FOR THAT RAG OF YOURS!
DO YOU HEAR ME, BENNY-BOY?
AND?
HE MADE A COUPLE OF PROMISES, JONAH.
YOUR NAME WAS MENTIONED.

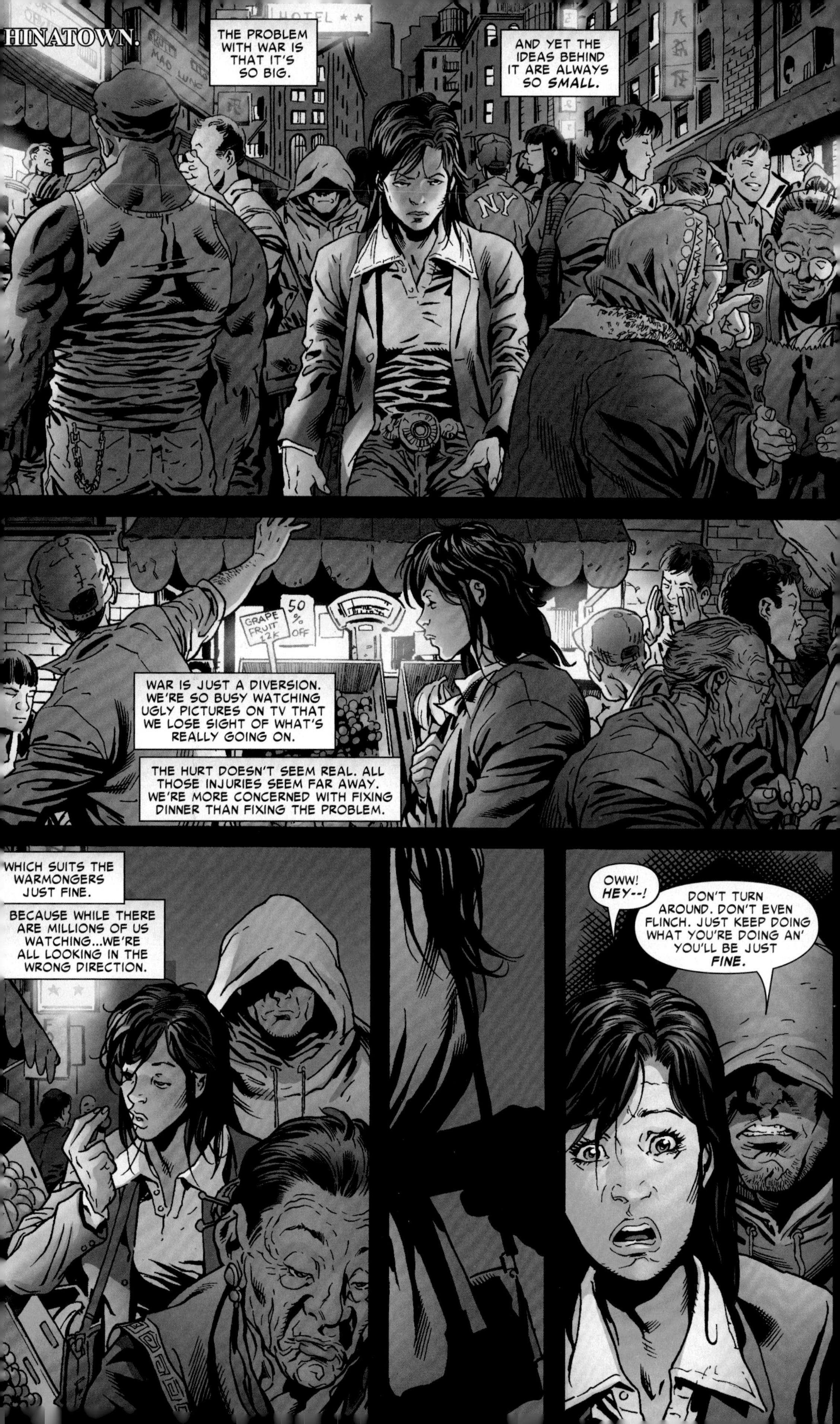
HINATOWN.
THE PROBLEM WITH WAR IS THAT IT'S SO BIG.
AND YET THE IDEAS BEHIND IT ARE ALWAYS SO SMALL.
HOTEL
NY
WAR IS JUST A DIVERSION. WE'RE SO BUSY WATCHING UGLY PICTURES ON TV THAT WE LOSE SIGHT OF WHAT'S REALLY GOING ON.
THE HURT DOESN'T SEEM REAL. ALL THOSE INJURIES SEEM FAR AWAY. WE'RE MORE CONCERNED WITH FIXING DINNER THAN FIXING THE PROBLEM.
GRAPE FRUIT
50 % OFF
WHICH SUITS THE WARMONGERS JUST FINE.
BECAUSE WHILE THERE ARE MILLIONS OF US WATCHING...WE'RE ALL LOOKING IN THE WRONG DIRECTION.
OWW! HEY--!
DON'T TURN AROUND. DON'T EVEN FLINCH. JUST KEEP DOING WHAT YOU'RE DOING AN' YOU'LL BE JUST FINE.

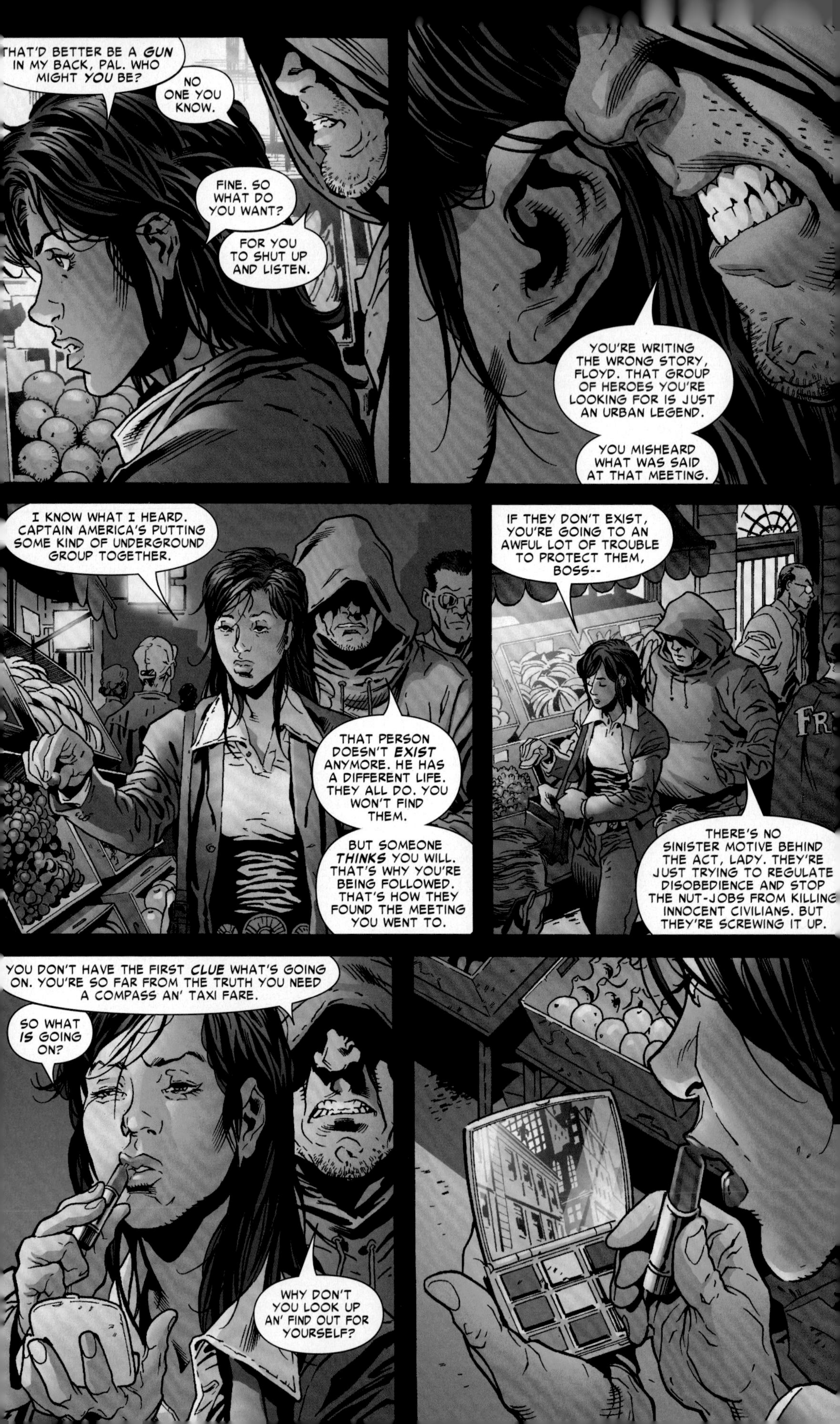

THAT'D BETTER BE A GUN IN MY BACK, PAL. WHO MIGHT YOU BE?
NO ONE YOU KNOW.
FINE. SO WHAT DO YOU WANT?
FOR YOU TO SHUT UP AND LISTEN.
YOU'RE WRITING THE WRONG STORY, FLOYD. THAT GROUP OF HEROES YOU'RE LOOKING FOR IS JUST AN URBAN LEGEND.
YOU MISHEARD WHAT WAS SAID AT THAT MEETING.
I KNOW WHAT I HEARD. CAPTAIN AMERICA'S PUTTING SOME KIND OF UNDERGROUND GROUP TOGETHER.
THAT PERSON DOESN'T EXIST ANYMORE. HE HAS A DIFFERENT LIFE. THEY ALL DO. YOU WON'T FIND THEM.
BUT SOMEONE THINKS YOU WILL. THAT'S WHY YOU'RE BEING FOLLOWED. THAT'S HOW THEY FOUND THE MEETING YOU WENT TO.
IF THEY DON'T EXIST, YOU'RE GOING TO AN AWFUL LOT OF TROUBLE TO PROTECT THEM, BOSS--
THERE'S NO SINISTER MOTIVE BEHIND THE ACT, LADY. THEY'RE JUST TRYING TO REGULATE DISOBEDIENCE AND STOP THE NUT-JOBS FROM KILLING INNOCENT CIVILIANS. BUT THEY'RE SCREWING IT UP.
YOU DON'T HAVE THE FIRST CLUE WHAT'S GOING ON. YOU'RE SO FAR FROM THE TRUTH YOU NEED A COMPASS AN' TAXI FARE.
SO WHAT IS GOING ON?
WHY DON'T YOU LOOK UP AN' FIND OUT FOR YOURSELF?

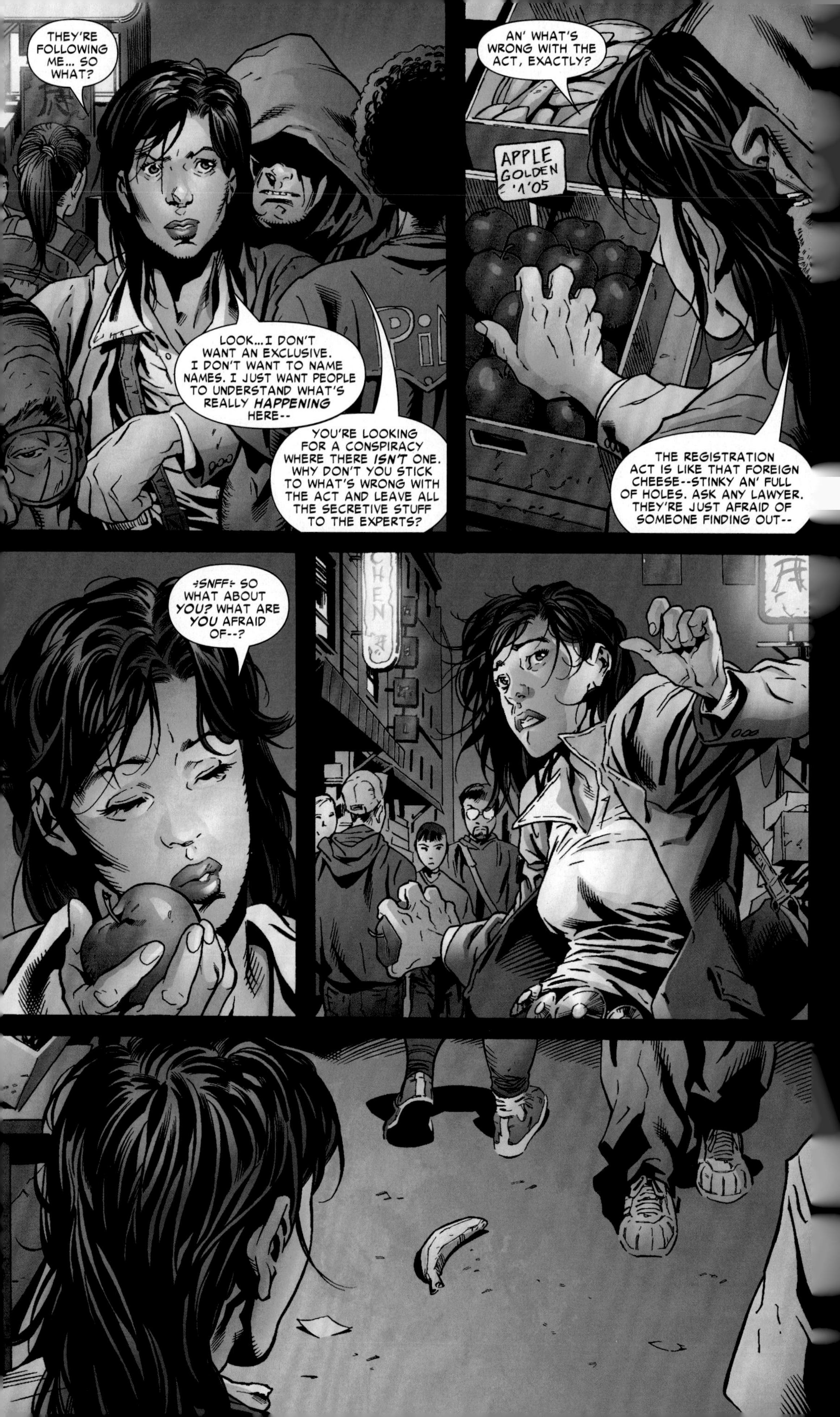

THEY'RE FOLLOWING ME... SO WHAT?
LOOK...I DON'T WANT AN EXCLUSIVE. I DON'T WANT TO NAME NAMES. I JUST WANT PEOPLE TO UNDERSTAND WHAT'S REALLY *HAPPENING* HERE--
YOU'RE LOOKING FOR A CONSPIRACY WHERE THERE *ISN'T* ONE. WHY DON'T YOU STICK TO WHAT'S WRONG WITH THE ACT AND LEAVE ALL THE SECRETIVE STUFF TO THE EXPERTS?
AN' WHAT'S WRONG WITH THE ACT, EXACTLY?
APPLE GOLDEN '1'05
THE REGISTRATION ACT IS LIKE THAT FOREIGN CHEESE--STINKY AN' FULL OF HOLES. ASK ANY LAWYER. THEY'RE JUST AFRAID OF SOMEONE FINDING OUT--
÷SNFF÷ SO WHAT ABOUT *YOU?* WHAT ARE *YOU* AFRAID OF--?
CHEN

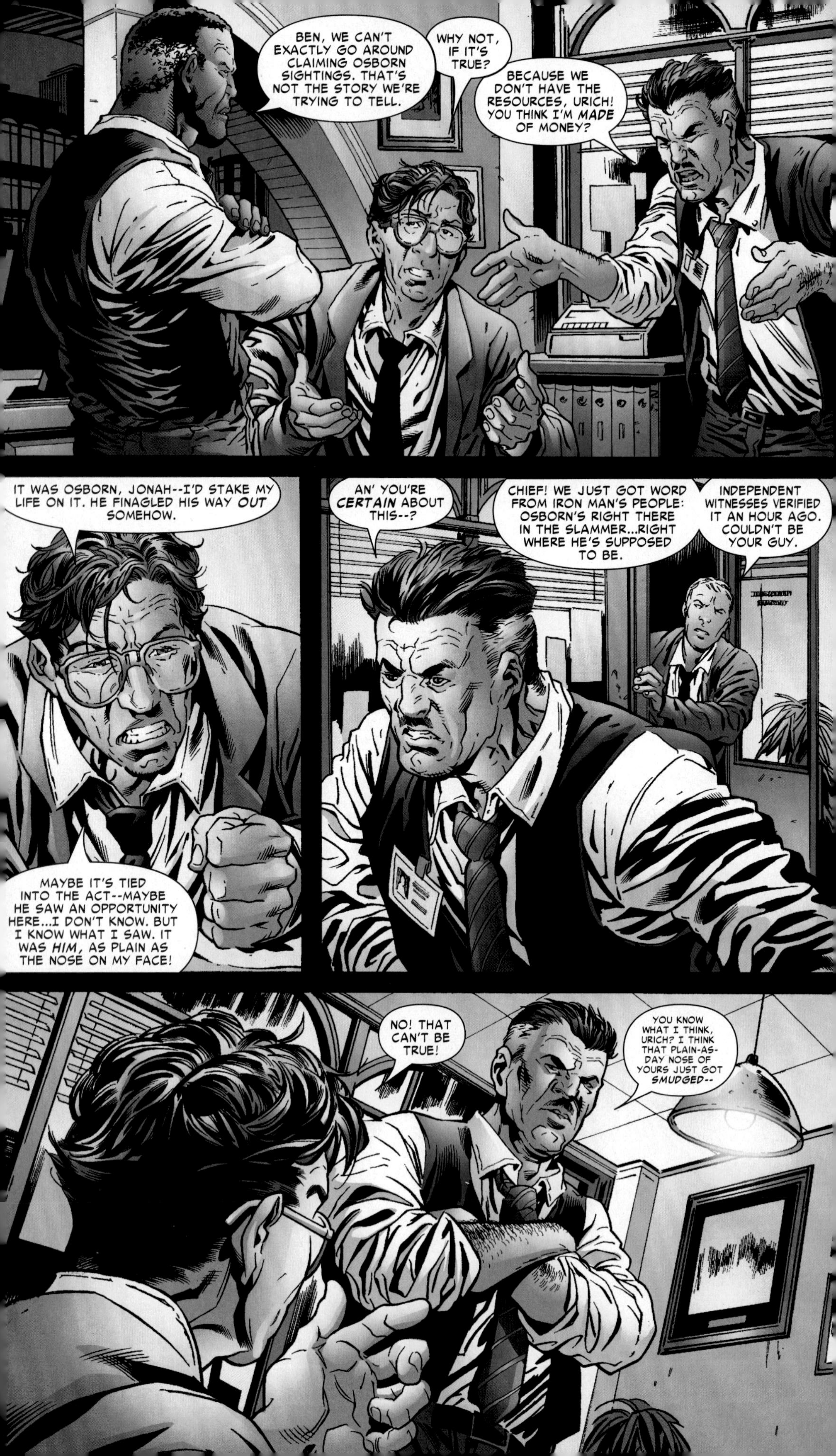
BEN, WE CAN'T EXACTLY GO AROUND CLAIMING OSBORN SIGHTINGS. THAT'S NOT THE STORY WE'RE TRYING TO TELL.
WHY NOT, IF IT'S TRUE?
BECAUSE WE DON'T HAVE THE RESOURCES, URICH! YOU THINK I'M *MADE* OF MONEY?
IT WAS OSBORN, JONAH--I'D STAKE MY LIFE ON IT. HE FINAGLED HIS WAY *OUT* SOMEHOW.
MAYBE IT'S TIED INTO THE ACT--MAYBE HE SAW AN OPPORTUNITY HERE...I DON'T KNOW. BUT I KNOW WHAT I SAW. IT WAS *HIM*, AS PLAIN AS THE NOSE ON MY FACE!
AN' YOU'RE *CERTAIN* ABOUT THIS--?
CHIEF! WE JUST GOT WORD FROM IRON MAN'S PEOPLE: OSBORN'S RIGHT THERE IN THE SLAMMER...RIGHT WHERE HE'S SUPPOSED TO BE.
INDEPENDENT WITNESSES VERIFIED IT AN HOUR AGO. COULDN'T BE YOUR GUY.
NO! THAT CAN'T BE TRUE!
YOU KNOW WHAT I THINK, URICH? I THINK THAT PLAIN-AS-DAY NOSE OF YOURS JUST GOT *SMUDGED*--

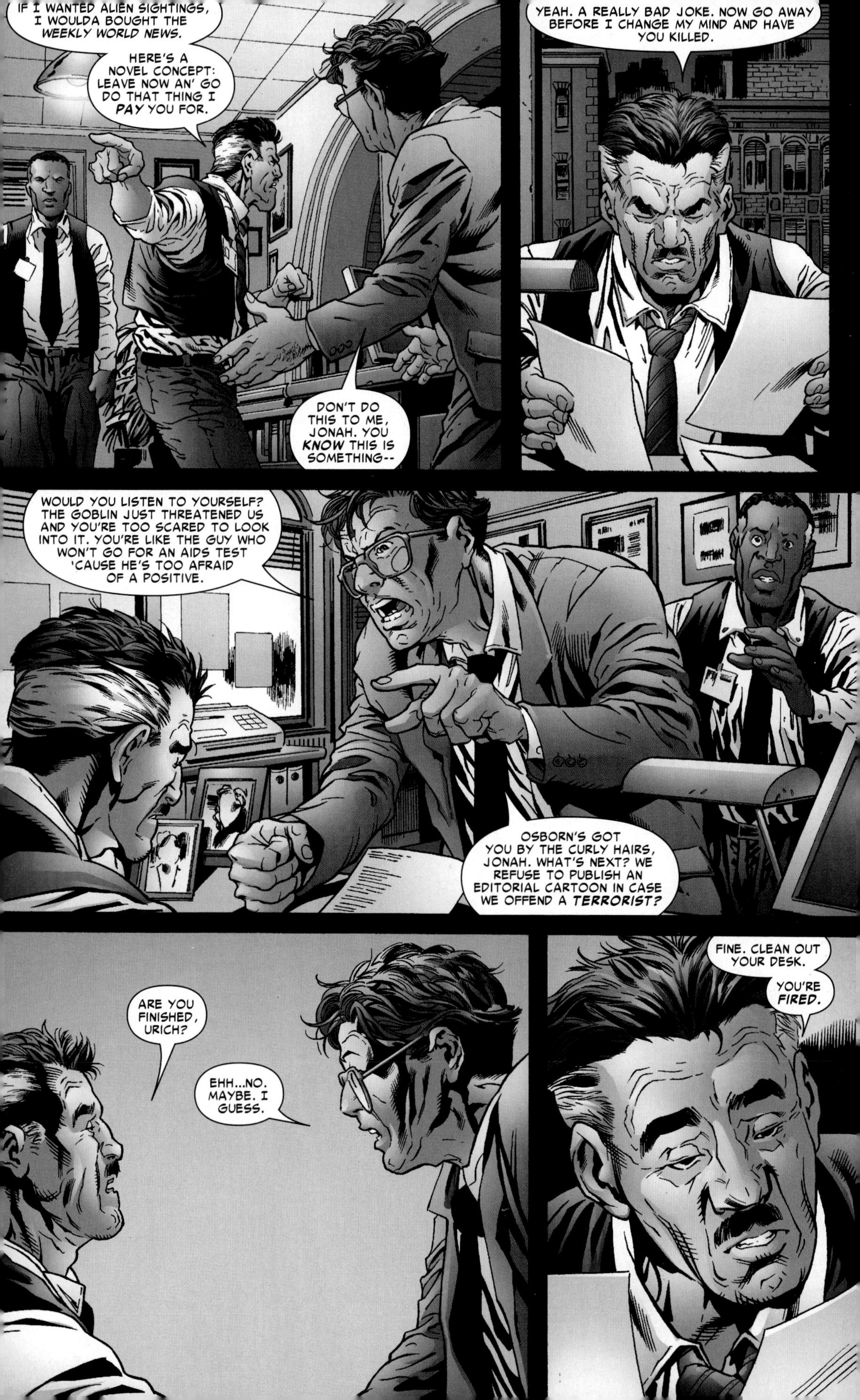
IF I WANTED ALIEN SIGHTINGS, I WOULDA BOUGHT THE *WEEKLY WORLD NEWS.*
HERE'S A NOVEL CONCEPT: LEAVE NOW AN' GO DO THAT THING I *PAY* YOU FOR.
DON'T DO THIS TO ME, JONAH. YOU *KNOW* THIS IS SOMETHING--
YEAH. A REALLY BAD JOKE. NOW GO AWAY BEFORE I CHANGE MY MIND AND HAVE YOU KILLED.
WOULD YOU LISTEN TO YOURSELF? THE GOBLIN JUST THREATENED US AND YOU'RE TOO SCARED TO LOOK INTO IT. YOU'RE LIKE THE GUY WHO WON'T GO FOR AN AIDS TEST 'CAUSE HE'S TOO AFRAID OF A POSITIVE.
OSBORN'S GOT YOU BY THE CURLY HAIRS, JONAH. WHAT'S NEXT? WE REFUSE TO PUBLISH AN EDITORIAL CARTOON IN CASE WE OFFEND A *TERRORIST?*
ARE YOU FINISHED, URICH?
EHH...NO. MAYBE. I GUESS.
FINE. CLEAN OUT YOUR DESK.
YOU'RE *FIRED.*

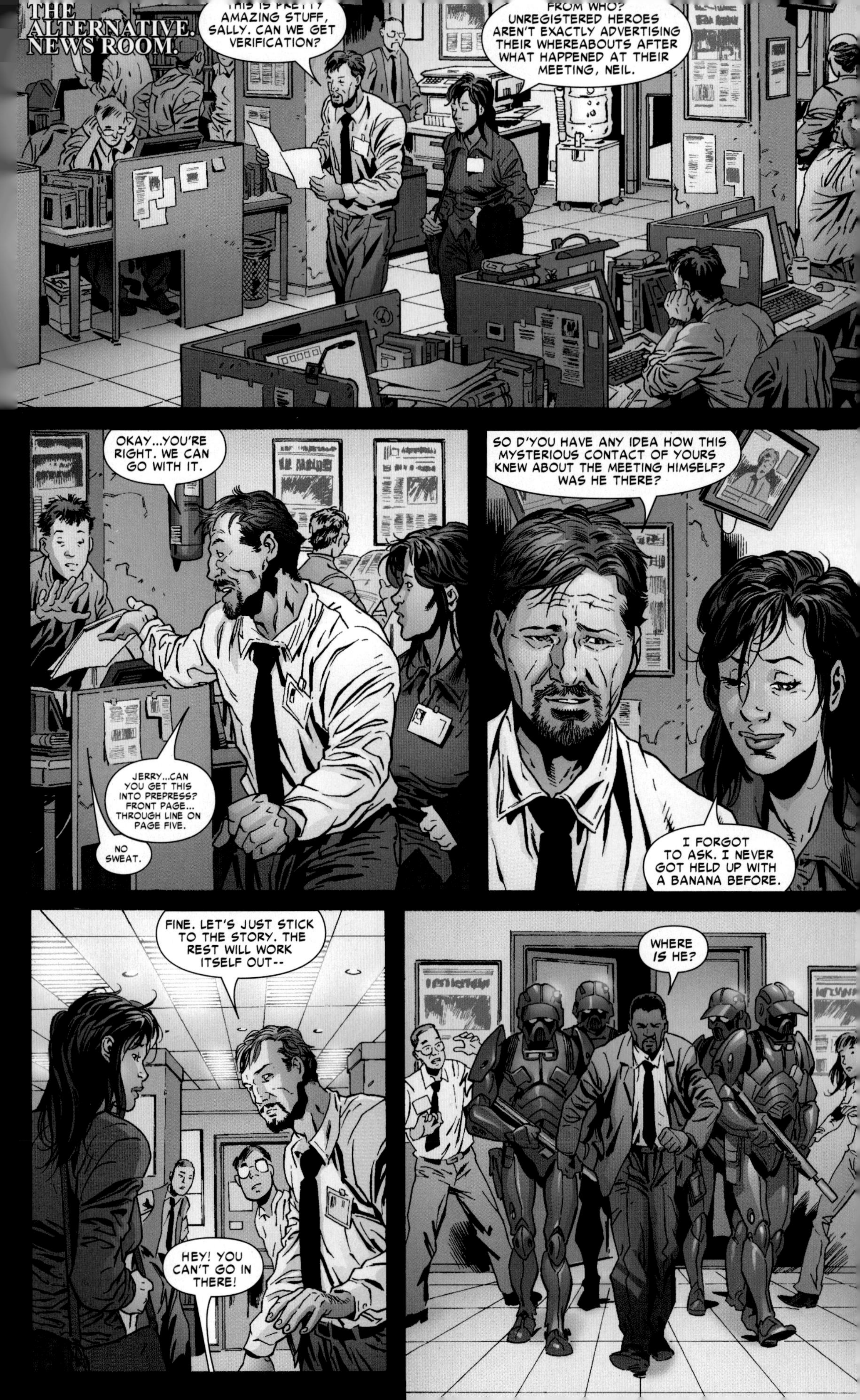
THE ALTERNATIVE. NEWS ROOM.
THIS IS PRETTY AMAZING STUFF, SALLY. CAN WE GET VERIFICATION?
FROM WHO? UNREGISTERED HEROES AREN'T EXACTLY ADVERTISING THEIR WHEREABOUTS AFTER WHAT HAPPENED AT THEIR MEETING, NEIL.
OKAY...YOU'RE RIGHT. WE CAN GO WITH IT.
JERRY...CAN YOU GET THIS INTO PREPRESS? FRONT PAGE... THROUGH LINE ON PAGE FIVE.
NO SWEAT.
SO D'YOU HAVE ANY IDEA HOW THIS MYSTERIOUS CONTACT OF YOURS KNEW ABOUT THE MEETING HIMSELF? WAS HE THERE?
I FORGOT TO ASK. I NEVER GOT HELD UP WITH A BANANA BEFORE.
FINE. LET'S JUST STICK TO THE STORY. THE REST WILL WORK ITSELF OUT--
HEY! YOU CAN'T GO IN THERE!
WHERE IS HE?

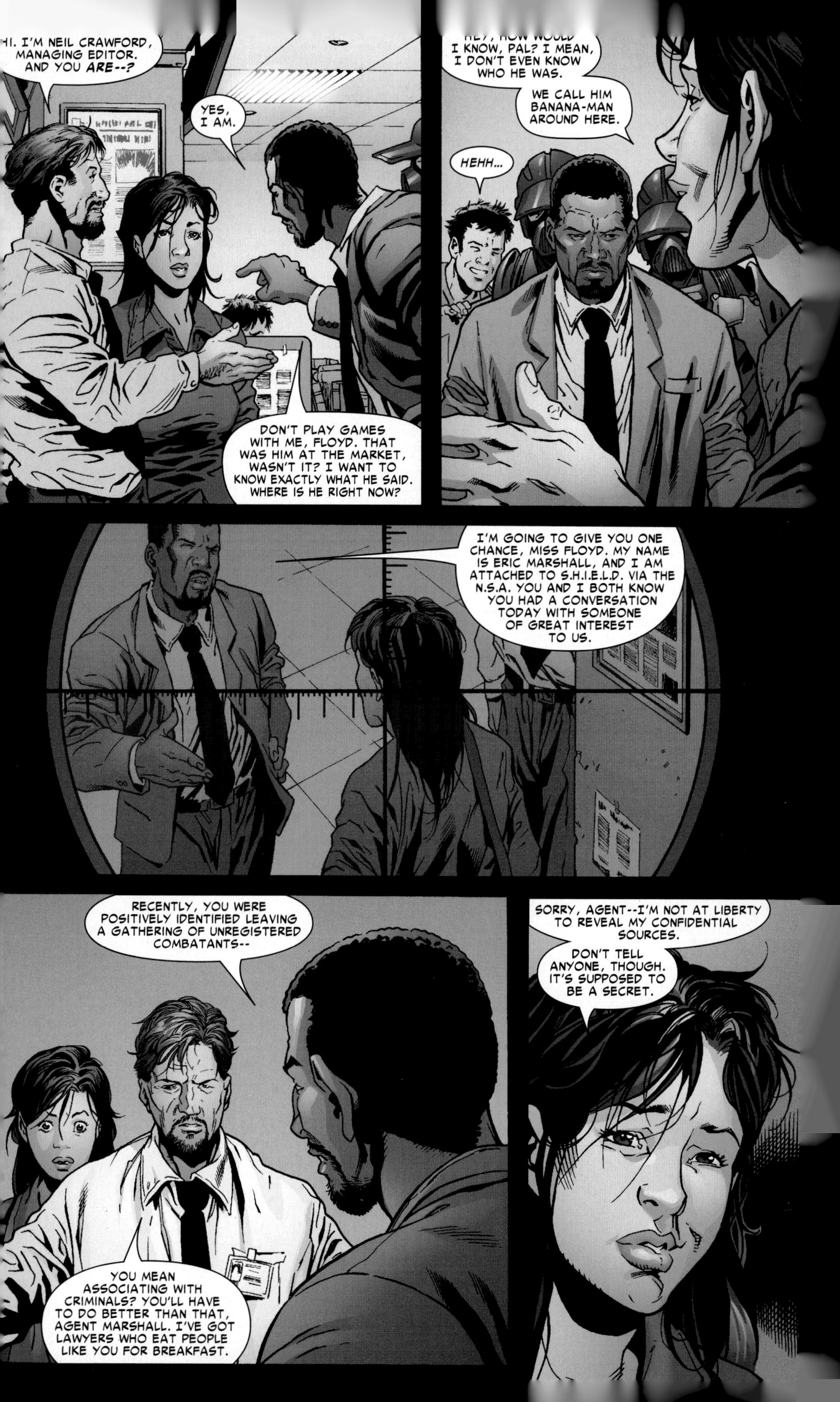

HI. I'M NEIL CRAWFORD, MANAGING EDITOR. AND YOU *ARE*--?
YES, I AM.
DON'T PLAY GAMES WITH ME, FLOYD. THAT WAS HIM AT THE MARKET, WASN'T IT? I WANT TO KNOW EXACTLY WHAT HE SAID. WHERE IS HE RIGHT NOW?
HEY, HOW WOULD I KNOW, PAL? I MEAN, I DON'T EVEN KNOW WHO HE WAS.
WE CALL HIM BANANA-MAN AROUND HERE.
HEHH...
I'M GOING TO GIVE YOU ONE CHANCE, MISS FLOYD. MY NAME IS ERIC MARSHALL, AND I AM ATTACHED TO S.H.I.E.L.D. VIA THE N.S.A. YOU AND I BOTH KNOW YOU HAD A CONVERSATION TODAY WITH SOMEONE OF GREAT INTEREST TO US.
RECENTLY, YOU WERE POSITIVELY IDENTIFIED LEAVING A GATHERING OF UNREGISTERED COMBATANTS--
YOU MEAN ASSOCIATING WITH CRIMINALS? YOU'LL HAVE TO DO BETTER THAN THAT, AGENT MARSHALL. I'VE GOT LAWYERS WHO EAT PEOPLE LIKE YOU FOR BREAKFAST.
SORRY, AGENT--I'M NOT AT LIBERTY TO REVEAL MY CONFIDENTIAL SOURCES.
DON'T TELL ANYONE, THOUGH. IT'S SUPPOSED TO BE A SECRET.

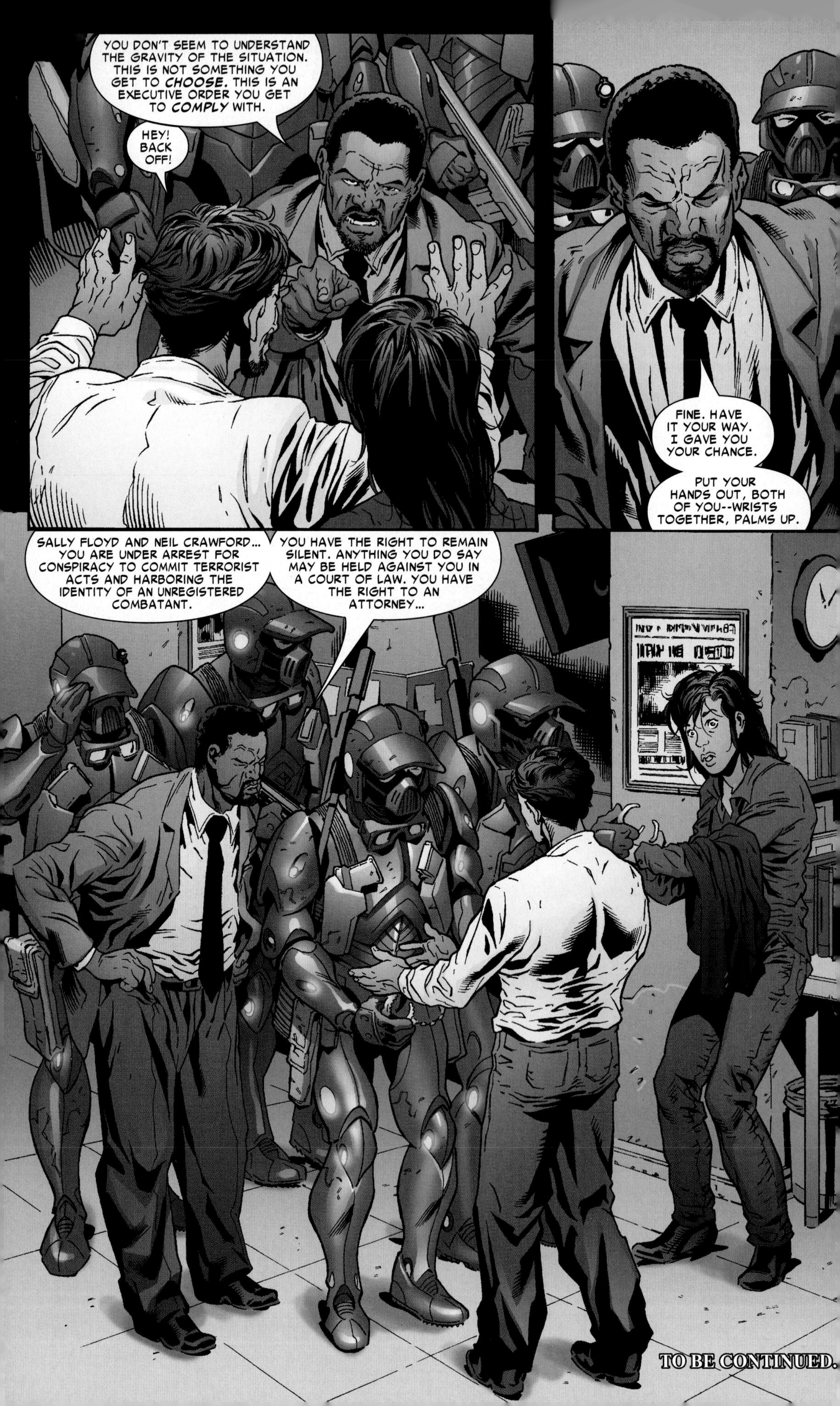
YOU DON'T SEEM TO UNDERSTAND THE GRAVITY OF THE SITUATION. THIS IS NOT SOMETHING YOU GET TO *CHOOSE*. THIS IS AN EXECUTIVE ORDER YOU GET TO *COMPLY* WITH.
HEY! BACK OFF!
FINE. HAVE IT YOUR WAY. I GAVE YOU YOUR CHANCE.
PUT YOUR HANDS OUT, BOTH OF YOU--WRISTS TOGETHER, PALMS UP.
SALLY FLOYD AND NEIL CRAWFORD... YOU ARE UNDER ARREST FOR CONSPIRACY TO COMMIT TERRORIST ACTS AND HARBORING THE IDENTITY OF AN UNREGISTERED COMBATANT.
YOU HAVE THE RIGHT TO REMAIN SILENT. ANYTHING YOU DO SAY MAY BE HELD AGAINST YOU IN A COURT OF LAW. YOU HAVE THE RIGHT TO AN ATTORNEY...
TO BE CONTINUED.

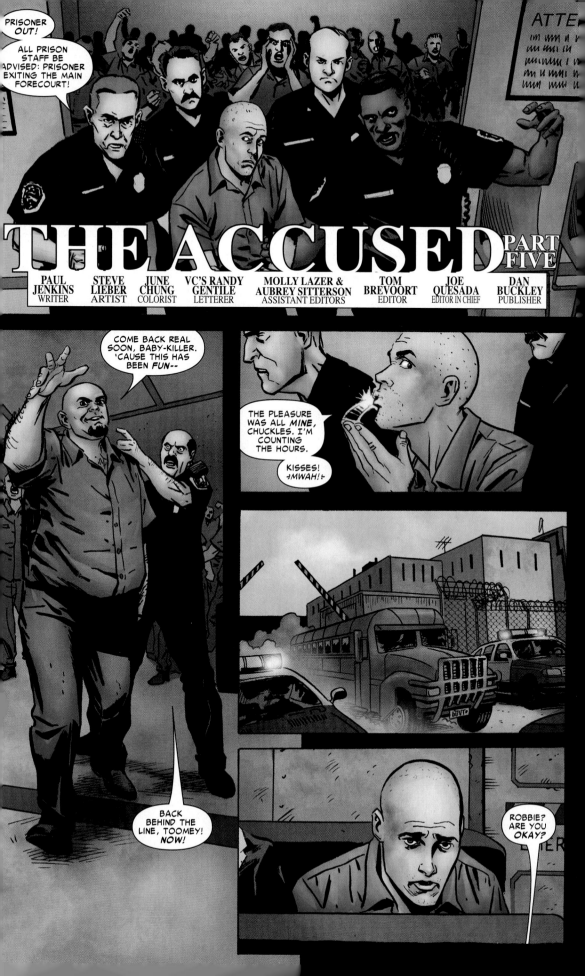

PRISONER OUT!

ALL PRISON STAFF BE ADVISED: PRISONER EXITING THE MAIN FORECOURT!

ATTE

THE ACCUSED PART FIVE

| PAUL JENKINS WRITER | STEVE LIEBER ARTIST | JUNE CHUNG COLORIST | VC'S RANDY GENTILE LETTERER | MOLLY LAZER & AUBREY SITTERSON ASSISTANT EDITORS | TOM BREVOORT EDITOR | JOE QUESADA EDITOR IN CHIEF | DAN BUCKLEY PUBLISHER |

COME BACK REAL SOON, BABY-KILLER. 'CAUSE THIS HAS BEEN FUN--

THE PLEASURE WAS ALL MINE, CHUCKLES. I'M COUNTING THE HOURS.

KISSES! ‡MWAH!‡

BACK BEHIND THE LINE, TOOMEY! NOW!

ROBBIE? ARE YOU OKAY?

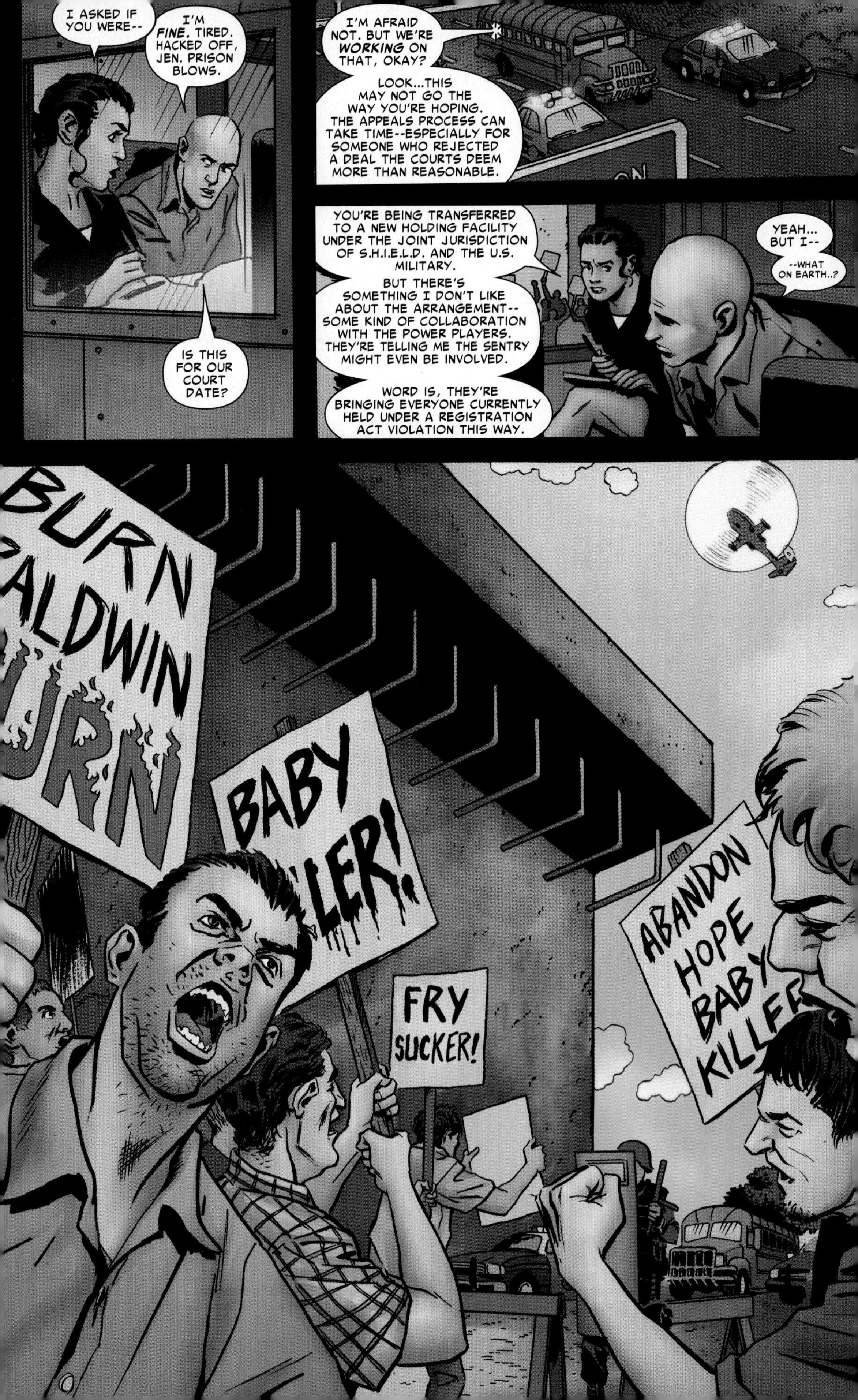
I ASKED IF YOU WERE--
I'M FINE. TIRED. HACKED OFF, JEN. PRISON BLOWS.
IS THIS FOR OUR COURT DATE?
I'M AFRAID NOT. BUT WE'RE WORKING ON THAT, OKAY?
LOOK...THIS MAY NOT GO THE WAY YOU'RE HOPING. THE APPEALS PROCESS CAN TAKE TIME--ESPECIALLY FOR SOMEONE WHO REJECTED A DEAL THE COURTS DEEM MORE THAN REASONABLE.
YOU'RE BEING TRANSFERRED TO A NEW HOLDING FACILITY UNDER THE JOINT JURISDICTION OF S.H.I.E.L.D. AND THE U.S. MILITARY.
BUT THERE'S SOMETHING I DON'T LIKE ABOUT THE ARRANGEMENT-- SOME KIND OF COLLABORATION WITH THE POWER PLAYERS. THEY'RE TELLING ME THE SENTRY MIGHT EVEN BE INVOLVED.
WORD IS, THEY'RE BRINGING EVERYONE CURRENTLY HELD UNDER A REGISTRATION ACT VIOLATION THIS WAY.
YEAH... BUT I--
--WHAT ON EARTH..?
BURN
ALDWIN
URN
BABY
LER!
FRY SUCKER!
ABANDON HOPE BABY KILLE

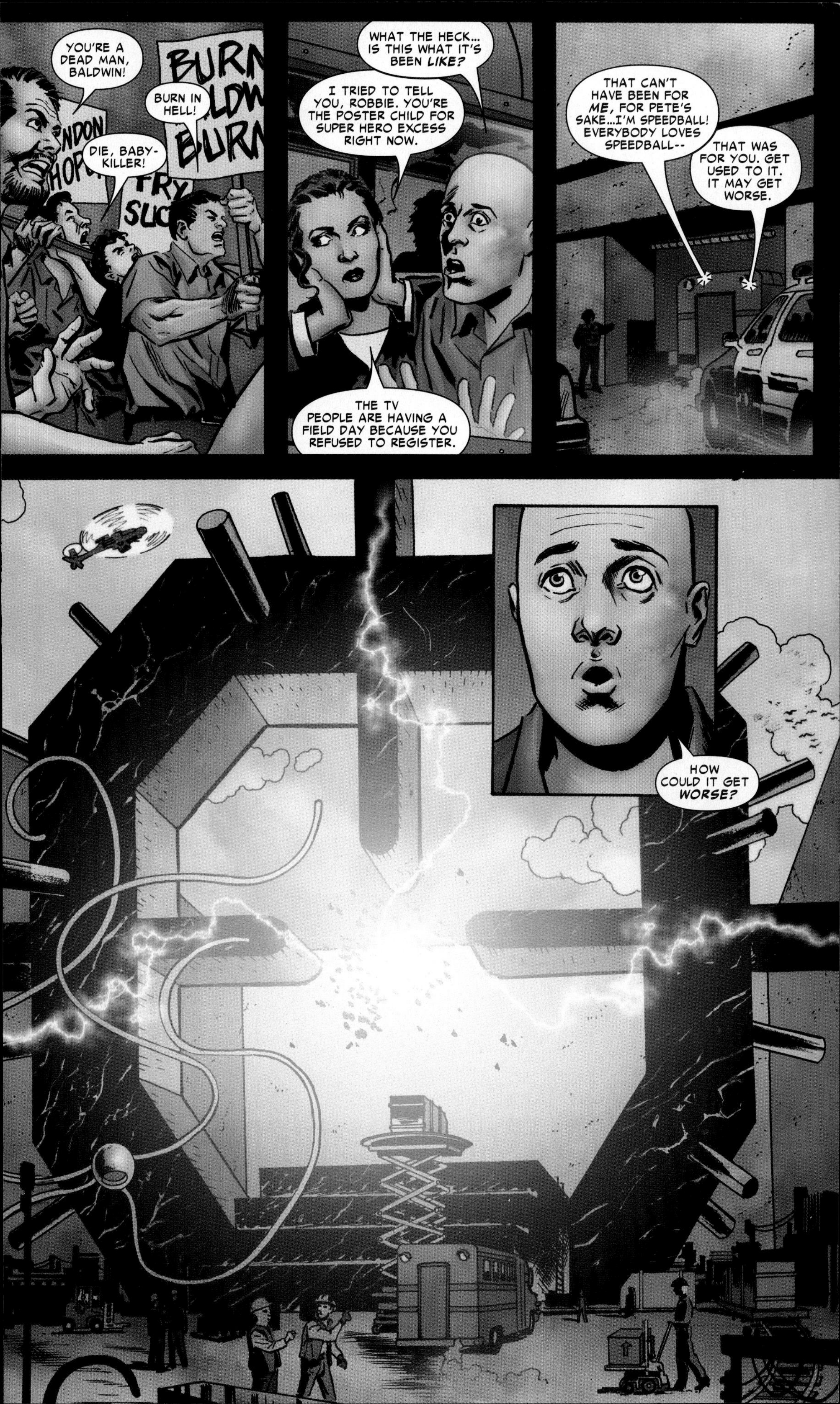

YOU'RE A DEAD MAN, BALDWIN!
BURN IN HELL!
DIE, BABY-KILLER!
WHAT THE HECK... IS THIS WHAT IT'S BEEN LIKE?
I TRIED TO TELL YOU, ROBBIE. YOU'RE THE POSTER CHILD FOR SUPER HERO EXCESS RIGHT NOW.
THE TV PEOPLE ARE HAVING A FIELD DAY BECAUSE YOU REFUSED TO REGISTER.
THAT CAN'T HAVE BEEN FOR ME, FOR PETE'S SAKE...I'M SPEEDBALL! EVERYBODY LOVES SPEEDBALL--
THAT WAS FOR YOU. GET USED TO IT. IT MAY GET WORSE.
HOW COULD IT GET WORSE?

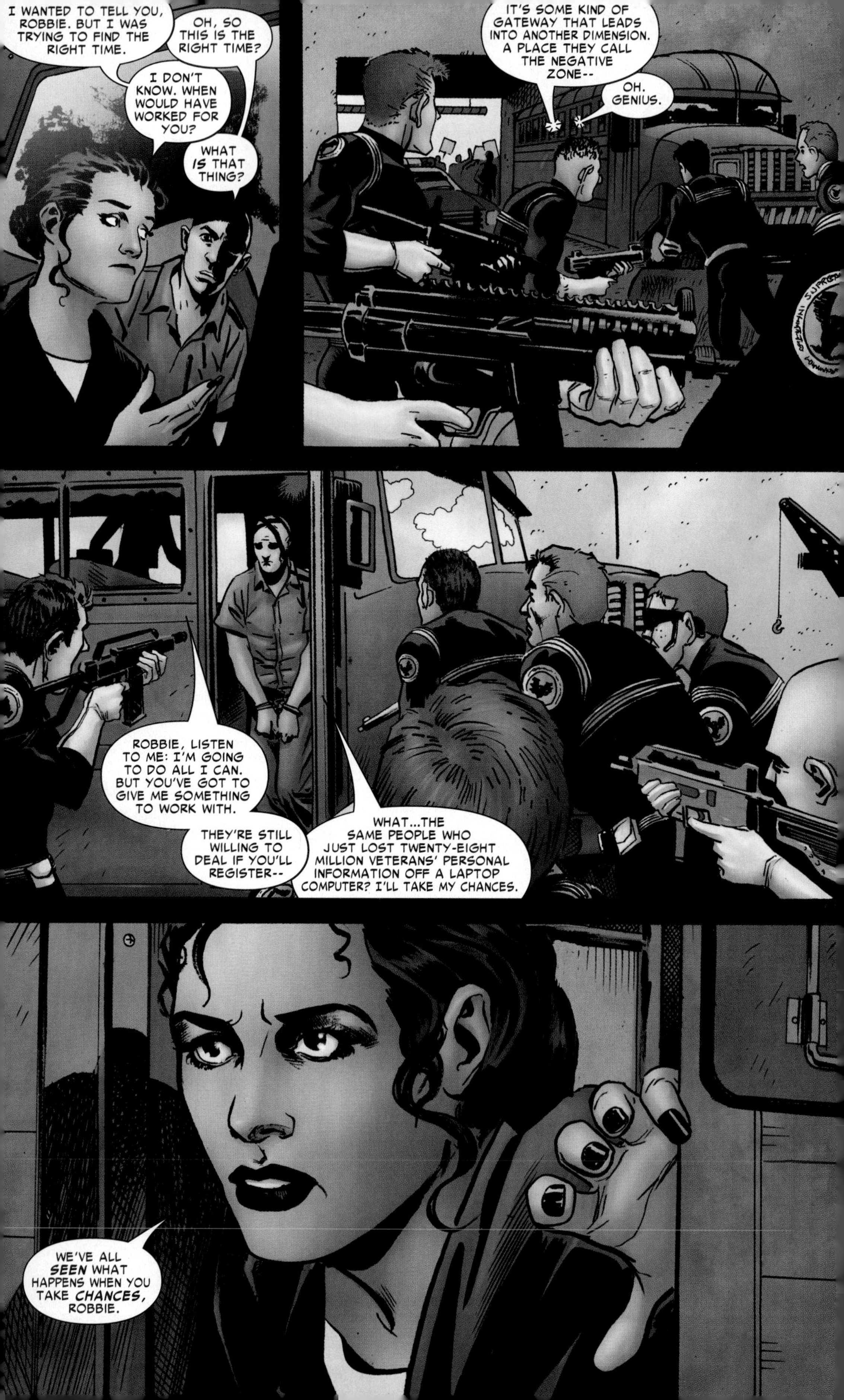
I WANTED TO TELL YOU, ROBBIE. BUT I WAS TRYING TO FIND THE RIGHT TIME.
OH, SO THIS IS THE RIGHT TIME?
I DON'T KNOW. WHEN WOULD HAVE WORKED FOR YOU?
WHAT *IS* THAT THING?
IT'S SOME KIND OF GATEWAY THAT LEADS INTO ANOTHER DIMENSION. A PLACE THEY CALL THE NEGATIVE ZONE--
OH. GENIUS.
ROBBIE, LISTEN TO ME: I'M GOING TO DO ALL I CAN. BUT YOU'VE GOT TO GIVE ME SOMETHING TO WORK WITH.
THEY'RE STILL WILLING TO DEAL IF YOU'LL REGISTER--
WHAT...THE SAME PEOPLE WHO JUST LOST TWENTY-EIGHT MILLION VETERANS' PERSONAL INFORMATION OFF A LAPTOP COMPUTER? I'LL TAKE MY CHANCES.
WE'VE ALL *SEEN* WHAT HAPPENS WHEN YOU TAKE *CHANCES*, ROBBIE.

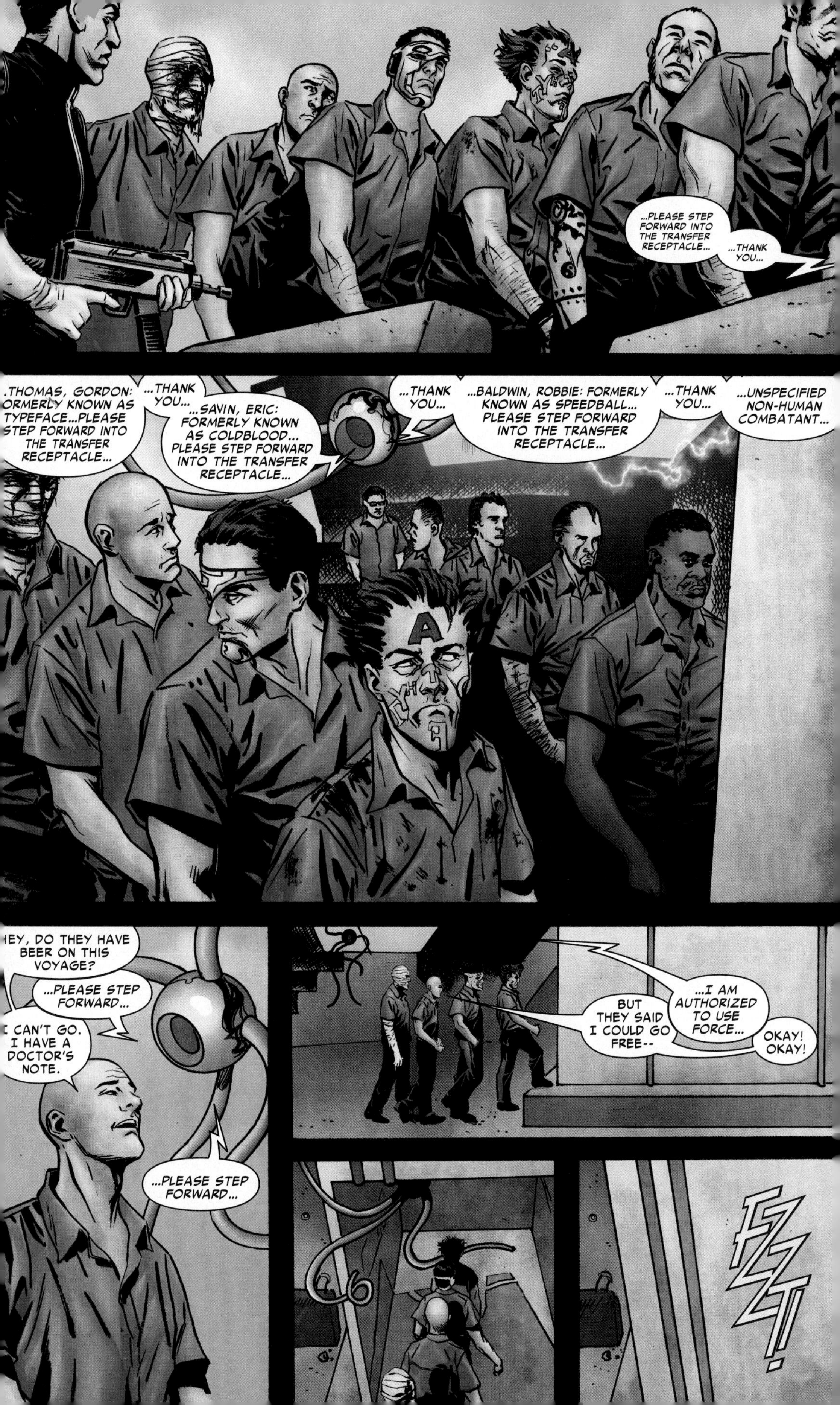

...PLEASE STEP FORWARD INTO THE TRANSFER RECEPTACLE...
...THANK YOU...
.THOMAS, GORDON: ORMERLY KNOWN AS TYPEFACE...PLEASE STEP FORWARD INTO THE TRANSFER RECEPTACLE...
...THANK YOU...
...SAVIN, ERIC: FORMERLY KNOWN AS COLDBLOOD... PLEASE STEP FORWARD INTO THE TRANSFER RECEPTACLE...
...THANK YOU...
...BALDWIN, ROBBIE: FORMERLY KNOWN AS SPEEDBALL... PLEASE STEP FORWARD INTO THE TRANSFER RECEPTACLE...
...THANK YOU...
...UNSPECIFIED NON-HUMAN COMBATANT...
HEY, DO THEY HAVE BEER ON THIS VOYAGE?
...PLEASE STEP FORWARD...
I CAN'T GO. I HAVE A DOCTOR'S NOTE.
...PLEASE STEP FORWARD...
BUT THEY SAID I COULD GO FREE--
...I AM AUTHORIZED TO USE FORCE...
OKAY! OKAY!
FZZT!

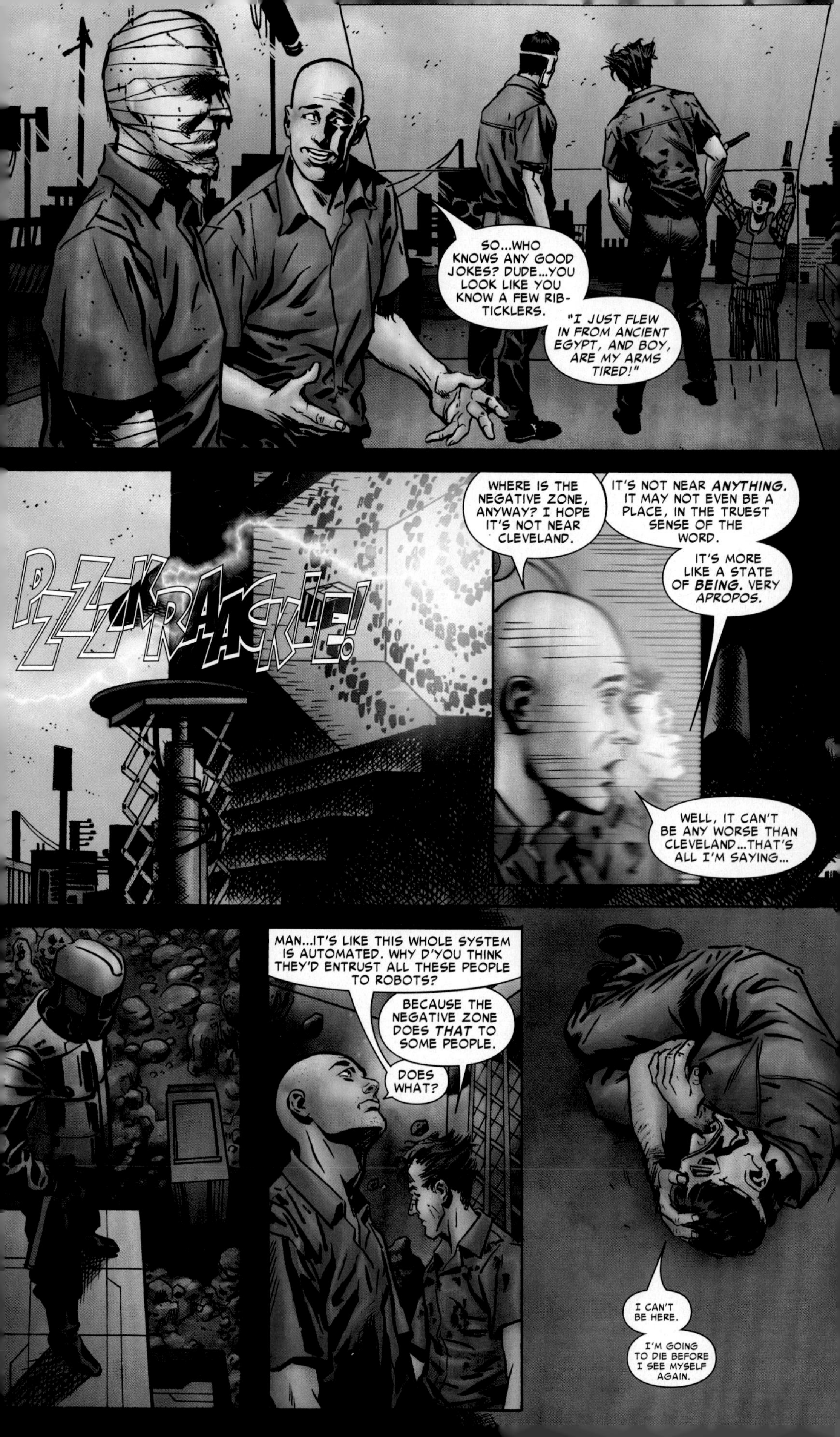
SO...WHO KNOWS ANY GOOD JOKES? DUDE...YOU LOOK LIKE YOU KNOW A FEW RIB-TICKLERS.
"I JUST FLEW IN FROM ANCIENT EGYPT, AND BOY, ARE MY ARMS TIRED!"
PZZZKRAACKLE!
WHERE IS THE NEGATIVE ZONE, ANYWAY? I HOPE IT'S NOT NEAR CLEVELAND.
IT'S NOT NEAR *ANYTHING.* IT MAY NOT EVEN BE A PLACE, IN THE TRUEST SENSE OF THE WORD.
IT'S MORE LIKE A STATE OF *BEING.* VERY APROPOS.
WELL, IT CAN'T BE ANY WORSE THAN CLEVELAND...THAT'S ALL I'M SAYING...
MAN...IT'S LIKE THIS WHOLE SYSTEM IS AUTOMATED. WHY D'YOU THINK THEY'D ENTRUST ALL THESE PEOPLE TO ROBOTS?
BECAUSE THE NEGATIVE ZONE DOES *THAT* TO SOME PEOPLE.
DOES WHAT?
I CAN'T BE HERE.
I'M GOING TO DIE BEFORE I SEE MYSELF AGAIN.

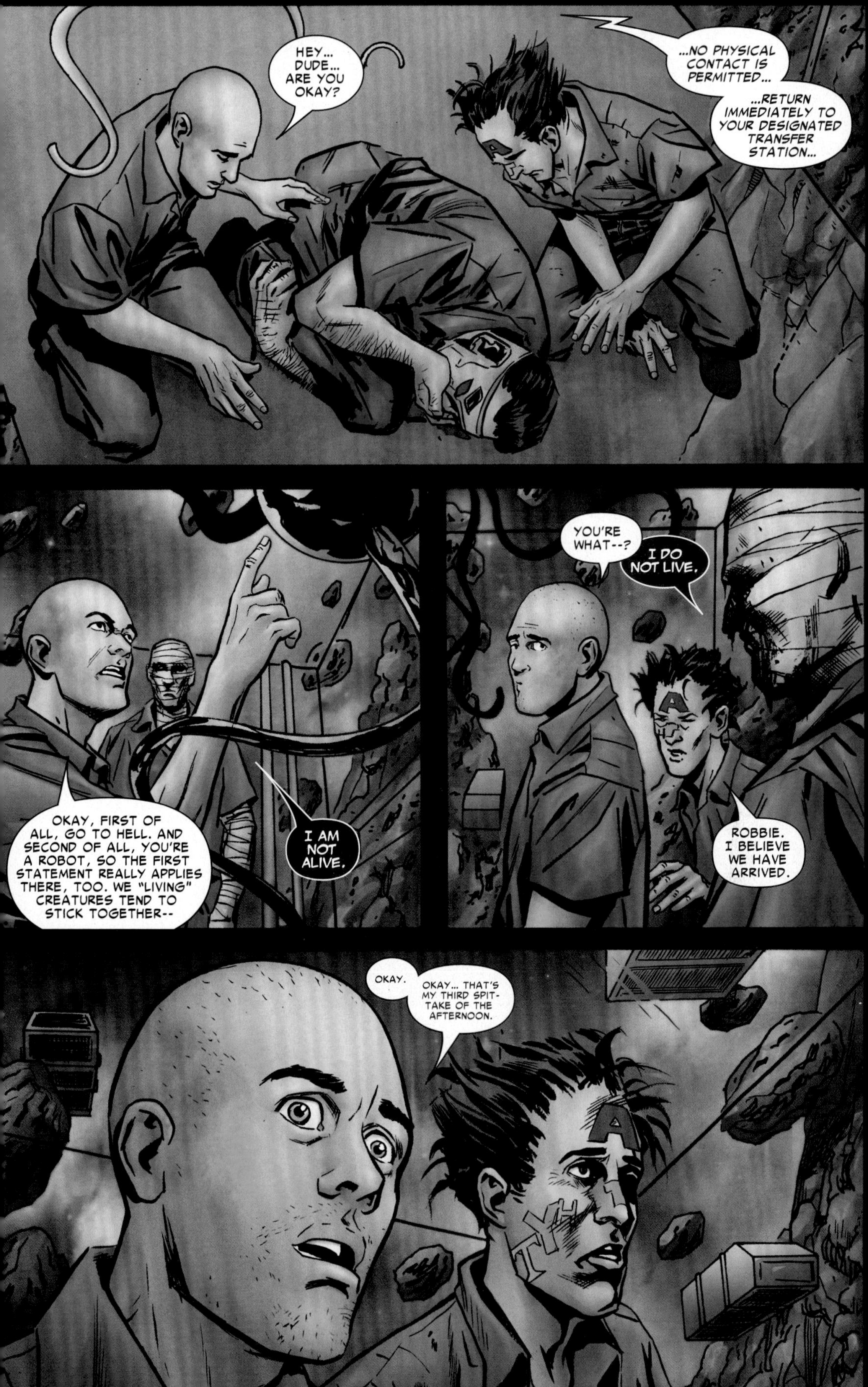
HEY... DUDE... ARE YOU OKAY?
...NO PHYSICAL CONTACT IS PERMITTED...
...RETURN IMMEDIATELY TO YOUR DESIGNATED TRANSFER STATION...
OKAY, FIRST OF ALL, GO TO HELL. AND SECOND OF ALL, YOU'RE A ROBOT, SO THE FIRST STATEMENT REALLY APPLIES THERE, TOO. WE "LIVING" CREATURES TEND TO STICK TOGETHER--
I AM NOT ALIVE.
YOU'RE WHAT--?
I DO NOT LIVE.
ROBBIE. I BELIEVE WE HAVE ARRIVED.
OKAY.
OKAY... THAT'S MY THIRD SPIT-TAKE OF THE AFTERNOON.

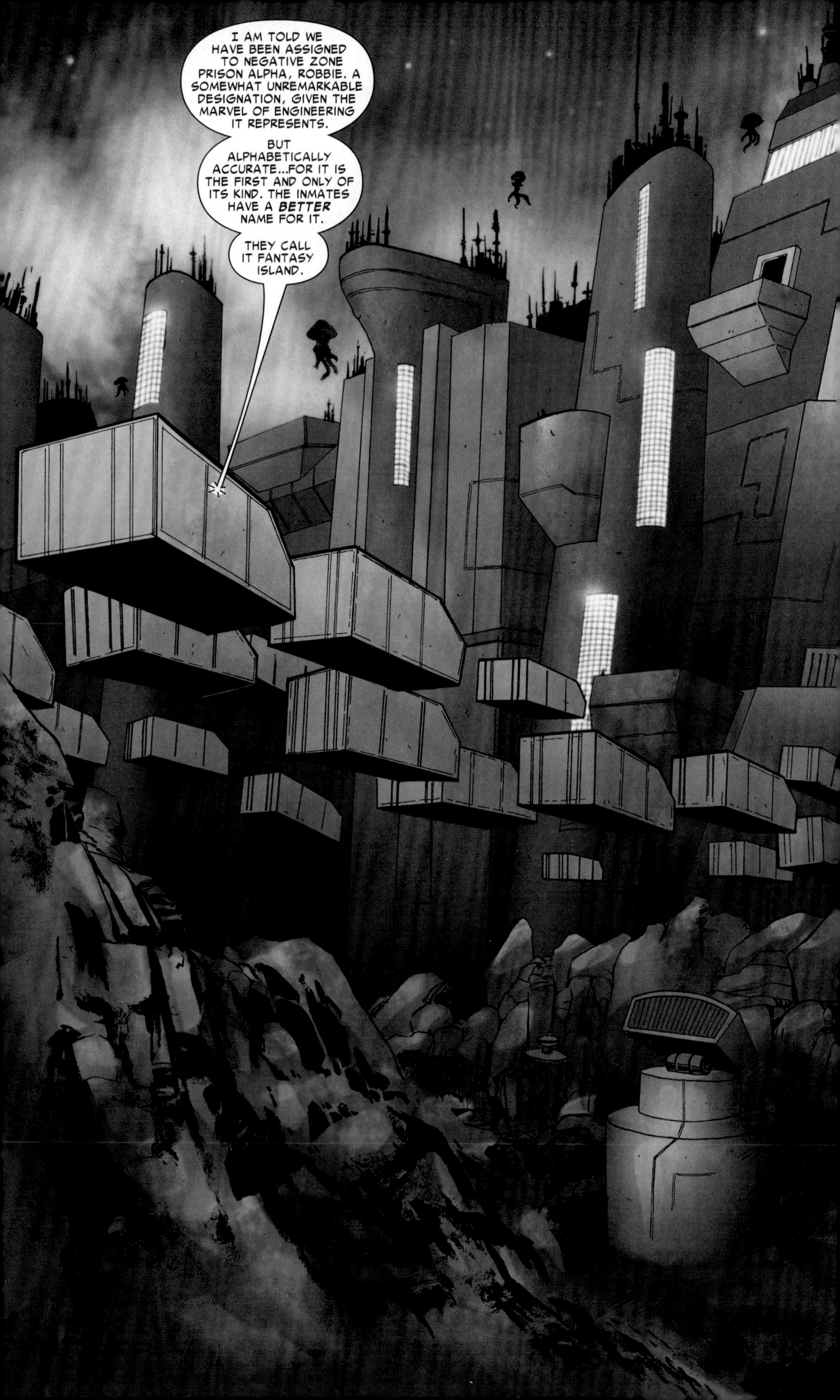
I AM TOLD WE HAVE BEEN ASSIGNED TO NEGATIVE ZONE PRISON ALPHA, ROBBIE. A SOMEWHAT UNREMARKABLE DESIGNATION, GIVEN THE MARVEL OF ENGINEERING IT REPRESENTS.
BUT ALPHABETICALLY ACCURATE...FOR IT IS THE FIRST AND ONLY OF ITS KIND. THE INMATES HAVE A *BETTER* NAME FOR IT.
THEY CALL IT FANTASY ISLAND.

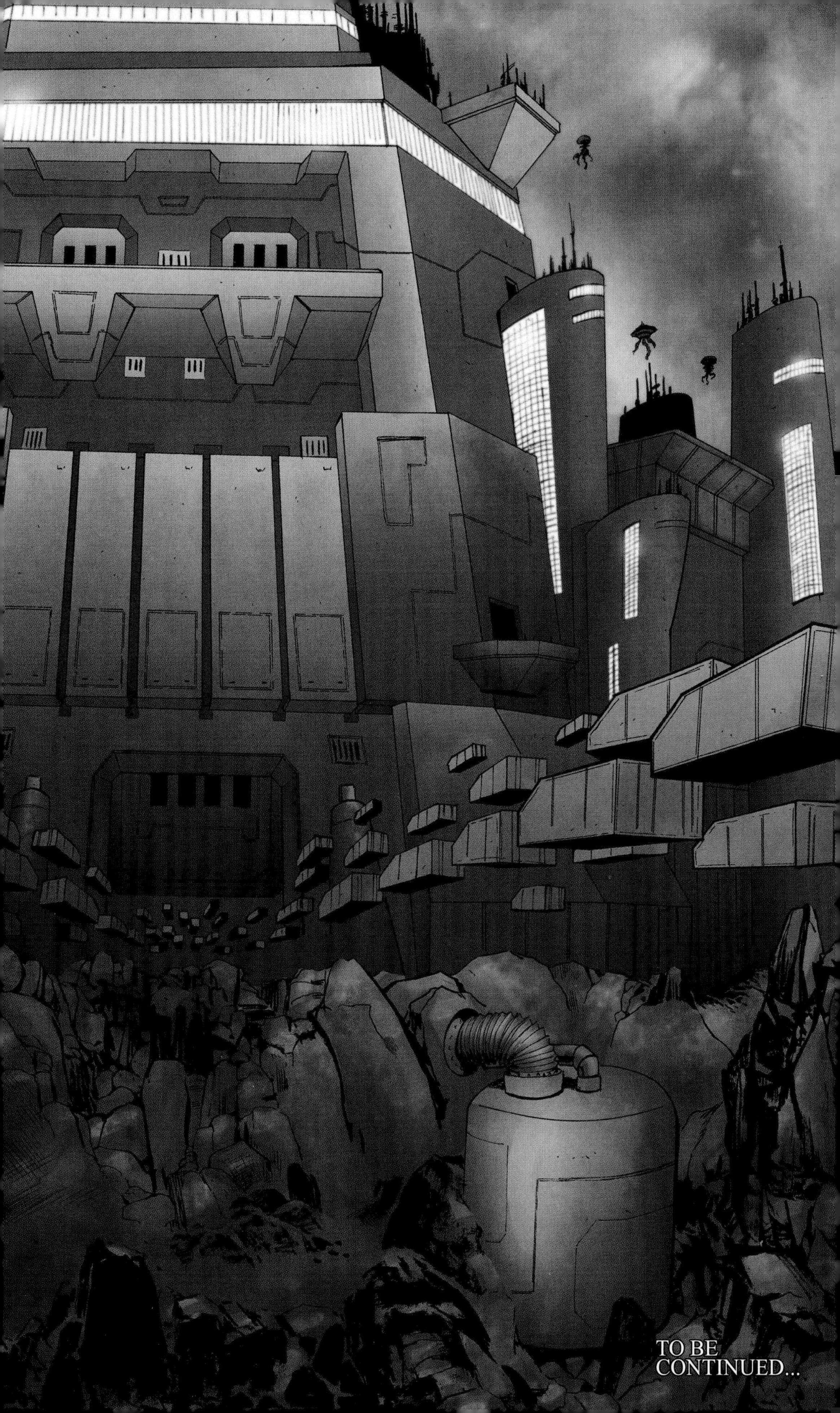
TO BE
CONTINUED...

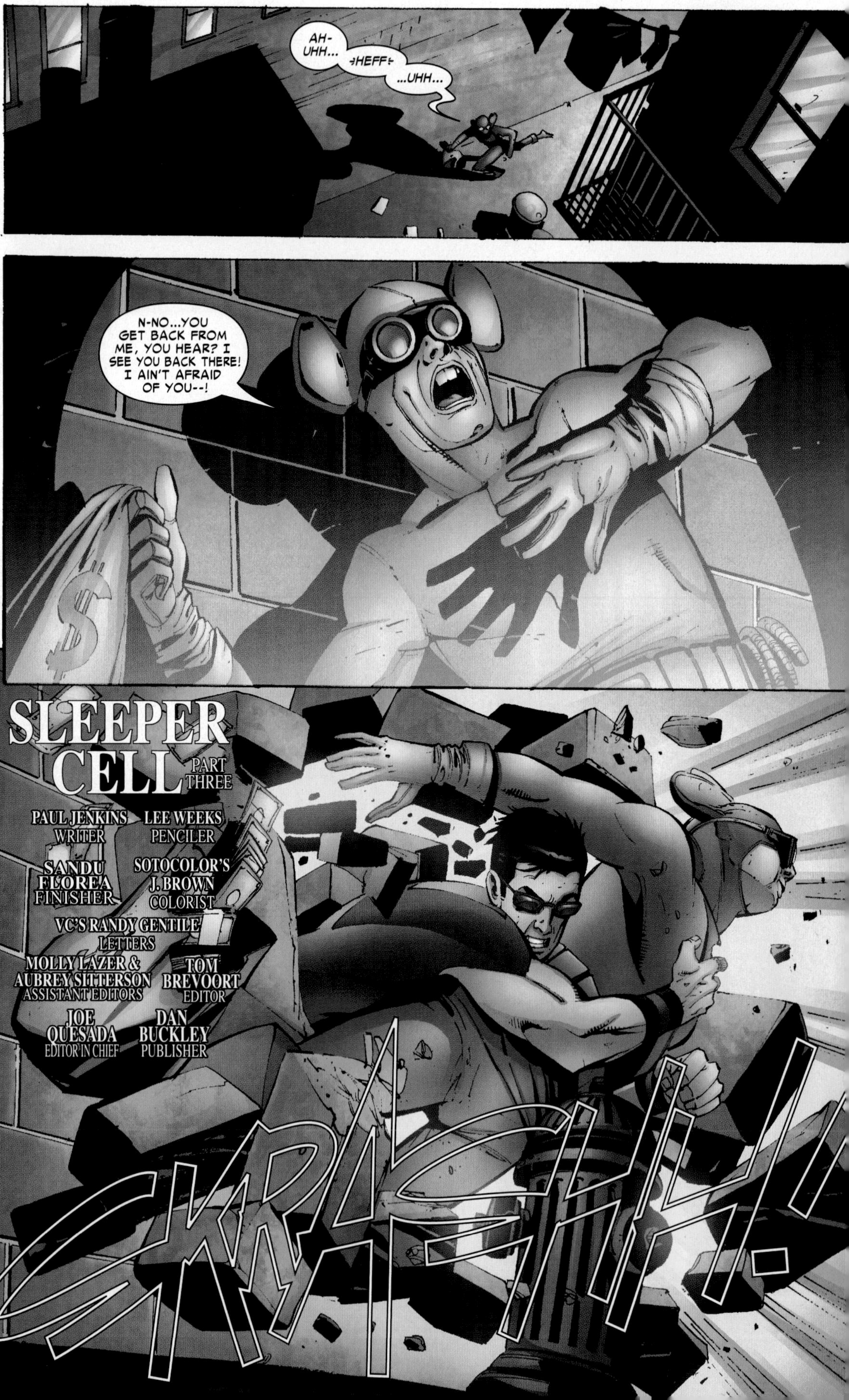

AH- UHH...
HEFF
...UHH...
N-NO...YOU GET BACK FROM ME, YOU HEAR? I SEE YOU BACK THERE! I AIN'T AFRAID OF YOU--!
SLEEPER CELL PART THREE
PAUL JENKINS WRITER
LEE WEEKS PENCILER
SANDU FLOREA FINISHER
SOTOCOLOR'S J. BROWN COLORIST
VC'S RANDY GENTILE LETTERS
MOLLY LAZER & AUBREY SITTERSON ASSISTANT EDITORS
TOM BREVOORT EDITOR
JOE QUESADA EDITOR IN CHIEF
DAN BUCKLEY PUBLISHER

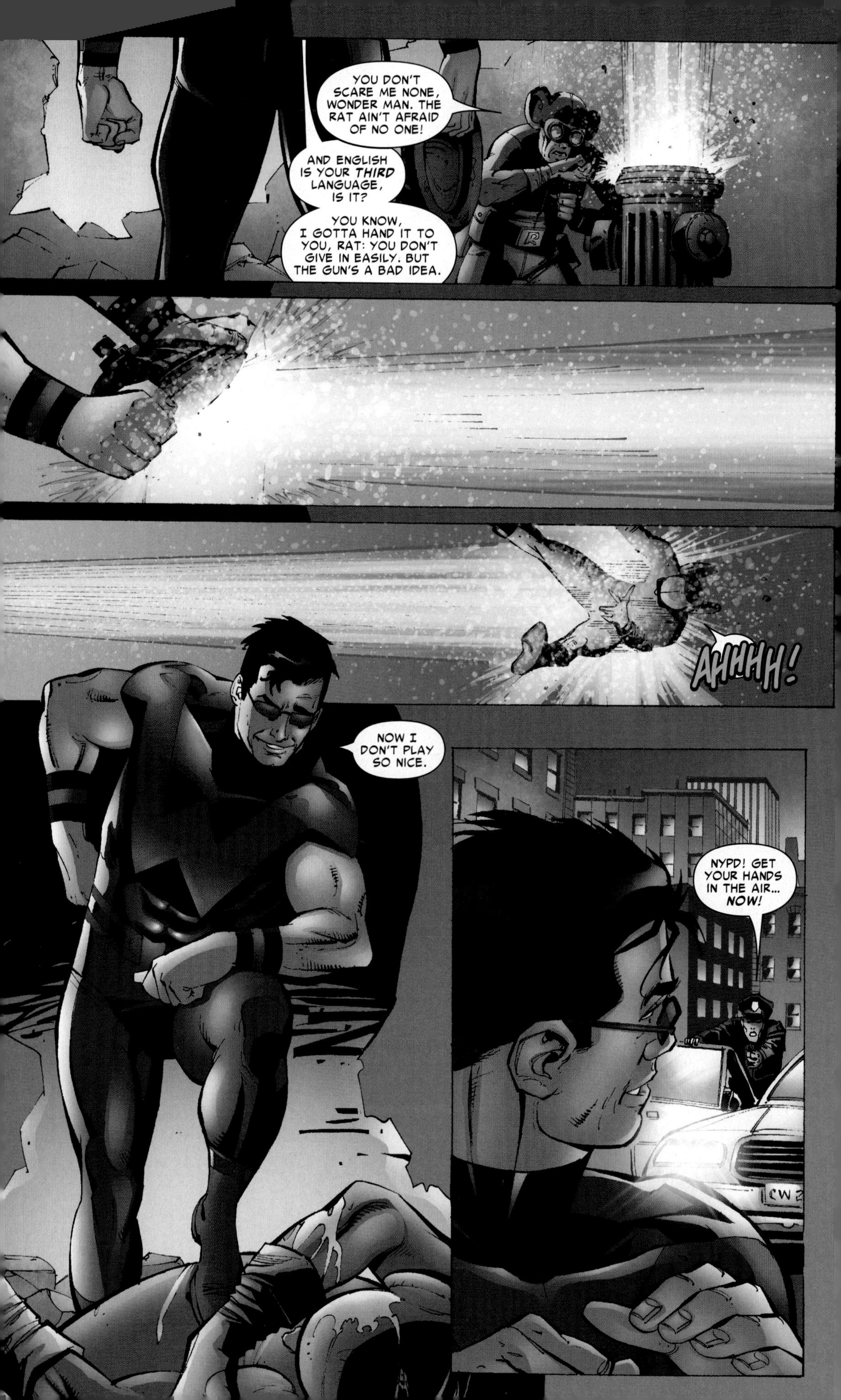

YOU DON'T SCARE ME NONE, WONDER MAN. THE RAT AIN'T AFRAID OF NO ONE!
AND ENGLISH IS YOUR *THIRD* LANGUAGE, IS IT?
YOU KNOW, I GOTTA HAND IT TO YOU, RAT: YOU DON'T GIVE IN EASILY. BUT THE GUN'S A BAD IDEA.
AHHHH!
NOW I DON'T PLAY SO NICE.
NYPD! GET YOUR HANDS IN THE AIR... *NOW!*

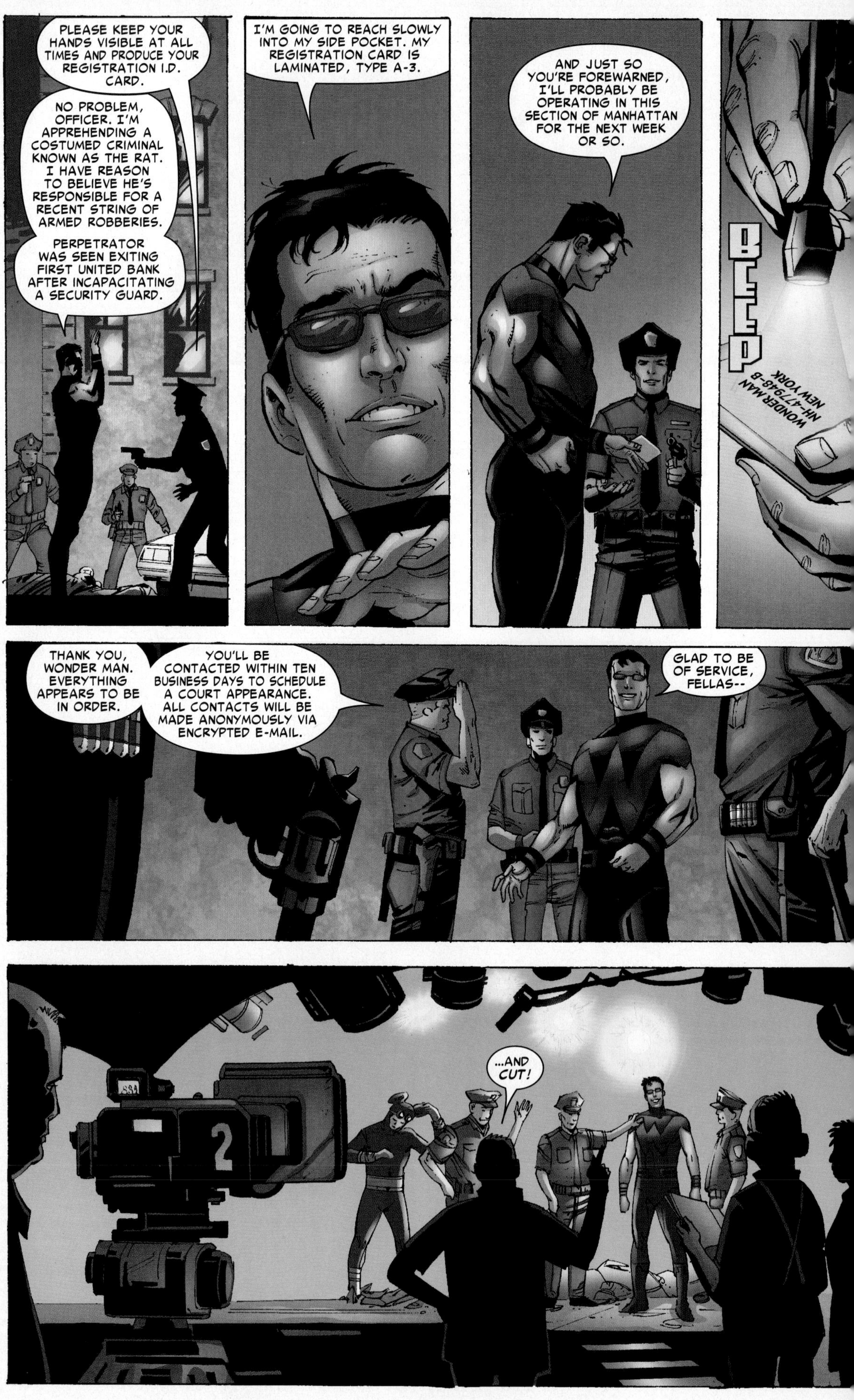
PLEASE KEEP YOUR HANDS VISIBLE AT ALL TIMES AND PRODUCE YOUR REGISTRATION I.D. CARD.
NO PROBLEM, OFFICER. I'M APPREHENDING A COSTUMED CRIMINAL KNOWN AS THE RAT. I HAVE REASON TO BELIEVE HE'S RESPONSIBLE FOR A RECENT STRING OF ARMED ROBBERIES.
PERPETRATOR WAS SEEN EXITING FIRST UNITED BANK AFTER INCAPACITATING A SECURITY GUARD.
I'M GOING TO REACH SLOWLY INTO MY SIDE POCKET. MY REGISTRATION CARD IS LAMINATED, TYPE A-3.
AND JUST SO YOU'RE FOREWARNED, I'LL PROBABLY BE OPERATING IN THIS SECTION OF MANHATTAN FOR THE NEXT WEEK OR SO.
BEEP
WONDER MAN
NH-47948-B
NEW YORK
THANK YOU, WONDER MAN. EVERYTHING APPEARS TO BE IN ORDER.
YOU'LL BE CONTACTED WITHIN TEN BUSINESS DAYS TO SCHEDULE A COURT APPEARANCE. ALL CONTACTS WILL BE MADE ANONYMOUSLY VIA ENCRYPTED E-MAIL.
GLAD TO BE OF SERVICE, FELLAS--
...AND CUT!
2

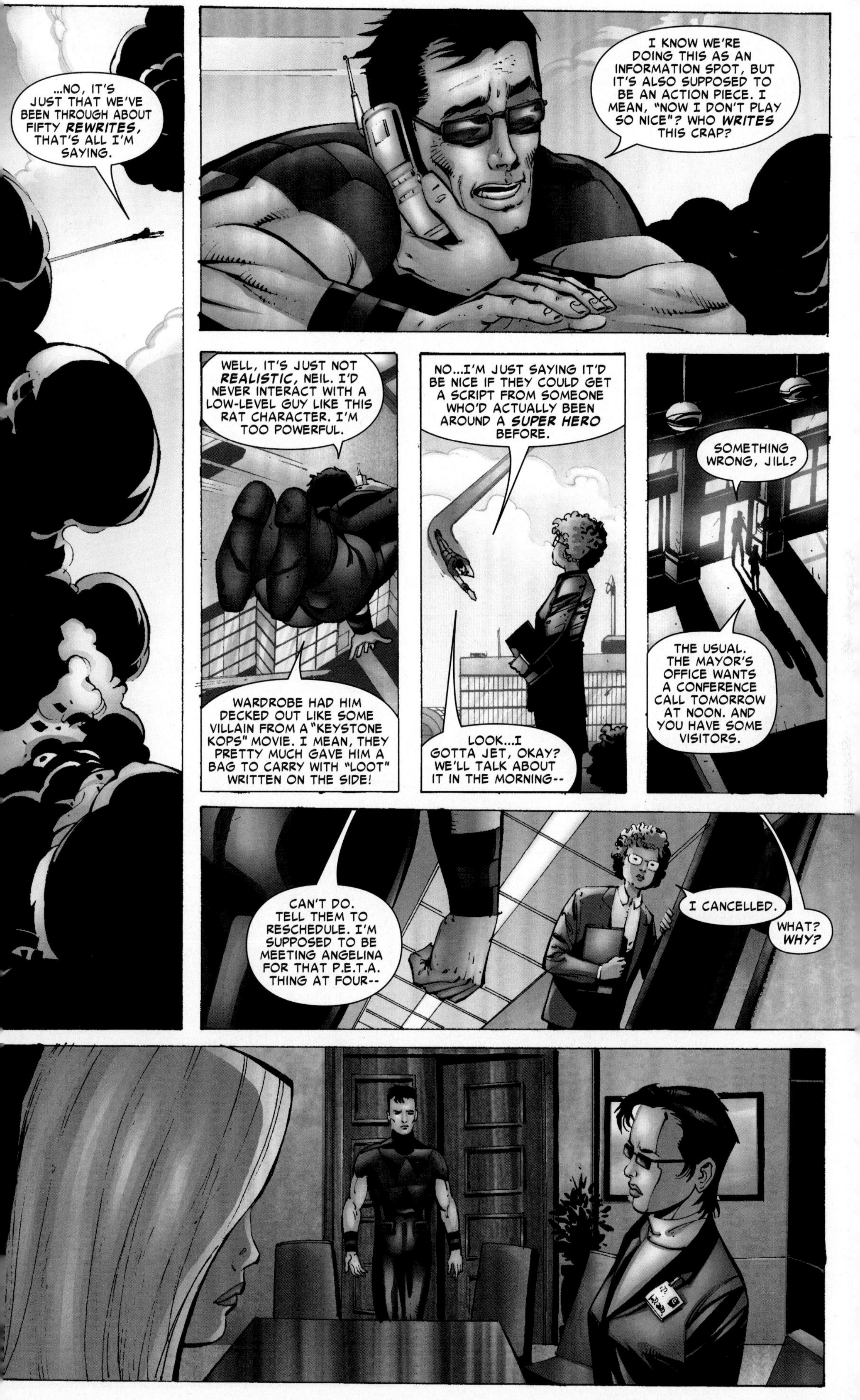

...NO, IT'S JUST THAT WE'VE BEEN THROUGH ABOUT FIFTY *REWRITES*, THAT'S ALL I'M SAYING.
I KNOW WE'RE DOING THIS AS AN INFORMATION SPOT, BUT IT'S ALSO SUPPOSED TO BE AN ACTION PIECE. I MEAN, "NOW I DON'T PLAY SO NICE"? WHO *WRITES* THIS CRAP?
WELL, IT'S JUST NOT *REALISTIC*, NEIL. I'D NEVER INTERACT WITH A LOW-LEVEL GUY LIKE THIS RAT CHARACTER. I'M TOO POWERFUL.
WARDROBE HAD HIM DECKED OUT LIKE SOME VILLAIN FROM A "KEYSTONE KOPS" MOVIE. I MEAN, THEY PRETTY MUCH GAVE HIM A BAG TO CARRY WITH "LOOT" WRITTEN ON THE SIDE!
NO...I'M JUST SAYING IT'D BE NICE IF THEY COULD GET A SCRIPT FROM SOMEONE WHO'D ACTUALLY BEEN AROUND A *SUPER HERO* BEFORE.
LOOK...I GOTTA JET, OKAY? WE'LL TALK ABOUT IT IN THE MORNING--
SOMETHING WRONG, JILL?
THE USUAL. THE MAYOR'S OFFICE WANTS A CONFERENCE CALL TOMORROW AT NOON. AND YOU HAVE SOME VISITORS.
CAN'T DO. TELL THEM TO RESCHEDULE. I'M SUPPOSED TO BE MEETING ANGELINA FOR THAT P.E.T.A. THING AT FOUR--
I CANCELLED.
WHAT? *WHY?*

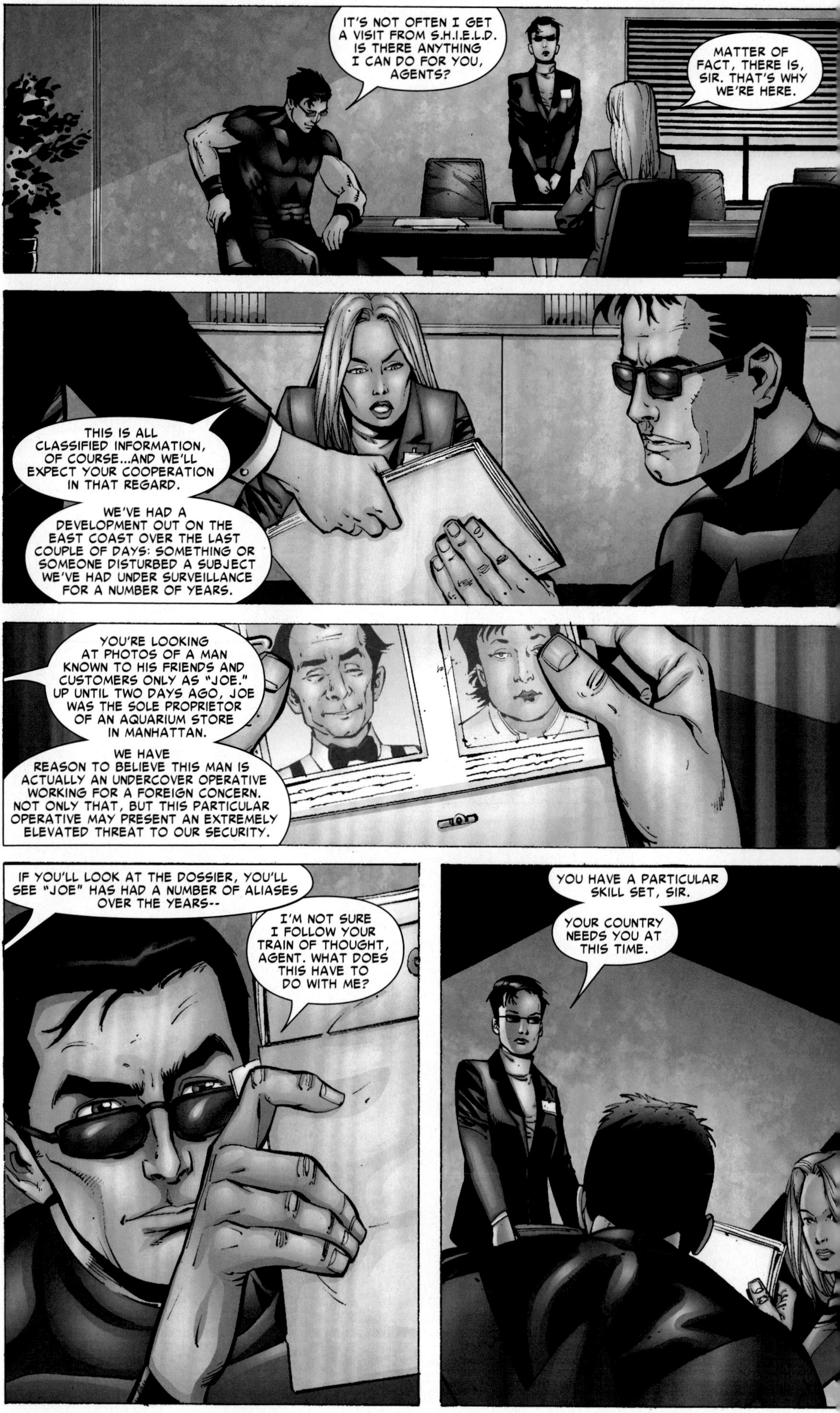

IT'S NOT OFTEN I GET A VISIT FROM S.H.I.E.L.D. IS THERE ANYTHING I CAN DO FOR YOU, AGENTS?
MATTER OF FACT, THERE IS, SIR. THAT'S WHY WE'RE HERE.
THIS IS ALL CLASSIFIED INFORMATION, OF COURSE...AND WE'LL EXPECT YOUR COOPERATION IN THAT REGARD.
WE'VE HAD A DEVELOPMENT OUT ON THE EAST COAST OVER THE LAST COUPLE OF DAYS: SOMETHING OR SOMEONE DISTURBED A SUBJECT WE'VE HAD UNDER SURVEILLANCE FOR A NUMBER OF YEARS.
YOU'RE LOOKING AT PHOTOS OF A MAN KNOWN TO HIS FRIENDS AND CUSTOMERS ONLY AS "JOE." UP UNTIL TWO DAYS AGO, JOE WAS THE SOLE PROPRIETOR OF AN AQUARIUM STORE IN MANHATTAN.
WE HAVE REASON TO BELIEVE THIS MAN IS ACTUALLY AN UNDERCOVER OPERATIVE WORKING FOR A FOREIGN CONCERN. NOT ONLY THAT, BUT THIS PARTICULAR OPERATIVE MAY PRESENT AN EXTREMELY ELEVATED THREAT TO OUR SECURITY.
IF YOU'LL LOOK AT THE DOSSIER, YOU'LL SEE "JOE" HAS HAD A NUMBER OF ALIASES OVER THE YEARS--
I'M NOT SURE I FOLLOW YOUR TRAIN OF THOUGHT, AGENT. WHAT DOES THIS HAVE TO DO WITH ME?
YOU HAVE A PARTICULAR SKILL SET, SIR.
YOUR COUNTRY NEEDS YOU AT THIS TIME.

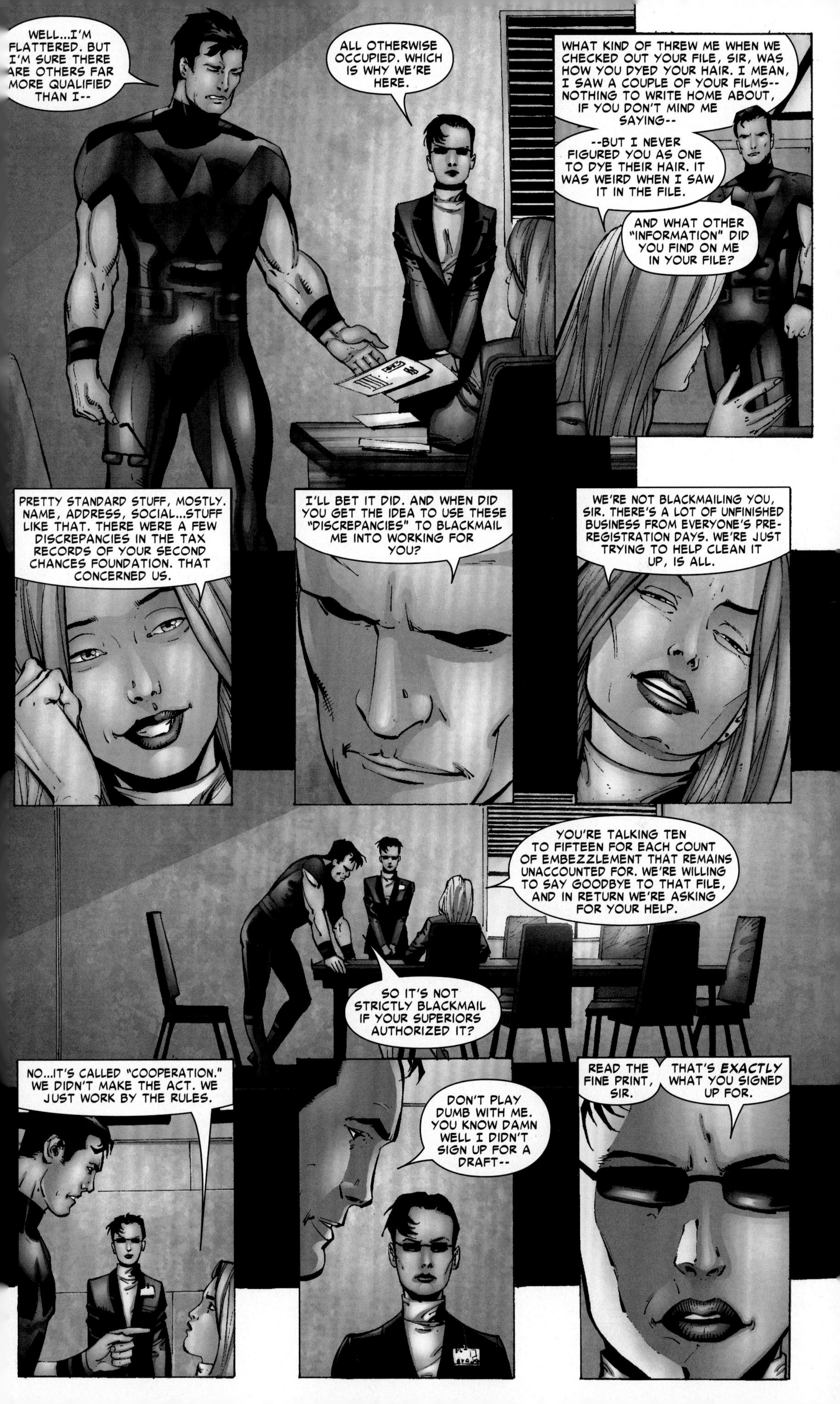

WELL...I'M FLATTERED. BUT I'M SURE THERE ARE OTHERS FAR MORE QUALIFIED THAN I--
ALL OTHERWISE OCCUPIED. WHICH IS WHY WE'RE HERE.
WHAT KIND OF THREW ME WHEN WE CHECKED OUT YOUR FILE, SIR, WAS HOW YOU DYED YOUR HAIR. I MEAN, I SAW A COUPLE OF YOUR FILMS--NOTHING TO WRITE HOME ABOUT, IF YOU DON'T MIND ME SAYING--
--BUT I NEVER FIGURED YOU AS ONE TO DYE THEIR HAIR. IT WAS WEIRD WHEN I SAW IT IN THE FILE.
AND WHAT OTHER "INFORMATION" DID YOU FIND ON ME IN YOUR FILE?
PRETTY STANDARD STUFF, MOSTLY. NAME, ADDRESS, SOCIAL...STUFF LIKE THAT. THERE WERE A FEW DISCREPANCIES IN THE TAX RECORDS OF YOUR SECOND CHANCES FOUNDATION. THAT CONCERNED US.
I'LL BET IT DID. AND WHEN DID YOU GET THE IDEA TO USE THESE "DISCREPANCIES" TO BLACKMAIL ME INTO WORKING FOR YOU?
WE'RE NOT BLACKMAILING YOU, SIR. THERE'S A LOT OF UNFINISHED BUSINESS FROM EVERYONE'S PRE-REGISTRATION DAYS. WE'RE JUST TRYING TO HELP CLEAN IT UP, IS ALL.
YOU'RE TALKING TEN TO FIFTEEN FOR EACH COUNT OF EMBEZZLEMENT THAT REMAINS UNACCOUNTED FOR. WE'RE WILLING TO SAY GOODBYE TO THAT FILE, AND IN RETURN WE'RE ASKING FOR YOUR HELP.
SO IT'S NOT STRICTLY BLACKMAIL IF YOUR SUPERIORS AUTHORIZED IT?
NO...IT'S CALLED "COOPERATION." WE DIDN'T MAKE THE ACT. WE JUST WORK BY THE RULES.
DON'T PLAY DUMB WITH ME. YOU KNOW DAMN WELL I DIDN'T SIGN UP FOR A DRAFT--
READ THE FINE PRINT, SIR.
THAT'S *EXACTLY* WHAT YOU SIGNED UP FOR.

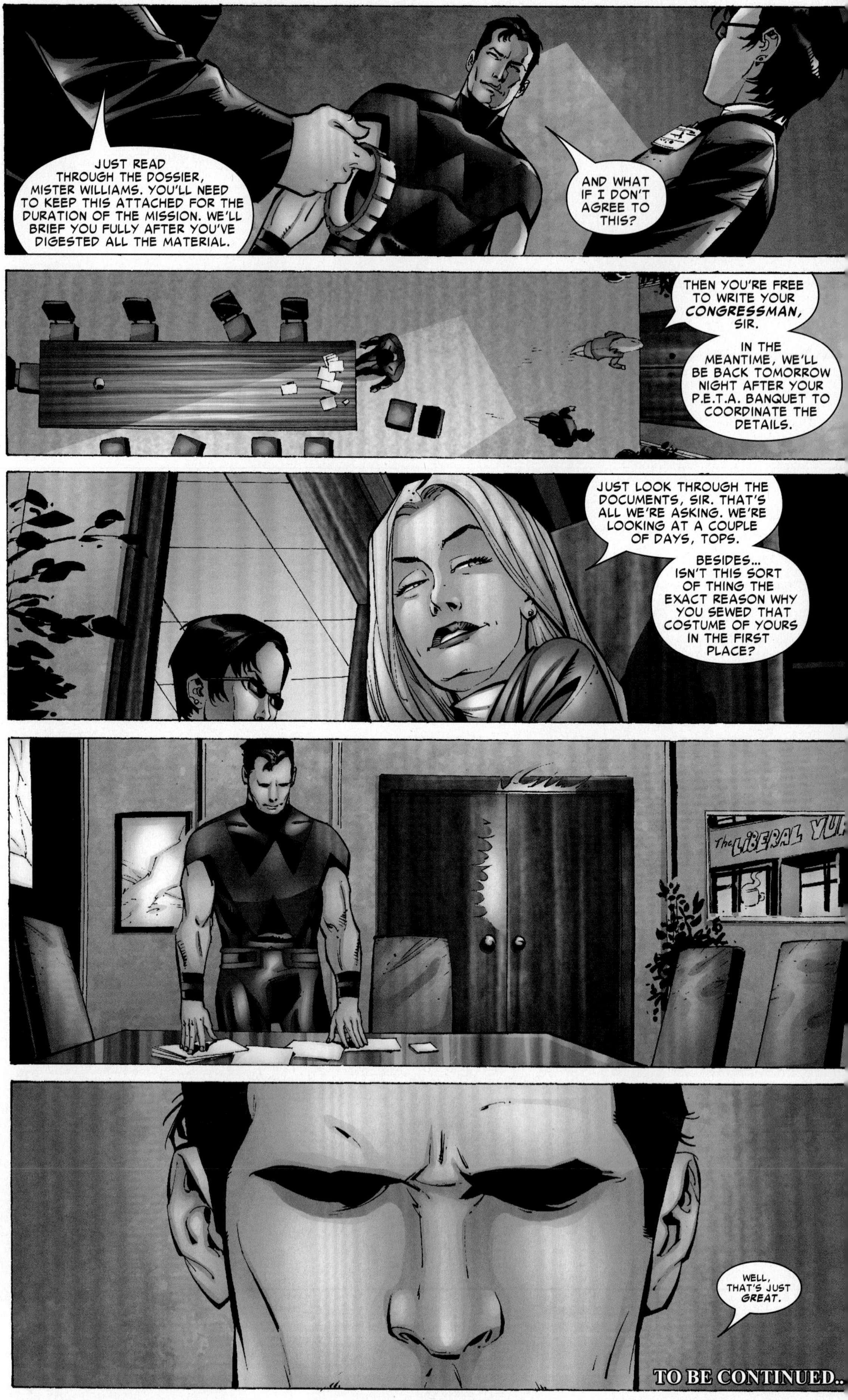
JUST READ THROUGH THE DOSSIER, MISTER WILLIAMS. YOU'LL NEED TO KEEP THIS ATTACHED FOR THE DURATION OF THE MISSION. WE'LL BRIEF YOU FULLY AFTER YOU'VE DIGESTED ALL THE MATERIAL.
AND WHAT IF I DON'T AGREE TO THIS?
THEN YOU'RE FREE TO WRITE YOUR CONGRESSMAN, SIR.
IN THE MEANTIME, WE'LL BE BACK TOMORROW NIGHT AFTER YOUR P.E.T.A. BANQUET TO COORDINATE THE DETAILS.
JUST LOOK THROUGH THE DOCUMENTS, SIR. THAT'S ALL WE'RE ASKING. WE'RE LOOKING AT A COUPLE OF DAYS, TOPS.
BESIDES... ISN'T THIS SORT OF THING THE EXACT REASON WHY YOU SEWED THAT COSTUME OF YOURS IN THE FIRST PLACE?
The LIBERAL YU
WELL, THAT'S JUST GREAT.
TO BE CONTINUED...

The Battle of Secessionville was fought near Charleston, South Carolina on June 16, 1862. It was the North's first major effort to take Charleston. During this battle, two brothers named James and Alexander Campbell fought on opposite sides--James as a Lieutenant in the Confederate army and Alexander as a Color Sergeant in the 79th Highlander Regiment. The brothers only later learned that they had fought directly against each other at Secessionville. The Charleston Courier called the two brothers "another illustration of the deplorable consequences of this fratricidal war."

PAUL JENKINS	ROY ALLEN MARTINEZ	SOTOCOLOR'S A. CROSSLEY	VC'S GENT	LAZER & SITTERSON	TOM BREVOORT	JOE QUESADA	DAN BUCKLEY
WRITER	ARTIST	COLORS	LETTERS	ASST. EDITORS	EDITOR	CHIEF	PUBLISHER

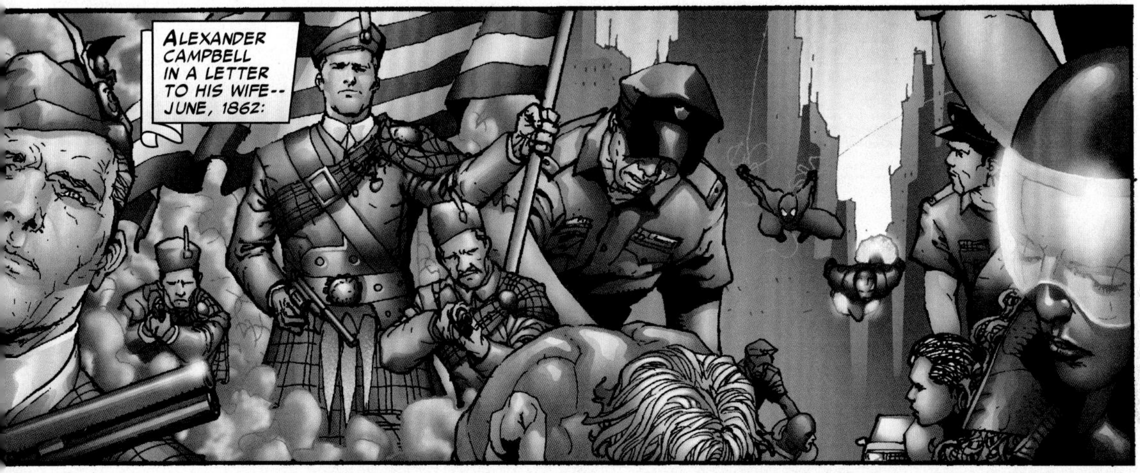

ALEXANDER CAMPBELL IN A LETTER TO HIS WIFE-- JUNE, 1862:

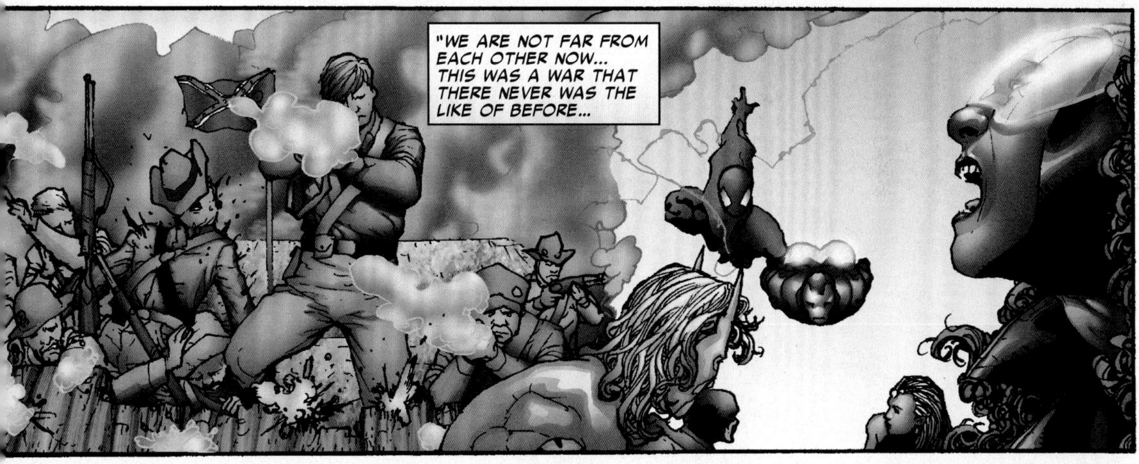

"WE ARE NOT FAR FROM EACH OTHER NOW... THIS WAS A WAR THAT THERE NEVER WAS THE LIKE OF BEFORE...

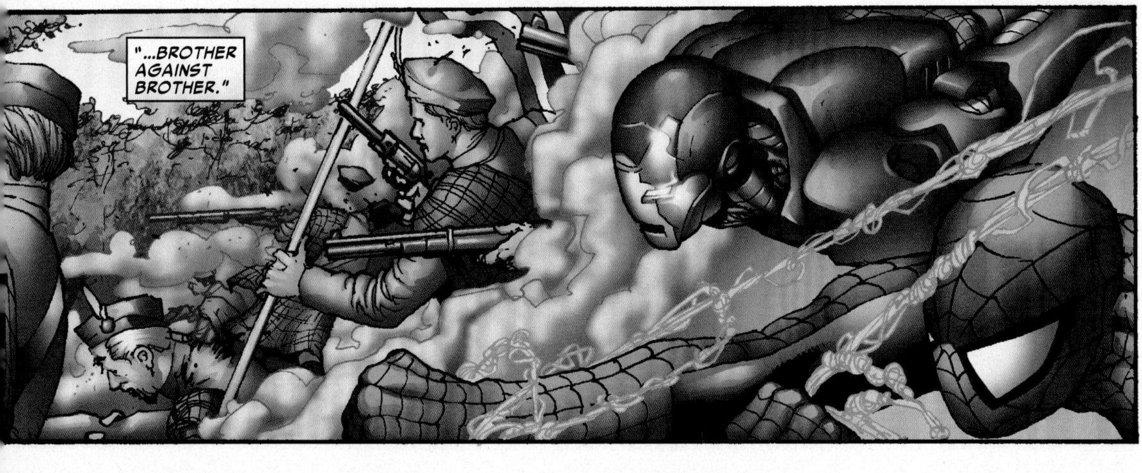

"...BROTHER AGAINST BROTHER."

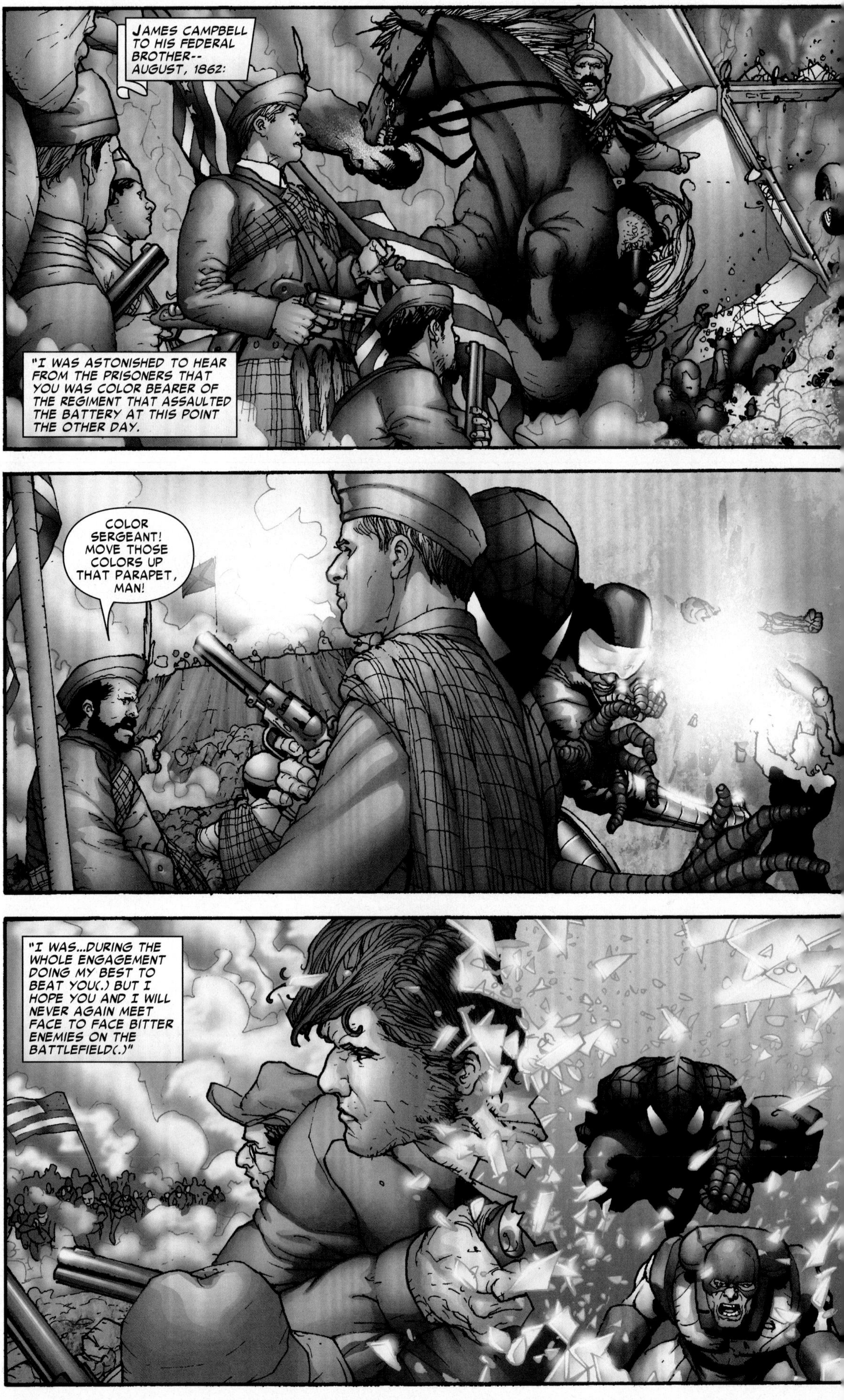
JAMES CAMPBELL TO HIS FEDERAL BROTHER-- AUGUST, 1862:
"I WAS ASTONISHED TO HEAR FROM THE PRISONERS THAT YOU WAS COLOR BEARER OF THE REGIMENT THAT ASSAULTED THE BATTERY AT THIS POINT THE OTHER DAY.
COLOR SERGEANT! MOVE THOSE COLORS UP THAT PARAPET, MAN!
"I WAS...DURING THE WHOLE ENGAGEMENT DOING MY BEST TO BEAT YOU(.) BUT I HOPE YOU AND I WILL NEVER AGAIN MEET FACE TO FACE BITTER ENEMIES ON THE BATTLEFIELD(.)"

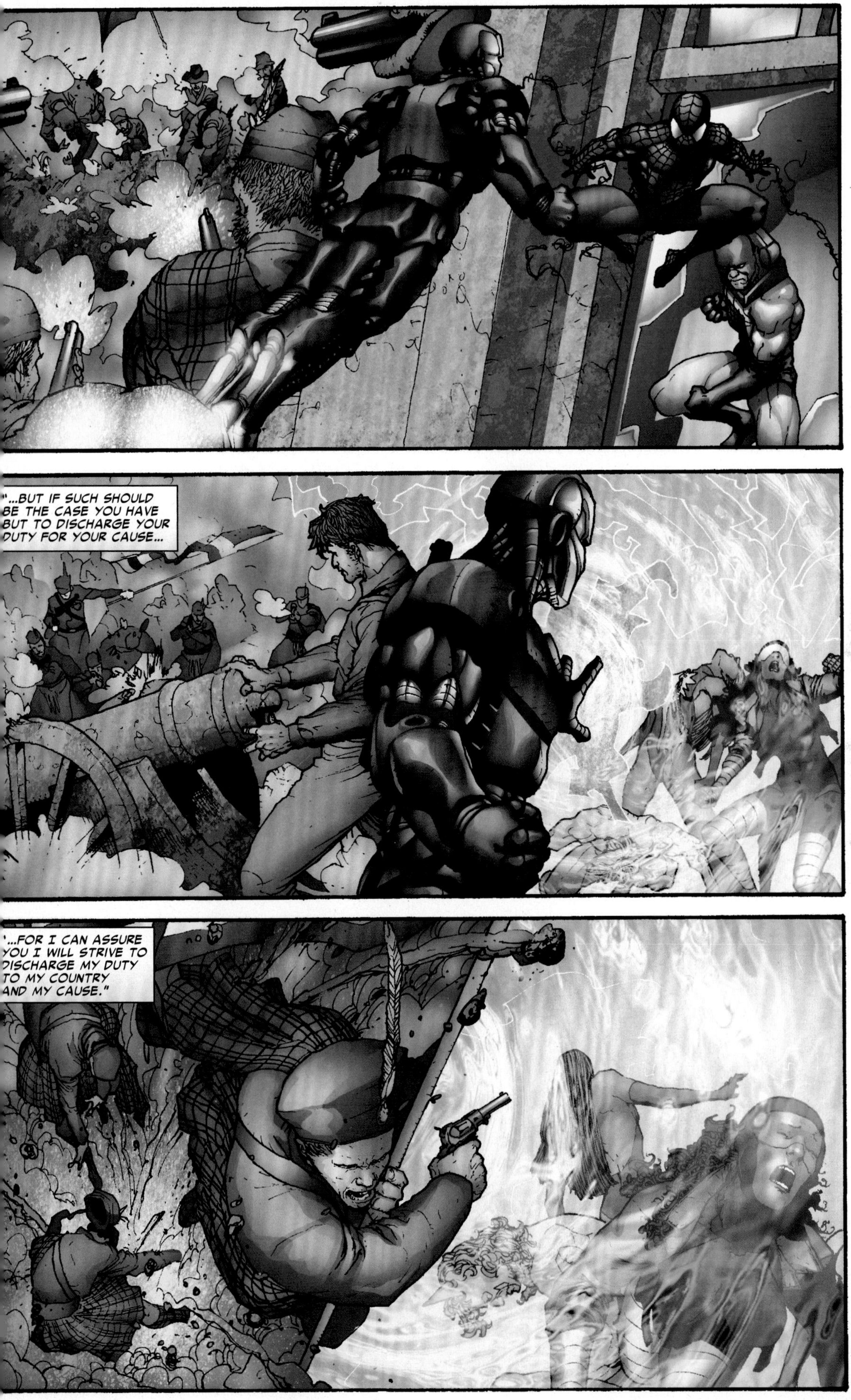
"...BUT IF SUCH SHOULD BE THE CASE YOU HAVE BUT TO DISCHARGE YOUR DUTY FOR YOUR CAUSE...
"...FOR I CAN ASSURE YOU I WILL STRIVE TO DISCHARGE MY DUTY TO MY COUNTRY AND MY CAUSE."

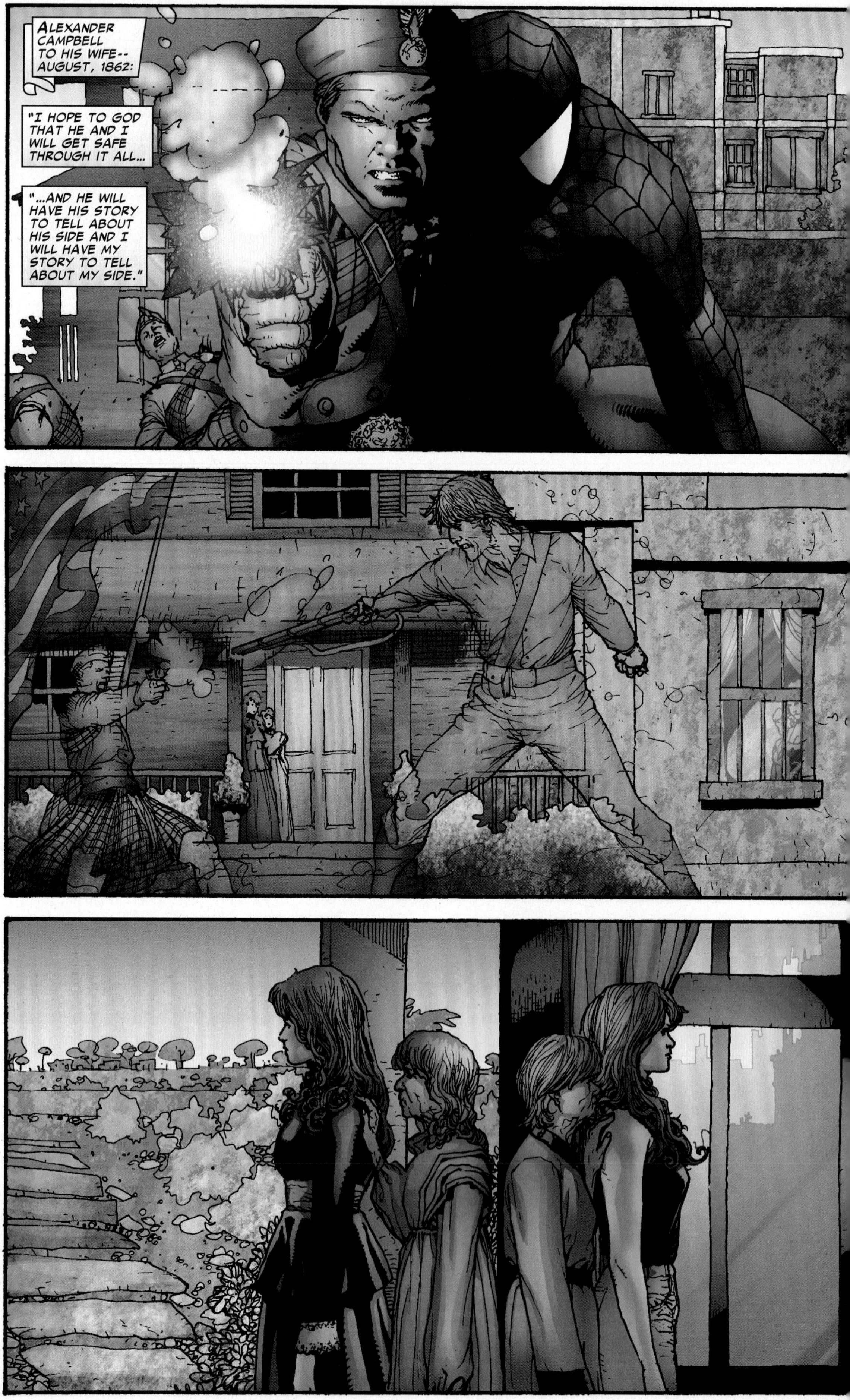
ALEXANDER CAMPBELL TO HIS WIFE-- AUGUST, 1862:
"I HOPE TO GOD THAT HE AND I WILL GET SAFE THROUGH IT ALL...
"...AND HE WILL HAVE HIS STORY TO TELL ABOUT HIS SIDE AND I WILL HAVE MY STORY TO TELL ABOUT MY SIDE."

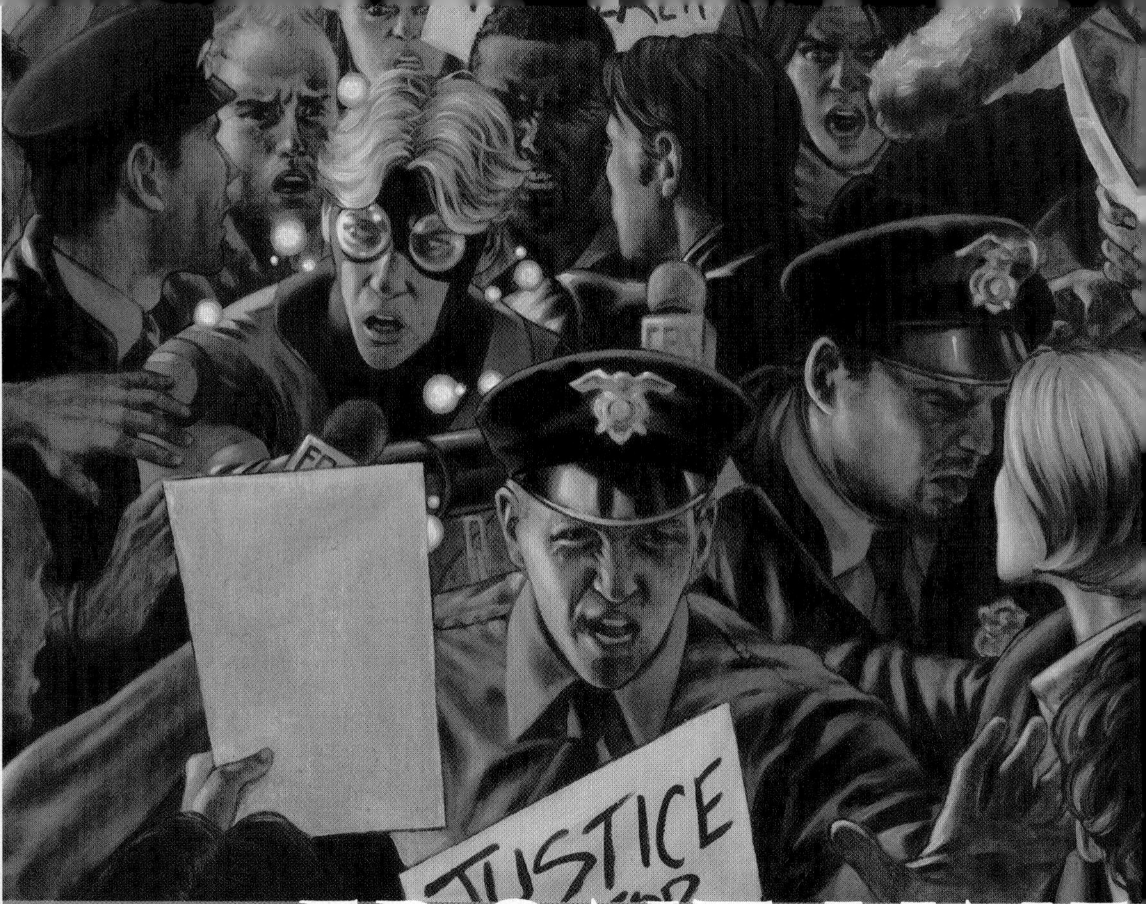
JUSTICE

FRONT LINE

A MARVEL COMICS EVENT

CIVIL WAR

CIVIL WAR: FRONT LINE #6

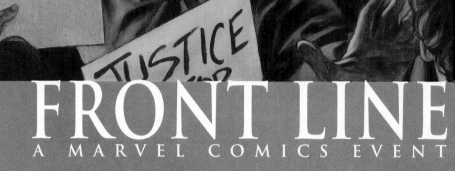

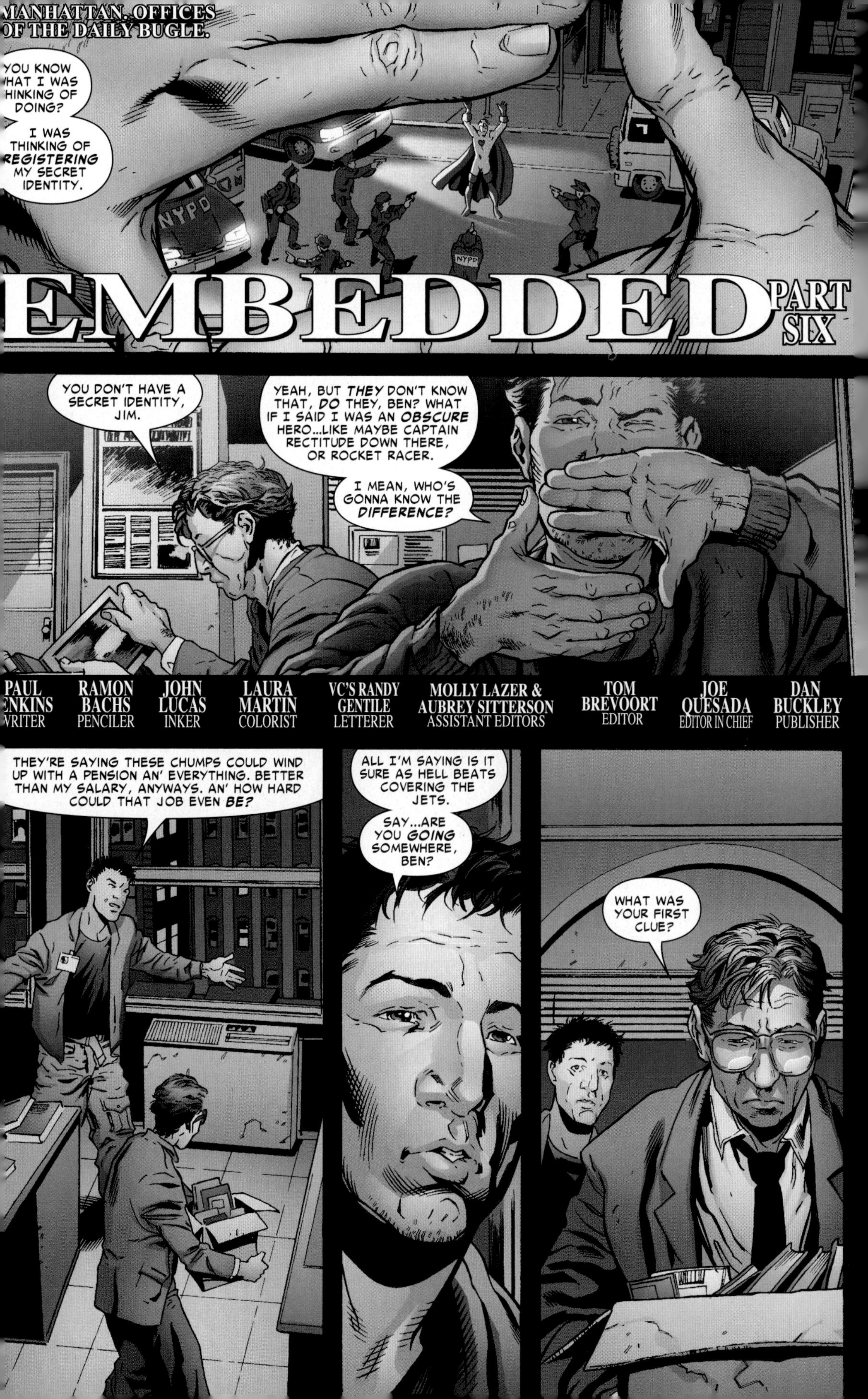
MANHATTAN. OFFICES OF THE DAILY BUGLE.
YOU KNOW WHAT I WAS THINKING OF DOING?
I WAS THINKING OF REGISTERING MY SECRET IDENTITY.
EMBEDDED PART SIX
YOU DON'T HAVE A SECRET IDENTITY, JIM.
YEAH, BUT THEY DON'T KNOW THAT, DO THEY, BEN? WHAT IF I SAID I WAS AN OBSCURE HERO...LIKE MAYBE CAPTAIN RECTITUDE DOWN THERE, OR ROCKET RACER.
I MEAN, WHO'S GONNA KNOW THE DIFFERENCE?
PAUL JENKINS WRITER
RAMON BACHS PENCILER
JOHN LUCAS INKER
LAURA MARTIN COLORIST
VC'S RANDY GENTILE LETTERER
MOLLY LAZER & AUBREY SITTERSON ASSISTANT EDITORS
TOM BREVOORT EDITOR
JOE QUESADA EDITOR IN CHIEF
DAN BUCKLEY PUBLISHER
THEY'RE SAYING THESE CHUMPS COULD WIND UP WITH A PENSION AN' EVERYTHING. BETTER THAN MY SALARY, ANYWAYS. AN' HOW HARD COULD THAT JOB EVEN BE?
ALL I'M SAYING IS IT SURE AS HELL BEATS COVERING THE JETS.
SAY...ARE YOU GOING SOMEWHERE, BEN?
WHAT WAS YOUR FIRST CLUE?

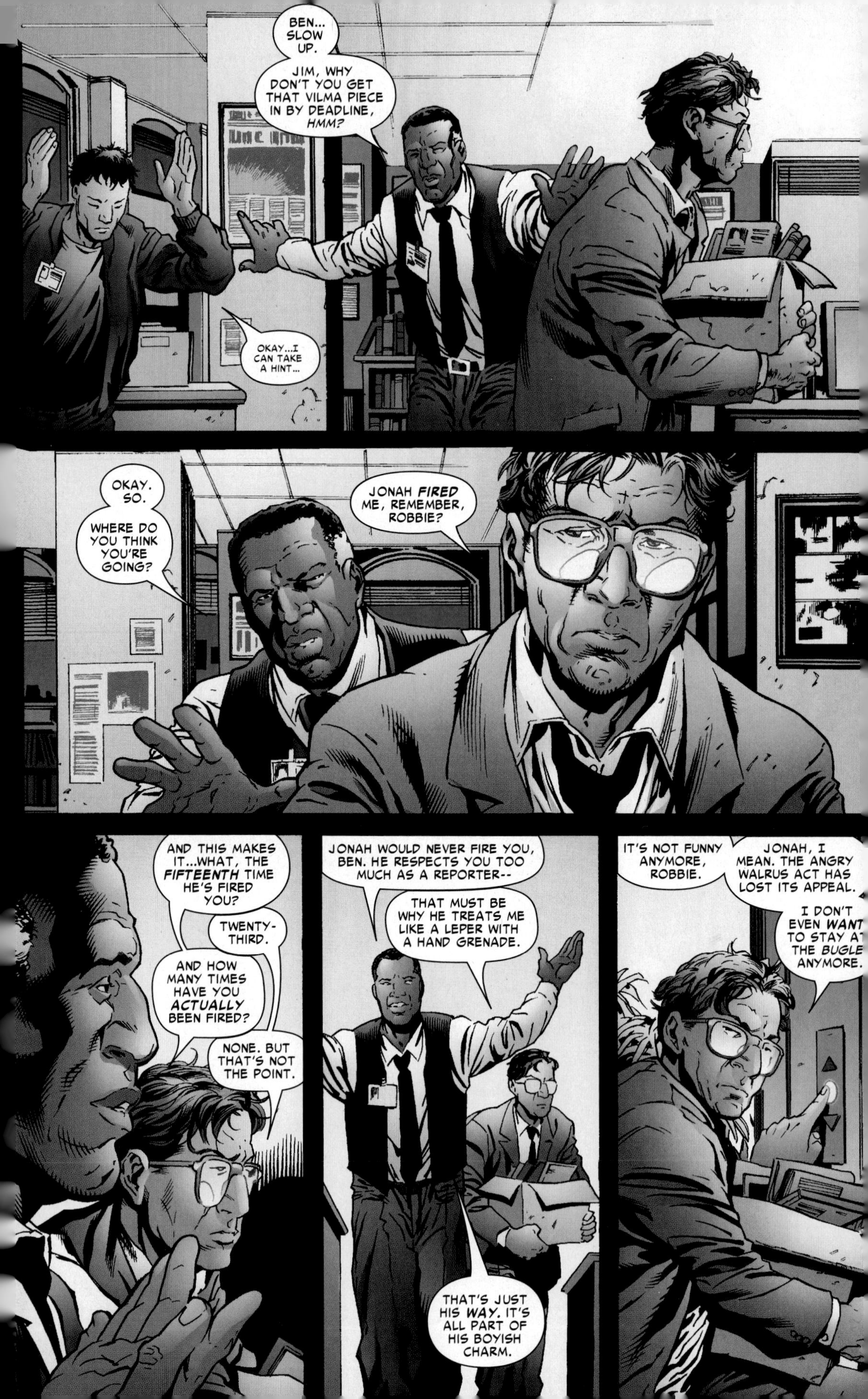
BEN... SLOW UP.
JIM, WHY DON'T YOU GET THAT VILMA PIECE IN BY DEADLINE, *HMM?*
OKAY...I CAN TAKE A HINT...
OKAY. SO.
WHERE DO YOU THINK YOU'RE GOING?
JONAH *FIRED* ME, REMEMBER, ROBBIE?
AND THIS MAKES IT...WHAT, THE *FIFTEENTH* TIME HE'S FIRED YOU?
TWENTY-THIRD.
AND HOW MANY TIMES HAVE YOU *ACTUALLY* BEEN FIRED?
NONE. BUT THAT'S NOT THE POINT.
JONAH WOULD NEVER FIRE YOU, BEN. HE RESPECTS YOU TOO MUCH AS A REPORTER--
THAT MUST BE WHY HE TREATS ME LIKE A LEPER WITH A HAND GRENADE.
THAT'S JUST HIS *WAY.* IT'S ALL PART OF HIS BOYISH CHARM.
IT'S NOT FUNNY ANYMORE, ROBBIE.
JONAH, I MEAN. THE ANGRY WALRUS ACT HAS LOST ITS APPEAL.
I DON'T EVEN *WANT* TO STAY AT THE *BUGLE* ANYMORE.

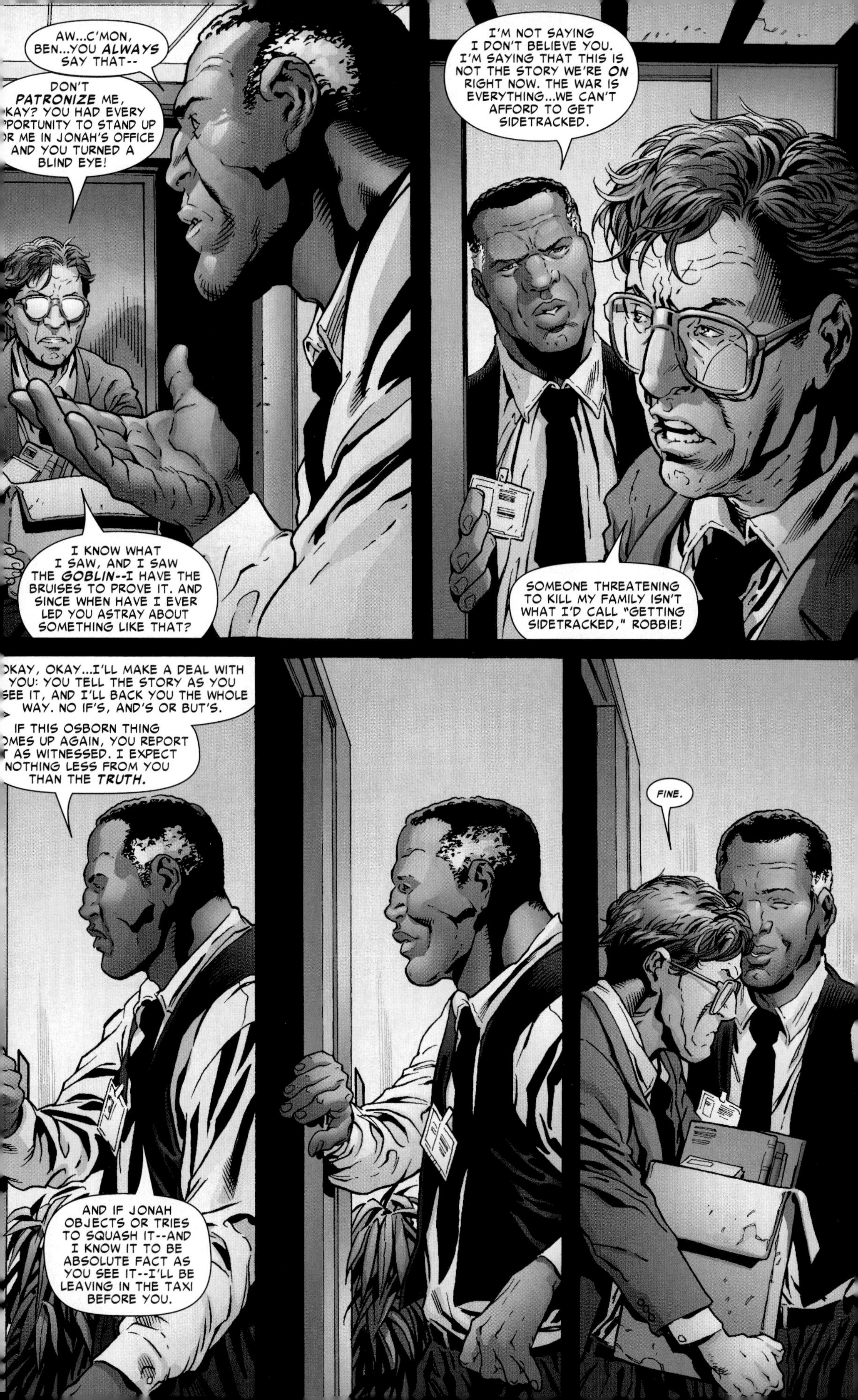
AW...C'MON, BEN...YOU ALWAYS SAY THAT--
DON'T PATRONIZE ME, OKAY? YOU HAD EVERY PPORTUNITY TO STAND UP R ME IN JONAH'S OFFICE AND YOU TURNED A BLIND EYE!
I KNOW WHAT I SAW, AND I SAW THE GOBLIN--I HAVE THE BRUISES TO PROVE IT. AND SINCE WHEN HAVE I EVER LED YOU ASTRAY ABOUT SOMETHING LIKE THAT?
I'M NOT SAYING I DON'T BELIEVE YOU. I'M SAYING THAT THIS IS NOT THE STORY WE'RE ON RIGHT NOW. THE WAR IS EVERYTHING...WE CAN'T AFFORD TO GET SIDETRACKED.
SOMEONE THREATENING TO KILL MY FAMILY ISN'T WHAT I'D CALL "GETTING SIDETRACKED," ROBBIE!
OKAY, OKAY...I'LL MAKE A DEAL WITH YOU: YOU TELL THE STORY AS YOU SEE IT, AND I'LL BACK YOU THE WHOLE WAY. NO IF'S, AND'S OR BUT'S.
IF THIS OSBORN THING OMES UP AGAIN, YOU REPORT T AS WITNESSED. I EXPECT NOTHING LESS FROM YOU THAN THE TRUTH.
AND IF JONAH OBJECTS OR TRIES TO SQUASH IT--AND I KNOW IT TO BE ABSOLUTE FACT AS YOU SEE IT--I'LL BE LEAVING IN THE TAXI BEFORE YOU.
FINE.

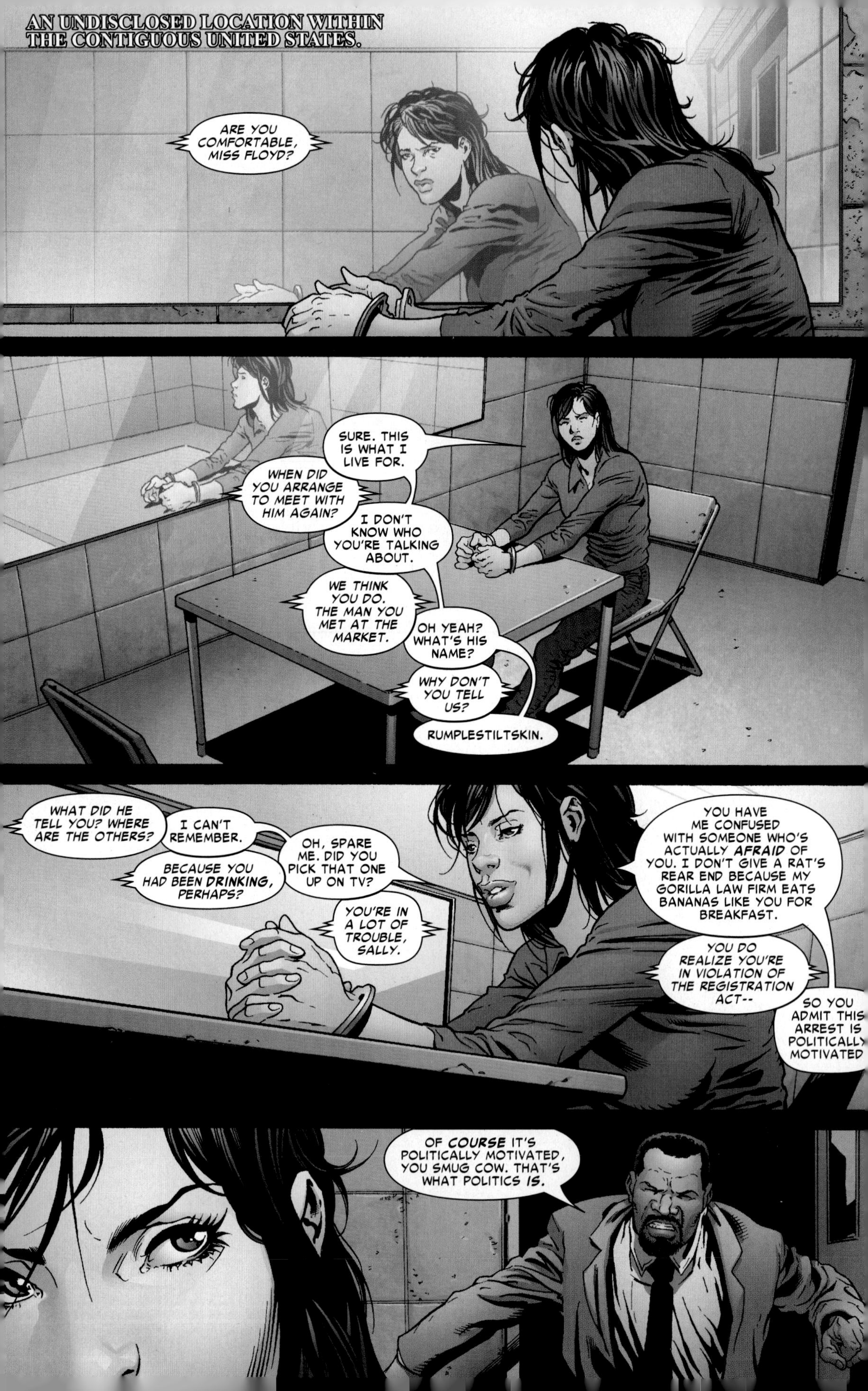
AN UNDISCLOSED LOCATION WITHIN THE CONTIGUOUS UNITED STATES.
ARE YOU COMFORTABLE, MISS FLOYD?
SURE. THIS IS WHAT I LIVE FOR.
WHEN DID YOU ARRANGE TO MEET WITH HIM AGAIN?
I DON'T KNOW WHO YOU'RE TALKING ABOUT.
WE THINK YOU DO. THE MAN YOU MET AT THE MARKET.
OH YEAH? WHAT'S HIS NAME?
WHY DON'T YOU TELL US?
RUMPLESTILTSKIN.
WHAT DID HE TELL YOU? WHERE ARE THE OTHERS?
I CAN'T REMEMBER.
BECAUSE YOU HAD BEEN DRINKING, PERHAPS?
OH, SPARE ME. DID YOU PICK THAT ONE UP ON TV?
YOU'RE IN A LOT OF TROUBLE, SALLY.
YOU HAVE ME CONFUSED WITH SOMEONE WHO'S ACTUALLY AFRAID OF YOU. I DON'T GIVE A RAT'S REAR END BECAUSE MY GORILLA LAW FIRM EATS BANANAS LIKE YOU FOR BREAKFAST.
YOU DO REALIZE YOU'RE IN VIOLATION OF THE REGISTRATION ACT--
SO YOU ADMIT THIS ARREST IS POLITICALLY MOTIVATED
OF COURSE IT'S POLITICALLY MOTIVATED, YOU SMUG COW. THAT'S WHAT POLITICS IS.

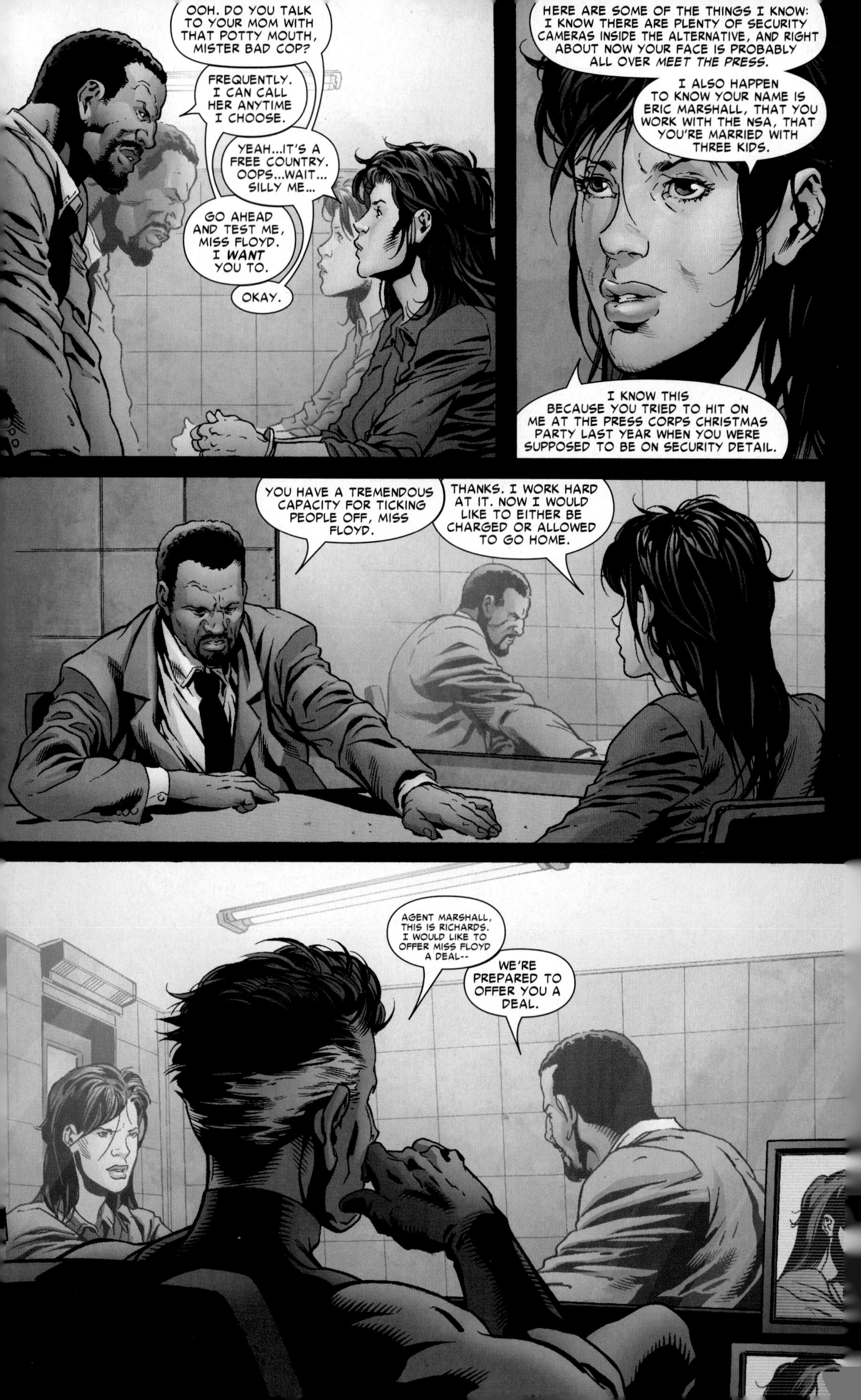
OOH. DO YOU TALK TO YOUR MOM WITH THAT POTTY MOUTH, MISTER BAD COP?
FREQUENTLY. I CAN CALL HER ANYTIME I CHOOSE.
YEAH...IT'S A FREE COUNTRY. OOPS...WAIT... SILLY ME...
GO AHEAD AND TEST ME, MISS FLOYD. I *WANT* YOU TO.
OKAY.
HERE ARE SOME OF THE THINGS I KNOW: I KNOW THERE ARE PLENTY OF SECURITY CAMERAS INSIDE THE ALTERNATIVE, AND RIGHT ABOUT NOW YOUR FACE IS PROBABLY ALL OVER *MEET THE PRESS.*
I ALSO HAPPEN TO KNOW YOUR NAME IS ERIC MARSHALL, THAT YOU WORK WITH THE NSA, THAT YOU'RE MARRIED WITH THREE KIDS.
I KNOW THIS BECAUSE YOU TRIED TO HIT ON ME AT THE PRESS CORPS CHRISTMAS PARTY LAST YEAR WHEN YOU WERE SUPPOSED TO BE ON SECURITY DETAIL.
YOU HAVE A TREMENDOUS CAPACITY FOR TICKING PEOPLE OFF, MISS FLOYD.
THANKS. I WORK HARD AT IT. NOW I WOULD LIKE TO EITHER BE CHARGED OR ALLOWED TO GO HOME.
AGENT MARSHALL, THIS IS RICHARDS. I WOULD LIKE TO OFFER MISS FLOYD A DEAL--
WE'RE PREPARED TO OFFER YOU A DEAL.

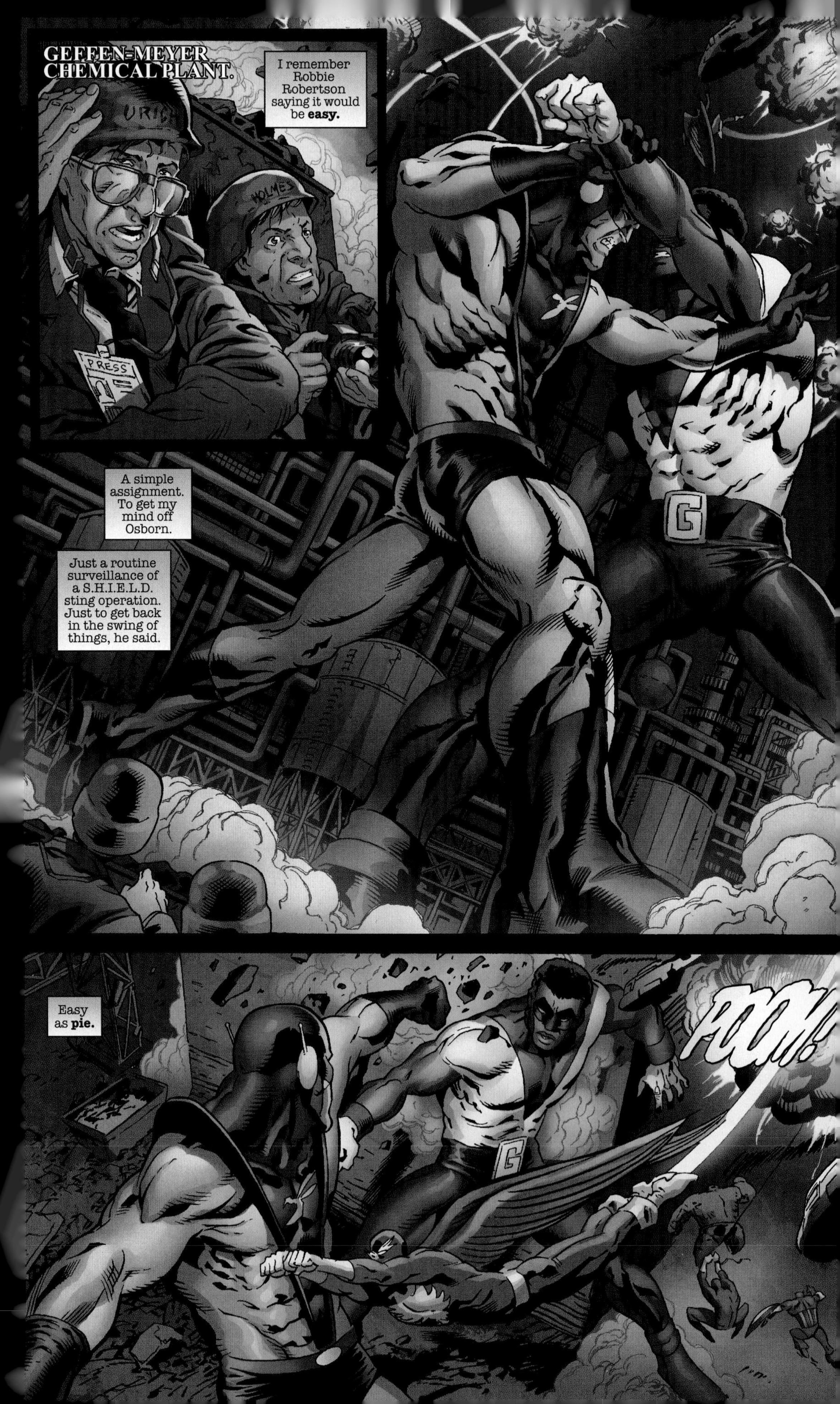
GEFFEN-MEYER CHEMICAL PLANT.
I remember Robbie Robertson saying it would be **easy.**
URICH
HOLMES
PRESS
A simple assignment. To get my mind off Osborn.
Just a routine surveillance of a S.H.I.E.L.D. sting operation. Just to get back in the swing of things, he said.
Easy as **pie.**
POOM!

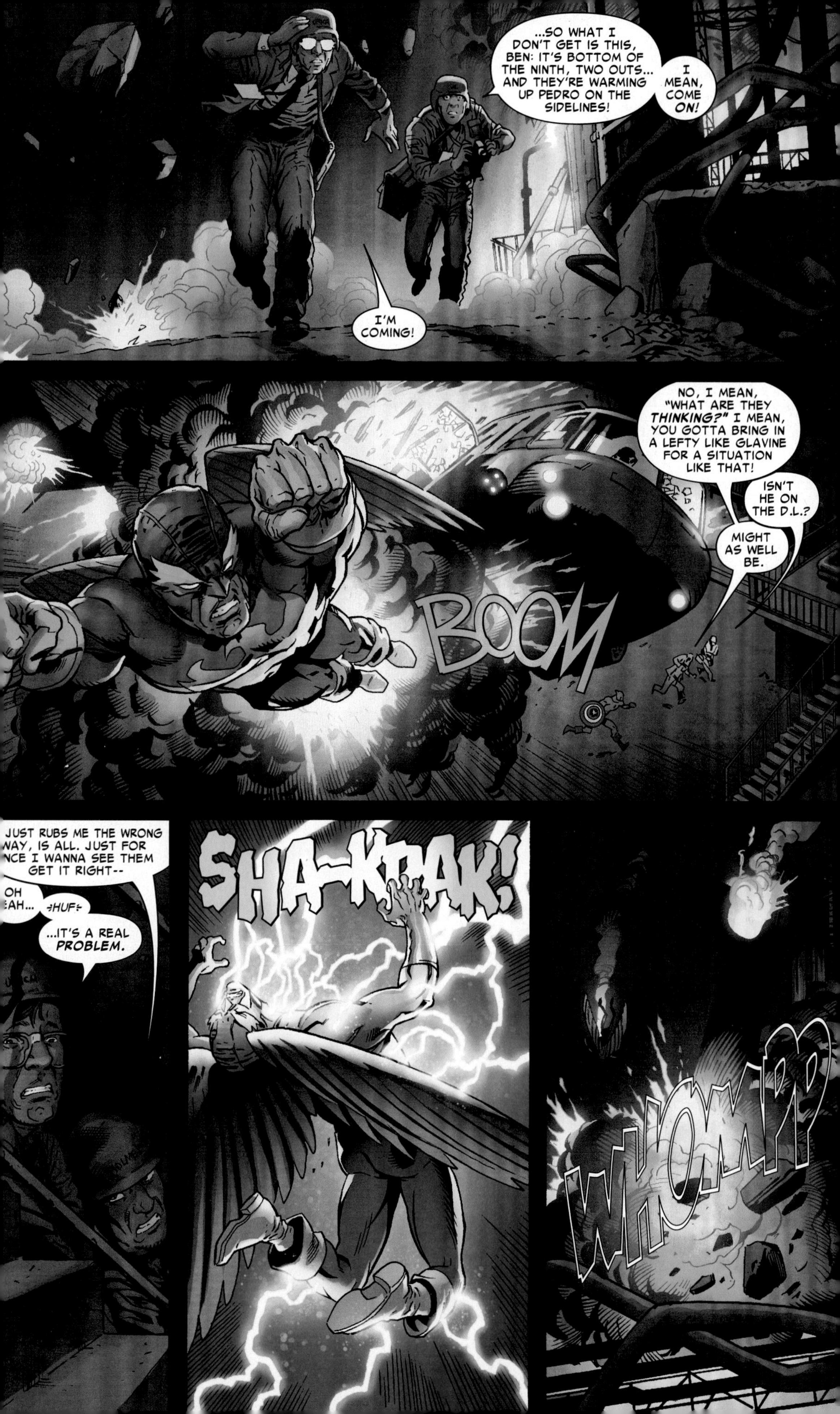
...SO WHAT I DON'T GET IS THIS, BEN: IT'S BOTTOM OF THE NINTH, TWO OUTS... AND THEY'RE WARMING UP PEDRO ON THE SIDELINES!
I MEAN, COME ON!
I'M COMING!
NO, I MEAN, "WHAT ARE THEY THINKING?" I MEAN, YOU GOTTA BRING IN A LEFTY LIKE GLAVINE FOR A SITUATION LIKE THAT!
ISN'T HE ON THE D.L.?
MIGHT AS WELL BE.
BOOM
JUST RUBS ME THE WRONG WAY, IS ALL. JUST FOR NCE I WANNA SEE THEM GET IT RIGHT--
OH EAH...
HUF
...IT'S A REAL PROBLEM.
SHA-KRAK!
WHOMP!

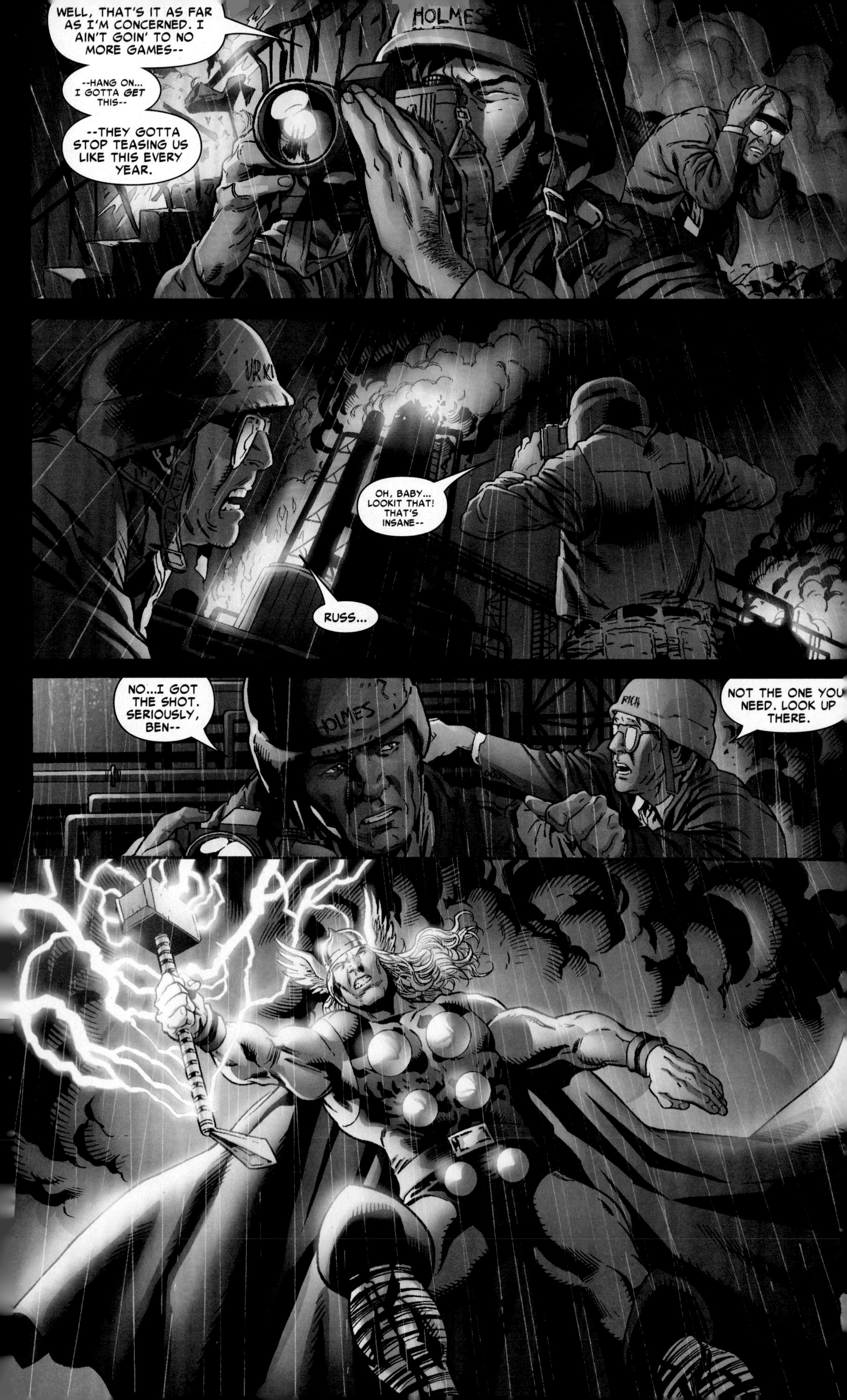
WELL, THAT'S IT AS FAR AS I'M CONCERNED. I AIN'T GOIN' TO NO MORE GAMES--
--HANG ON... I GOTTA GET THIS--
--THEY GOTTA STOP TEASING US LIKE THIS EVERY YEAR.
HOLMES
OH, BABY... LOOKIT THAT! THAT'S INSANE--
RUSS...
NO...I GOT THE SHOT. SERIOUSLY, BEN--
NOT THE ONE YOU NEED. LOOK UP THERE.
HOLMES

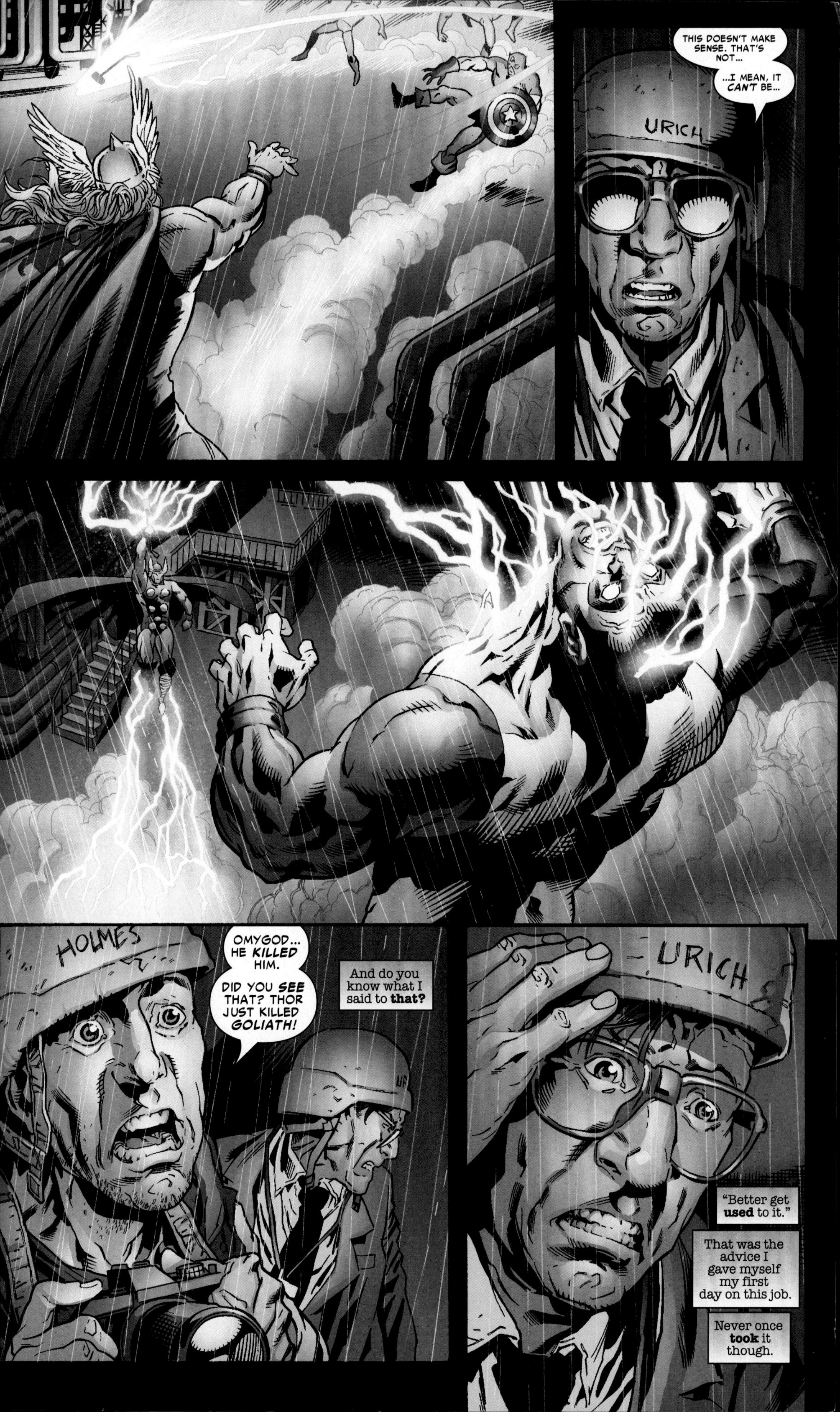

THIS DOESN'T MAKE SENSE. THAT'S NOT...
...I MEAN, IT CAN'T BE...
URICH
HOLMES
OMYGOD... HE KILLED... HIM.
DID YOU SEE THAT? THOR JUST KILLED GOLIATH!
And do you know what I said to that?
URICH
"Better get used to it."
That was the advice I gave myself my first day on this job.
Never once took it though.

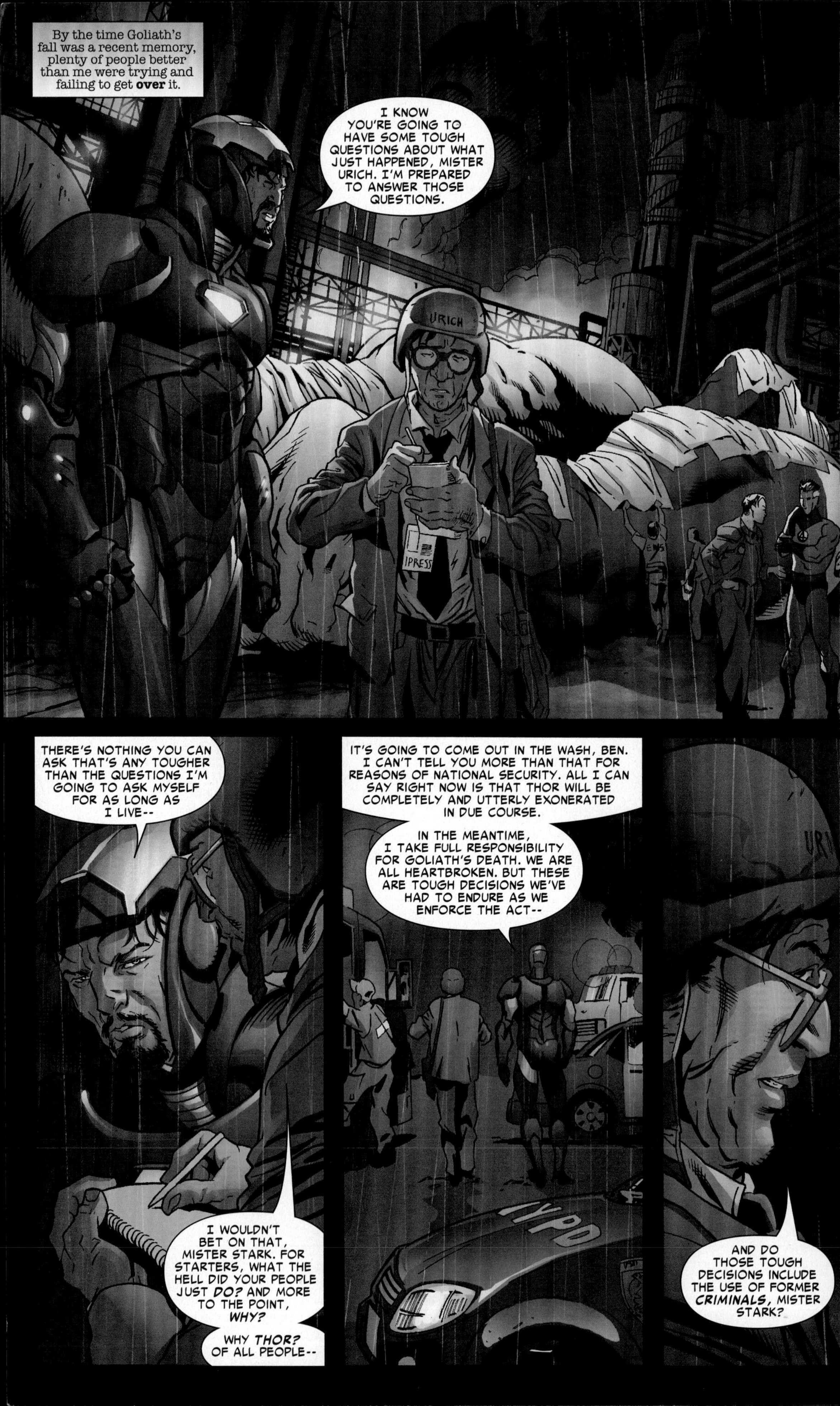

By the time Goliath's fall was a recent memory, plenty of people better than me were trying and failing to get **over** it.
I KNOW YOU'RE GOING TO HAVE SOME TOUGH QUESTIONS ABOUT WHAT JUST HAPPENED, MISTER URICH. I'M PREPARED TO ANSWER THOSE QUESTIONS.
URICH
PRESS
THERE'S NOTHING YOU CAN ASK THAT'S ANY TOUGHER THAN THE QUESTIONS I'M GOING TO ASK MYSELF FOR AS LONG AS I LIVE--
I WOULDN'T BET ON THAT, MISTER STARK. FOR STARTERS, WHAT THE HELL DID YOUR PEOPLE JUST *DO?* AND MORE TO THE POINT, *WHY?*
WHY *THOR?* OF ALL PEOPLE--
IT'S GOING TO COME OUT IN THE WASH, BEN. I CAN'T TELL YOU MORE THAN THAT FOR REASONS OF NATIONAL SECURITY. ALL I CAN SAY RIGHT NOW IS THAT THOR WILL BE COMPLETELY AND UTTERLY EXONERATED IN DUE COURSE.
IN THE MEANTIME, I TAKE FULL RESPONSIBILITY FOR GOLIATH'S DEATH. WE ARE ALL HEARTBROKEN. BUT THESE ARE TOUGH DECISIONS WE'VE HAD TO ENDURE AS WE ENFORCE THE ACT--
NYPD
AND DO THOSE TOUGH DECISIONS INCLUDE THE USE OF FORMER *CRIMINALS,* MISTER STARK?

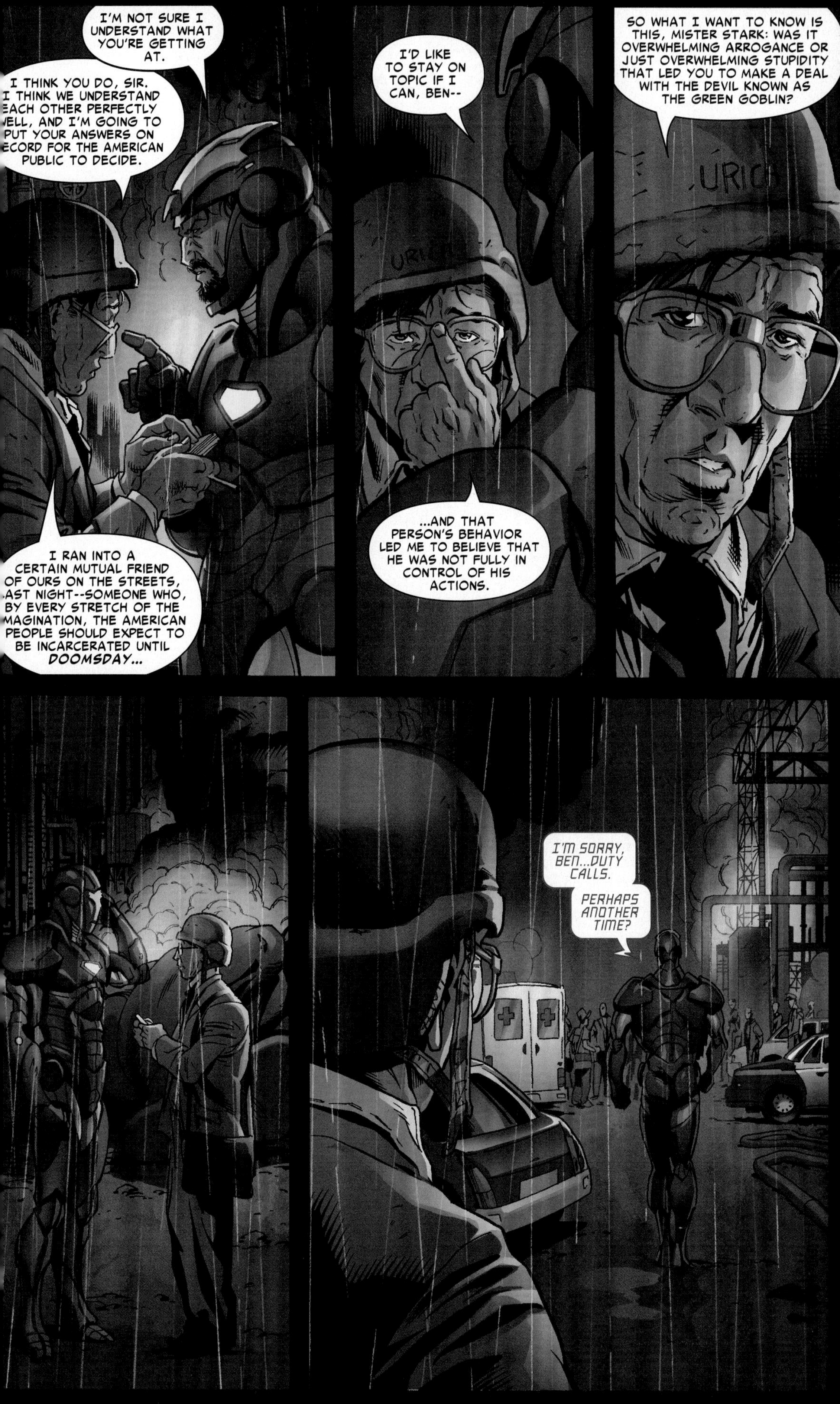
I'M NOT SURE I UNDERSTAND WHAT YOU'RE GETTING AT.
I THINK YOU DO, SIR. I THINK WE UNDERSTAND EACH OTHER PERFECTLY WELL, AND I'M GOING TO PUT YOUR ANSWERS ON RECORD FOR THE AMERICAN PUBLIC TO DECIDE.
I RAN INTO A CERTAIN MUTUAL FRIEND OF OURS ON THE STREETS, LAST NIGHT--SOMEONE WHO, BY EVERY STRETCH OF THE IMAGINATION, THE AMERICAN PEOPLE SHOULD EXPECT TO BE INCARCERATED UNTIL DOOMSDAY...
I'D LIKE TO STAY ON TOPIC IF I CAN, BEN--
...AND THAT PERSON'S BEHAVIOR LED ME TO BELIEVE THAT HE WAS NOT FULLY IN CONTROL OF HIS ACTIONS.
SO WHAT I WANT TO KNOW IS THIS, MISTER STARK: WAS IT OVERWHELMING ARROGANCE OR JUST OVERWHELMING STUPIDITY THAT LED YOU TO MAKE A DEAL WITH THE DEVIL KNOWN AS THE GREEN GOBLIN?
I'M SORRY, BEN...DUTY CALLS.
PERHAPS ANOTHER TIME?

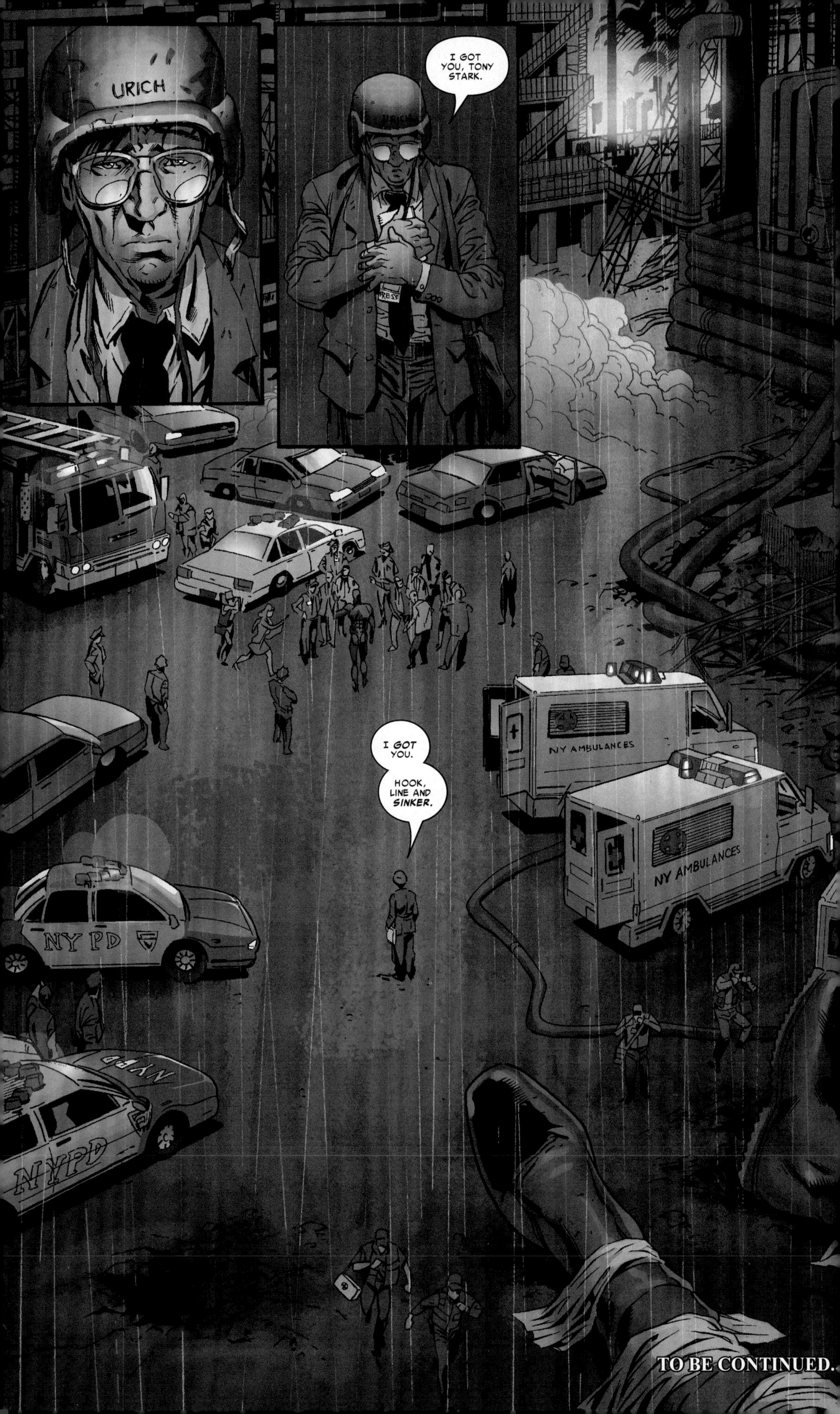
URICH
I GOT YOU, TONY STARK.
PRESS
I GOT YOU.
HOOK, LINE AND SINKER.
NY AMBULANCES
NY AMBULANCES
NYPD
NYPD
NYPD
TO BE CONTINUED.

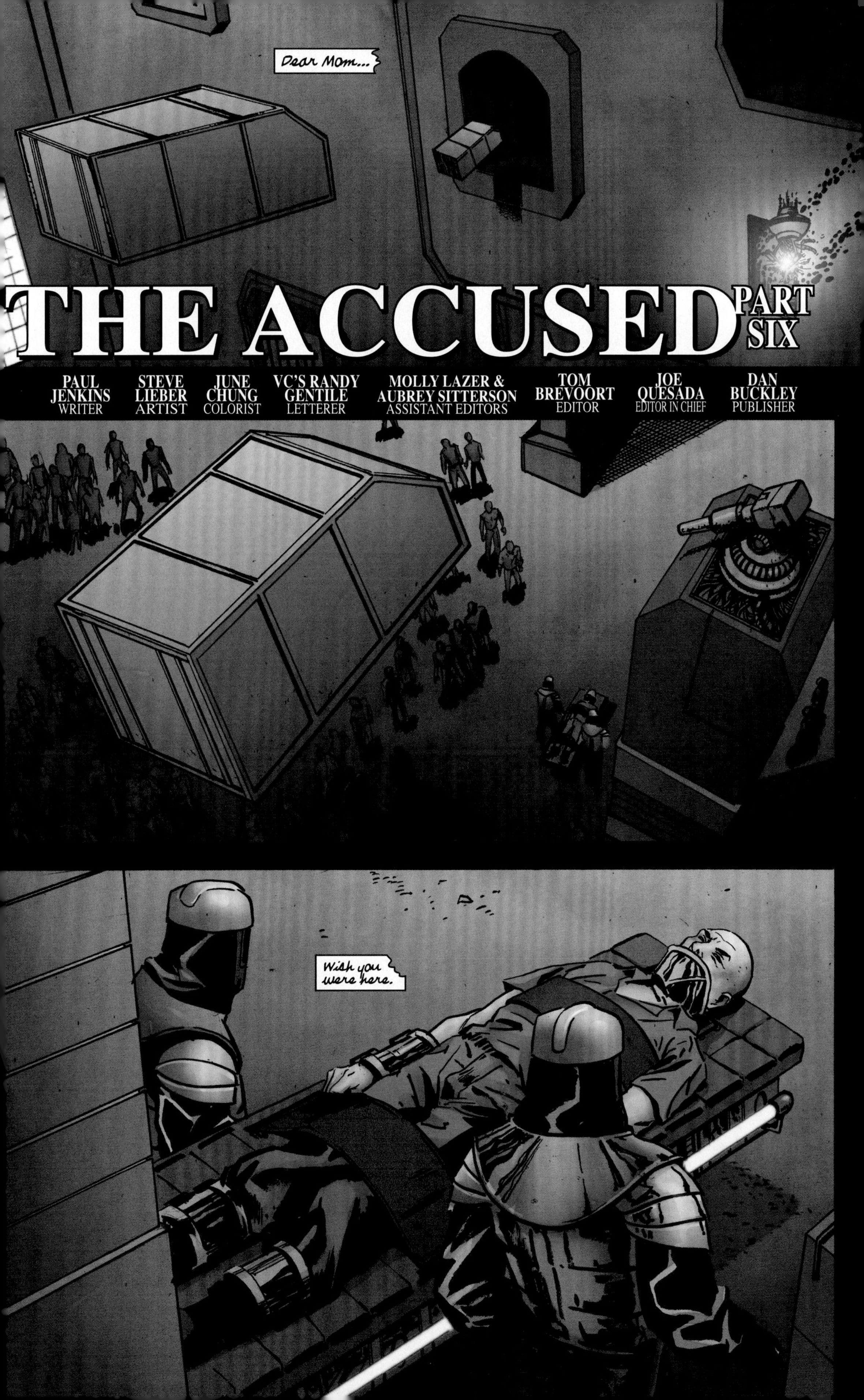
Dear Mom...
THE ACCUSED PART SIX
PAUL JENKINS WRITER
STEVE LIEBER ARTIST
JUNE CHUNG COLORIST
VC'S RANDY GENTILE LETTERER
MOLLY LAZER & AUBREY SITTERSON ASSISTANT EDITORS
TOM BREVOORT EDITOR
JOE QUESADA EDITOR IN CHIEF
DAN BUCKLEY PUBLISHER
Wish you were here.

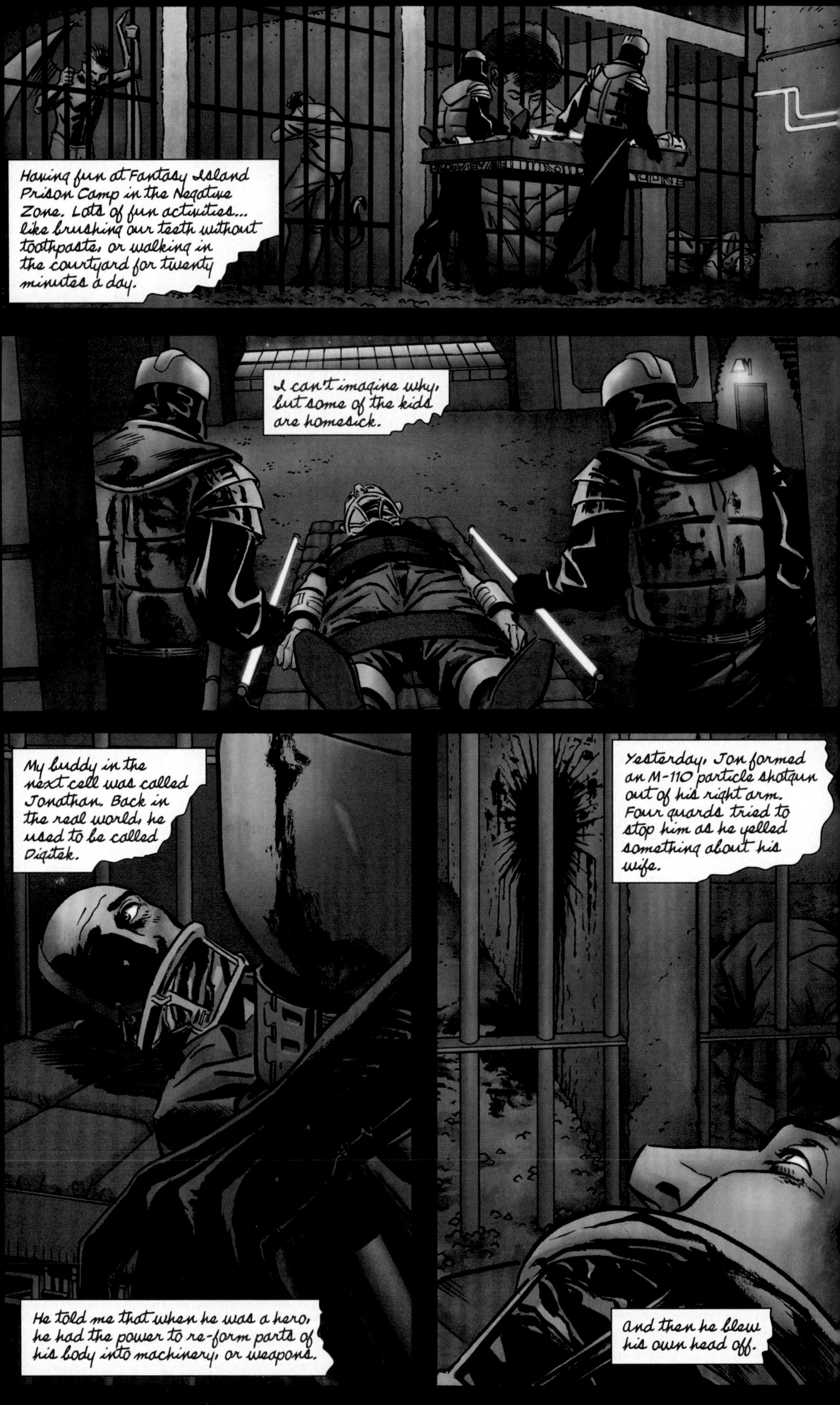

Having fun at Fantasy Island Prison Camp in the Negative Zone. Lots of fun activities... like brushing our teeth without toothpaste, or walking in the courtyard for twenty minutes a day.
I can't imagine why, but some of the kids are homesick.
My buddy in the next cell was called Jonathan. Back in the real world, he used to be called Digitek.
He told me that when he was a hero, he had the power to re-form parts of his body into machinery, or weapons.
Yesterday, Jon formed an M-110 particle shotgun out of his right arm. Four guards tried to stop him as he yelled something about his wife.
And then he blew his own head off.

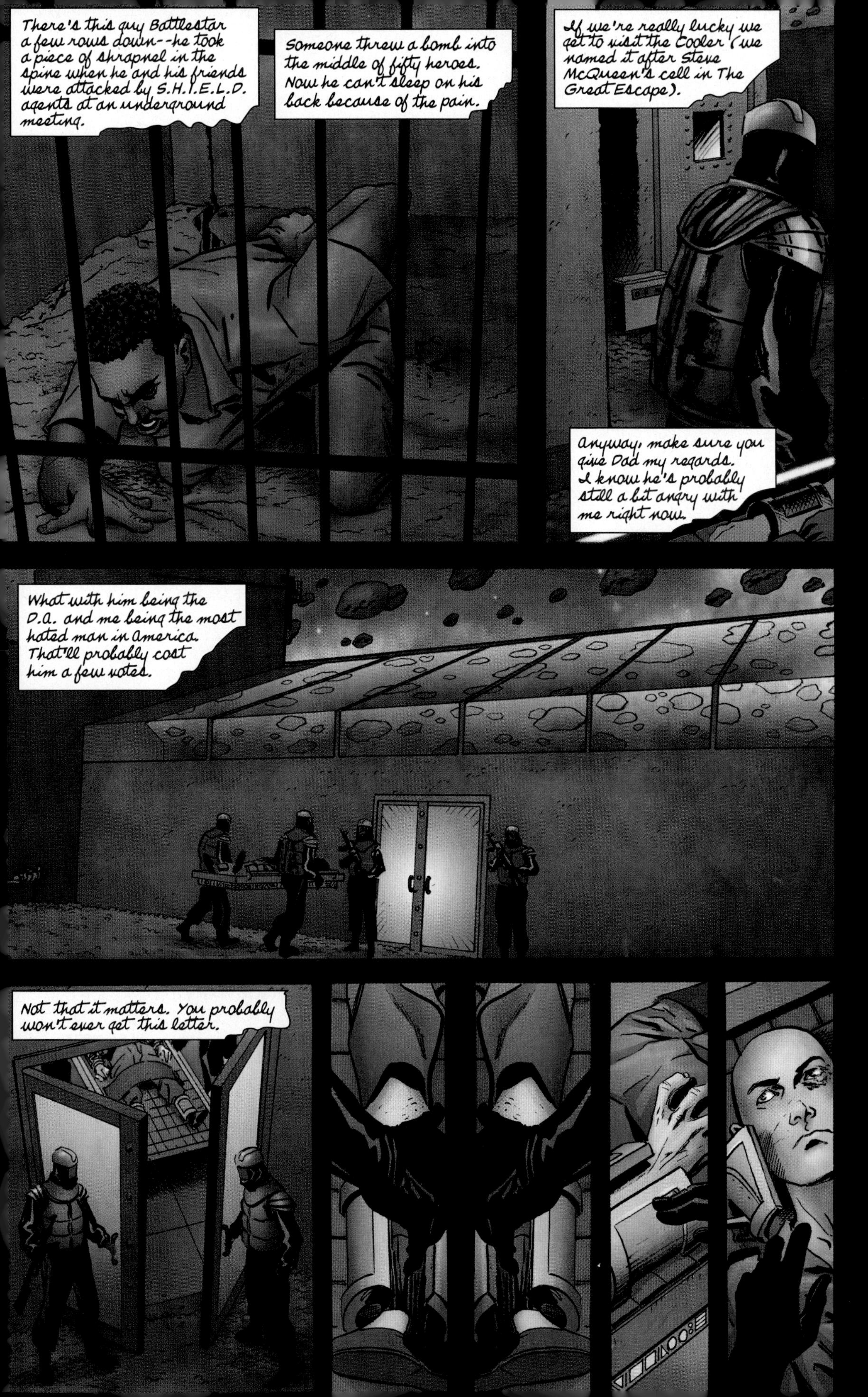
There's this guy Battlestar a few rows down--he took a piece of shrapnel in the spine when he and his friends were attacked by S.H.I.E.L.D. agents at an underground meeting.
Someone threw a bomb into the middle of fifty heroes. Now he can't sleep on his back because of the pain.
If we're really lucky we get to visit the Cooler (we named it after Steve McQueen's cell in The Great Escape).
Anyway, make sure you give Dad my regards. I know he's probably still a bit angry with me right now.
What with him being the D.A. and me being the most hated man in America. That'll probably cost him a few votes.
Not that it matters. You probably won't ever get this letter.

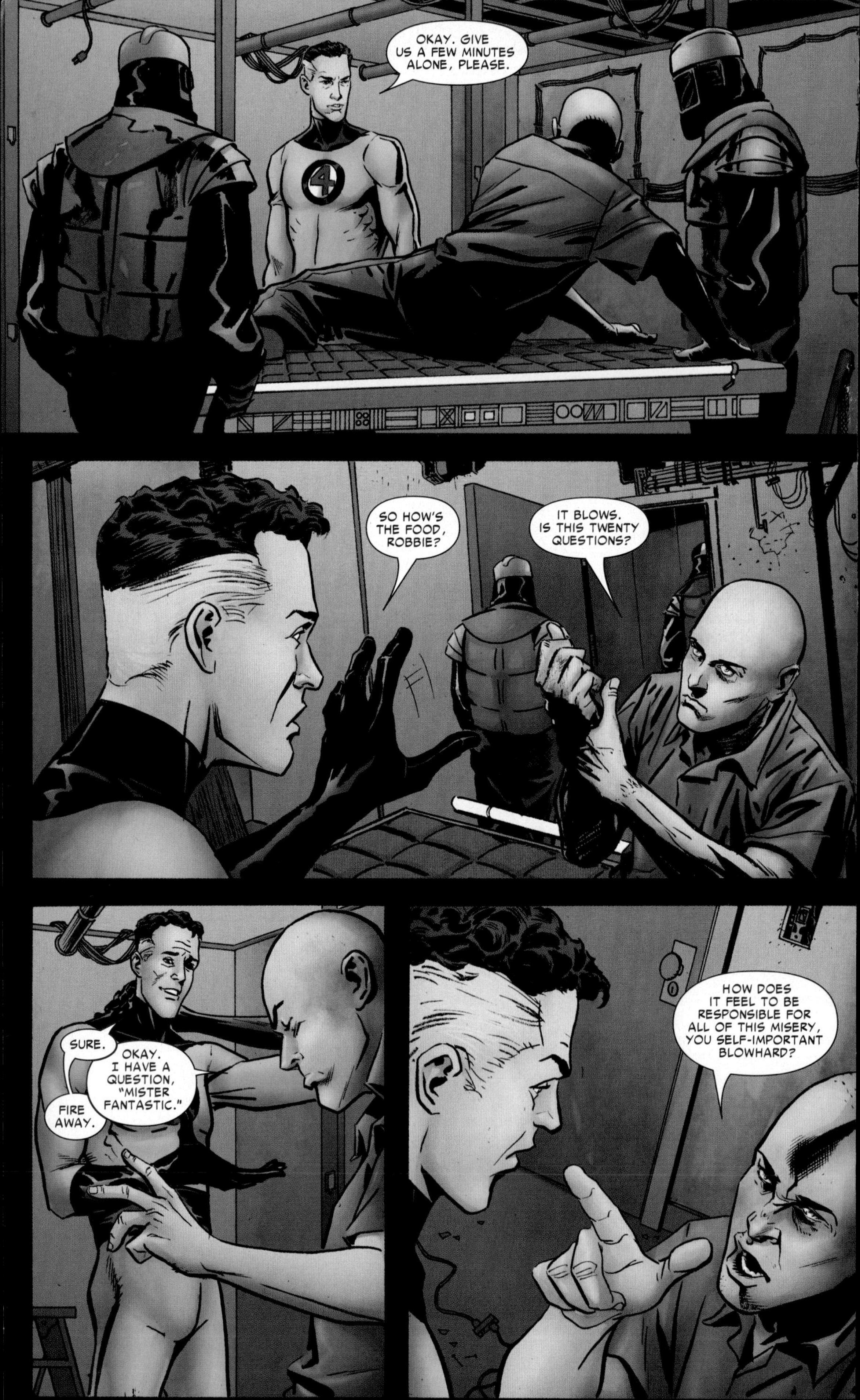

OKAY. GIVE US A FEW MINUTES ALONE, PLEASE.
SO HOW'S THE FOOD, ROBBIE?
IT BLOWS. IS THIS TWENTY QUESTIONS?
SURE.
FIRE AWAY.
OKAY. I HAVE A QUESTION, "MISTER FANTASTIC."
HOW DOES IT FEEL TO BE RESPONSIBLE FOR ALL OF THIS MISERY, YOU SELF-IMPORTANT BLOWHARD?

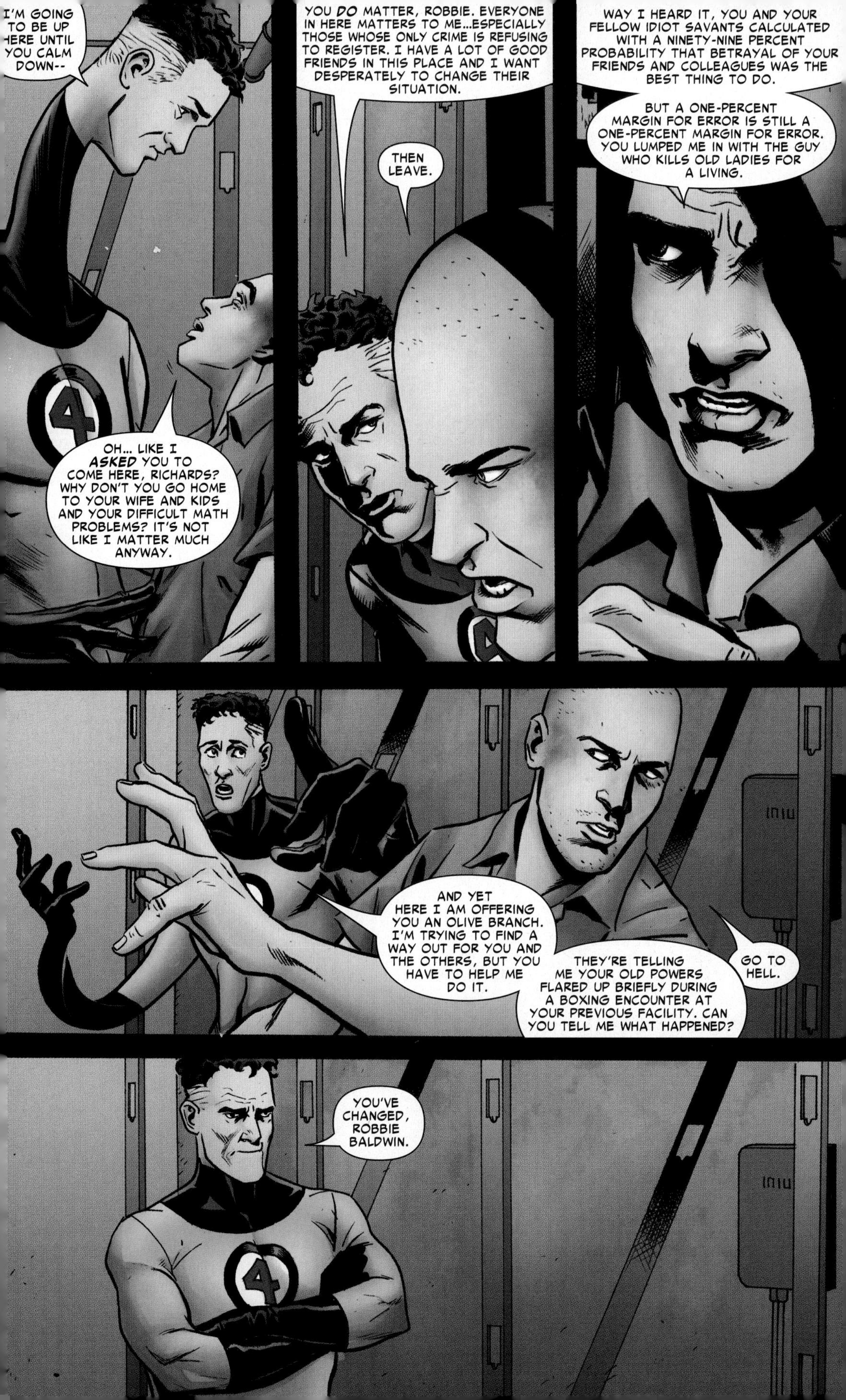
I'M GOING TO BE UP HERE UNTIL YOU CALM DOWN--
OH... LIKE I *ASKED* YOU TO COME HERE, RICHARDS? WHY DON'T YOU GO HOME TO YOUR WIFE AND KIDS AND YOUR DIFFICULT MATH PROBLEMS? IT'S NOT LIKE I MATTER MUCH ANYWAY.
YOU *DO* MATTER, ROBBIE. EVERYONE IN HERE MATTERS TO ME...ESPECIALLY THOSE WHOSE ONLY CRIME IS REFUSING TO REGISTER. I HAVE A LOT OF GOOD FRIENDS IN THIS PLACE AND I WANT DESPERATELY TO CHANGE THEIR SITUATION.
THEN LEAVE.
WAY I HEARD IT, YOU AND YOUR FELLOW IDIOT SAVANTS CALCULATED WITH A NINETY-NINE PERCENT PROBABILITY THAT BETRAYAL OF YOUR FRIENDS AND COLLEAGUES WAS THE BEST THING TO DO.
BUT A ONE-PERCENT MARGIN FOR ERROR IS STILL A ONE-PERCENT MARGIN FOR ERROR. YOU LUMPED ME IN WITH THE GUY WHO KILLS OLD LADIES FOR A LIVING.
AND YET HERE I AM OFFERING YOU AN OLIVE BRANCH. I'M TRYING TO FIND A WAY OUT FOR YOU AND THE OTHERS, BUT YOU HAVE TO HELP ME DO IT.
THEY'RE TELLING ME YOUR OLD POWERS FLARED UP BRIEFLY DURING A BOXING ENCOUNTER AT YOUR PREVIOUS FACILITY. CAN YOU TELL ME WHAT HAPPENED?
GO TO HELL.
YOU'VE CHANGED, ROBBIE BALDWIN.

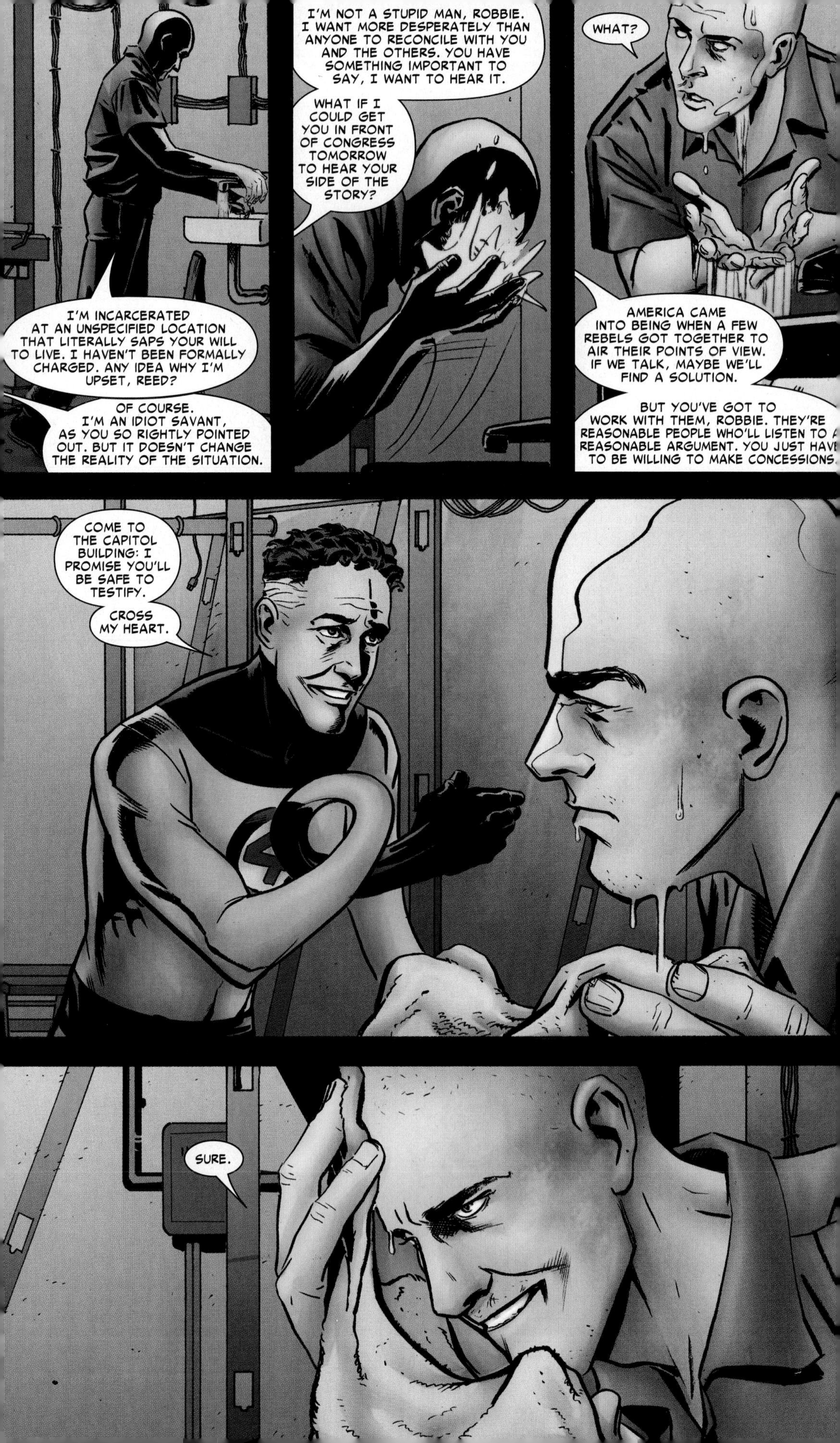
I'M INCARCERATED AT AN UNSPECIFIED LOCATION THAT LITERALLY SAPS YOUR WILL TO LIVE. I HAVEN'T BEEN FORMALLY CHARGED. ANY IDEA WHY I'M UPSET, REED?
OF COURSE. I'M AN IDIOT SAVANT, AS YOU SO RIGHTLY POINTED OUT. BUT IT DOESN'T CHANGE THE REALITY OF THE SITUATION.
I'M NOT A STUPID MAN, ROBBIE. I WANT MORE DESPERATELY THAN ANYONE TO RECONCILE WITH YOU AND THE OTHERS. YOU HAVE SOMETHING IMPORTANT TO SAY, I WANT TO HEAR IT.
WHAT IF I COULD GET YOU IN FRONT OF CONGRESS TOMORROW TO HEAR YOUR SIDE OF THE STORY?
WHAT?
AMERICA CAME INTO BEING WHEN A FEW REBELS GOT TOGETHER TO AIR THEIR POINTS OF VIEW. IF WE TALK, MAYBE WE'LL FIND A SOLUTION.
BUT YOU'VE GOT TO WORK WITH THEM, ROBBIE. THEY'RE REASONABLE PEOPLE WHO'LL LISTEN TO A REASONABLE ARGUMENT. YOU JUST HAVE TO BE WILLING TO MAKE CONCESSIONS.
COME TO THE CAPITOL BUILDING: I PROMISE YOU'LL BE SAFE TO TESTIFY.
CROSS MY HEART.
SURE.

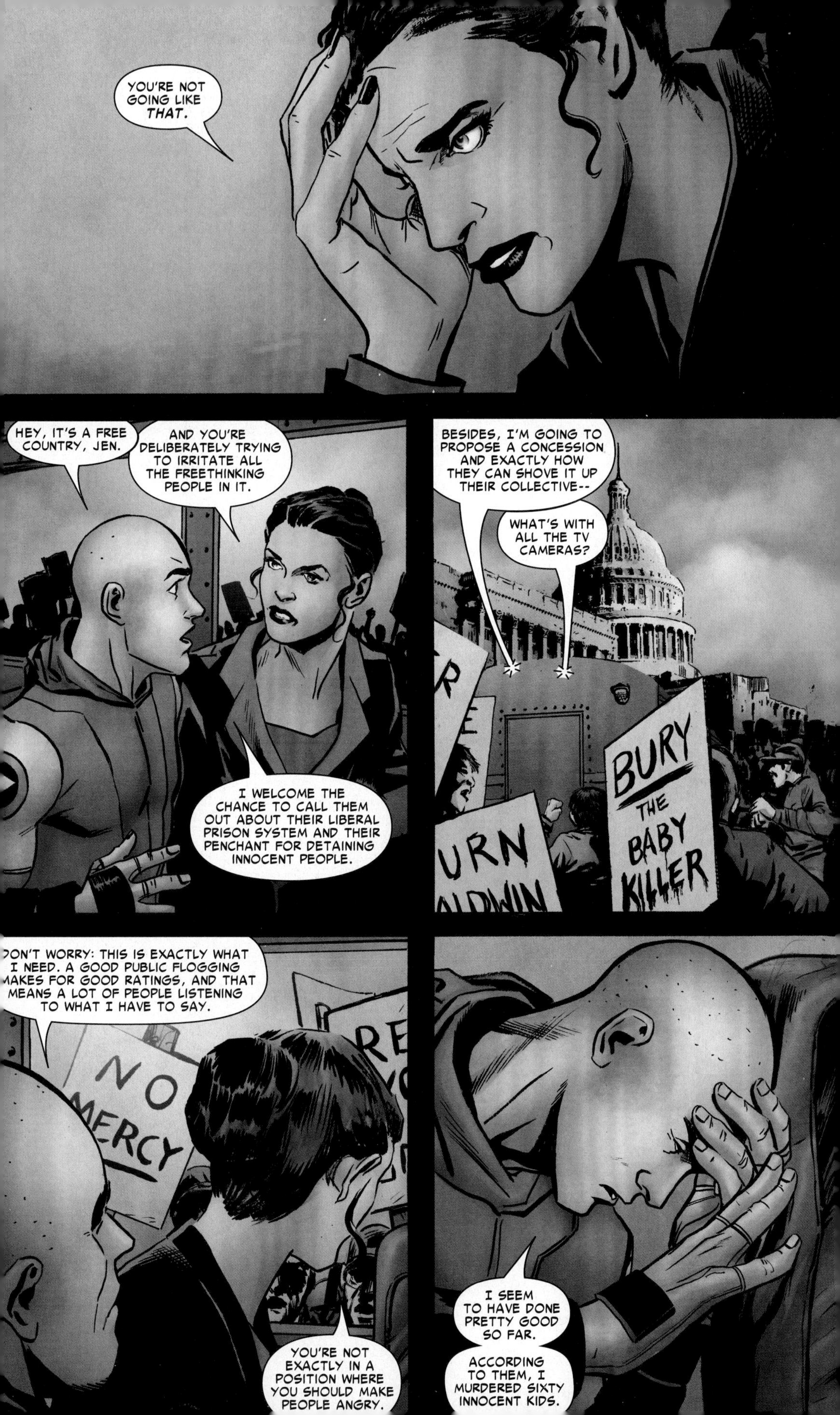
YOU'RE NOT GOING LIKE *THAT.*
HEY, IT'S A FREE COUNTRY, JEN.
AND YOU'RE DELIBERATELY TRYING TO IRRITATE ALL THE FREETHINKING PEOPLE IN IT.
I WELCOME THE CHANCE TO CALL THEM OUT ABOUT THEIR LIBERAL PRISON SYSTEM AND THEIR PENCHANT FOR DETAINING INNOCENT PEOPLE.
BESIDES, I'M GOING TO PROPOSE A CONCESSION AND EXACTLY HOW THEY CAN SHOVE IT UP THEIR COLLECTIVE--
WHAT'S WITH ALL THE TV CAMERAS?
BURY THE BABY KILLER
DON'T WORRY: THIS IS EXACTLY WHAT I NEED. A GOOD PUBLIC FLOGGING MAKES FOR GOOD RATINGS, AND THAT MEANS A LOT OF PEOPLE LISTENING TO WHAT I HAVE TO SAY.
NO MERCY
YOU'RE NOT EXACTLY IN A POSITION WHERE YOU SHOULD MAKE PEOPLE ANGRY.
I SEEM TO HAVE DONE PRETTY GOOD SO FAR.
ACCORDING TO THEM, I MURDERED SIXTY INNOCENT KIDS.

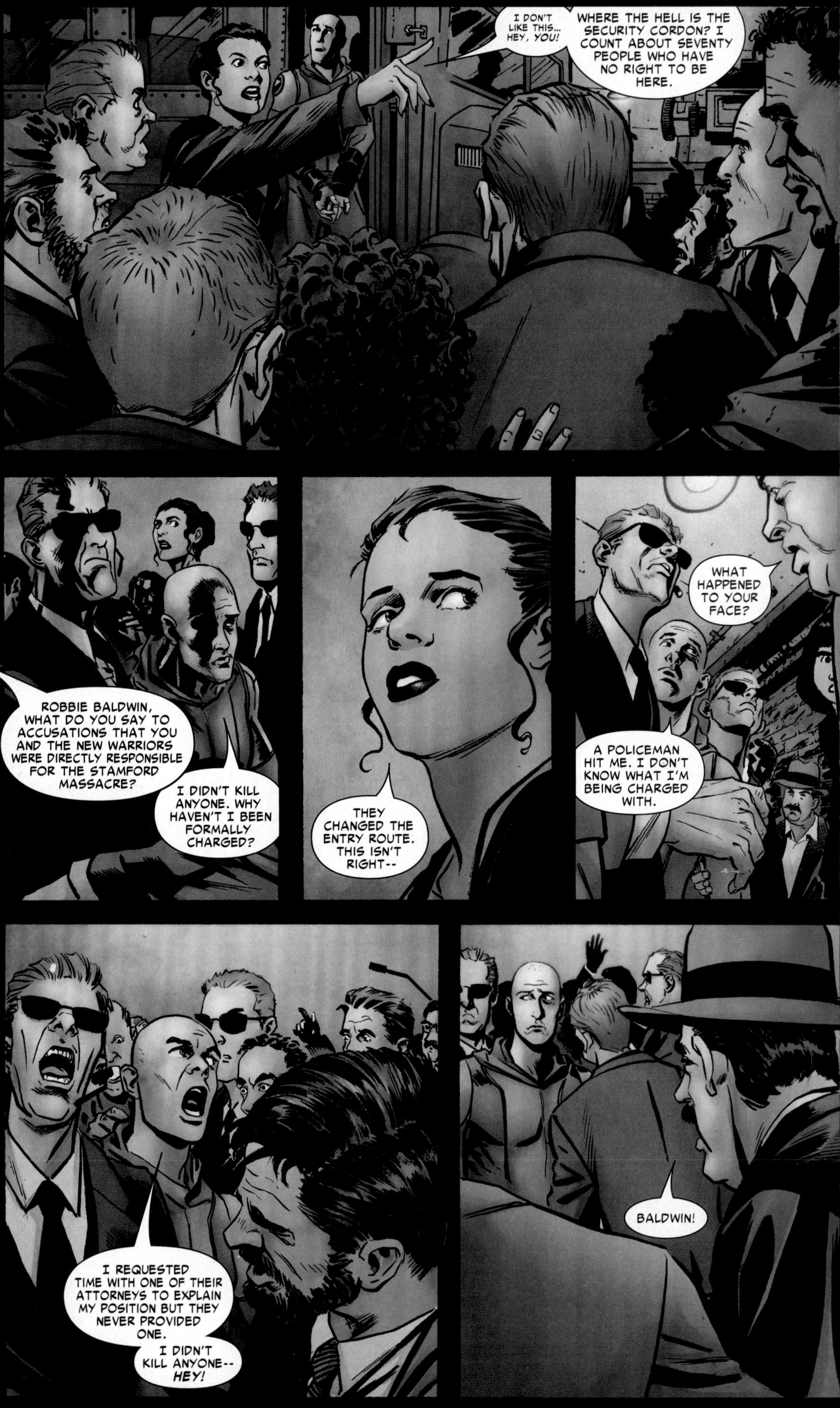
I DON'T LIKE THIS... HEY, YOU!
WHERE THE HELL IS THE SECURITY CORDON? I COUNT ABOUT SEVENTY PEOPLE WHO HAVE NO RIGHT TO BE HERE.
ROBBIE BALDWIN, WHAT DO YOU SAY TO ACCUSATIONS THAT YOU AND THE NEW WARRIORS WERE DIRECTLY RESPONSIBLE FOR THE STAMFORD MASSACRE?
I DIDN'T KILL ANYONE. WHY HAVEN'T I BEEN FORMALLY CHARGED?
THEY CHANGED THE ENTRY ROUTE. THIS ISN'T RIGHT--
WHAT HAPPENED TO YOUR FACE?
A POLICEMAN HIT ME. I DON'T KNOW WHAT I'M BEING CHARGED WITH.
I REQUESTED TIME WITH ONE OF THEIR ATTORNEYS TO EXPLAIN MY POSITION BUT THEY NEVER PROVIDED ONE.
I DIDN'T KILL ANYONE-- HEY!
BALDWIN!

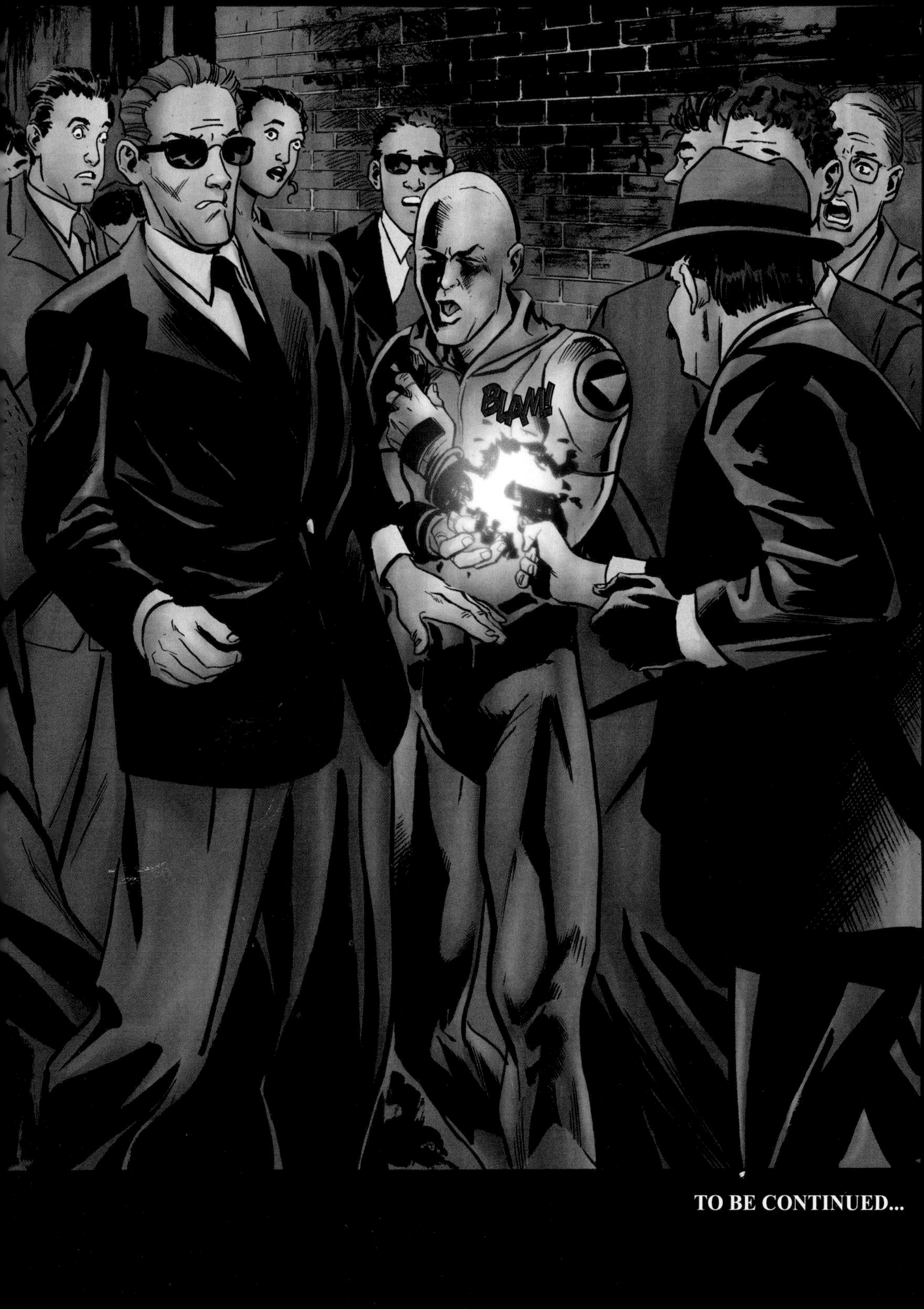
BLAM!

TO BE CONTINUED...

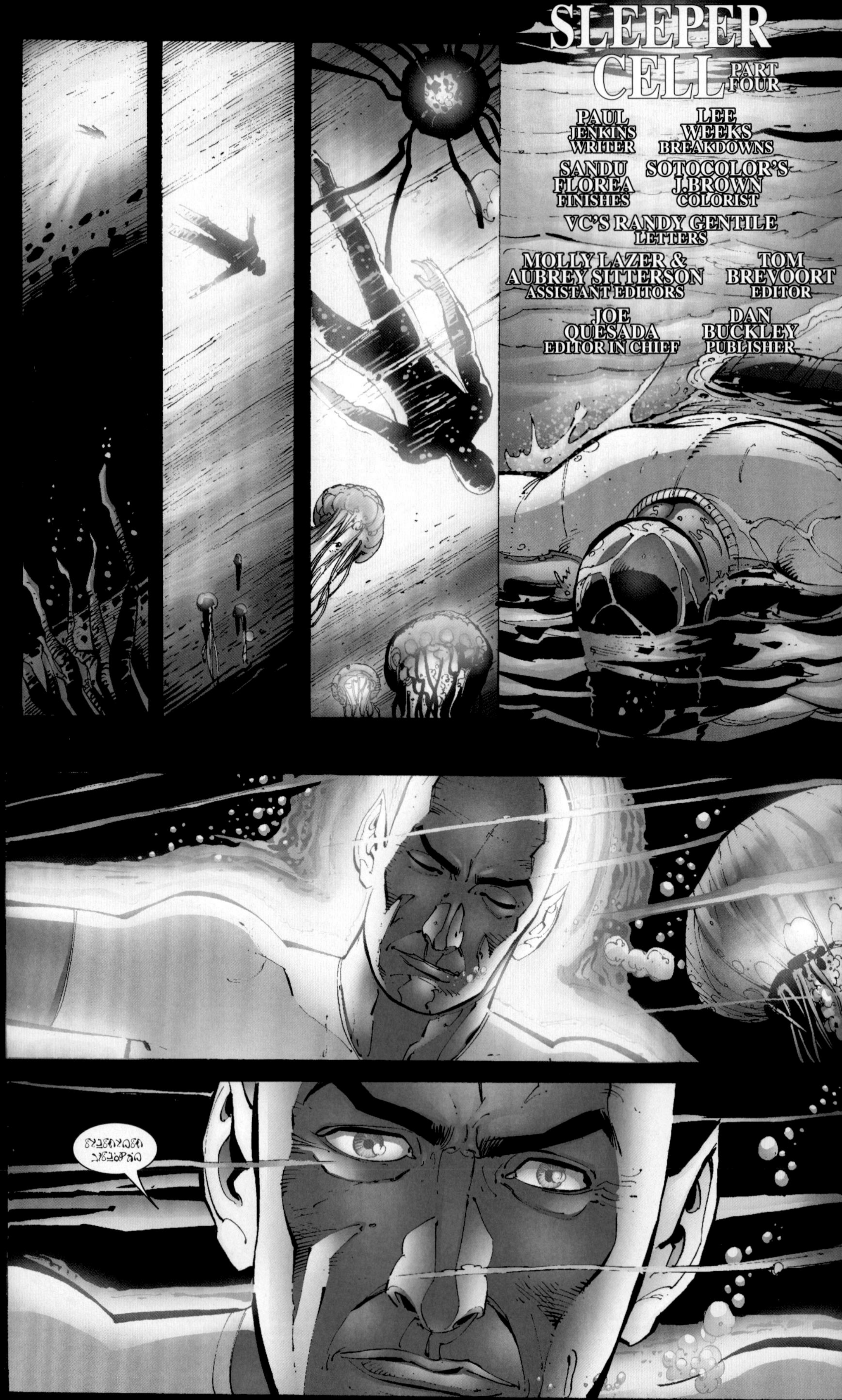
SLEEPER CELL
PART FOUR
PAUL JENKINS WRITER
LEE WEEKS BREAKDOWNS
SANDU FLOREA FINISHES
SOTOCOLOR'S J.BROWN COLORIST
VC'S RANDY GENTILE LETTERS
MOLLY LAZER & AUBREY SITTERSON ASSISTANT EDITORS
TOM BREVOORT EDITOR
JOE QUESADA EDITOR IN CHIEF
DAN BUCKLEY PUBLISHER

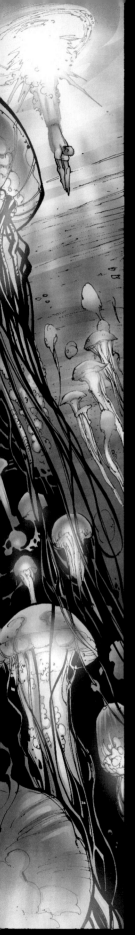

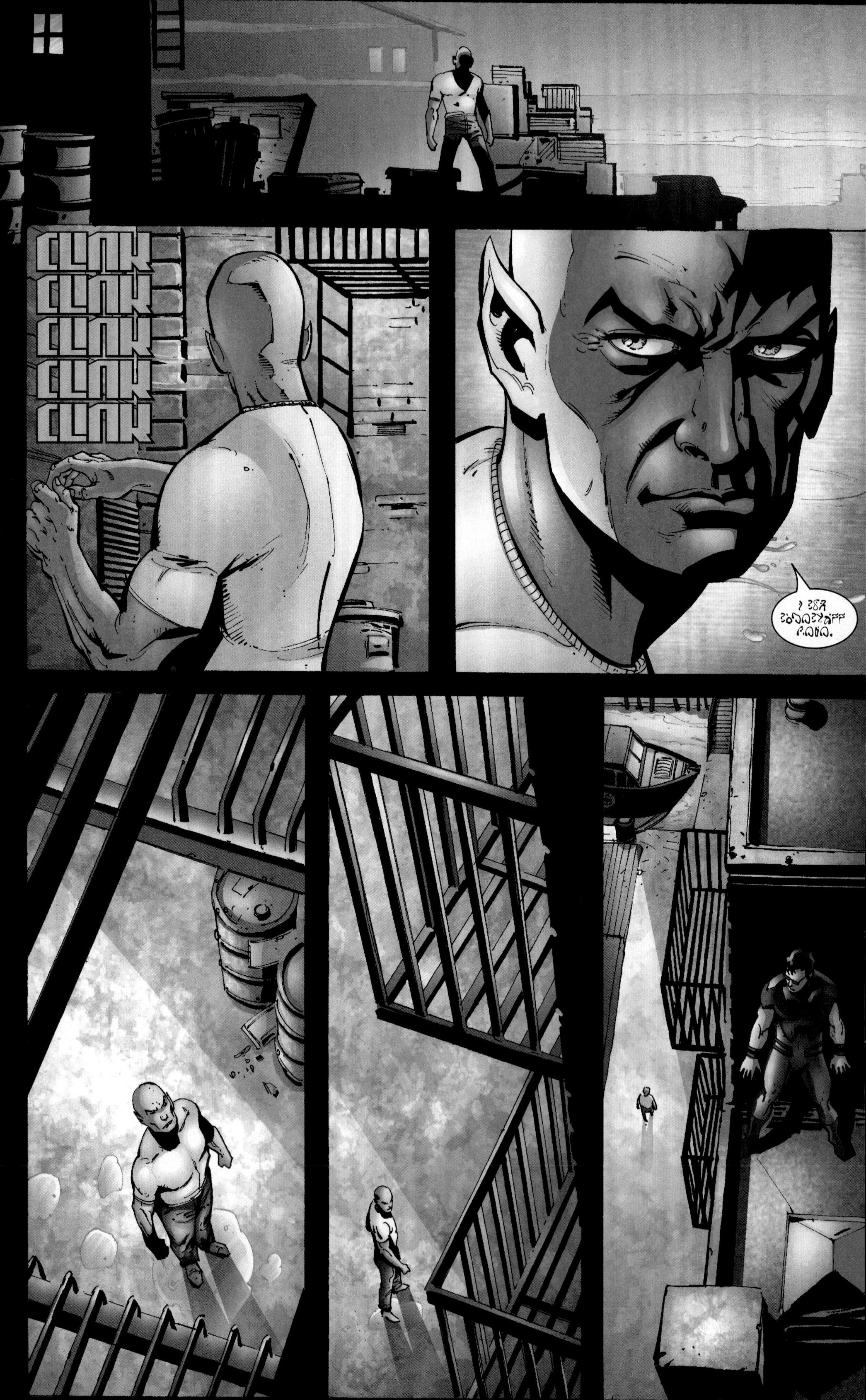
CLAK
CLAK
CLAK
CLAK
CLAK

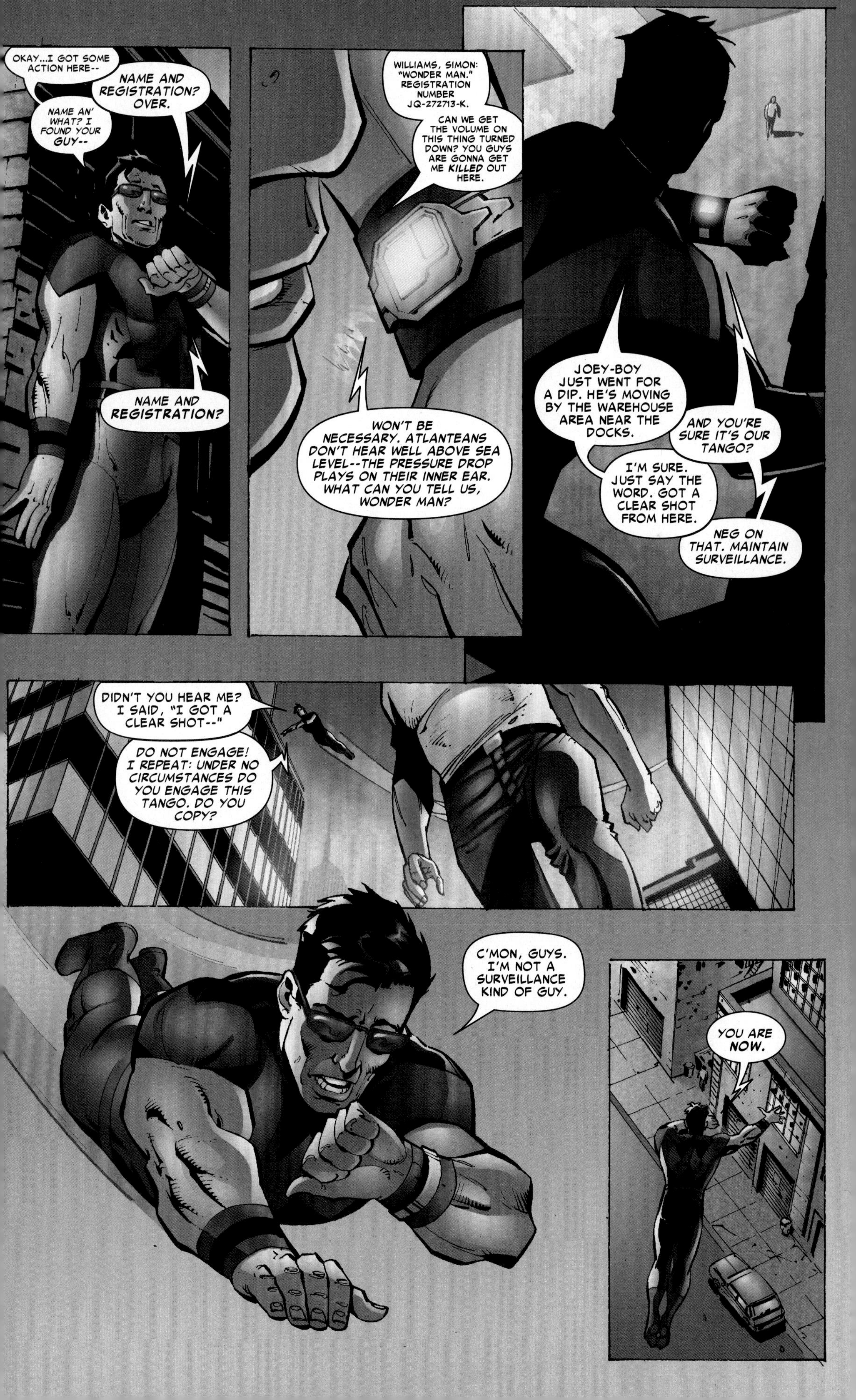
OKAY...I GOT SOME ACTION HERE--
NAME AND REGISTRATION? OVER.
NAME AN' WHAT? I FOUND YOUR GUY--
NAME AND REGISTRATION?
WILLIAMS, SIMON: "WONDER MAN." REGISTRATION NUMBER JQ-272713-K.
CAN WE GET THE VOLUME ON THIS THING TURNED DOWN? YOU GUYS ARE GONNA GET ME KILLED OUT HERE.
WON'T BE NECESSARY. ATLANTEANS DON'T HEAR WELL ABOVE SEA LEVEL--THE PRESSURE DROP PLAYS ON THEIR INNER EAR. WHAT CAN YOU TELL US, WONDER MAN?
JOEY-BOY JUST WENT FOR A DIP. HE'S MOVING BY THE WAREHOUSE AREA NEAR THE DOCKS.
AND YOU'RE SURE IT'S OUR TANGO?
I'M SURE. JUST SAY THE WORD. GOT A CLEAR SHOT FROM HERE.
NEG ON THAT. MAINTAIN SURVEILLANCE.
DIDN'T YOU HEAR ME? I SAID, "I GOT A CLEAR SHOT--"
DO NOT ENGAGE! I REPEAT: UNDER NO CIRCUMSTANCES DO YOU ENGAGE THIS TANGO. DO YOU COPY?
C'MON, GUYS. I'M NOT A SURVEILLANCE KIND OF GUY.
YOU ARE NOW.

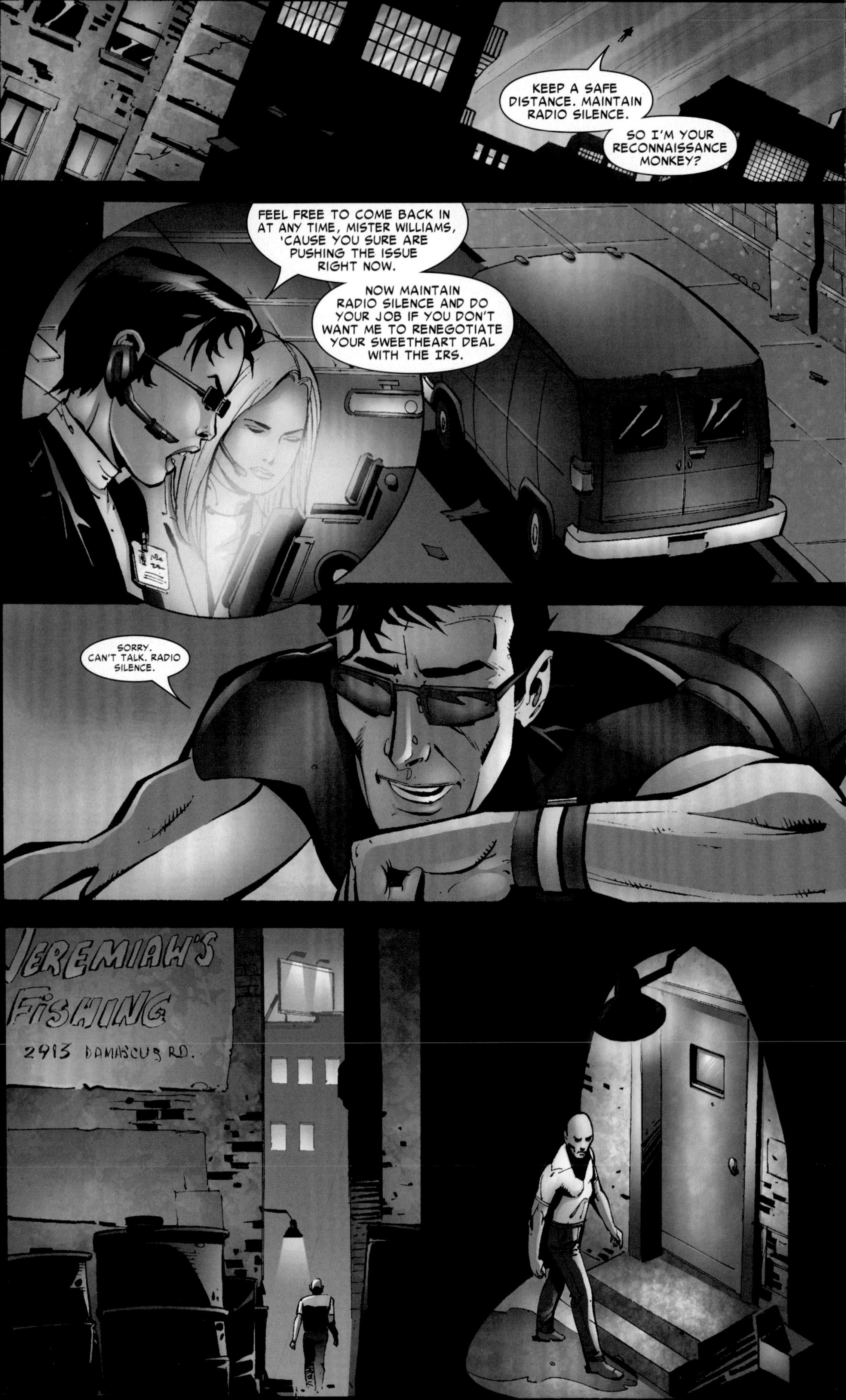
KEEP A SAFE DISTANCE. MAINTAIN RADIO SILENCE.
SO I'M YOUR RECONNAISSANCE MONKEY?
FEEL FREE TO COME BACK IN AT ANY TIME, MISTER WILLIAMS, 'CAUSE YOU SURE ARE PUSHING THE ISSUE RIGHT NOW.
NOW MAINTAIN RADIO SILENCE AND DO YOUR JOB IF YOU DON'T WANT ME TO RENEGOTIATE YOUR SWEETHEART DEAL WITH THE IRS.
SORRY. CAN'T TALK. RADIO SILENCE.
JEREMIAH'S FISHING
2913 DAMASCUS RD.

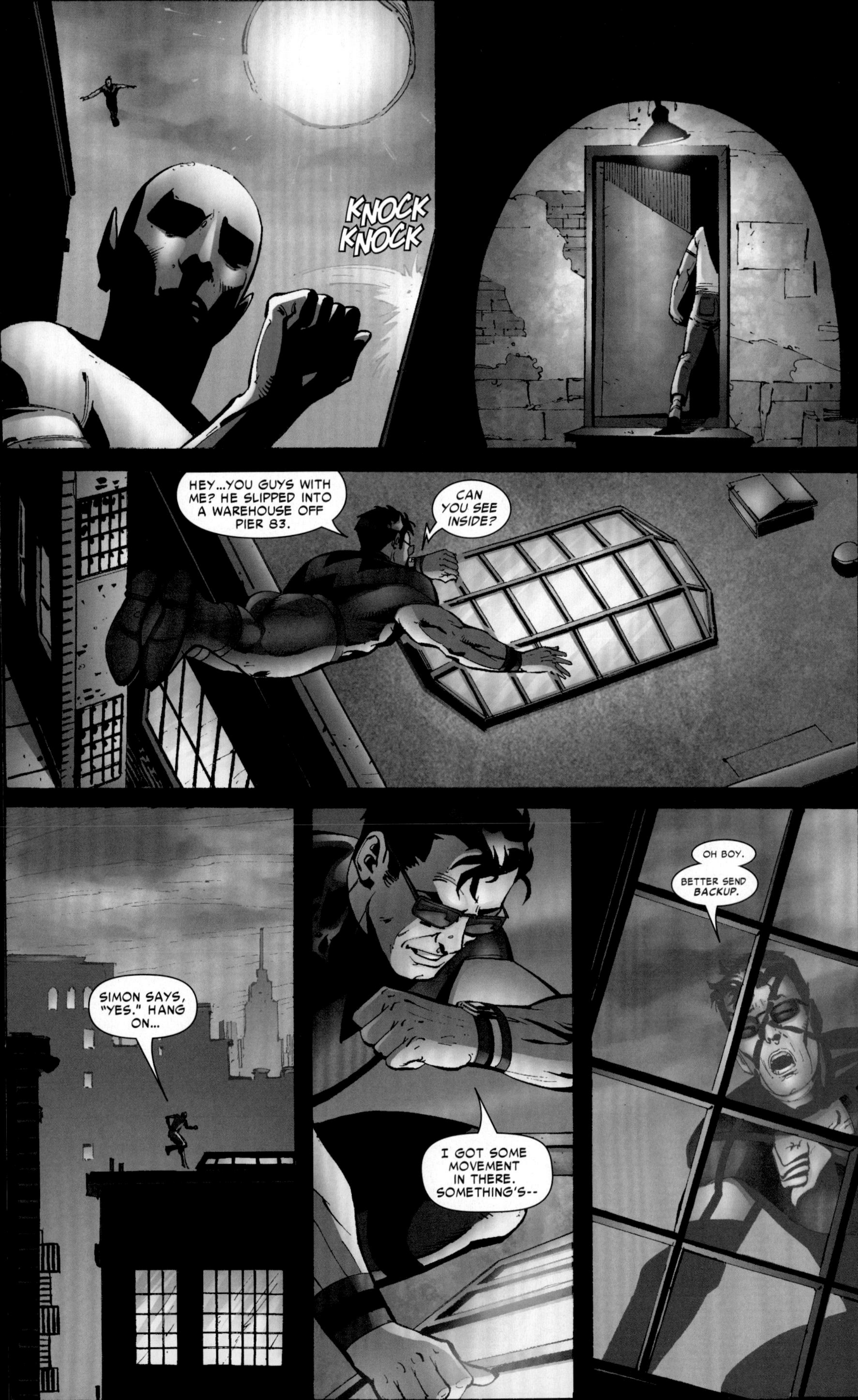
KNOCK KNOCK
HEY...YOU GUYS WITH ME? HE SLIPPED INTO A WAREHOUSE OFF PIER 83.
CAN YOU SEE INSIDE?
SIMON SAYS, "YES." HANG ON...
I GOT SOME MOVEMENT IN THERE. SOMETHING'S--
OH BOY.
BETTER SEND BACKUP.

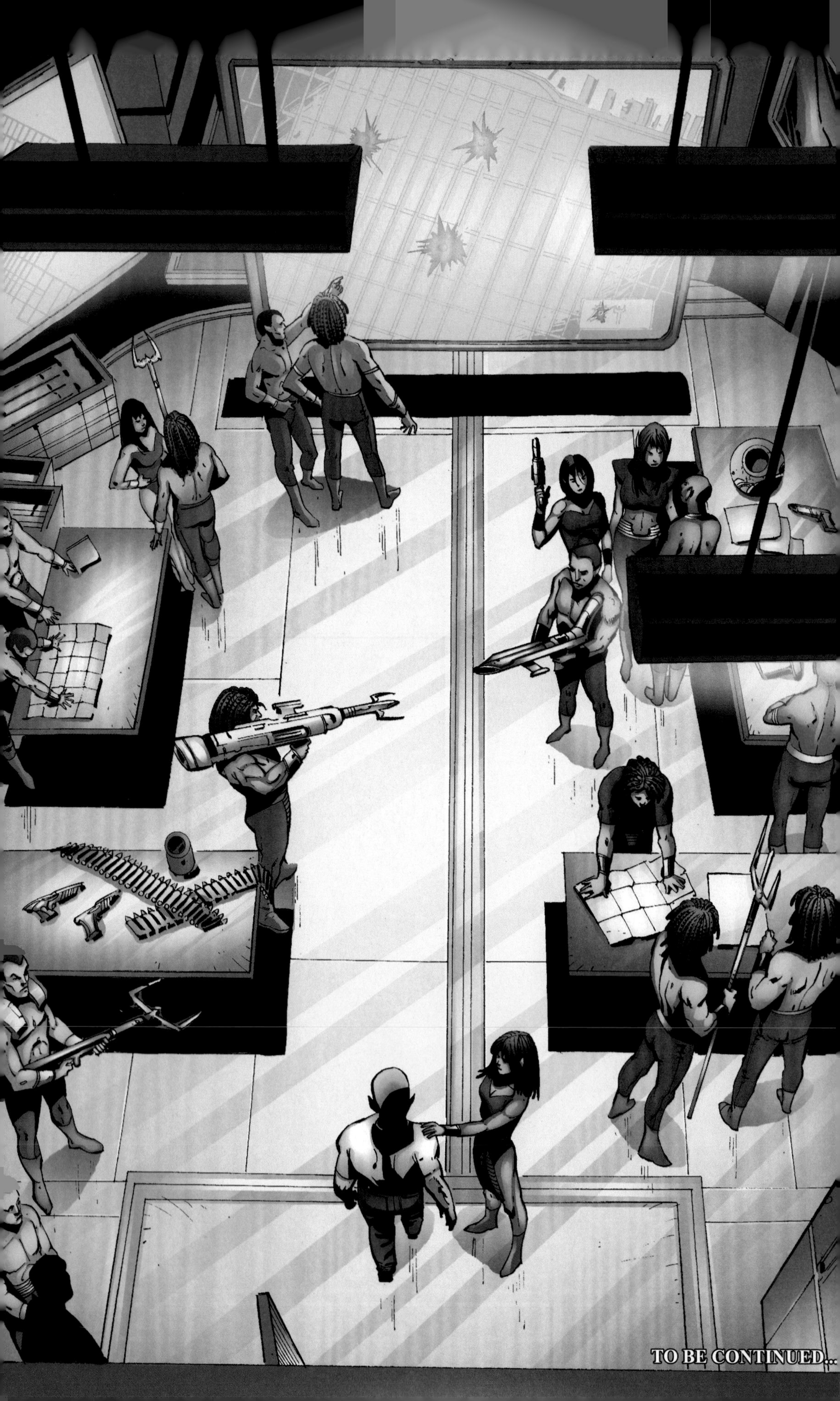
TO BE CONTINUED...

In the spring and summer of 1940, Adolf Hitler implemented a bombing campaign known as "blitzkrieg" or "thunder war" to destroy the British resistance and pave the way for a German invasion of Britain. Hitler knew if he controlled the skies, he would soon control the land.

His German Luftwaffe under the command of General Hermann Göering outnumbered his opponents by approximately eleven-to-one, and yet it was the Royal Air Force who won the Battle of Britain.

For the only thing greater than the British wartime spirit was the skill of its pilots--referred to by Winston Churchill in his famous speech to Parliament as "the Few..."

...and the incredible flying machine known as the Spitfire!

The following poem was written by Royal Canadian Air Force pilot, John G. Magee on September 3rd, 1941, some three months before he was killed on December 11th of that same year.

Of the sonnet, he wrote to his parents, saying, "I am enclosing a verse I wrote the other day. It started at 30,000 feet, and was finished soon after I landed."

President Ronald Reagan quoted from the first and last lines in a televised address to the nation after the explosion of the space shuttle Challenger in 1986.

PAUL JENKINS WRITER | **JORGE LUCAS** ARTIST | **VC'S GENT** LETTERS | **LAZER & SITTERSON** ASST. EDITORS | **TOM BREVOORT** EDITOR | **JOE QUESADA** CHIEF | **DAN BUCKLEY** PUBLISHER

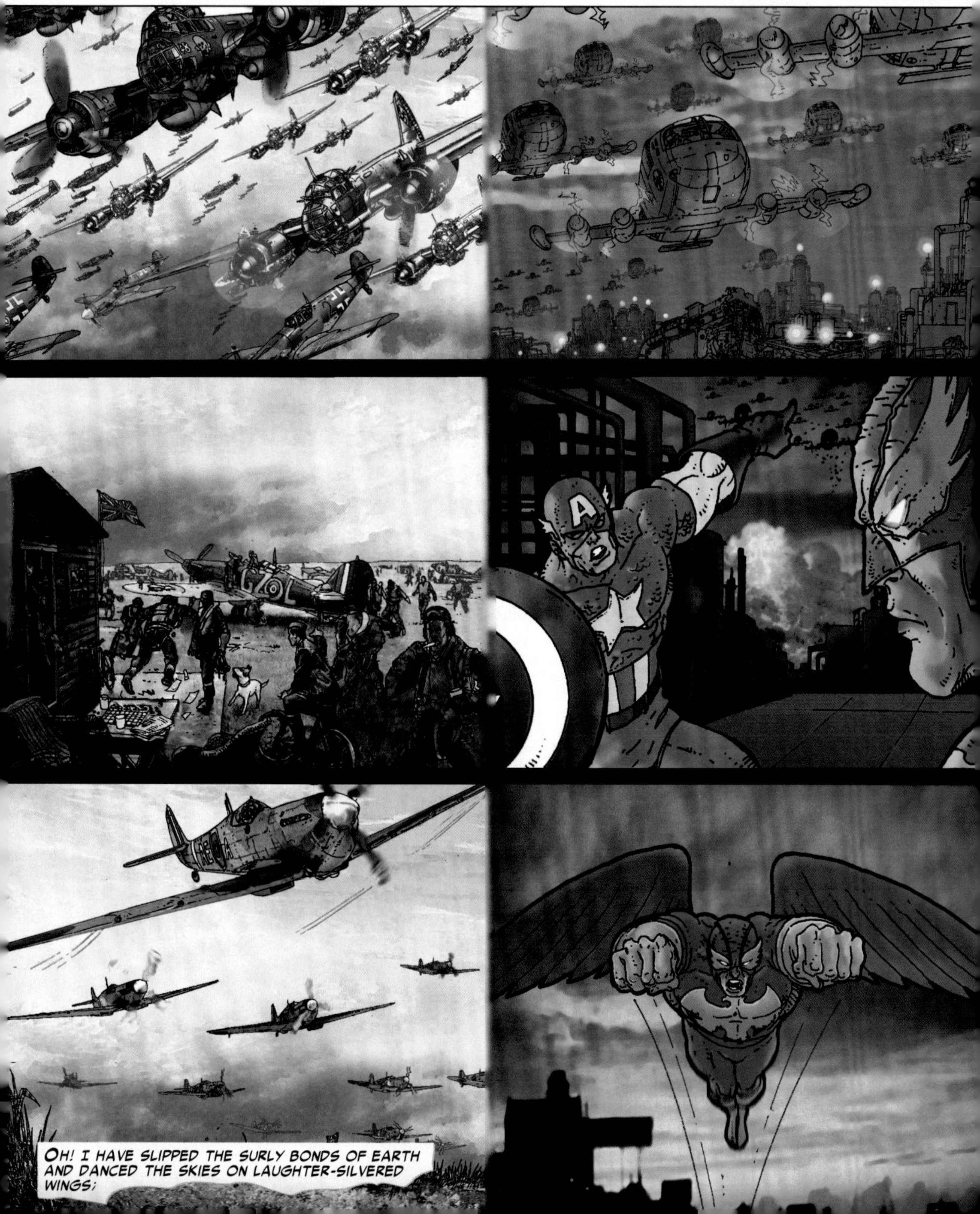
OH! I HAVE SLIPPED THE SURLY BONDS OF EARTH AND DANCED THE SKIES ON LAUGHTER-SILVERED WINGS;

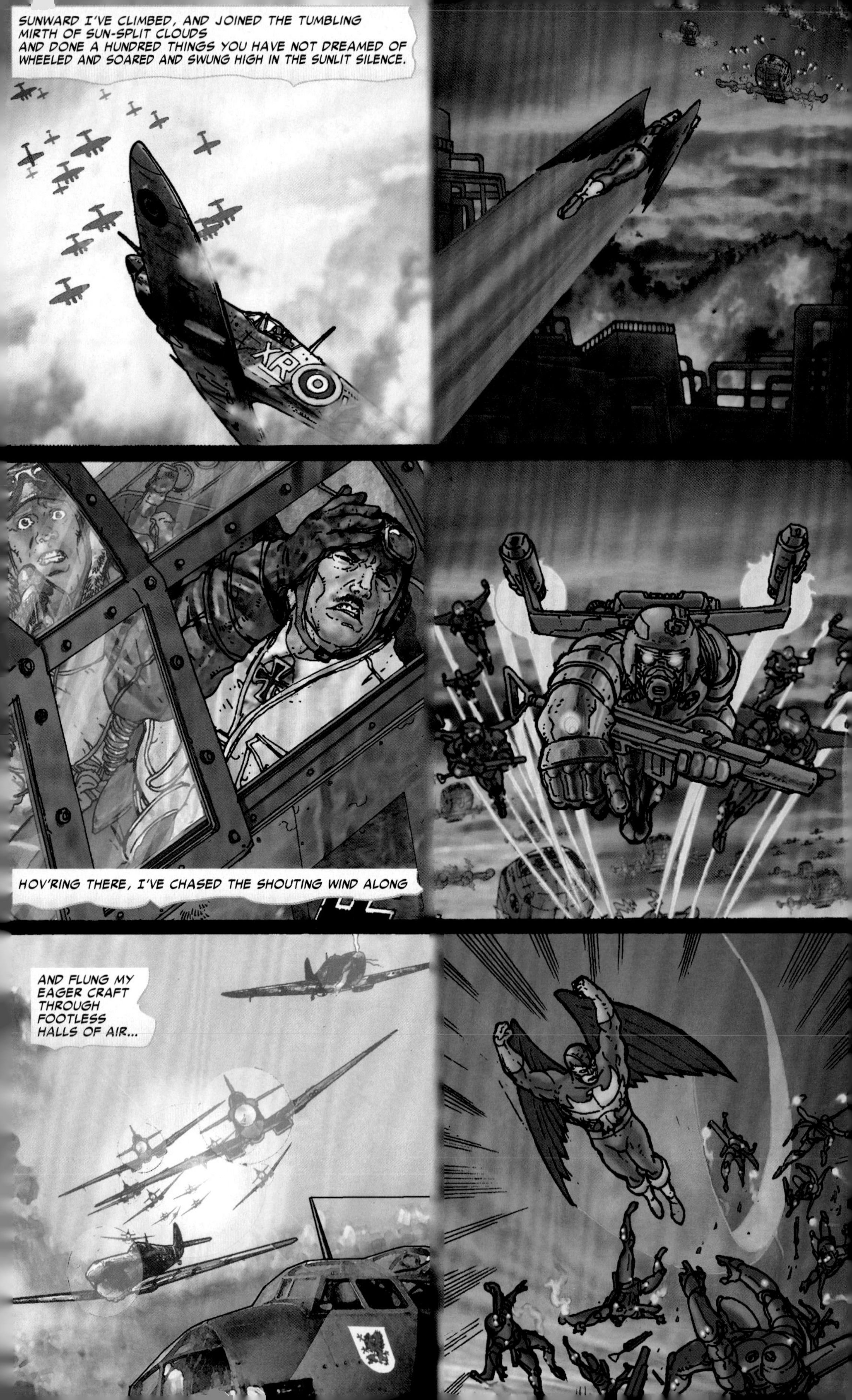
SUNWARD I'VE CLIMBED, AND JOINED THE TUMBLING MIRTH OF SUN-SPLIT CLOUDS
AND DONE A HUNDRED THINGS YOU HAVE NOT DREAMED OF
WHEELED AND SOARED AND SWUNG HIGH IN THE SUNLIT SILENCE.
HOV'RING THERE, I'VE CHASED THE SHOUTING WIND ALONG
AND FLUNG MY EAGER CRAFT THROUGH FOOTLESS HALLS OF AIR...

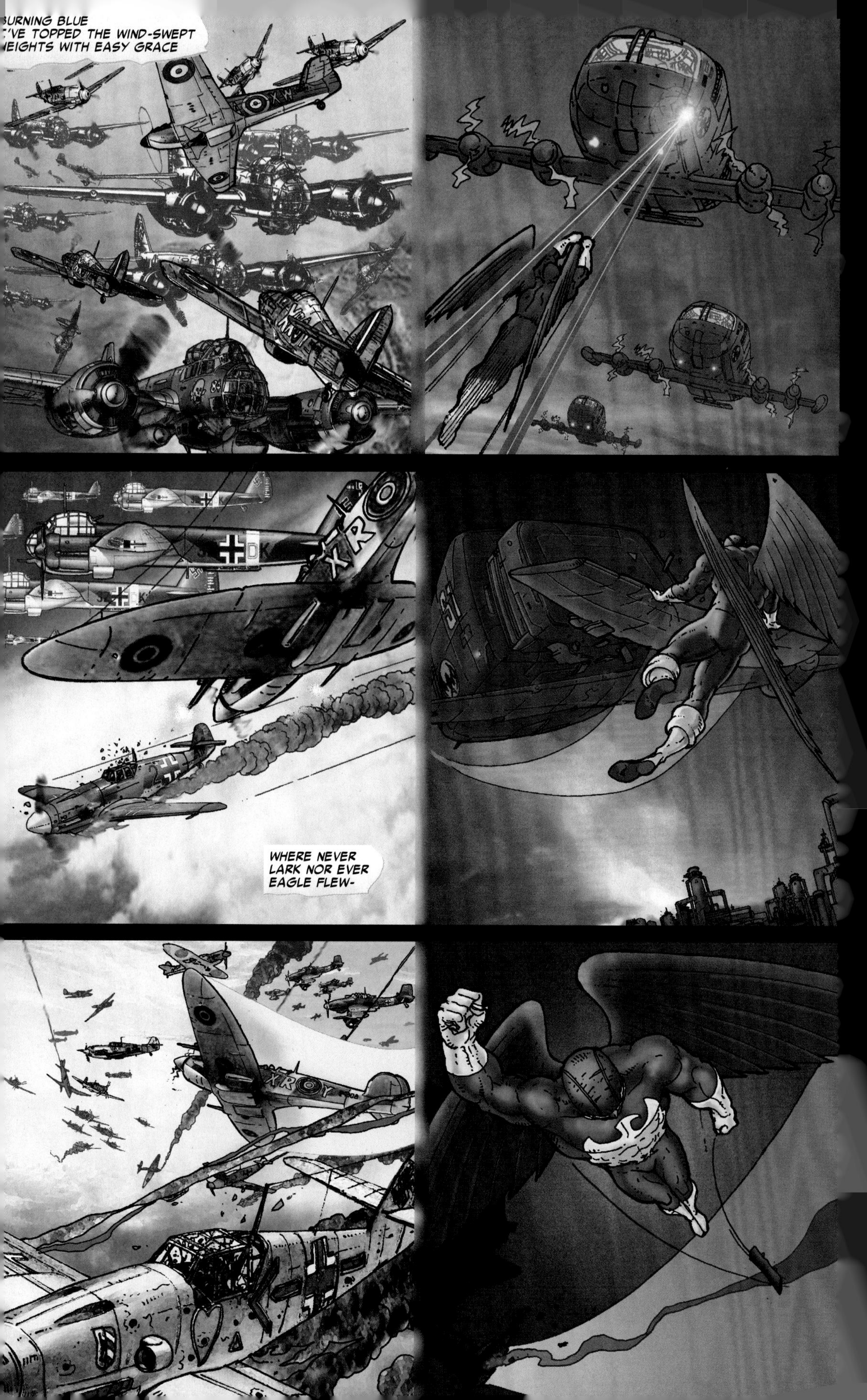

BURNING BLUE
I'VE TOPPED THE WIND-SWEPT HEIGHTS WITH EASY GRACE
WHERE NEVER LARK NOR EVER EAGLE FLEW-

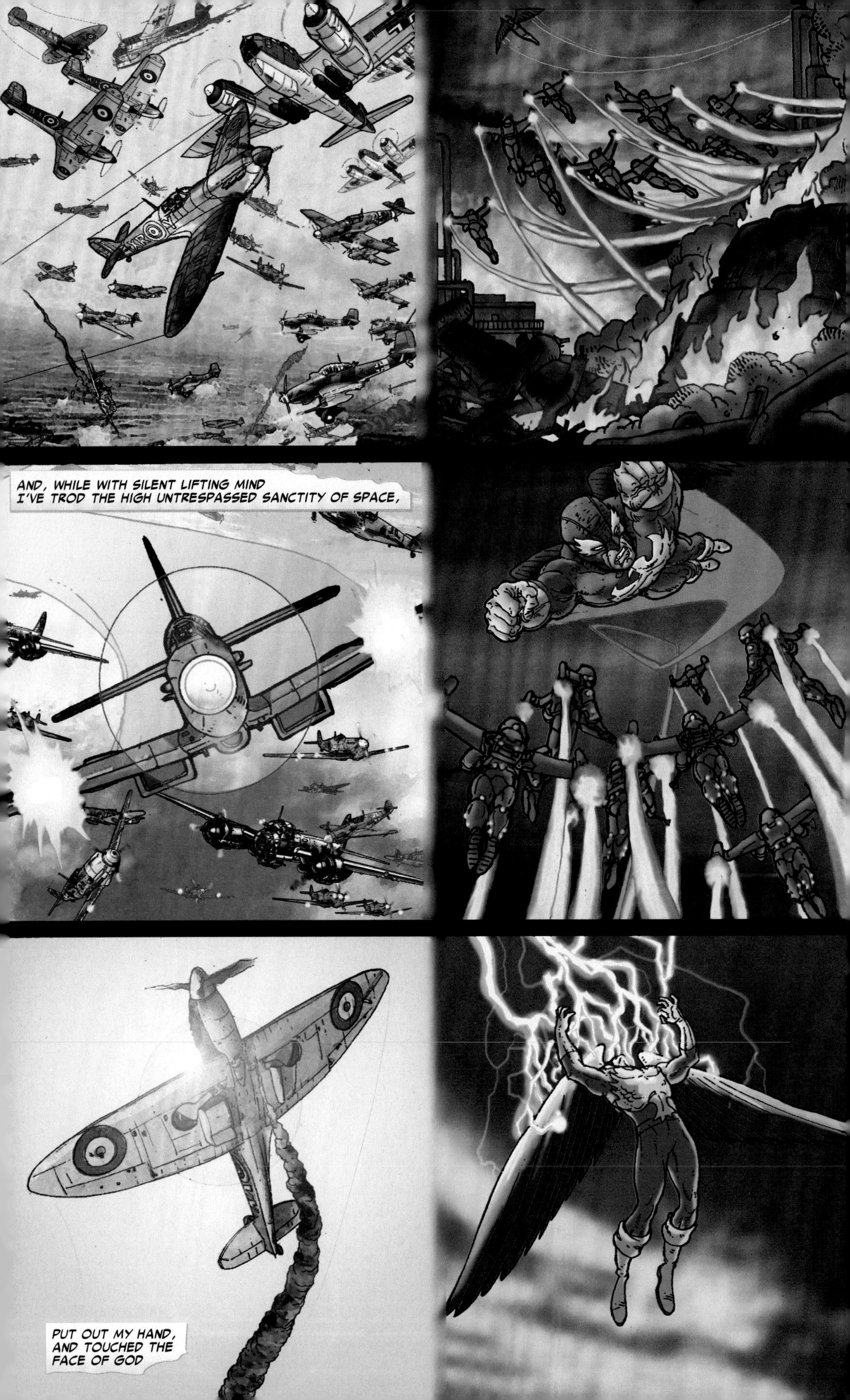
AND, WHILE WITH SILENT LIFTING MIND
I'VE TROD THE HIGH UNTRESPASSED SANCTITY OF SPACE,
PUT OUT MY HAND,
AND TOUCHED THE
FACE OF GOD

HISTORY: Once-typical teenager Robbie Baldwin has faced many trials in his young life, but he always bounces back. He grew up in the small city of Springdale under the often-smothering guidance of his parents, no-nonsense assistant district attorney Justin Baldwin and free-spirited actress Madeline Naylor-Baldwin. His parents disagreed on many topics and argued endlessly about everything, including whether Robbie's future lay with the law or in the arts. Robbie himself was an unremarkable student at Springdale Central High, where he got respectable grades and was reasonably well-liked. After school, he worked part-time as a gofer for research scientist Dr. Nicholas Benson at the local Hammond Research Lab.

Curious about one of Benson's secret experiments, Robbie secretly watched as Benson and his colleagues accessed and tapped an extradimensional energy source that originated, unknown to them, from a realm composed entirely of kinetic energy. An accidental rupture in the energy's flow stream shorted out the lab's lights and released a swarm of energy bubbles that enveloped both Robbie and Benson's pet cat, Niels. Undetected by the scientists, a panicked Robbie ran to the washroom, trying to scrub off the bubbles, and discovered that he had been transformed: his physique was enhanced, his hair was strangely animated, his voice was warped, and his clothes had morphed into a weird orange and blue costume. Afraid to let anyone see him like this, Baldwin retreated to the roof, happening upon masked bandits planning to rob the lab. When they knocked him off the roof, Robbie bounced off the ground and back into their midst, unharmed. His body now generated a kinetic energy field that absorbed any impact directed against him and converted it into increased kinetic energy, such that Robbie would bounce back with increasing force the harder he was hit. Unable to control his new ability, Baldwin bounced around wildly but held off the criminals long enough for the police to arrive. The robbers fled, dying minutes later when their van went off the road, leaving only Robbie to greet the police. Having reverted to his normal form, Robbie claimed he had nothing to do with the fight, but the police were suspicious. Officer Al LaGuardia in particular took an active interest in Baldwin thereafter, bordering on harassment; however, the more fair-minded veteran officer Burnatt was supportive of the Baldwin family, even when Robbie's parents were wrongly accused of murdering their old friend Alexander Bow.

Robbie became anxious and isolated, partly because he realized that any accidental impact could trigger his kinetic field and expose his secret. He dropped out of sports, avoided roughhousing and spent less time with his friends, but he soon found a use for his new powers. When vengeful ex-convict Johnny Roarke tried to kill Robbie's parents, Robbie shifted into his kinetic-charged form and attacked, saving his parents. Thus began Robbie's career as Springdale's only local superhero, popularly referred to as the "Masked Marvel" by Springdale residents and the local press; however, Robbie himself chose the title of Speedball, the Masked Marvel, based on Roarke's calling him a "little speedball" during their fight. His mother became one of Speedball's biggest admirers, but his father vehemently disapproved of any super-vigilante operating in his town. In fact, Springdale was one of the first places in America to outlaw superheroes, making Robbie even more determined to conceal his secret identity from his parents.

Despite Springdale's anti-superhero laws, Speedball protected the city from an odd array of two-bit criminals and minor menaces such as Crooked Face, the Sticker, the Graffiti Guerillas, Leaper Logan, the Proletariat, the Ghost of Springdale High, the Basher, the Two-Legged Rat, the Bug-Eyed Voice, the Harlequin Hitmen, Bonehead, the Feathered Felon, Jolly Roger, the Bouncer and mad scientist Clyde, who later outrageously claimed responsibility for equipping or empowering most of Springdale's other second-rate villains; however, Baldwin's most frustrating early opponent was probably Dr. Benson's cat Niels, who developed the same kinetic energy powers as Speedball. Robbie was assigned to catch the bouncing feline so that Benson could study him, but Niels remained

REAL NAME: Robert "Robbie" Baldwin
ALIASES: The Masked Marvel, "Baby-Killer", "Toothpick", "Speedy"
IDENTITY: Publicly known
OCCUPATION: Adventurer; former television star, student, television show intern, engineering intern, lab worker
CITIZENSHIP: U.S.A. with a criminal record
PLACE OF BIRTH: Springdale, Connecticut
KNOWN RELATIVES: Justin Baldwin and Madeline Naylor (parents)
GROUP AFFILIATION: Formerly New Warriors, Damage Control staff; applied unsuccessfully for Avengers membership
EDUCATION: High school (unfinished)
FIRST APPEARANCE: Amazing Spider-Man Annual #22 (1988)

---

elusive. Certainly the most tragic of Speedball's Springdale foes was his one-time girlfriend Shara, alias Vibrania; a dying, mutated girl, she went on a destructive rampage when her African homeland Kwarrai was destroyed, but ultimately sacrificed herself to save Robbie's life.

Speedball encountered and befriended fellow super-beings such as Spider-Man, Daredevil, and Robbie's enigmatic "Freak of Science" classmate Rico; the Masked Marvel even tried out for membership in the Avengers alongside fellow applicants Blue Shield, Gladiatrix and Mechanaut (Fabian Stankowicz), though Captain America rejected them all as too inexperienced, advising them to continue honing their skills and reapply at a later date. During a subsequent visit to Manhattan, Speedball teamed with several other young super-heroes

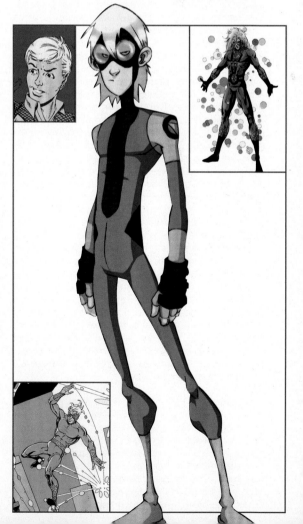

to defeat the alien menace Terrax. Together these heroes formed the New Warriors, gradually maturing into a successful crime-fighting team. Training with and fighting alongside the Warriors brought new discipline to Robbie's heroics, and he gradually refined his control over his kinetic powers.

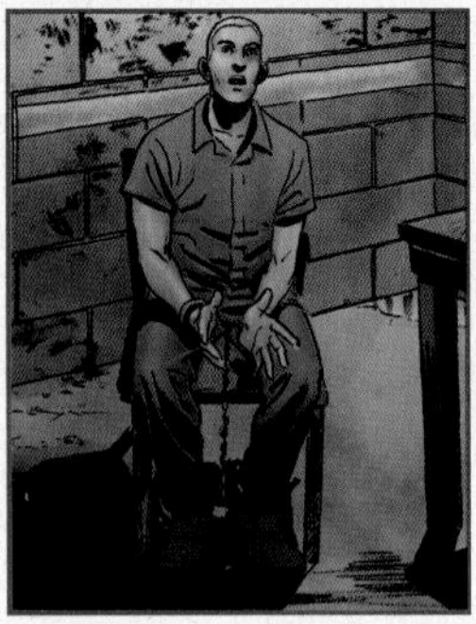

The Warriors became Baldwin's closest friends, especially later recruit Rage; however, Robbie's schoolwork suffered due to his super-hero responsibilities, and his family life continued to deteriorate. When his parents finally got divorced, Robbie moved to Manhattan with his mother, largely to be closer to the Warriors. By this time, Robbie had already shared his secret identity with his mother when he helped the Warriors rescue Madeline from her one-time associates Project: Earth, controversial environmentalists who turned out to be ruthless eco-terrorists. Robbie's father eventually discovered Speedball's secret as well. This bitterly estranged the father and son, though they later reconciled their differences. Meanwhile, Robbie's classmate Carlton LaFroyge also discovered Speedball's secret identity and blackmailed his way into the Warriors as technical advisor Hindsight Lad.

When vastly powerful megalomaniac the Sphinx scattered the Warriors throughout the timestream, Speedball was trapped in the kinetic energy dimension that spawned his powers. Robbie's time-spanning presence there was detected in the year 2092 by father-and-son research scientists Kyle and Darrion Grobe, who used that dimension to power their time travel invention, the bioelectric time shell. Pressured into prematurely testing the time shell after corporate backers Alchemax threatened to cut off their funding, Kyle time-shifted into the past, but a molecular inversion transformed him into the mad time-warping cyborg Advent, whose temporal manipulations threatened all existence. Seeking to undo this disaster via time travel but unwilling to risk becoming another Advent, Darrion devised an alternate means of time travel via the kinetic dimension, but only Speedball could survive that dimension's energies for long. To get around this limitation, Darrion created a complete mental and physical duplicate of Speedball and downloaded his own consciousness into it. As the duplicate Speedball, Grobe went back through time via the kinetic dimension to the modern era, where he impersonated Robbie and Speedball for nearly a year. Wanting to minimize disruption of the past, Grobe submerged his own consciousness within the duplicate Speedball's mind, genuinely believing himself to be Speedball during most of this time period, though he had planned to awaken his own consciousness in time to thwart Advent's time disruptions. Realizing Grobe would fail in his mission because his own consciousness had been suppressed too long and too thoroughly within the Speedball duplicate, a reformed Sphinx killed Grobe as part of a complex plan to involve the time-shifting Warriors member Timeslip, who used information from the dying Grobe to thwart Advent as the Sphinx intended. The Grobes' time alterations were all undone, Kyle and Darrion Grobe were both restored to normal in their native time period (Earth-928), and a time beacon automatically activated in the past by the duplicate Speedball warned the future-era Grobes against repeating their time travel mistakes. Just before the time alterations were all undone, Grobe had helped the time-displaced Warriors return to their own era via the kinetic dimension, and they brought the true Speedball back home.

Quickly adjusting to his lost months, Robbie began getting closer to new teammate Timeslip, though the Warriors drifted apart and broke up before anything came of it. Unwilling to accept the Warriors' dissolution, Speedball later convinced several veteran members and new recruits to join him in reassembling the group, though the team never recaptured the success of its earlier incarnation and soon broke up again (but not before Speedball and teammate Nova collaborated in an unsuccessful attempt to produce a New Warriors movie). When Warriors founder Night Thrasher revived the group again, this time as stars of a crime-fighting reality television series, attention-loving showoff Speedball was one of the more enthusiastic participants. The new gig turned tragic, however, when Speedball and his teammates Microbe, Namorita and Night Thrasher tried to arrest super-criminals Cobalt Man, Coldheart, Nitro and Speedfreek on camera in the town of Stamford. During the battle, Nitro caused an explosion that killed hundreds — including, seemingly, all of the Warriors.

Speedball was later found alive (albeit barely), his powers apparently burned out. The media and the authorities made him the scapegoat for the Stamford disaster, which sparked widespread anti-superhero sentiment and prompted the passing of a law requiring superheroes to register with the authorities. The government decided to make an example of Robbie, holding him without bail or trial while he was abused repeatedly by both guards and fellow inmates. His secret identity leaked to the press, hated by the public, disowned by his parents after he refused to admit to any wrongdoing, Robbie was offered a deal: he would be released if he became a government-registered super-hero, helping train other super-agents and hunting down unauthorized super-heroes. Robbie repeatedly turned down the deal on principle, and was later shot by a protester on his way to testify before Congress.

HEIGHT: (Baldwin) 5'6"; (Speedball) 5'10"
WEIGHT: (Baldwin) 133 lbs.; (Speedball) 170 lbs.
EYES: Blue HAIR: Blond

ABILITIES/ACCESSORIES: As Speedball, Baldwin's body generated an energy field that absorbed, amplified and redirected kinetic energy; it also weirdly distorted his voice and often surrounded him with multicolored kinetic energy "bubbles." The field activated anytime any portion of Baldwin's body experienced a significant impact, though Baldwin gradually developed enough control over the field to suppress it if the activating impact was slight enough. Speedball's most frequent use of his kinetic field was to engage in high-speed, high-impact bouncing, building up greater speed and force with every additional impact while he remained in motion. After a series of sufficiently numerous or forceful bounces to build up power, he could hurl himself into a given target with tremendous impact. Later, he could consciously thrust his kinetic energy field outward, delivering extremely forceful kinetic-powered punches, generating a wider kinetic force field that could more gently push targets away from him, or releasing streams of pure kinetic energy which struck their targets with great impact. He also learned to drain kinetic energy from outside sources, slowing or halting the motion of other people and objects. With his kinetic field activated, Speedball was almost completely immune to physical harm; it also slightly enhanced his physical mass and strength and converted whatever clothing he was wearing into his Speedball costume, presumably created by Robbie's subconscious from otherdimensional kinetic energy (he later discovered that he could alter the costuming's appearance to some extent at will). Robbie developed some proficiency in unarmed combat during his time with the Warriors.

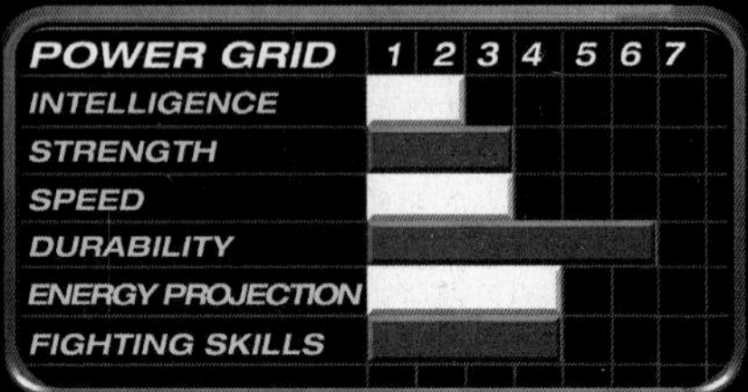
POWER GRID
1 2 3 4 5 6 7
INTELLIGENCE
STRENGTH
SPEED
DURABILITY
ENERGY PROJECTION
FIGHTING SKILLS